1-800-HELP!
with Windows™ 3.1

1-800-HELP!
with
Windows™ 3.1

by Carl Townsend

SAMS

A Division of Prentice Hall Computer Publishing
11711 North College, Carmel, Indiana 46032 USA

©1992 by Sams Publishing

First Edition

All rights reserved. No part of this book shall be reproduced, stored in a retrieval system, or transmitted by any means, electronic, mechanical, photocopying, recording, or otherwise, without written permission from the publisher. No patent liability is assumed with respect to the use of the information contained herein. Although every precaution has been taken in the preparation of this book, the publisher and author assume no responsibility for errors or omissions. Neither is any liability assumed for damages resulting from the use of the information contained herein. For information, address Sams Publishing, 11711 N. College Ave., Carmel, IN 46032.

International Standard Book Number: 0-672-30246-2
Library of Congress Catalog Card Number: 92-60382

95 94 93 92   8 7 6 5 4 3

Interpretation of the printing code: the rightmost number of the first series of numbers is the year of the book's printing; the rightmost number of the second series of numbers is the number of the book's printing. For example, a printing code of 92-1 shows that the first printing of the book occurred in 1992.

Printed in the United States of America

Publisher
Richard Swadley

Associate Publisher
Marie Butler-Knight

Managing Editor
Elizabeth Keaffaber

Acquisitions Editor
Stephen R. Poland

Product Development Manager
Lisa Bucki

Manuscript Editor
Diana Francoeur

Editorial Assistant
Hilary Adams

Cover Design
Tim Amrhein

Book Designer
Michele Laseau

Indexer
Jeanne Clark

Production Team
Claudia Bell
Paula Carroll
Michelle Cleary
Christine Cook
Keith Davenport
Terri Edwards
Mark Enochs
Brook Farling
Tim Groeling
Carla Hall-Batton
Carrie Keesling
Laurie Lee
Jay Lesandrini
Caroline Roop
Linda Seifert
Sandra Shay
Angie Trzepacz
Kelli Widdifield
Lisa Wilson
Allan Wimmer
Phil Worthington

Directory Assistance

Chapter 3   Help with Starting Windows   59

Chapter 4   Help with Program Manager   113

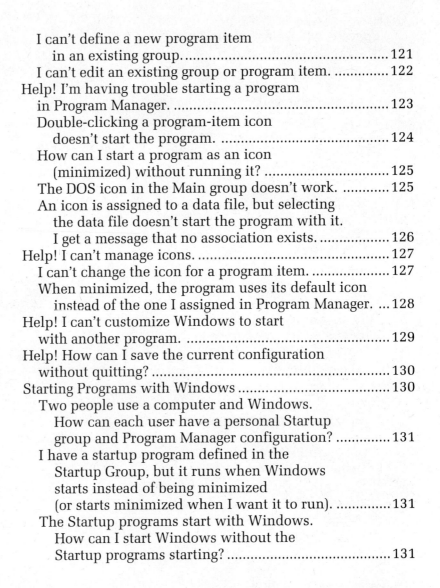

Chapter 6   Help Using Windows Applications   187

Chapter 7   Help with Display Problems   209

Chapter 8   Help with Font Management   237

Chapter 9　Help with Printing　291

Chapter 10 Help with DOS Applications   323

Chapter 11   Help in Sharing Objects and Data with Applications   385

1-800-HELP! with Windows 3.1

1-800-HELP! with Windows 3.1

Appendix A Managing Memory for Speed and Performance   501

1-800-HELP! with Windows 3.1

INTRODUCTION

With over 9 million copies sold, Windows is the most-used
graphical user interface on the market, outselling even the
Macintosh system. Windows' popularity is, in large part, due to
its ease of use. Even first-time users can quickly get the hang of
using Windows. However, when problems do arise, users are
often frustrated over how to solve them. Many find themselves
without directions in a large and dark forest. This book is a
guidebook for getting out of this forest.

What, really, is Windows? Is it an environment, operating
system, or what? Microsoft calls it an operating system, but
does calling it one make it one?

An *operating system* is the manager or supervisor of a
computer system. By this definition, not even DOS is an operating system, since it gives the resources of the computer
(memory, printer, processor, etc.) to whichever program is
running. Only OS/2 or Windows NT could be called true
microcomputer operating systems with this definition. DOS is
more like a control program, providing file management and
program-launching access for the user. Early Windows versions were environments, or shells, that acted "on top" of DOS
to provide a graphical user interface.

With Windows 3.1, Windows has become more like a true
operating system. After booting the system to DOS, DOS hands
the resources of the computer to Windows, just as it would
with any DOS application. Windows then owns all the resources of the computer, managing memory, the printer, and

the processor. Windows applications run under, and are managed by, Windows. If the new FastDisk is installed, even file management is done from Windows and DOS is used only for running DOS applications. If the system crashes, the resources are still owned by Windows and you are returned to the familiar Windows interface. Windows provides multitasking, system management, and resource control for all Windows applications that are executing.

To take full advantage of Windows, then, you should be switching to Windows applications as quickly as possible. Already many corporations are saying that any new program purchases for their PCs must be Windows applications.

This book is a guidebook for both beginner and advanced users as you negotiate in this new world. For DOS/Windows, one could say, "The King is dead. Long live the King!"

How to Use This Book

Each chapter of this book focuses on a particular topic related to using Windows. The chapter consists of problems—and solutions— that are related to this topic. The problems are ones that you may encounter during key Windows operations— installing and starting Windows, printing, running applications, choosing the right hardware options, sharing data, and more. Simply consult the Contents at the beginning of the book to find out which chapter holds the solution to your problem.

Within each chapter, you'll find appropriate background information as well as handy charts that identify specific problems and summarize solutions for each. You can simply work from a chart, or read the text that follows it for a more in-depth explanation of how to resolve the problem.

Conventions Used in This Book

This book uses some typographic conventions as aids for you, the reader. New terms appear in *italics* the first time they are introduced. Anything that you would be entering, such as a value or a command appears in a bold monospace type. For example, the instruction "Type `WIN /r`" means that you type the characters `WIN /r`. Anything that you would see on a screen, such as a message or a line in a WINDOWS file, appears in regular monospace type, such as the `DEVICE=` line.

The selection letter for a menu or for a command appears in boldface type. For example, in the instruction "Choose **E**dit **C**opy," you would press the letter **E** for the Edit menu and then the letter **C** for the Copy command.

Disk Offer

As a service to readers, the shareware programs that are referred to in this book are available on an IBM-compatible, 5 1/4-inch diskette. To order the shareware diskette containing over 20 programs, fill out the Disk Offer Form at the back of the book.

INTRODUCTION

Acknowledgments

The author expresses a deep appreciation to Microsoft and the many vendors who supplied software and hardware to make this book possible. A special acknowledgment is due to Media Vision, Inc., for supplying the sound card.

Trademarks

All terms mentioned in this book that are known to be trademarks or service marks are listed below. In addition, terms suspected of being trademarks or service marks have been appropriately capitalized. Sams cannot attest to the accuracy of this information. Use of a term in this book should not be regarded as affecting the validity of any trademark or service mark.

Adobe Type Manager is a trademark, and ATM, PageMaker, and PostScript are registered trademarks, of Adobe Systems Incorporated.

Ami Pro is a trademark of Samna Corporation, a wholly owned subsidiary of Lotus Development Corporation.

CorelDRAW! is a trademark of Corel Systems.

DESQview and Quarterdeck QEMM/386 are trademarks of Quarterdeck Office Systems.

IBM is a registered trademark of International Business Machines Corporation.

LaserJet and HP are registered trademarks, and DeskJet is a trademark, of Hewlett-Packard Co.

TOP 10 WINDOWS PROBLEMS

Although you will find more than 400 problems and their solutions in this book, here is an overview of the ten most common ones. For each problem, you'll find an easy solution. If you need more help, refer to the chapter or appendix listed with the solution.

1. A Windows 3.0 application won't work with Windows 3.1.

Some Windows 3.0 applications won't work with Windows 3.1. Contact the manufacturer for an update. At the time of Windows 3.1 release (April 6, 1992), the following applications would not run or had problems under Windows 3.1:

Ace Software AceFile
Adobe Illustrator 1.1
Adobe TypeAlign
Aldus Freehand 3.0
Aldus Persuasion
Bitstream FaceLift 1.2
Borland C 3.0 Winsight
Campbell Services On Time 1.0
Central Point PC Tools version 7.1
Channel Computing Forest and Trees 2.0a

Claris Hollywood version 1.0
Coda Finale
Computer Support Arts and Letters 3.10
Computer Support Picture Wizard
First Byte Monologue for Windows
hDC FirstApps Memory Viewer 1.0
Hewlett-Packard NewWave
Lotus Ami Pro 1.0
Microsoft Bookshelf for Windows (1990)
Microsoft PowerPoint 2.0e
Microsoft Productivity Pack 1.0
Microsoft Word for Windows 1.1
NBI Legacy
Norton Desktop 1.0
PFS: WindowWorks
Powersoft PowerBuilder
SoftNet FAXit for Windows
Software Publishing: Harvard Graphics for Windows
WordPerfect for Windows (Find Files feature)
WordStar for Windows

2. The system hangs when booting or when starting Windows.

See Chapter 3 for more information.

If the system hangs on booting, watch for error messages during the bootup to identify the problem source. The most likely cause is a memory conflict in the upper memory area

(640K–1MB) when drivers are being loaded high (see Chapter 6). If you are using DOS 5 and loading drivers high (`DEVICEHIGH=` used in CONFIG.SYS or `LOADHIGH=` used in AUTOEXEC.BAT), change these lines so that the drivers and TSRs are loaded to conventional memory. For example, in CONFIG.SYS

```
DEVICEHIGH=C:\MOUSE.SYS
```

becomes

```
DEVICE=C:\MOUSE.SYS
```

If this works, you have identified the problem. Modify the line that loads EMM386.EXE to:

```
DEVICE=E:\WIN\EMM386.EXE noems x=A000-FFFF
```

This excludes *all* of the upper memory area, and should enable booting. See Appendix G for information about editing CONFIG.SYS and AUTOEXEC.BAT.

If Windows hangs on booting, you have either a hardware or a memory conflict. If there is a hardware conflict, use the /m parameter with HIMEM.SYS to specify the type of hardware or use a custom install. If there is a memory conflict, Windows will run in standard mode but not in 386 enhanced. Exclude memory by adding the `EMMExclude=` parameter to the `[386]` section of SYSTEM.INI.

3. I can't get a Windows utility that I need.

A large number of bulletin board systems (BBS), as well as CompuServe, support free and shareware utilities for Windows. On CompuServe, dial into the Microsoft area

(GO MICROSOFT) or check the various application vendor
forums on CompuServe. This author supports the Catacombs
BBS with Windows software. You can reach Catacombs by
dialing 503-284-5130. Also watch *PC Magazine* for its Windows column. You can order trial copies of the shareware
utilities mentioned in this book (see the Disk Order Form at the
end of the book).

4. A video (or printer) driver doesn't work with Windows 3.1.

See Chapter 7 for more information.

Windows interfaces to the video and printer by using a software driver. The same video and printer drivers are generally
used for all Windows applications. Drivers (both video and
printer) designed for Windows 3.0 will not work with Windows 3.1. Purchase a new driver from the manufacturer of the
video adapter or printer or use the one with Windows 3.1.

5. With a disk compression TSR (such as Stacker), Windows doesn't install or run properly.

Various *disk compressions utilities* are available for compressing the files on the disk so that the disk appears larger to DOS.

The Stacker utility is one such example. Stacker runs as a *TSR*, or memory resident utility. It works with the *disk driver* (the software that interfaces with the disk) to increase the storage space on the disk. For the most reliable operation of Windows, avoid using a disk compression utility such as Stacker.

All disk drivers must be located on noncompressed drives. They should also be listed in CONFIG.SYS before the lines that install compressed drives. SMARTDrive should not be used to cache compressed drives. (See Appendix G for information on editing CONFIG.SYS.)

6. FastDisk doesn't work.

See Appendix B for more information.

FastDisk is a file management system in Windows 3.1 that can be used when running in the 386 enhanced mode. It is available only for systems containing disk controllers using the Western Digital 1003 disk controller standard. The FastDisk system uses a 32-bit file management system that bypasses DOS and is therefore very fast.

If the installation detects that FastDisk might work on your system, a check box appears in the dialog box. To reach the check box, start Control Panel, choose 386 Enhanced and **V**irtual Memory, and click Change. This check box does not appear in the dialog box if other disk controllers are used. If the check box appears in the dialog box, it is NOT turned on by default. You must turn it on. If FastDisk is installed (check box is checked) and fails to work properly on your system, the system will hang; but you should not lose any data from the disk.

7. The video display is not working properly under Windows.

See Chapter 7 for more information.

Make sure that there are no memory conflicts in the UMB area (see Chapter 6). The video driver may not support Windows 3.1. Upgrade to a new video driver.

8. An application crashed in Windows.

If an application crashed in Windows 3.0, your only solution was to reboot. With Windows 3.1, however, recovery is greatly improved. If an application crashes, press Ctrl+Alt+Del. You will get a message screen providing three options:

- Press Enter to close the current application and provide an option to save your work.
- Press Ctrl+Alt+Del again to really reboot the system (and lose everything).
- Press Esc for no action.

9. A DOS application doesn't run properly under Windows.

See Chapter 10 for more information.

A *PIF file* is a file created with Windows' PIF Editor. The PIF defines certain system parameters for a DOS application. It often has the same filename as the program executable file but has a PIF extension, such as WORD.PIF. If you have a problem running under Windows, the PIF file is probably incorrect.

10. Protected-mode software doesn't run under Windows.

See Appendix A for more information.

Protected-mode software programs are ones that use the older VCPI standard for addressing extended memory. Windows does not support VCPI or programs that use this standard. Appendix A describes these two standards and lists the software that uses the VCPI standard and should not be run under Windows. Upgrade to an application version that supports the newer DPMI standard, or use QEMM-386.

1

C H A P T E R

PREPARING TO INSTALL WINDOWS

The way you install and configure Windows largely determines the performance of your system and all applications that you run on your system under Windows. This chapter will give you guidelines to prepare for installation so that you can head off problems before they happen.

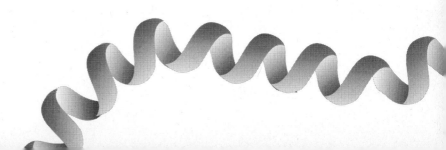

Planning

Before installing Windows, you should plan the installation carefully. First, be sure you have adequate resources to run Windows. Here is the minimum computer configuration for running Windows:

■ An MS-DOS compatible computer with a processor that supports the particular version of Windows you are installing. You will need an 80286, 80386, or 80486 processor with at least 1 megabyte of memory. At least 256K of it must be configured as extended memory. (Although Microsoft says an 80286 will support Windows, it's not very realistic.)

■ A hard disk with at least 10 megabytes of free space. Windows applications, fonts, and clip art use a lot of disk space, so an 80-megabyte disk is a minimum working size.

■ DOS 3.1 or later.

■ A printer and video terminal supported by the Microsoft Windows environment.

■ A mouse. This is optional but highly suggested.

■ An optional Hayes-compatible modem if you want to use communication applications.

■ An optional pen. Windows 3.1 supports pens. Pens can be used with Windows applications that are not specifically designed for pens (such as ObjectVision) or with special Windows applications.

■ Optionally, for multimedia extensions, an MPC-compatible CD-ROM system and an MPC-compatible audio board with amplifier and speakers. Windows 3.1 supports multimedia.

For maximum productivity with Windows, you should have a 386-type or 486-type processor with 4 megabytes of memory, of which 3 megabytes is extended memory.

Windows supports two modes: standard and 386 enhanced. To run the *standard mode,* you need an 80286 or later processor and at least 1 megabyte of memory (640K conventional memory and 256K of extended). To run *386 enhanced mode,* you need an 80386 processor or later and at least 2 megabytes of memory (640 conventional and 1024K of extended).

Secrets and Surprises: Some systems, such as an IBM XT with a 386 Inboard, require a special version of Windows. Some PC clones may not support Windows or may require a special version of Windows. Check with your manufacturer.

Here are some questions that Windows will ask you as part of the installation process. You will need to provide answers in order to proceed with the installation.

- What drive and directory will be used for Windows? (You should have more than 10 megabytes of free space.)
- What is the manufacturer and model number of your printer? What port will the printer use?

Here are some additional questions that Windows will ask. Although you should know the answers to these questions, in most cases the installation can determine the answers automatically by using the express install.

What is the manufacturer and model number of your computer? What processor does it use (286, 386, etc.)?

What type of video display do you have (VGA, EGA, etc.)?

How much memory do you have (RAM)?

What is the manufacturer and model number of your mouse?

What is your keyboard type?

If you are on a network, what type of network? What version? Does this version support Windows?

Planning to Prevent Installation Problems

The following planning guidelines are general ones that work for many users:

Use subdirectories, but don't make the levels too deep. In most cases, the root directory should contain only the bootup routines (AUTOEXEC.BAT and the SYS files).

Put all the DOS routines in a \DOS directory.

Put all batch files in a \BAT directory.

Put each application program (including each Windows application) in its own directory.

Separate data files by project, and create subdirectories for each project. (This is where you may want more hierarchical levels.)

Put utilities in their own \UTIL subdirectory. If a utility has several files (such as PC Tools), put it in its own directory.

- Read the Setup documentation in the manuals.

- Be sure you have enough disk space on the available drive for installing Windows. You will need 8 to 10 megabytes just for Windows, and additional space for Windows applications you intend to use. Windows automatically checks to see if sufficient disk space is available when it starts installation. Setup will terminate if there is not enough space.

- Install Windows applications *after* installing Windows. Installing applications will modify the WIN.INI file. (If you are already using Windows, first save the old WIN.INI file under a different name, such as WIN.SAV.)

- Use short directory names. For example, install Windows to C:\WIN instead of C:\WINDOWS. The PATH statement in AUTOEXEC.BAT is limited in length, and this permits more directories in the statement. Use C:\WIN instead of C:\WIN31. It's shorter, and gives a generic directory name for batch files or paths referencing Windows files.

- Contact your computer manufacturer to see if any special directions are necessary when installing Windows with your system.

Precautions to Prevent Installation Problems

Before you install Windows, you should be somewhat familiar with the roles that the AUTOEXEC.BAT and CONFIG.SYS files play and with procedures for editing them. See Appendix G for this information and also consult your DOS manuals.

Here are some precautions to take for installation:

For installation, be sure none of the DOS APPEND, JOIN, GRAPHICS, FASTOPEN, PRINT, or SHARE commands are used in AUTOEXEC.BAT. Remove all TSRs (memory-resident programs), which may have a startup command in AUTOEXEC.BAT. Use the DOS EDLIN command or any text editor to edit AUTOEXEC.BAT (see Appendix G). If any of these commands are used or if TSRs are there, delete the line containing the command or TSR, or comment them out temporarily by adding **REM** before the line, for example:

```
REM SHARE.EXE
```

Some nonstandard DOS partitioning schemes don't work with Windows if SMARTDrive is installed. Be sure that your disk partitioning is supported, or don't install SMARTDrive. Check with your system manufacturer.

Some PC computers are not supported or require special installation steps. When using clones, check with the manufacturer to see if Windows is supported or if a special version of Windows is needed. It is always a good idea to check with the manufacturer before installing Windows. With some computers, Windows can't detect certain hardware aspects and you must use a custom install.

Anticipate the method that you will use to make backups, and then design your directories to support this. For example, temporary projects could have their own directories so that they could be backed up easily. Program files, which are seldom backed up, should be on separate directories.

Deinstall any current memory manager. Start with Windows' memory manager and then work from that.

Make sure that **FILES=40** is in the CONFIG.SYS file.

▪ Verify that your video adapter and mouse are supported by Windows.

▪ Be sure you are using the correct DOS for your computer. Type **VER** at the DOS prompt to see the DOS version. If the name in the copyright notice doesn't match your computer, check with your computer manufacturer to be sure the DOS version will work.

▪ Be sure you have enough hard disk space. A good starting point is 10 megabytes. Setup will let you know upon starting if it needs more. In addition, you should have about 1.5 megabytes of additional disk space for starting Windows.

▪ If the mouse is on COM3 or COM4, install it to another port. The Windows mouse does not work on COM3 or COM4.

▪ Make sure that everything is working under DOS: the mouse, printer, and video.

Modify the AUTOEXEC.BAT file to contain a PATH command that includes the Windows directory; the \DOS, \BAT, and \UTIL directories, and the directories for the application programs.

Performance Tip: When DOS searches for a file, it starts in the current directory and then proceeds down the directories of the PATH command left to right. Directories used most frequently should be first so that you can maximize speed. Since Windows is highly disk intensive, you generally should put its directory early in the list.

As an example of a PATH command, you might have in your file the commands shown in Figure 1.1. These commands set the path, define a symbolic name for the D:\TEMP sub-directory that Windows will use, define a new DOS prompt that will include the current directory, and clear the screen. Notice that the D:\WIN directory is listed first.

Figure 1.1

A printout of a typical AUTOEXEC.BAT file.

```
PATH D:\WIN;D:\DOS;C:\BAT;D:\UTIL;C:\
SET TEMP=D:\TEMP
PROMPT $p$g
CLS
```

After modifying the AUTOEXEC.BAT file, you will need to modify the CONFIG.SYS file in order to increase the number of files and buffers in use at one time. Add the lines shown in Figure 1.2 to your CONFIG.SYS file. (See Appendix G.)

Figure 1.2

A printout of a typical CONFIG.SYS file.

```
SHELL=C:\COMMAND.COM /P /E:512 /F
STACKS=0,0
FILES=40
BUFFERS=20
BREAK=ON
```

The first line of the file shown in Figure 1.2 defines the location of COMMAND.COM. Other parameters here force COMMAND.COM to run with AUTOEXEC.BAT and open the environment to 512K bytes.

The second line turns off the stacks for saving interrupts, which are no longer needed in DOS 3.3 or later. If you have DOS 3.2, set the stack line to **STACKS=9,192**. For a later version, use **STACKS=0,0**. For DOS 3.1, omit the STACKS line. If you have DOS 3.1, the /e parameter of the first line should be **/E:32**. Use **/E:512** for DOS 3.2 or later. For DOS 3.1, don't use the /e parameter in the first line or in the STACKS= line.

Most of the modifications of the AUTOEXEC.BAT and the CONFIG.SYS files are automatic during Windows installation. Save the originals and let the Setup program modify them. You should, however, have some understanding of what is happening and be able to tune the installation to your specific needs. Refer to your DOS manual if you need more help with this.

Be sure there are no APPEND, JOIN, FASTOPEN, or SHARE commands in the AUTOEXEC.BAT file. Remove all TSRs. Windows doesn't like them.

Preinstallation

Before starting the installation, make sure that the following conditions are met: unused files are deleted, the system is backed up, you've created a boot diskette, the TEMP directory is defined, you've run CHKDSK on every drive, the disk is compressed, and all TSRs are removed.

Deleting Unused Files

Another tip for improved performance is to clear files you are no longer using from the disk by deleting them. This is particularly true of the files in the \TEMP directory.

Backing Up the System

Your next task should be to back up your system. If you have invested in a tape system, back up to tape and then verify the backup tapes. Otherwise, use a program that can back up the hard disk to diskettes. Back up all drives.

If you are currently using Windows 3.0 in the 386 enhanced mode, delete the permanent swap file before backing up the system and installing the update from 3.0 to 3.1. This will minimize the number of backup diskettes and tapes as well as save time. To delete the permanent swap file from Windows 3.0, start Windows in the real mode (**WIN /r**). Use **F**ile **R**un to execute SWAPFILE.EXE on the WIN\SYSTEM directory.

At this time you may wish to create copies of both CONFIG.SYS and AUTOEXEC.BAT on the hard disk, since Windows will modify these files. Use names like CONFIG.SAV and AUTOEXEC.SAV. Don't use the extension .OLD because Windows will use this extension.

Creating a Boot Diskette

If you haven't already, you should create a boot diskette. This enables you to boot the system if you can no longer boot from the hard disk. It also is a very valuable disk for backup work.

For example, I use a boot diskette when backing up to tape cartridges with SYSTOS. This quickly eliminates all TSRs and enables the backup to be done from a simple configuration.

To create the boot diskette, format a new diskette and put it in drive A. Then enter the following command to copy the system files to the diskette:

```
C>SYS A:
```

You can also use **FORMAT A:** /**S** to create a boot diskette. This command copies both the system files and COMMAND.COM. If you used the command **SYS A:**, you will now need to copy COMMAND.COM to this same diskette.

Create any basic CONFIG.SYS file for your system. Normally this is simply a matter of creating a two-line file:

```
FILES=40
BUFFERS=20
```

If you have a third-party disk manager such as SpeedStor, you may need to add a DEVICE= line to the file. Add any other support you think is important, but avoid any TSRs or extra drivers. It's also a good idea to place a simple editor on the disk.

Once you've created the diskette, check it out. Be sure you can boot from it and read the hard disk.

Defining the TEMP Directory

Windows and many applications (including some DOS applications) use temporary files for storing data. These are automatically stored in a TEMP or TMP directory, if it exists. Define a TEMP directory for your system by adding two lines to AUTOEXEC.BAT:

```
SET TEMP=C:\TEMP
SET TMP=C:\TEMP
```

Be sure to include both lines because some programs use one variable and some the other.

> **Performance Tip:** Add a line to AUTOEXEC.BAT to clear these temporary directories upon booting. Otherwise, they can get cluttered and may cause abnormal program terminations in Windows. (See Appendix G.)

Clearing Lost Clusters with CHKDSK

DOS stores and retrieves information from the hard disk in cluster entities. A *cluster* is the smallest addressable storage unit on a disk and is normally about 2K in size.

To allocate clusters for files, DOS (and Windows) uses a *FAT* (File Allocation Table) stored at the beginning of the disk. This table defines which clusters are in use and identifies the chain of clusters used for each file on the disk. To maximize the speed of the disk, DOS does most of its directory updating by using a memory buffer, and it updates the hard disk directory only after the file is closed. If a program should have an abnormal termination, one or more files may not have their directory entries properly updated. The result is *lost clusters*; that is, the FAT on the disk shows that the clusters are in use, but DOS can't find any file in the directory using the clusters.

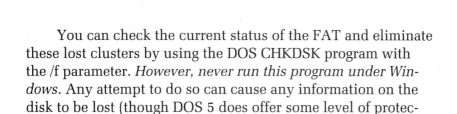

You can check the current status of the FAT and eliminate these lost clusters by using the DOS CHKDSK program with the /f parameter. *However, never run this program under Windows.* Any attempt to do so can cause any information on the disk to be lost (though DOS 5 does offer some level of protection). Exit Windows, and then run CHKDSK directly from DOS by typing the following command when you see the prompt:

CHKDSK /F

You may get a message about lost clusters. Go ahead and press Y to let DOS fix them. After the program terminates, the clusters will be in files with a CHK extension. If you wish, you can examine these files with an editor, but in most cases you can simply delete them.

Note: Getting messages about lost clusters with CHKDSK doesn't mean the disk is going bad. It simply means that one or more programs weren't terminated properly. You may have rebooted without closing a program, ended a program without closing a data file, or turned the computer off while a program was still active.

Run CHKDSK periodically, such as before backups, before compressing a disk, or before changing the disk interleave. Also run it after any unexpected disk crash. It should be run on each drive. No recovery is made unless the /f parameter is specified, regardless of the message you get. For best results, run CHKDSK before each backup.

Compressing the Disk

DOS stores files on the disk as one or more clusters, with the size of the cluster varying between systems. Normally, a cluster is about 2K or 4K. With DOS 5 and 127 megabytes of logical drive or less, clusters are 2K. Over this, DOS uses 4K clusters. A 2.4K file, for example, really takes two clusters, or 4K. When you delete a file from the disk, its clusters are made available for other files. When a new file is saved, it uses any free clusters it can find, and often the clusters are scattered on the disk. As you continue to use the disk, pieces of files become scattered on the disk and access times for an entire file deteriorate.

To improve disk performance, you need to compress the disk occasionally. You can use any of the various compression utilities such as Central Point's PC Tools, Norton Utilities, or Mace Utilities. These utilities physically move the files on the disk so that all the clusters for each file are physically adjacent on the disk. The directory is also updated to reflect the new location of the files. All the free space on the disk is placed after the files. Thus, new files can be saved (at least for a while) in sequential clusters.

The best time to compress the disk is when you are backing it up. You also must compress any drive used for a permanent swap file before the permanent swap file is installed.

Before installing Windows, compress the hard disk drive that will contain the Windows routines by using a compression utility, such as PC Tools' Compress. Compressing the disk will ensure the most efficient operation of Windows.

When you are using a permanent swap file in 386 enhanced mode, the space for this file must use *contiguous clusters;* that is, they must be serially adjacent. If there is an

Preparing to Install Windows

insufficient number of contiguous clusters, the permanent swap file can't be created. Compressing the disk is the best way of making the most number of contiguous clusters available.

Removing all TSRs, Unused Drivers, and Memory Managers

Before starting, remove all TSRs (memory-resident programs), unused drivers, and memory managers from the system. Edit the AUTOEXEC.BAT and CONFIG.SYS files (see Appendix G), commenting out the lines with the TSRs, unused drivers, and memory managers by adding **REM** at the beginning of each. Then reboot. For example, edit

`SHARE /F:2048 /L:20`

to read

`REM SHARE /F:2048 /L:20`

> **Performance Tip:** Once the installation is complete, you may want to add the SHARE.EXE program (if it is not already there) by inserting the preceding SHARE line (minus the **REM**) in AUTOEXEC.BAT. SHARE.EXE prevents two programs from writing to the same file at the same time. Since Windows is a multitasking environment, this program is a good idea.

Remove any drivers from CONFIG.SYS if they are not essential to the system operation. For example, remove any

virus-checking, CD-ROM, audio board, and other unusual drivers. Leave any special drivers for the disk in place.

Most recent versions of memory managers will work with Windows, but you should check with the manufacturer to be sure that you are using the latest version and that Windows 3.1 is supported. In addition, you may need to change the configuration before starting the installation. For 386MAX, for example, the EXT parameter should never be below 64. Setting the parameter to 0 can cause the system to hang.

TSRs vary in their ability to work with Windows. For installation, it is safer to remove them. In all probability, however, you will want to use some TSRs with Windows. Try the following to get some information on what works and what doesn't work with the installation and Windows:

- Read SETUP.TXT on the first Windows 3.1 Setup disk for the latest information on TSRs and your version of Windows.

- Read the file for the [incompTSR1] section of SETUP.INF, which defines TSRs that can't be loaded during installation. A second section of SETUP.INF, [incompTSR2], defines TSRs that can't be used with Setup or when Windows is running. SETUP.INF appears in uncompressed form on the first Windows disk.

- Run SETUP /t from the DOS prompt to force the Setup program to do an analysis of currently running TSRs. You'll get a report similar to the one shown in Figure 1.3. Don't put too much trust in this report, however.

Some TSRs should be removed just during Setup. You can then use them with Windows. Others should be run from Windows as stand-alone programs. Others should not be used with Windows under any condition. In many cases, the

Windows installation can catch any troublesome TSRs that you may have installed and can stop its installation. Don't, however, depend on this. Popular mouse programs (such as Logitech's Click and Logicmenu) as well as some DOS TSRs (JOIN, SHARE, APPEND, etc.) can cause problems.

```
Windows Setup

    Setup has found the programs listed below on your system. When Setup
    or Windows runs with some versions of these programs, your system may
    fail. It is recommended that you quit Setup now and look in the
    file SETUP.TXT for information about using these programs with Setup
    or Windows. Then run Setup again.

    Note: SETUP.TXT is a text file located on disk 1 of your Windows
    disk set. If you need information about accessing SETUP.TXT, see
    Troubleshooting in your Windows documentation.

    CED.COM        running        CED Command Line Editor
    CED.EXE        running        PCED Command Line Editor




      • Press ENTER or F3 to quit Setup.
      • Press C to continue Setup.
 ENTER=Exit  F3=Exit  C=Continue
```

Figure 1.3
SETUP /t analyzes which TSRs are currently running on your system.

Updating from Windows 3.0

If you are upgrading from a previous version of Windows, you can install the new version over the old version and automatically keep your program groups and special edits of the INI files. There is a disadvantage, however. You may find that some applications will not run on Windows 3.1, and you will thus need your old version for them. In addition, you are trusting Windows to update properly, and it may not.

The safest way to upgrade is to install the new version of Windows to a separate directory. If you are too short on disk space to do this, back up the old version and install Windows 3.1 over it. Here are a few precautions:

■ Don't install the new version to something like \WIN31. You need to avoid long path names, such as one with a version number in it. Also, always using \WIN ensures that all references to the Windows files and to the batch files using Windows will still work.

■ Don't rename the old directory to something like \WINOLD and install the new version to a new directory with the old name, such as \WIN. Some files in the old version contain references to specific files in specific directories, for example, the GRP files. If you rename a Windows directory, it won't work any more.

Secrets and Surprises: The jury is still out on the question of whether to load Windows 3.1 over Windows 3.0 when upgrading or whether to place Windows 3.1 in a new directory. The Windows installation is supposed to be smart enough to permit you to load the new version over the old. The advantage of this method is that you preserve original program groups, any previous multi-media installation, and parameters in the WIN.INI file. What is true in theory, however, is often not true in practice. With some systems, this method just won't work. Some Windows 3.0 programs won't run with 3.1. Whichever way you do it, back up all system drives before installing so that you can get back home if you need to.

If you elect to install Windows 3.1 over an older Windows 3.0, SETUP.INF on the first Setup diskette is already set up to define the procedure. SETUP.INF is a text file that has several sections identified by headings such as [win.copy]. During Windows installation:

- Files listed in [win.copy], [win.copy.net], or [win.copy.win386] and [update.files] are copied to the appropriate directories.
- Files listed in [delFiles] are deleted.
- WIN.INI is updated based on [ini.upd.31].
- Program Manager groups are redefined based on [new.groups].
- WINVER.EXE is updated.

Secrets and Surprises: If you elect to install Windows 3.1 in a separate directory and keep Windows 3.0, copy all the INI and GRP files from the Windows 3.0 directory into the new directory you will use for Windows before you install Windows 3.1. This will preserve groups and customizations. Otherwise, you will need to rebuild groups.

Installing Windows with DOS 5

If possible, you should upgrade to DOS 5 before installing Windows. DOS 5 is specifically designed for better support of Windows 3. You will have fewer Windows problems, better memory management, and more utilities.

DOS 5 permits loading DOS in the high memory area (HMA), giving more conventional memory for programs (see

Chapter 3). You can also load some drivers high in the upper memory blocks, or UMBs (see Appendix A), giving even more conventional memory. The following drivers can be loaded high: ANSI.SYS, DISPLAY.SYS, DRIVER.SYS, EGA.SYS, PRINTER.SYS, and RAMDRIVE.SYS. The following DOS TSRs can also be loaded high: DOSKEY.COM, DOSSHELL.COM, GRAPHICS.COM, KEYB.COM, NLSFUNC.EXE, PRINT.EXE, MODE.COM, and SHARE.EXE. Don't use APPEND.COM with Windows. If you are already using SHARE.EXE, disable it during installation (comment it out) and then add it in again after installation. Don't load HIMEM.SYS, SMARTDrive.SYS, or EMM386.SYS high. Don't try tricky things, such as placing files or buffers high.

If DOS 5 is installed to high memory (the HMA), make sure that no other DOS applications use this area. Turn off the use of the area in the application's PIF file. Also turn it off in the _DEFAULT.PIF file after Windows is installed.

To load DOS 5 high (to HMA), you must have at least a 286-based system with enough extended memory. Then add these lines to CONFIG.SYS:

```
DEVICE=C:\DOS\HIMEM.SYS
DOS=HIGH
```

Loading DOS high is generally automatic on DOS 5 installation. Also, with DOS 5 you will probably wish to add the EMM386.DRV driver so that you can load all drivers high in the UMB area (see Appendix A and Chapter 14).

You may still wish to use a third-party memory manager with DOS 5, such as QEMM-386. Most third-party memory managers have features not included with DOS 5, such as better management of the UMB area.

Windows 3.1 Installation

Now you've prepared your system and you're ready to install Windows 3.1. This section contains the instructions for doing so. If you encounter any problems when you run Setup, refer to Chapter 2 for "Help with Installation Problems."

Here are a few tips on installation:

- Save a copy of WIN.INI under a different name.

- The files on the Windows diskettes are in a compressed format. Don't try to install Windows by copying them to the hard disk. If necessary to recover a selected file, use the EXPAND utility on the diskettes.

- Create copies of the installation diskettes and install from the copies. Using copies ensures that you don't damage the master diskettes.

If you wish to use custom Setup options, the switches you can use (type) with Setup are described in Table 1.1.

Switch	Purpose
/a	Installs Windows to a network server. Files will be read-only (see Chapter 14).
/b	Forces Setup to monochrome display.
/i	Bypasses automatic hardware detection in Setup.
/n	Sets up shared copy of Windows on a network server (see Chapter 14).

Table 1.1

Switches Available with Windows 3.1 Setup

continues

Windows 3.1 Installation

21

Table 1.1

continued

Switch	Purpose
/t	Searches driver for incompatible software with Windows.
/h:*filespec*	Runs a batch mode for Setup without user intervention.
/o:*filepath*	Uses *filepath* for Setup instead of SETUP.INF.
/s:*filepath*	Specifies *filepath* for SETUP.INF and the Windows installation disks.

You can verify the switches by typing **SETUP /?**. For a network installation, see Chapter 14.

To install Windows, reboot to use the new AUTOEXEC.BAT and CONFIG.SYS files. Place the first disk in the drive that you want to use for the installation and switch to that drive. Type the command:

A:SETUP

and then follow the directions on the screen.

Secrets and Surprises: At one place in the installation, Windows will ask for some information about your name and company and will then write it to the installation diskette. The safest method is to use copies of the installation disks. At any rate, always use a copy of the diskette that has the open write-protect slot.

Preparing to Install Windows

If you need help during Setup, press the F1 key. Read the prompts for additional help during installation. After finishing the installation, you are given the option of starting Windows immediately.

With Windows 3.1, the Setup program will ask if you wish an express install or a custom install. With the *express install*, Windows will automatically sense the hardware you are using and will install Windows appropriately for that hardware. If you are installing Windows for the first time, the default installation is to the C:\WINDOWS directory. If you are upgrading from Windows 3.0, Windows will prompt you with the current directory and give you the option of changing it. You can change the default directory by editing the `defdir` parameter in SETUP.INF before installation. This file is on the first disk. It permits you to do an express install to any directory without requiring that a previous version of Windows be on the hard disk.

You need the *custom install* only if Windows can't sense your hardware appropriately or if you are installing Windows for the first time to a directory other than the default directory defined by SETUP.INF. Check with your hardware manufacturer to see if a custom install is needed for your system and what hardware to specify.

At the end of the installation, Setup will ask if it should update AUTOEXEC.BAT and CONFIG.SYS. Let Windows do it. You should have backup copies, and you can always use the boot diskette if it's needed. Let Windows do everything if possible. The only exception to updating these files is if you are installing Windows to OS/2. You will then need to reboot before starting Windows.

HELP WITH INSTALLATION PROBLEMS

Installing Windows is usually a straightforward process, but sometimes you may encounter error messages or your system will simply *hang* (that is, stop and become unresponsive) during installation. With most installation problems, Windows will display a message and you can take appropriate action. In some cases, however, you may find that the system hangs during Setup and displays no message. In this case, the most likely cause is a TSR that is still installed or a hardware conflict. This chapter will address various types of installation problems and how to resolve them.

The first part of this chapter gives some guidelines for solving general Setup problems.

Help! My system hangs during Setup.

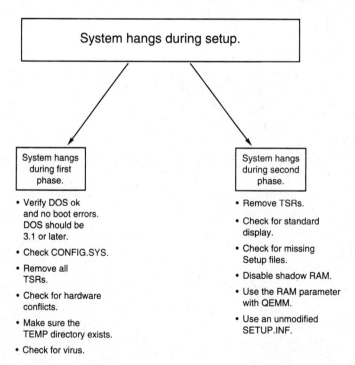

System hangs during setup.

System hangs during first phase.

- Verify DOS ok and no boot errors. DOS should be 3.1 or later.
- Check CONFIG.SYS.
- Remove all TSRs.
- Check for hardware conflicts.
- Make sure the TEMP directory exists.
- Check for virus.

System hangs during second phase.

- Remove TSRs.
- Check for standard display.
- Check for missing Setup files.
- Disable shadow RAM.
- Use the RAM parameter with QEMM.
- Use an unmodified SETUP.INF.

Setup is actually a two-step process:

- The first step (typing **SETUP** at the DOS prompt) is actually a DOS program. This step determines your configuration and does some initial checking for the Windows mode to use (see Appendix B).

- Once this is done, the Setup process loads Windows and then completes the Setup under *standard mode* (Windows 3.1) or *real mode* (Windows 3.0) by copying the appropriate files for standard or enhanced mode, installing the driver and PIF files, and building the Program Manager groups.

Setup is two programs bound in a single executable file. To identify the problem, you need to ascertain whether Windows successfully completed the first step. Windows has completed the first step if Setup is displaying a graphic screen asking for your name and company. This is the third diskette when you are installing Windows 3.1.

My system hangs during the first phase of Setup.

When this happens, it means that the system hung while still running under DOS. Check the following:

- Be sure the system is working properly for DOS programs. There should be no hangups during DOS program execution, and there should be no error messages, such as a memory failure. If there is a problem here, use a diagnostic utility, MEM, or MSD to find the cause. MEM is provided with DOS, and MSD is provided with Windows. MSD is on disk 5 in uncompressed form.

Reboot and verify there are no error messages during bootup. If there are error messages, fix the problem in bootup first.

Be sure you are using DOS 3.1 or later. Windows will not run on earlier versions of DOS. Type **VER** at the DOS prompt to find out which version of DOS you are using. Update DOS if necessary.

☐ Make sure that CONFIG.SYS contains the following lines. (Use any text editing program or EDLIN to edit CONFIG.SYS. See Appendix G.)

```
FILES=40
BUFFERS=20
```

☐ The most common cause of lockup during the first phase of install is a TSR interference. You may or may not see an error message. Setup first tries to sense troublesome TSRs and will indicate their names. Make sure that all TSRs are removed and that you have rebooted to a TSR-free system. You can use the DOS MEM command to verify this (type **MEM** and press Enter).

Note: The best way to remove TSRs for Setup is to edit the AUTOEXEC.BAT and CONFIG.SYS files, putting **REM** before each TSR or driver that you don't need, for example, **REM DOSSHELL**. This gives you an "audit trail" for putting things back together after the installation. See Appendix G.

☐ Another common cause of lockup during the first phase of install is a hardware conflict. If all TSRs are removed and Windows still won't get to the second phase, it's probably a hardware conflict. If you suspect a hardware conflict, try starting the install by typing **SETUP /i**. This bypasses the automatic hardware sensing. Windows then displays a default generic system definition. Select the appropriate settings manually and then complete the installation.

The most common type of hardware conflict that Windows has trouble sensing is video driver type. Some older display drivers just aren't recognized properly by Windows. If this happens, install by using the command **SETUP /i**. Try using a more generic driver (EGA or VGA) and see if that works.

Note: When you use the /i option, choosing the wrong hardware can crash your hard disk. Back up the disk first.

Check the dates on any drivers in CONFIG.SYS. There should be no drivers 1987 or older. To obtain the date of the driver, use the DIR command with each driver, for example, **DIR DVRMGR.SYS**.

You should also try to contact your system manufacturer for any special instructions for Windows installation. Many types of hardware require special installation instructions.

◻ Be sure the TEMP directory is defined by AUTOEXEC.BAT. Check to see that there are no spaces before or after the equal (=) sign in the SET command of AUTOEXEC.BAT (SET TEMP=C:\TEMP).

◻ Make sure the system is virus-free by using a program to scan for viruses.

My system hangs during the second phase of Setup.

During the second phase of Setup, Windows tries to start in the standard (Windows 3.1) or the real (Windows 3.0) mode. A system hangup here generally indicates that a TSR is installed or that there is a hardware conflict, most probably with the display. Check the following:

- Verify that all TSRs are removed (see "My system hangs during the first phase of Setup.").

- Check for standard video display. Then use **SETUP** /**i** and select a basic generic display, such as EGA or VGA, as appropriate.

- A second possible cause is a missing Setup file. Compare the disk copies you're using to the original diskettes.

- Disable shadow RAM if your system uses it. The method for doing this varies with the hardware manufacturer. Consult the documentation that came with your system. Some systems use a special area of memory for high-speed BIOS that is in the UMB. If Windows can't sense this, you can have troubles.

- If you are using QEMM-386, make sure the RAM parameter is used in AUTOEXEC.BAT, as follows:

  ```
  DEVICE=C:\QEMM\QEMM386.SYS RAM
  ```

- Finally, remember that Setup is driven from the SETUP.INF file. If you have modified this file, this can cause the Setup to hang. Recover the original file from the Windows disk.

Help! I have floppy disk problems during Setup.

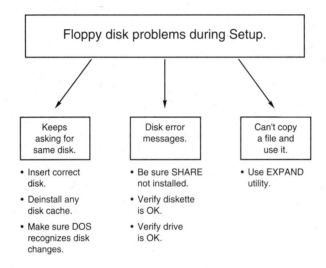

Messages about the floppy disk drive can generally be divided into two categories: error messages that indicate something is wrong with the drive, and messages that indicate the wrong diskette is in the drive.

I keep getting a prompt for the same disk or a beep and the screen doesn't change.

▪ You are trying to put the wrong diskette in the drive. Check the diskette label.

▪ Try disabling any disk cache utility by removing that line from CONFIG.SYS. (Don't forget to reboot after doing so.)

Help! I have floppy disk problems during Setup.

31

■ Another possibility is that DOS does not recognize that the diskette in the drive has changed. Add a `DRIVEPARM` line to the CONFIG.SYS file. (See the DOS documentation and also Appendix G; use a text editing program or EDLIN to edit AUTOEXEC.BAT.) For a 1.2MB drive in A, this line would be

```
DRIVEPARM=/d:0 /f:1
```

Then remove the Setup disk, reboot the computer, and try the install again.

I get disk error messages on installing.

■ Make sure the SHARE utility is not installed (check AUTOEXEC.BAT).

■ The floppy disk might be bad, causing an error. Copy the original Windows disks on another system by using the DOS DISKCOPY command and then rerun Setup from the copy.

■ Check to see if the drive has problems reading diskettes from DOS. In this case, repair or replace the drive.

I copied an installation file to the hard disk, but it won't work.

You normally don't need to copy an installation file to the hard disk during installation. You would need to do this only if you suspected that a file was damaged or missing from the hard disk.

The files on the Setup diskettes are compressed. You can identify a file as compressed because its filename extension includes an underscore. To restore an individual file, you must use the EXPAND utility on the diskettes (disk 2 for Windows 3.1). The proper format is

EXPAND *x:\filename1 y:\filename2*

where *x:\filename1* is the source and *y:\filename2* is the destination; that is, use EXPAND like you would the COPY command.

Video, Keyboard, and Printer Drivers

Your system's monitor, keyboard, and printer(s) each require a special software routine called a *driver*. The driver is the physical program code that interfaces Windows with your particular hardware. Once installed, any Windows application can use that device.

Windows contains a wide base of drivers for many types of hardware. It is impossible, however, for Microsoft to provide all the necessary drivers with Windows. The drivers use the DRV extension and are placed in the \WINDOWS\SYSTEM directory.

The video driver, network driver, and keyboard driver are provided with Windows. Setup senses the hardware and installs most of the appropriate drivers automatically. The printer is installed during Setup when the user selects the desired printer from a displayed list.

If you need a driver for a new printer or video that is not supported by the version of Windows that you have, you should contact the manufacturer to obtain the driver.

Note: Many drivers designed for Windows 3.0 are not compatible with Windows 3.1, since Windows 3.1 supports 32-bit device drivers. Use the drivers included with Windows 3.1 instead of the drivers included with your video or printer unless you are assured that your old drivers will work with Windows 3.1.

Help! I can't install a video device.

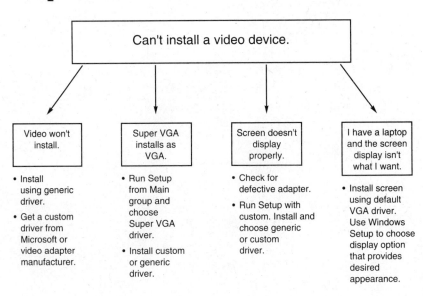

As the preceding discussion explains, device drivers can inhibit effective Windows installation. In general, video driver installation problems will appear in one of three forms:

▢ The adapter won't install at all.

- Super VGA installs as VGA.
- After installing, the screen doesn't display properly.

My video adapter wouldn't install.

- Choose the generic VGA or Super VGA adapter during Setup.
- Get a custom driver from Microsoft or the manufacturer of the video adapter card and install it.

I have a Super VGA adapter, but it installed as VGA.

- After Windows is installed, choose the Windows Setup icon from the Main program group by double-clicking on the icon. Use the **O**ptions **C**hange System Settings command from the Windows Setup dialog box. Choose **Di**splay in the Change System Settings dialog box (see Figure 2.1) to install the Super VGA driver.

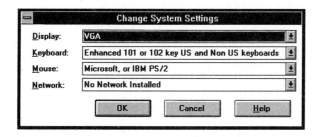

Figure 2.1
Changing the driver with the Change System Settings dialog box.

Help! I can't install a video device.

35

Another alternative is to install the custom driver that came with the video adapter board. Use the directions provided on the disk that comes with the adapter. Super VGA can run as 16 colors or 256 colors. Using 16 colors will improve the speed dramatically unless the adapter board has a coprocessor or accelerator. If installing a third-party (custom) driver, be sure it works with Windows 3.1. If not, use the generic drivers with Windows.

Windows are not displayed correctly or the screen is blank.

The display driver may be defective. See Chapter 7.

Try running Setup using a custom install and choose a generic driver from Microsoft or a custom driver from a video card manufacturer.

I have a laptop, and the screen display is not what I want. How do I install the screen for a laptop?

Install by using the default VGA driver. After Windows is installed, use Windows Setup on the Main group of Program Manager. Select **C**hange System Settings from the **O**ptions menu and select the type of display: LCD Default, LCD Reversed Dark, LCD Reversed Light, or Plasma Power Saver. Windows is normally dark on a light screen. The "Reversed" options reverse this, placing light characters on a dark screen. This will save power with a portable, which has a finite battery life.

Help! I can't set up another keyboard.

```
┌─────────────────────────────────────────────────────┐
│                                                       │
│               Can't set up keyboard.                  │
│                                                       │
└─────────────────────────────────────────────────────┘
                           │
                           ▼
```

- Make sure the driver file is in the \WIN directory.
- Edit the keyboard.dle line in SYSTEM.INI.
- For a portable or laptop, install the keyboard to emulate a 101-key Enhanced AT keyboard.

Troubleshoot keyboard problems just as you would problems with the video display. Try the keyboard with DOS first to verify that the problem is not with the keyboard hardware. If the keyboard works with DOS, the problem is with the keyboard driver in Windows on the \WINDOWS\SYSTEM directory. A bad driver can cause some keys to display garbage or not work at all, yet the same keys work fine in DOS.

To change the keyboard, start Windows Setup from the Main group of Program Manager. Select Change System Settings from the Options menu. Select the Keyboard option; then select the type of keyboard. Windows will prompt for any diskette that is needed.

When you choose a new keyboard layout by running Windows Setup from the Main program group, you may get messages about inserting diskettes. If so, try the following:

Help! I can't set up another keyboard.

37

■ Make sure the keyboard driver file is already in the Windows (\WINDOWS\SYSTEM) directory. To install the keyboard driver without copying it into the Windows directory and editing SYSTEM.INI, just insert the diskette with the driver file and Windows will take care of it. Copying the driver and editing SYSTEM.INI is taking the long way around. Why work when you can get the software to work for you?

■ If the driver file is in the right directory, edit the line in SYSTEM.INI that reads:

```
keyboard.dll=filename
```

to include the filename of the desired layout. To do so, make a backup copy of SYSTEM.INI in case you need to revert to its present version, open SYSTEM.INI in the Windows Notepad application or another text editor, make the necessary change, save SYSTEM.INI, and restart Windows. (See Appendix G.)

■ If the keyboard is not installed properly on a portable or laptop, install the keyboard to emulate a 101-key Enhanced AT keyboard, even though it has only 80 keys.

Help! I can't install my printer.

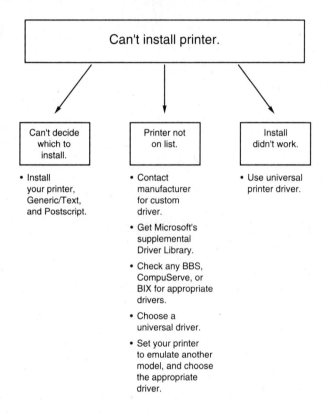

The printer is installed during the installation step from a list of printers in a dialog box. When you install Windows, the Setup procedure will install a default printer for immediate use.

Secrets and Surprises: If you wish to install more printers, double-click the Control Panel icon in the Main program group and double-click the Printers icon. From the Printers dialog box (see Figure 2.2), choose the Add Printer button, select a printer, and choose the Install button. Insert the Setup disk requested, and press Enter or click OK. The correct files are copied. Then, you must connect the printer to a port, configure the printer to work the way you want with Windows, and make it the active printer. See your *Windows User's Guide* for more information on these operations.

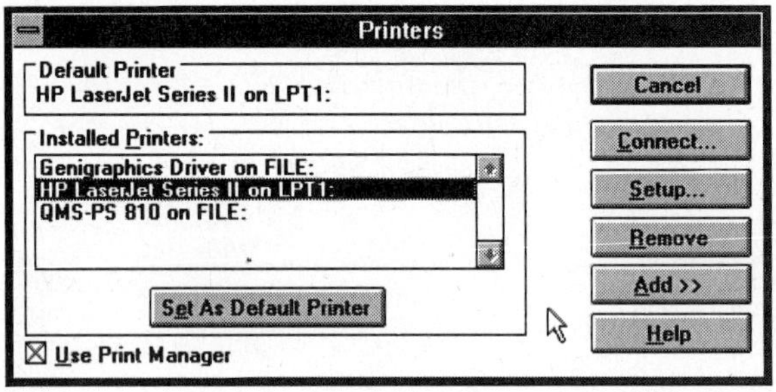
Printers
Default Printer
HP LaserJet Series II on LPT1:
Installed Printers:
Genigraphics Driver on FILE:
HP LaserJet Series II on LPT1:
QMS-PS 810 on FILE:
Set As Default Printer
Use Print Manager
Cancel
Connect...
Setup...
Remove
Add >>
Help

Figure 2.2
Setting up a new printer.

I can't decide which printer to install.

- It's a good idea to install drivers for each printer you are using, including both the Generic/Text printer and the PostScript printer drivers, even if the hardware isn't there. Start by installing one during the actual installation process. Use the Control Panel as described in the preceding Secrets and Surprises tip to set up additional printers. The Generic/Text printer driver is useful for printing to a file because it gives you an ASCII text file that you can import to Notepad or Write. The PostScript driver is useful for creating PostScript printer files, which can be used with commercial printers for high-quality printing. For example, you can set up a brochure with PageMaker and print it on your laser printer at 300 dpi. Once you like the draft, you can print to a file by using the PostScript printer driver. Then you can take the file to a commercial printer and print a master at 1200 dpi or more.

When installing a PostScript printer, be sure that error handling is enabled. To enable error handling, choose **O**ptions from the Setup dialog box and press Alt+E (even if not on the dialog box). Click OK as necessary to exit.

My printer isn't on Setup's list.

Avoid using Windows 3.0 printer drivers if you are using Windows 3.1. Here are some options you can use:

- Contact your printer manufacturer and obtain a custom driver file.

- Contact Microsoft or your hardware dealer to obtain the Windows Supplemental Driver Library (SDL). You will find many additional drivers here and the cost is low— about $20. Microsoft's number for the SDL is 800 426-9400.

- Check the various bulletin board services (BBS), CompuServe, and BIX. Many drivers are on these boards. Be sure, however, to download a Windows 3.1 driver if that's what you are using.

- Windows 3.1 includes some universal drivers for most printers. For example, the PostScript driver with

Windows 3.1 will work with almost any PostScript printer, and the PCL drivers will work for almost any laser printer. Use the universal printer driver instead of the driver provided with the printer for Windows unless you are sure the printer driver will work with Windows 3.1.

Some printers can emulate other printers. If this is true of your printer, you can set your printer for this particular emulation (see the printer documentation to learn how) and then install for that printer.

The printer installation didn't work.

Use the universal printer driver for your printer provided with Windows instead of any third-party driver.

Help! I get a message during Setup and then Setup aborts.

> After an error, Setup aborts.

- Remove TSRs and run Setup.
- Remove SHARE and SUBST and run Setup.
- Edit WIN.INI to make it smaller and run Setup.

There are several messages that can appear during Setup. The basic solution is to read the message and respond by correcting the error.

- You might get a message about a TSR being installed. Windows does not support some TSRs. Read the information in the SETUP.TXT file (which comes with Windows) about TSRs that won't work with Windows. Follow any specific directions given. Remove the TSR from AUTOEXEC.BAT and try running Setup from the DOS prompt again. After installation, try using the TSR as a stand-alone program. Many TSRs will work that way.

- If you get a message about SHARE or SUBST being installed, remove the SHARE or SUBST TSR line in AUTOEXEC.BAT, reboot, and restart Setup. You can put the SHARE loading line back in after installation.

- If you get a Setup Error #S020 error message, you are installing Windows over an older version and the WIN.INI used with that version is too large. Edit the file to make it smaller by eliminating unused programs and fonts. Then try running Setup again. (See Appendix G.)

Help! I get a message during Setup and then Setup aborts.

43

Help! I have hard disk problems.

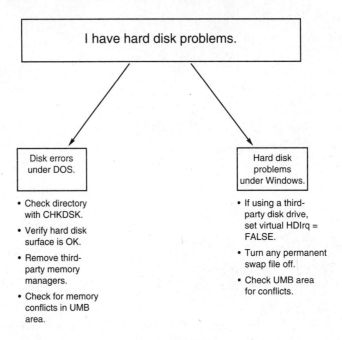

You may have hard disk problems before, during, or after running Setup. First, make sure your hard disk is working correctly.

I get disk errors under DOS.

If you followed the preparation steps in Chapter 1, you checked the hard disk before starting the installation by using both CHKDSK (which checks the directory only) and the compression utility, which often can verify that the disk is good. If you didn't do it then, do it now.

- If you are getting hard disk errors under DOS before installing Windows, make sure this problem is fixed before running Setup. Use a disk utility (such as Central Point's PC Tools) to verify that the disk surface is good. Use CHKDSK to verify that there are no lost clusters or defective allocations.

- Remove any memory managers currently installed by editing CONFIG.SYS (see Appendix G) and reboot. Reinstall after setting up Windows.

- Check for any memory conflicts in the UMB area (see Chapter 7 and Appendix A) by moving all drives and TSRs into conventional memory and then rebooting. Use the DOS MEM utility or other diagnostics to identify conflicts.

During or after running Setup, I have hard disk errors and lost data.

- If you are using Windows 3 and a third-party partitioning software program, such as SpeedStor or Disk Manager, you may have problems with Windows if either of two conditions is true. In the first condition, the drive has fewer than 1024 cylinders, the BIOS settings don't match the driver parameters, and you have DOS 3.3 or later. In the second condition, the drive has more than 1024 cylinders, and you are using DOS 3.3 or earlier.

  The problem will cause a loss of data from the hard disk. Back up your system before installing Windows! To see if the problem exists on your system, check with your system manufacturer. The rules can vary with hardware, DOS version, and Windows version.

You may have to disable SMARTDrive (by removing the line from CONFIG.SYS with a text editor—see Appendix G). In most cases, Windows will sense the driver and disable SMARTDrive automatically. Place the following line in the [386enh] section of SYSTEM.INI (see Appendix G for more on editing .INI files):

`VirtualHDIrq=FALSE`

■ Avoid using a permanent swap file or FastDisk (see Appendix B) with this type of system.

■ As with DOS errors, you may have a conflict in the UMB area (see Chapter 7 for solution methods).

Help! My system won't boot after I run Setup.

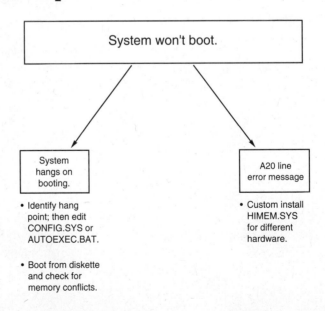

Help with Installation Problems

If your system fails to boot after you run Setup, the installation modified the CONFIG.SYS or AUTOEXEC.BAT file in such a way that the current hardware is no longer supported. In most cases, the hardware is recognized improperly during installation. Boot from a DOS disk rather than from the hard drive and modify the files as appropriate.

My system hangs on booting.

☐ Watch the screen during the boot and notice at what point the system hangs. Then check AUTOEXEC.BAT or CONFIG.SYS at that point.

☐ If you have a memory manager and are loading drivers and TSRs high, you may have a memory conflict, particularly in the UMB area. Boot from a diskette and then edit the line that installs the EMM386.SYS driver (or memory manager) to exclude the memory in the UMB area that is causing the problem.

I get the error message "Cannot install A20 line" when booting.

☐ This error message indicates that the HIMEM.SYS driver, which is loaded from CONFIG.SYS, is not working properly. The type of hardware you have is not being recognized by the driver. Try installing HIMEM.SYS by adding

Help! My system won't boot after I run Setup.

47

the /M:*x* switch to its command line in CONFIG.SYS, where *x* indicates the hardware type. See Table 2.1 for the appropriate number to substitute for *x*. When HIMEM.SYS is properly installed, you should see the message `Installed A20 handler number` *x*, where *x* is a number corresponding to a particular hardware.

Table 2.1

Hardware
Switch Codes
for
HIMEM.SYS

Code (x)	Hardware
1	IBM AT compatible
2	IBM PS/2
3	Phoenix Cascade BIOS
4	HP Vectra
5	AT&T 6300 Plus
6	Acer 1100
7	Toshiba 1600 & 1200XE
8	Wyse 12.5 Mhz 286
9	Tulip SX
10	Zenith ZBIOS
11	IBM PC/AT
12	IBM PC/AT (alternate), CSS Labs
13	IBM PC/AT (alternate), Phillips
14	HP Vectra
15	IBM 7552
16	Bull Mocral 60

Note: Use the numbers listed in Table 2.1 with care. If you enter the wrong number, you can scramble the FAT of the hard disk. Back up the system first!

Help! I'm using a disk compression TSR (such as Stacker) and Windows didn't install properly.

> I'm using a disk compression TSR and Windows didn't install properly.

- Many disk compression utilities won't work with Windows 3.1.

- If utility will work with Windows 3.1, locate all DRV files on noncompressed drives.

Many disk compression utilities will not work with Windows 3.1 at all.

☐ Check with the manufacturer to see if your utility is designed to work with Windows 3.1.

☐ If you can use the utility with Windows 3.1, all disk drivers (DRV files) must be located on noncompressed drives. The drivers should also be listed in CONFIG.SYS

Help! I'm using a disk compression TSR and Windows didn't install properly.

49

before the lines that install compressed drives. SMARTDrive should not be used to cache compressed drives. Permanent swap files should not be on compressed drives.

Help! I'm using Digital Research's DR DOS and have problems installing Windows 3.1.

```
I'm using DR DOS and can't install
            Windows 3.1
```

- Remove all TSRs from memory.
- Contact Digital Research for version of DR DOS that works with Windows 3.1.

☐ Be sure all TSRs are removed from memory.

☐ If Windows still doesn't install, contact Digital Research for a version of DR DOS that works with Windows 3.1.

Changing the Setup After Installation

After installing Windows, you may wish to change the Setup at a later time. Typical issues include changing the video driver, changing the keyboard driver, changing the mouse driver, or changing the display font. You can make these changes by running Windows Setup again from the Main group.

Using the Setup program from Windows' Program Manager (the Main program group) permits you to change a video, mouse, or network device driver. When you initially install Windows, Setup tries to detect the video, mouse, keyboard, and any network device you are using and then installs for them.

If this method fails, you must either use the Setup program from Windows to change one or more of these drivers or reinstall Windows from scratch. Use **SETUP** */i* or a custom install, in this case, to override the automatic sensing. If you change the system unit or disk controller, reinstall Windows from scratch.

How do I change the video drivers?

After you have installed Windows, you may wish to change the video driver at a later time. For example, you may be upgrading to a higher-resolution screen or you may wish to use a different driver for display purposes other than the one that normally is installed.

If the installation involves selecting a new driver from Windows, the installation is simple. Start Setup by double-clicking on its icon. Then select Change System Settings from the Options menu to display the Change System Settings dialog box (see Figure 2.1 shown earlier). Select Display to change the display. Select the new driver and OK. Then restart Windows.

Installing a third-party video driver supplied with an adapter board is a tricky task to try, and often the directions provided with the video adapter can actually crash your Windows installation or hang the computer. To be safe, back up your system first and then install the video driver manually. Here are two methods for doing it:

Method 1

If there is an OEMSETUP.INF file on the driver disk, you can use this method.

1. Back up the system.

2. Run Setup from DOS.

3. Select Other as the last item in the Display list.

4. Insert the new driver disk. Setup reads OEMSETUP.INF, which copies the files and modifies your SYSTEM.INI file.

Method 2

1. Back up the computer.

2. Copy any drivers on the new driver disk (DRV extension) as well as any files with a 386 extension to the WINDOWS\SYSTEM directory.

3. Use Windows Notepad to examine the SETUP.INF file on the new driver disk. This includes the parameters you will need for the SYSTEM.INI file. Print a copy of this file.

4. Examine new SETUP.INF on the driver disk for a section labeled [display]. You should see a list with some DRV filenames. Highlight the lines for the drivers you are using and use **E**dit **C**opy to place the lines in the Clipboard.

5. Open the old SETUP.INF in the Windows directory. Locate the [display] section and paste the new lines from the Clipboard at the end of the section. This will make the new display driver available for the normal Setup program.

6. Run Windows Setup from DOS to select the new driver. Select Other as the last item in the Display list.

7. Restart Windows.

To upgrade your display to a higher resolution, you must first run Setup from the Main group of Program Manager to change to the new mode. Then change the video adapter card and perhaps change to a monitor that supports the higher resolution. Restart Windows. The Super VGA 800 x 600 resolution requires a monitor with a 35-kHz horizontal scan rate. To use a 1024 x 768 resolution, you will need a 49-kHz scan rate. Windows drivers for the new higher-resolution displays are often available from the video adapter manufacturer and from Microsoft, CompuServe, or local bulletin boards. For more information on displays, see Chapter 7.

The specifications for the driver in SETUP.INF may look mysterious, particularly the three numbers 100,96,96. The last two numbers are the vertical and the horizontal resolution, respectively, in dots per logical inch. The first number is the ratio of the resolutions multiplied by 100 [(96/96)*100].

To understand the logical inch, assume you have a piece of paper 8.5 inches wide. With a left and a right margin of approximately 1 inch, assume that this leaves a 6.6-inch line width. With 10 display characters per inch, the line width would be 66 characters, or 6.6 characters/inch. Now assume that this width has to be mapped to the 640-pixel width of the VGA display. The fraction 640/6.6 gives 96.7 pixels per inch, the same as the specification in the SETUP.INF file.

How do I change other drivers?

Windows uses its own mouse driver, which is in the \WIN directory. DOS applications use the mouse driver in the root directory of the C drive. To change the mouse driver, edit the SYSTEM.INI file accordingly (see Appendix G) and be sure the corresponding driver is in the \WINDOWS\SYSTEM directory. Alternatively, you can add any driver to the SETUP.INF file (as with a display driver) by using an editor (see Appendix G). The same is true of the keyboard driver.

How do I change the display font?

The new proportional system font introduced with Windows 3.0 makes working with the screen all day a pleasurable experience, but you may wish to change the font to allow more lines on the screen (or perhaps fewer). With Windows 3, you can experiment without having to do a complete Windows reinstallation. (It's still a good idea to back up the system first, however.)

As an example, let's assume your screen font is too small. You have a screen with a 400-line mode, and Windows installed the EGA fonts for 350 lines. This means you've got small fonts. You wish to change these to the larger VGA fonts. Here's how:

1. Copy the VGA*.FON files (VGASYS.FON, VGAFIX.FON, and VGAOEM.FON) from the installation disks to the \WINDOWS\SYSTEM directory.

2. Expand each with the EXPAND utility.

3. Back up SYSTEM.INI if you haven't already. That's the file you're changing.

4. Open SYSTEM.INI in Notepad or Sysedit and locate the lines:

```
[boot]
fixfon.fon=egafix.fon
oemfonts.fon=egaoem.fon
fonts.fon=egasys.fon
```

5. Substitute **vga** for ega in each line and save the file.

6. Restart Windows.

The display fonts will now be larger and easier to read. You don't need to replace the EGA typographic fonts (such as HELVB.FON). The VGA varieties here don't look very good at 400 lines.

If you have Super VGA with a 1024 x 768 resolution, you have another situation that may call for a larger system font. The VGA fonts, designed for 480 scan lines, now look too small. Try the 8514 fonts. The steps are the same, just use "8514" instead of "ega" or "vga." If you like the new fonts, you may wish to try the typographic fonts here as well. Expand TMSRF.FON, HELVF.FON, COURF.FON, and SYMBOLF.FON. Now edit these changes to WIN.INI in the [fonts] section, changing HELVE.FON to HELVF.FON for example. See Chapter 7 for more on the filename designations.

Customizing the Setup for Installing to Several Systems

At some time you may wish to create a customized Setup process. For example, you may be installing Windows in 100 machines and wish to add special printer drivers, application groups, or applications as a part of each Setup. This minimizes Setup problems at each location and ensures that each computer is set up identically. SETUP.INF is on the first Windows disk and is not compressed. Back it up before editing it.

SETUP.INF is the "driver" file for Setup and contains all the information (filenames, disks, comments, etc.) that are needed during Setup. You can edit this file with any text editor and create a customized Setup. (Don't use a word processor unless you can save the file in an ASCII form.) See Appendix G.

> **Tip:** Before changing SETUP.INF, be sure to make a backup copy.

The SETUP.INF file looks much like the familiar INI files. Section names appear in brackets, and the parameters for each section are defined. Table 2.2 lists the sections of interest to you. For more information on modifying the SETUP.INF file, see the *Windows Resource Kit* published by Microsoft.

Table 2.2

Sections of the SETUP.INF File

Section Name	Description
[run]	Specifies programs that should be run at the end of Setup, such as MIRROR.
[dialog]	Defines dynamic strings used in Setup dialogs.
[data]	Contains the default settings for Setup.

Section Name	Description
[disks]	Defines the input disks. If you wish to add disks to the Setup (such as for another printer driver), add them here.
[shell]	Defines the shell program to use.
[display]	Defines display types for windows in the following format: driver name, description, resolution, 286 Grabber, logo code, virtual display driver, 386 Grabber, EGA driver request (EGA.SYS), and logo bit map file. Modify this to add a custom driver. You will also see some numbers with each file to identify the disk containing the file, such as 1:8514.DRV.
[pointingdevice]	Defines supported pointing devices in the following format: profile name, driver, description, enhanced mode support file, and DOS mouse driver name. Again, numeric prefixes indicate the disk number. The designation x:*vmd indicates a virtual file that is built into WIN386.EXE.
[network]	Defines network information for installation in the form: profile=driver name, description, help file, optional file, section name in WIN.INI, section name in SYSTEM.INI, and enhanced support files. There may also be additional network-specific sections.

2

CHAPTER

Troubleshooting an Error on Installation

First run Setup with the /L parameter, using the following command:

SETUP /L

This won't fix the problem, but it will show where in the installation the problem occurred. Each step is saved to a log, and you can examine the log to see how much of Windows was installed and where the error occurred.

Caution: The Windows 3.1 Setup program performs several checks on installation. During this time, it can remove TSRs or drivers without warning. This is why you should back up all drives before installing Windows.

Help with Installation Problems

3

C H A P T E R

HELP WITH STARTING WINDOWS

This chapter begins with general troubleshooting guidelines for starting Windows and then gives specific strategies for specific problems.

General Strategies for Starting Windows

Before tackling the specific problem you are having when you start Windows, you might try these general strategies:

Check the last thing you did. If you modified WIN.INI, AUTOEXEC.BAT, or CONFIG.SYS, the last modification could be the source of the problem.

If you have made hardware changes in the system, use Windows Setup to reconfigure for a new display, mouse, or keyboard. You may need to do a complete reinstall if you have changed the disk controller, such as upgrading from an ESDI (Enhanced Small Device Interface) to an SCSI (Small Computer-System Interface).

Read all the TXT files that came with Windows.

Try the problem action in DOS. For example, if you have a print problem in Windows, see if the same problem exists when you print from a DOS application.

If the display is gone and you can't use the mouse, try the action with the keyboard. For example, Alt+F4 should still close the active application.

Check the location and space of the TEMP directory. Printing large files and some scanning programs can really eat up space here. Sometimes a program (and/or Windows) is friendly when this space runs out, but sometimes the system crashes. Sometimes you get a general error message (like "generic printer failure") that doesn't mean anything. Use a shareware program to monitor the available TEMP space. Clear the directory on booting. Try moving it temporarily to a drive with more space.

- Remove TSRs from the system and boot again. You should always create and keep on-hand a bootable diskette that can be used for starting the system when all else fails. Check the diskette (be sure it boots) before putting it away. Avoid using any TSRs that require expanded memory.

- Be sure the PATH statement in AUTOEXEC.BAT is less than 128 bytes. That's the limit for DOS, and long PATH statements can overwrite part of DOS and create unusual effects. Use shorter directory names to fix this.

- Check the system SETUP program that defines the system clock time and the type of hard disk. (This is not a Windows or a DOS Setup program, but one provided with some hardware systems and stored in ROM.) Some application programs can overwrite this area of memory.

- When using a memory manager, be sure the device driver for the memory manager is the first line in CONFIG.SYS. For example, the first line might be

```
DEVICE=HIMEM.SYS
```

The memory manager must be loaded before any other device drivers that may depend on it, such as SMARTDRV.SYS.

- If running Windows 3.0, be sure you are not running Windows from Windows. To do this, type **EXIT**, and see if you exit to Windows. With Windows 3.1, you can't run Windows from Windows. You will get a message and the attempt is blocked.

Be sure there is no interrupt conflict. Adapter boards often have a switch that sets the interrupt to use. Two boards can't use the same interrupt. In addition, some are reserved by the PC. (See Appendix C.)

Make sure there is no conflict in the upper memory between 640K and 1 megabyte. Windows is supposed to be smart enough to prevent such conflicts, but this is checked only when Windows is loaded. If adapter software decides to use some of this memory after Windows is loaded, there can be a conflict. The best trick to explore this in the 386 enhanced mode is to modify the `[386enh]` section of SYSTEM.INI to exclude all memory from A000 to CFFF:

`EMMExclude=A000-CFFF`

If this modification solves the problem, then modify the SYSTEM.INI file to exclude less memory until the problem reappears. Then back off to a working set of parameters.

In running Windows 3.0, you can run out of system resources if the desk gets too cluttered. Use the **A**bout option of the **H**elp menu to check system resources. Then clean up the desk.

If you have two versions of Windows installed, be sure there are no conflicts between the files of both versions. For example, if both Windows 3.0 and 3.1 are installed, make sure that the CONFIG.SYS file installs the HIMEM.SYS for 3.1.

Note: Some computers, such as an XT with an Intel Inboard, require special versions of Windows. Be sure your hardware supports the version of Windows you are using.

Performance Tips for All Windows Applications

Certain general rules apply for working with all Windows applications:

- In painting and spreadsheet programs, you will generally want to maximize windows to get the most working area.

- It's generally easier to double-click the title bar to maximize than to try to aim at those tiny buttons located at the upper right corner of the window. You can also define shortcut keys for maximizing (if you aren't using a mouse) with the Recorder.

- Remember to use Alt+Tab to rotate between applications. This will work to catch even minimized applications. Rotate to the minimized icon and then release the keys.

- Use Ctrl+F6 to rotate between documents in an application.

Help! I can't start Windows.

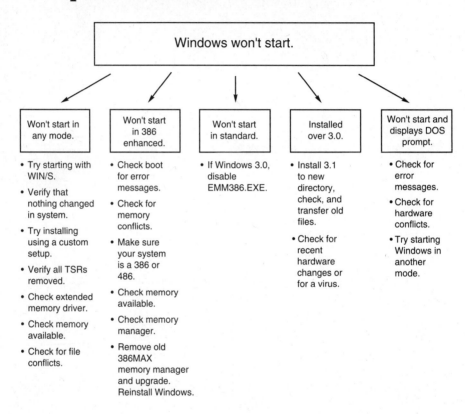

Windows is generally started by typing **WIN** at the DOS prompt. A logo appears briefly, Windows loads, and the Program Manager starts. Various program groups are displayed, and an icon for each program is shown. See Figure 3.1.

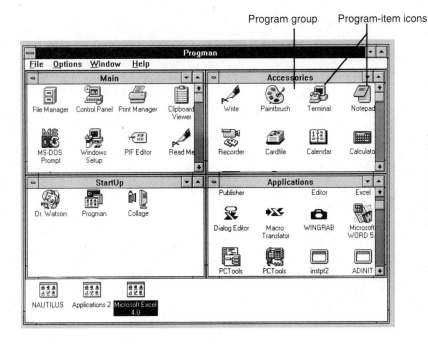

Program group   Program-item icons

Figure 3.1
Windows as it looks on startup with Program Manager.

Windows 3.1 starts in one of two modes: *standard* or *386 enhanced*. Windows senses the hardware resources you have and automatically starts in the appropriate mode each time. Think of Windows 3.1 as a combination of two products: a standard mode Windows and a 386 enhanced mode Windows. During each startup, Windows decides which of these two products to load. You can always find out which mode Windows is using by selecting **A**bout Program Manager from the **H**elp menu of Program Manager.

Windows 3.0 supports an additional *real mode* for running older Windows 2.x applications. Real mode is no longer supported in Windows 3.1, and Windows 2.x applications should be updated to the new versions for Windows 3.1.

Help! I can't start Windows.

You can start Windows by using the /b switch to track down hangups during startup:

WIN /b

This creates the file BOOTLOG.TXT that shows what loaded. The last line will list the file that failed to load properly.

For tracing UAEs with Windows 3.0 or for tracing general errors with Windows 3.1, use the Dr. Watson program (DRWATSON.EXE). Set up an icon for this program in the Startup group, and it will always be there as an icon for trapping problems. When an error condition occurs, Dr. Watson automatically becomes active and traps information about the cause to its log. You can then use the log with the application developer or Microsoft to find the cause of the error.

Windows won't start in any mode after installing.

Try starting Windows 3.1 in standard mode by using **WIN /S** or for Windows 3.0 starting in real mode by using **WIN /R**. You can use the standard mode if you have a 286, 386, or 486 processor and at least 1MB of memory (including 384K extended). If you don't have FastDisk installed (Appendix B), you may find that standard is the best mode to use when you are running only Windows applications on a 386/486 computer.

Since part of the Windows 3.1 installation is from the standard mode of Windows, failure to start in this mode indicates some conditions must have changed since installation. Be sure that HIMEM.SYS (which isn't used in real mode) is the one supplied with your version of

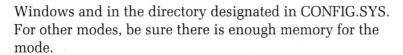

Windows and in the directory designated in CONFIG.SYS. For other modes, be sure there is enough memory for the mode.

■ If you have changed something in your system since you last used Windows or since you installed it, suspect this change and examine the change. A new printer driver, new display, or perhaps a modified WIN.INI are possibilities. If you have lost memory to a TSR loaded since installation, that may be the problem.

■ The installation may have detected the wrong hardware. Try installing using a custom setup. Be sure the A20 handler is correct. You can use the /m directive with HIMEM.SYS to install the correct handler.

■ Be sure any TSRs are removed. Run them as stand-alone programs.

■ Be sure the SMARTDrive or RAMDrive is not taking too much memory. Be sure the extended memory manager is compatible with the Windows version you are using. Don't use the HIMEM.SYS for Windows 3.0 with Windows 3.1, for example. Be sure HIMEM.SYS is identifying your hardware correctly. Be sure there are no error messages during bootup.

■ Also, be sure you have sufficient memory: 256K of extended memory for standard mode and 1024K for 286 enhanced. You may think you have enough, but network and other drivers can load the existing memory to a point that there isn't enough free memory for Windows to load. Use MEM or CHKDSK to find the available memory.

■ If you have two versions of Windows installed, be sure there are no conflicts between the files of both versions.

For example, if Windows 3.0 and 3.1 are both installed, be sure the CONFIG.SYS file installs the HIMEM.SYS for 3.1.

Windows starts in the standard mode but not in 386 enhanced mode.

The 386 enhanced mode is the most advanced Windows mode. Many Windows features are supported only when executing in this mode. To use this mode, you must have a 386 or 486 processor and a total of 2MB or more of memory, including 1MB or more of extended memory. In this mode the processor is supporting multiple *virtual processors*, each running in its own protected memory with its own application (see Appendix A). This is the best mode to use when running DOS applications under Windows.

If your hardware resources support 386 enhanced mode, Windows should automatically start in this mode. You can also force a startup in this mode by entering **WIN /3** at the DOS prompt, assuming of course that the hardware resources are available.

■ Reboot the system and verify that there are no error messages during the bootup. If there are, fix this problem and reboot.

■ If the problem is only in the 386 enhanced mode, you may need to exclude some memory from the UMB area (use **emmexclude=** in SYSTEM.INI) to run in the 386 enhanced mode. Windows is supposed to be smart enough to know what else is in the UMB area, but sometimes it fails. Display drivers, network drivers, memory managers, and shadow RAM are often the elusive culprits here. If using

QEMM-386, be sure it's installed correctly. As a test (for Windows 3.1), start Windows by using `WIN /d:x`. If this works, there is probably a conflict in the UMB area (640K–1MB). Use the MSD utility with Windows and the DOS MEM program to check this area for conflicts. Then add the `emmexclude=` statement to SYSTEM.INI in the `[386enh]` area to exclude this memory (see Appendix A and Chapter 7).

Try starting Windows by using `WIN /d:v`. If this works, you need to add the line `VIRTUALHDIRQ=FALSE` to the SYSTEM.INI `[386enh]` section. (See Appendix G for more on editing .INI files.)

There are many variables in 386 enhanced mode that you can change to alter the configuration for your needs. Most of them are in the `[386enh]` section of SYSTEM.INI. The best route here is to understand how memory is managed in this mode (Appendix A) and then adjust the parameters to match your needs.

■ Make sure that your computer has a 386 or 486 processor, that the HIMEM.SYS driver is installed from CONFIG.SYS, and that it is the version with your Windows. Don't use a Windows 3.0 HIMEM.SYS with Windows 3.1. Be sure that `FILES=` in CONFIG.SYS is set to at least 40 and that `BUFFERS=` to at least 20 (10 if SMARTDrive is installed). (See Appendix G for more on editing CONFIG.SYS.) If using EGA, be sure the EGA.SYS driver is installed.

■ Check the space allocated to device drivers and see if enough memory is really available. If either RAMDrive or SMARTDrive is installed too large, there won't be enough left for the memory manager to start the 386 enhanced mode. See also the special 386 enhanced section in Appendix A.

If you have an expanded memory driver installed and are using DOS 5, you may need to use the undocumented /y switch when loading the expanded memory driver (see Appendix B). Use this option to specify where the EMM386.EXE file is located.

Make sure that WINA20.386 is in the root directory of the C drive. If it is missing, you will get a message indicating this fact. Place the file (included with Windows) in the root directory of the boot drive. Alternatively, you can add **SWITCHES=/W** in CONFIG.SYS and add a DEVICE statement to specify where this file is located, for example:

```
DEVICE=C:\DOS\WINA20.386
```

(See Appendix G for information on editing CONFIG.SYS.) If you are using QEMM-386, check to see that the RAM parameter is used in loading the driver with CONFIG.SYS, as follows:

```
DEVICE=C:\QEMM\QEMM386.SYS RAM
```

This permits QEMM-386 to use the upper memory area between 640K and 1MB. If for some reason you wish to exclude part of this area, use the EXCLUDE parameter:

```
DEVICE=C:\QEMM\QEMM386.SYS RAM EXCLUDE=C000-C7FF
```

If you are using a version of 386MAX memory manager older than 6, and it was installed when Windows 3.1 was installed, remove it and reinstall Windows. Upgrade the 386MAX memory manager.

Windows starts in 386 enhanced mode but not in standard.

▢ If you are using Windows 3.0 and DOS 5 with EMM386.EXE to load drivers or TSRs to UMBs, you won't be able to start in standard mode. Upgrade to Windows 3.1 or disable EMM386.EXE and the loading high of drivers and TSRs.

I installed Windows 3.1 over Windows 3.0 and it doesn't run.

During the installation, Windows had to run to complete the installation. Something must have happened since the installation, possibly a hardware change or a virus. Try these steps:

▢ Install Windows 3.1 to a new directory. Be sure it is working. Rename GRP files as GRN; rename INI files as INN.

Copy all these files to the directory containing the old Windows. Try Windows again—this will be the working Windows with the GRP and INI files in the old directory.

If Windows still fails to run, rename the old INI files to INO and the INN files to INI. Restart. If Windows runs now, there is an error in the INO files.

▢ If Windows still fails to run, check for any recent hardware changes or a virus.

Help! I can't start Windows.

Windows fails to start and displays a DOS prompt.

Remember, Windows did start during the installation process. Something has happened since then.

▣ Check for messages.

▣ Try starting in another mode.

Help! I have other problems starting Windows.

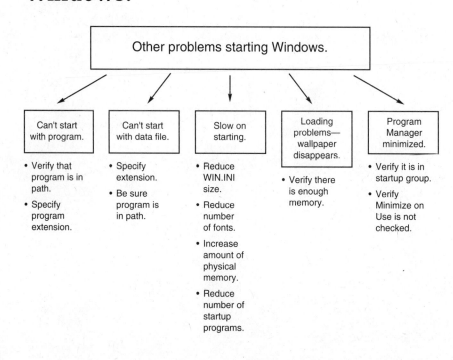

Other problems starting Windows.

Can't start with program.	Can't start with data file.	Slow on starting.	Loading problems— wallpaper disappears.	Program Manager minimized.
• Verify that program is in path. • Specify program extension.	• Specify extension. • Be sure program is in path.	• Reduce WIN.INI size. • Reduce number of fonts. • Increase amount of physical memory. • Reduce number of startup programs.	• Verify there is enough memory.	• Verify it is in startup group. • Verify Minimize on Use is not checked.

Occasionally, the startup problem occurs not because Windows or the memory is improperly configured, but because Windows is having trouble working with other application files, data files, and so on. Following are tactics you can use to alleviate such problems.

I can't start Windows with the program I wish to use.

You can start Windows with a program directly, leaving Program Manager as a minimized icon on the desktop. You can start Windows with an application program by specifying the program in the command line, for example:

WIN EXCEL

This assumes that the directory paths for Windows and the program are in the PATH statement of AUTOEXEC.BAT, as follows:

`PATH C:\WINDOWS;D:\EXCEL`

If your application won't start with Windows, check the following:

- Verify that the program is in the PATH statement of AUTOEXEC.BAT (see Appendix G).

- Specify the program extension (.EXE, etc.) when you start Windows.

I can't start Windows with a data file parameter.

You can start Windows with a data file by switching to the directory containing the data file and entering the data file name as a startup parameter. For example, the following command starts Windows with Excel and the data file BUDGET.XLS:

```
WIN BUDGET.XLS
```

■ Be sure to enter the file extension. This assumes that the file extension has been associated with a program. To create an association, use the **A**ssociate command of the **F**ile menu in File Manager. You can also create an association by manually editing the [extensions] section of WIN.INI.

■ Check AUTOEXEC.BAT to be sure that the PATH command includes the directory for the program (see Appendix G).

Secrets and Surprises: An undocumented feature of Windows permits you to start it without the startup logo screen by typing a space and a colon after the program name. That is, you type **WIN :**. If you use a startup option, place it before the colon and precede it with a space: **WIN /S:**. You may even wish to create a batch file that starts Windows without the logo or with your own logo. Eliminating the logo, however, will not make the startup much faster. All startup options (data filenames, program names, mode, etc.) should be placed before the colon).

You can configure your system so that Windows starts automatically when you boot your computer. To do this, add the Windows prompt as a separate line in the AUTOEXEC.BAT file (see Appendix G) as shown here:

```
WIN :
```

Performance Tip: You can configure your system so that you can start Windows by pressing a single function key. To do this, first be sure the ANSI device driver is installed. To install it, include the line `DEVICE=C:\DOS\ANSI.SYS` in the CONFIG.SYS file. Once this is done, you can add a PROMPT statement to AUTOEXEC.BAT to start Windows. For example, you could add the line `PROMPT $p$g$E[0;133;"WIN :";13p`. (See Appendix G for more on editing these files.) Then reboot. Pressing F11 will now start Windows. For safety's sake, create this as a TEMP.BAT file first. Try it out and then append it to the AUTOEXEC.BAT file. This precaution ensures that you don't lose the system on booting. The 133 value assigns the specified command string to the F11 key. Other key values would be:

Key	Value
F1	59
F2	60
F3	61
F4	62
F5	63
F6	64
F7	65

continues

Help! I have other problems starting Windows.

continued

F8	66
F9	67
F10	68
F11	133
F12	134
Shift+F11	135
Shift+F12	136
Ctrl+F11	137
Ctrl+F12	138
Alt+F11	139
Alt+F12	140

You can also make multiple assignments with a single PROMPT command. For example, you could use F11 to start Windows in standard mode and then use F12 to start Windows in 386 enhanced mode. Avoid using the keys F1 to F9 because they are often used for other purposes in applications. If you have questions, look up the PROMPT command in your DOS manual.

Windows is slow on starting.

☐ Minimize the size of the WIN.INI file.

☐ Reduce the number of fonts used in your data files.

☐ Increase the amount of physical memory. (This requires extra memory chips or an add-on board.)

☐ Minimize the number of programs in the Startup group and those defined by the `load=` parameter in WIN.INI (see Appendix G).

I have Windows loading problems or wallpaper disappears.

■ There may not be enough memory for loading. Try starting in standard mode. Be sure any extended memory used for a video driver or a network is excluded (see SYSTEM.INI file). Windows needs 2 megabytes in 386 enhanced mode. To run a DOS application in this mode, you need another megabyte. Remove TSRs temporarily and try loading.

Your display adapter may support nonmaskable interrupts (NMI) to switch video modes more efficiently. You should be able to press Alt+F4 and Enter to exit Windows if this is true. The drivers shipped with Windows do not support NMI. To solve the problem, check with the display adapter manual to find out how to turn this mode off or support it. Many of these adapters include a video driver for Windows that handles NMI correctly. If so, install this driver.

When I start Windows, I see only the desktop and Program Manager minimized.

Figure 3.2 shows how the Program Manager looks in this situation. Double-click the Program Manager icon to open Program Manager. Then try the following techniques:

■ Make sure that Program Manager (PROGMAN.EXE) is in the Startup group. If not, open File Manager and drag the filename from the Windows directory to the Startup group.

Figure 3.2
The Program Manager is minimized on startup.

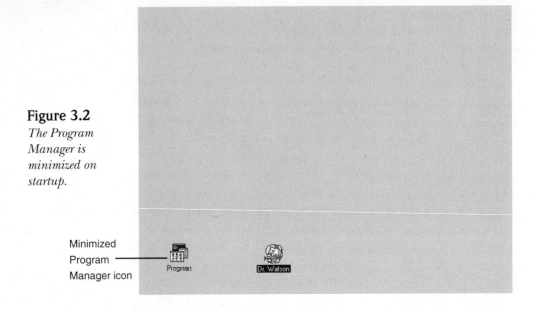

Minimized Program Manager icon

Progman

Dr. Watson

□ On the **O**ptions menu, be sure **M**inimize on Use is NOT checked. Be sure **S**ave Settings on Exit is checked. Exit Windows. Restart Windows; Program Manager should open.

Help! I get a message on starting Windows.

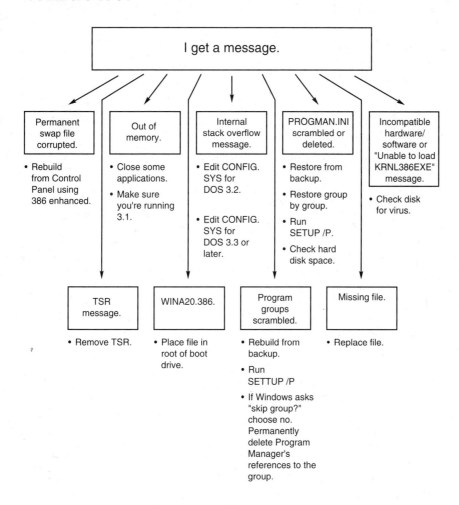

Help! I get a message on starting Windows.

79

Many error messages relating to TSRs, memory, and other problems may appear when you start Windows. Here are some effective strategies for dealing with such messages when you encounter them.

I get a message that my permanent swap file is corrupted.

☐ Compress the disk drive containing the swap file. For Windows 3.0, restart Windows in the real mode and then create the swap file again by using **File** **R**un and executing SWAPFILE.EXE. For Windows 3.1, start Control Panel by double-clicking on its icon and choosing the 386 Enhanced icon. From the 386 Enhanced dialog box, choose **V**irtual Memory (the permanent swap file creates the virtual memory). From the Virtual Memory dialog box (shown in Figure 3.3), choose the **C**hange>> button, and rebuild virtual memory.

I get a message about a TSR.

☐ Try running the TSR program as a stand-alone program from an icon instead of using a hot key. Initiate it from the icon with a shortcut key. If the TSR uses INT2A, add `ReflectDOSInt2A=true` in the `[386enh]` section of SYSTEM.INI.

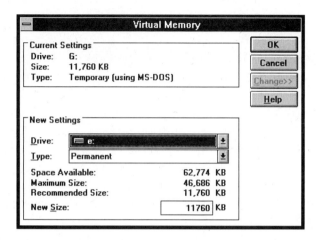

Figure 3.3
Rebuilding the permanent swap file.

I have extended memory but get "Out of Memory" messages. Windows reports that I have free memory.

□ With Windows 3.0, Windows creates two buffer areas called *USER* and *GDI local heaps.* Each area is limited to 64K. Using **A**bout Program Manager, you should see that, although memory is available, the percent of "Free System Resources" is low. For either version of Windows, close some applications and, if necessary, restart Windows.

□ Windows 3.1 manages the resource area better, and you are less likely to see the message. Make sure you are running version 3.1.

Help! I get a message on starting Windows.

81

On starting, I get the message "You must have WINA20.386 in the root directory of the drive you booted from."

▪ Place this file (included with Windows) in the root directory of the boot drive. Alternatively, you can add `SWITCHES=/W` in CONFIG.SYS (see Appendix G) and add a DEVICE statement to specify where this file is located, such as:

```
DEVICE=C:\DOS\WINA20.386
```

I get an internal stack overflow message.

▪ If you are using MS-DOS 3.2, add this line to the CONFIG.SYS file (see Appendix G) and reboot:

```
stacks=0,192
```

▪ If you are using MS-DOS 3.3 or later, add this line:

```
stacks=0,0
```

I get a message that my program groups are scrambled or missing.

▪ With some versions of Windows, scrambled or missing program groups are a common problem. Your best insurance is to keep the group files backed up. Then recover from the backed-up files. This can also be a problem if you have tried to move your Windows to another drive or directory. Some of the file locations are "hardwired" into certain Windows files during Setup. One file you might check is PROGMAN.INI (see Appendix G). This holds the location of the group files, and the pointers here are probably still pointing to the old files. Sometimes just editing this file will solve the problem. You might try to edit the INI files, but the safer method is not to move Windows. Reinstall the groups from scratch if you need to place Windows at another disk location.

☐ If you can't recover the last group configuration, you can easily recreate the original groups. Start Windows and then File Manager. Choose **R**un from the **F**ile menu and enter **SETUP /P**. This will recreate the initial groups. (This trick won't work from DOS. You must be in Windows.)

☐ If a group file is missing, you are asked whether you want to skip this group on further loadings. You can answer No and permanently delete the Program Manager's references to the group.

I get a message that my PROGMAN.INI file is scrambled or deleted.

☐ The best solution to restore PROGMAN.INI from a backup disk or tape if one is available.

☐ If a backup of PROGMAN.INI is not available, you should have at least a printout of the former file. To restore, from the Program Manager, select **F**ile **N**ew. Select Program **G**roup and OK. When a filename is requested, enter the name of one file, such as MAIN.GRP from the printout of PROGMAN.INI. The entire set will be reconstructed. Repeat for each group.

■ You can also restore Windows to the original groups by entering **SETUP** **/P** from within Windows as described in the preceding section.

■ Check your hard disk space. This is a common problem when running low on disk space. Also, take better precautions and keep a backup copy of your INI and GRP files.

I get a message about a missing file on starting.

■ When Windows is started, it loads all programs in the Startup group as well as any programs specified by the run= and load= parameters of WIN.INI (see Appendix G). Verify that all of these programs are in the specified paths.

I get a message "Incompatible hardware/ software installed" or "Unable to load KRNL386EXE."

■ A virus has been detected and Windows will not load. Check the disk for viruses.

Help! I have disk problems.

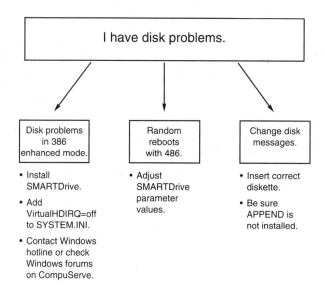

Windows is very *disk intensive*—it spends a lot of its time reading and writing the hard disk. This means you need the disk interface as fast as possible. Compress and back up the disk often. Monitor the FAT area of each drive for errors by using CHKDSK. Use SMARTDrive. If possible, use a permanent swap file (see Appendix B). Avoid third-party disk managers, which make the use of a permanent swap file impossible.

When purchasing hard disks, ask for the average access time of the disk. Modern disks use access times of 20 ms or less. Don't use anything rated over 30 ms. The *interleave factor* is another important rating. It defines how many times the disk must rotate for the computer to read one track. An interleave of 1:2 means the disk must rotate twice to read one track. Purchase disks with interleaves of 1:1 so that the entire track can be read in one rotation.

I have disk problems in 386 enhanced mode.

▢ If SMARTDrive is not loaded, the 386 enhanced mode supports only standard ST506 and ESDI controllers. To use SCSI or nonstandard controllers, you must have SMARTDrive loaded. In such cases, SMARTDrive generally must be double-buffered to resolve the interface problem. (See Appendix B.)

▢ If you get disk read or write error messages or disk drive not ready messages, try adding this line to the `[386enh]` section of SYSTEM.INI (see Appendix G):

`VirtualHDIRQ=off`

In this case, SMARTDrive must be installed without the /b switch. This will force all disk I/O through the ROM routines. It will be slower, but it should solve the problem.

▢ Try the Windows hotline (800 323-3577) for specific questions or specific setups, or try the Windows forums on CompuServe. Later versions of SMARTDrive sense any risk conditions and won't install, even if you add it to CONFIG.SYS.

I get random reboots using a 486-based computer.

▢ Try setting the minimum and maximum memory values for SMARTDrive the same (see Appendix B). If this doesn't work, you may have a bad Setup or hardware problem.

When trying to open a file, I get the message "Change Disk – Cannot find *xxxx.xx.* Please insert in drive A."

■ You can get this message when a Setup program (including Windows' own) is looking for a file and can't find it. Be sure the right diskette is inserted in the right drive.

■ An APPEND command is active. Don't use the DOS APPEND command with Windows. Check the AUTOEXEC.BAT file (see Appendix G) to be sure that no APPEND command is included.

Help! My clock doesn't work right.

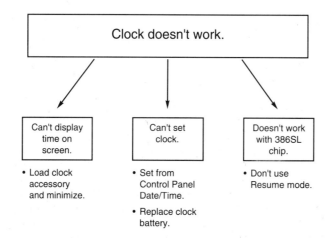

Clock doesn't work.

| Can't display time on screen. | Can't set clock. | Doesn't work with 386SL chip. |

- Load clock accessory and minimize.

- Set from Control Panel Date/Time.
- Replace clock battery.

- Don't use Resume mode.

The clock is a useful utility for monitoring your time. It's so useful, in fact, that you may wish to keep it minimized as an icon on the screen where it constantly displays the time.

If you have Windows 3.0, you may prefer the Clock program that is used with it. If so, copy it to the new Windows directory and start it as an icon.

How can I display the time on my screen whenever Windows is running?

Start the Clock program from Windows (its icon is in the Accessories group). Use the **C**lock menu to set it to an analog or digital clock. Then minimize Clock to an icon. The clock will keep running as an icon, as shown in Figure 3.4.

If you wish to have the clock load as an icon automatically each time you start Windows, place it in the Startup group or edit the load= parameter in the WIN.INI file (see Appendix G) as:

```
load=clock.exe
```

Help with Starting Windows

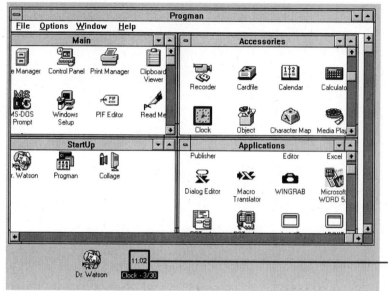

Figure 3.4
Keeping a clock on the screen.

The clock minimized to an icon

I can't set the clock.

For 286 computers and later, the clock is run from a battery when the computer is off. The clock is set from a special Setup program that is part of the computer system. For example, to access this program on a Dell computer, you use Ctrl+Alt+Enter. Windows uses this system clock to display the time. You can also use the DATE and TIME programs of DOS to set the clock. To use Control Panel in Windows to set the clock, double-click on the Date/Time icon.

If the clock loses time when the computer is off, the battery is disconnected or needs to be replaced.

Help! My clock doesn't work right.

The clock doesn't work right under Windows on a laptop using a 386SL chip.

When Windows is started, it gets the correct time from the system clock and then keeps its own time. On some laptops, certain modes (such as Resume) stop the CPU clock. When the laptop is restarted, the clock picks up from where it left off. Zenith MastersPort has this problem. When you are using PIM programs that are time dependent, the only solution is not to use the Resume mode. If Resume is more important than tracking time, use it.

Help! I want a customized desktop.

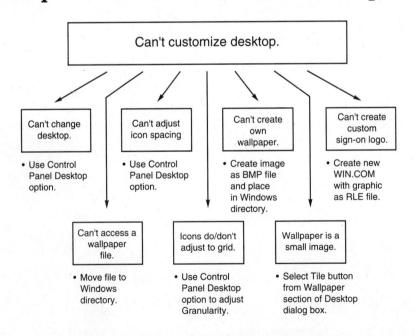

Can't customize desktop.

Can't change desktop.
• Use Control Panel Desktop option.

Can't adjust icon spacing
• Use Control Panel Desktop option.

Can't create own wallpaper.
• Create image as BMP file and place in Windows directory.

Can't create custom sign-on logo.
• Create new WIN.COM with graphic as RLE file.

Can't access a wallpaper file.
• Move file to Windows directory.

Icons do/don't adjust to grid.
• Use Control Panel Desktop option to adjust Granularity.

Wallpaper is a small image.
• Select Tile button from Wallpaper section of Desktop dialog box.

You can customize the desktop by choosing Desktop from Control Panel. You can control the icon spacing and the background wallpaper, use a screen saver, and create an invisible "magnetic" grid for placing windows.

I can't change the desktop pattern.

To change the background pattern, start Control Panel by double-clicking on the Control Panel icon in the Main group. Double-click on the Desktop icon to display the Desktop dialog box, shown in Figure 3.5. Under Pattern, select the **N**ame dropdown list box and choose a pattern name.

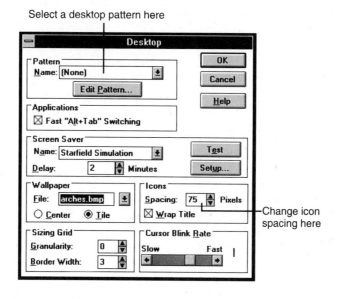

Select a desktop pattern here

Figure 3.5
Changing the wallpaper.

Change icon spacing here

I can't access some bit-mapped files for wallpaper that are on the disk.

Windows defaults to displaying the available windows on a white background known as *wallpaper*. Wallpaper files should be in bit-mapped format (BMP extension) and kept in the Windows directory. You can, however, also use the RLE format.

■ Bit-mapped files for wallpaper must be on the Windows (\WINDOWS) directory. Icons can be kept anywhere.

Secrets and Surprises: Instead of using Control Panel's desktop, you can also use the new wallpaper by changing the `Wallpaper=` line in the WIN.INI file (see Appendix G) to point to the new file:

```
Wallpaper=space.bmp
```

I can't adjust icon spacing on the desktop.

■ Choose the Desktop icon after starting Control Panel, and set the **S**pacing option in the Icons area. To wrap titles, be sure that **W**rap Title is on. (See Figure 3.5.)

My icons jump into place (or don't jump) to an invisible grid on the desktop.

■ Choose the Desktop icon after starting Control Panel, and set the **G**ranularity option. This defines an invisible grid to which the icons are aligned. Each value is 8 pixels. Set the value to 0 if you wish no grid.

I can't create my own wallpaper.

You can change the wallpaper to something far more interesting, such as a graphic image or even your company logo. Windows contains a few standard wallpapers, some of which are very good. These can be changed by using the Desktop option of Control Panel, as described earlier. It's more fun, however, to create your own wallpaper.

■ You can create BMP images with Paintbrush in the Accessories group. Use **F**ile Save **A**s to save the image from Paintbrush in BMP format, saving it to the Windows (\WINDOWS) directory. Then choose it by using the Desktop option of Control Panel, as described earlier in this section under "I can't access some bit-mapped files for wallpaper that are on the disk."

Secrets and Surprises: If you wish to use a GIF image from CompuServe or a public bulletin board, use the WINGIF shareware program to convert it to a bit-mapped format.

The wallpaper is a small image.

■ If you're using a small bit map for wallpaper, you must select the Tile button from the Wallpaper section of the Desktop dialog box. This lays copies of the bit map edge-to-edge to cover the screen. Otherwise, the small image is displayed once, right in the middle of the screen, where it can be covered by windows and make you think that your wallpaper isn't working right.

How can I change the sign-on logo?

You can also change Windows' sign-on logo or eliminate it entirely. First, here's an overview of what happens on starting. Typing **WIN** starts WIN.COM, which is actually three program modules: WIN.CNF, VGALOGO.LGO (if you have a VGA), and VGALOGO.RLE (for a VGA). WIN.CNF determines from the system resources which mode to use, and this determines which modules will load. VGALOGO.LGO switches the video adapter to the VGA mode, and VGALOGO.RLE is the default logo. The filenames will be different for a different adapter. The basic strategy is then to change the RLE file and combine the three files in a new WIN.COM with a new name.

■ To create your own starting logo with perhaps your company name:

1. Create the sign-on screen image as a BMP file.

2. Use WINGIF to convert the image to a compressed RLE file. Assume that the name is NEWLOGO.RLE.

3. Create a new WIN.COM by typing:

```
COPY /B WIN.CNF+VGALOGO.LGO+NEWLOGO.RLE NEWWIN.COM
```

Now run NEWWIN.COM to start Windows and see the new logo. There is one restriction: NEWWIN.COM must be less than 64K in size. Keep the new logo small enough to achieve this.

Remember that if you install a new video adapter using Windows Setup, WIN.COM will be created again and will overwrite this version.

Help! I have keyboard problems.

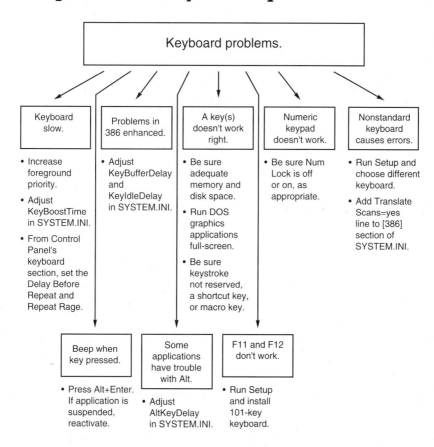

To resolve keyboard problems, use the same technique described for resolving video, printer, and mouse problems: check the problem from DOS first. If the problem is there with DOS, it's probably the hardware. If it's only under Windows, suspect the Windows keyboard driver.

My keyboard response is slow.

▪ The keyboard is always assigned to the foreground task. Use Control Panel's 386 Enhanced option to increase foreground priority.

▪ Also try adding the line **KeyBoostTime=.005** (or use a larger value) to the [386enh] section of SYSTEM.INI (see Appendix G).

▪ Set the Delay Before Repeat and Repeat Rage from the Keyboard section of Control Panel.

I hear a beep when I press a certain key.

▪ The application may be suspended. For example, you may have tried to run a DOS application in a window when it won't run in a window. Try pressing Alt+Enter in this case to return to full-screen. If the application is suspended, reactivate the application. You may also get a beep on error conditions.

I have keyboard problems in the 386 enhanced mode.

▪ Increase the values for the `KeyBufferDelay` line and decrease the values for the `KeyIdleDelay` line in the `[386enh]` section of SYSTEM.INI (see Appendix G).

Some applications have trouble with the Alt key.

▪ Try adjusting the value for the `AltKeyDelay` line in SYSTEM.INI (see Appendix G).

A key or keystroke series doesn't seem to work right.

Be sure the key is working right in DOS. If the key misbehaves in DOS, you probably have a keyboard problem. If the problem is just in Windows, check these ideas:

▪ If the problem is in switching away from a program, you may be low on memory or hard disk space.

▪ Check the key in DOS. Be sure the key is functioning properly.

▪ If the problem occurs when you are using a DOS graphics application (through Windows) in a window on a VGA screen, run the application full-screen (Alt+Enter) or in a text mode.

▪ Verify that the keystroke is not a reserved keystroke in the DOS application's PIF file or Windows application. If the keystroke is switching you to a DOS application, it probably has been assigned in the PIF file as a shortcut key for starting that application. The keystroke is assigned by Recorder to a macro.

My F11 and F12 keys don't work as expected.

◻ Windows installed to an 84-key keyboard. (Check this with the Setup program.) Run Setup from the Main group and install a 101-key keyboard.

My numeric keypad doesn't work right.

◻ The Num Lock key switches the keypad numeric mode on or off. When using the direction keys, be sure the Num Lock light is off. When entering numeric values, press the Num Lock key to turn the light on. Holding down the Shift key when using the numeric keypad reverses the mode. The asterisk on the keypad may not work with some applications.

I have a nonstandard keyboard, and some keys send incorrect values to the computer.

◻ Try running Setup from the Main group and choosing a different keyboard.

◻ If that doesn't work, add a `TranslateScans=yes` line in the [386] section of SYSTEM.INI (see Appendix G).

Help! I have mouse problems.

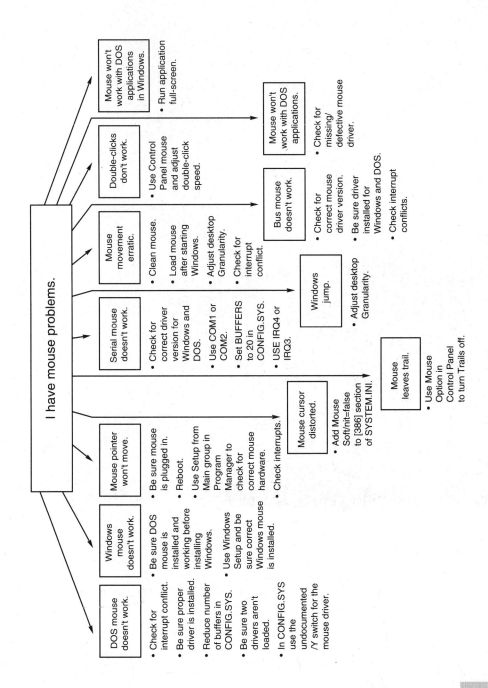

I have mouse problems.

DOS mouse doesn't work.
- Check for interrupt conflict.
- Be sure proper driver is installed.
- Reduce number of buffers in CONFIG.SYS.
- Be sure two drivers aren't loaded.
- In CONFIG.SYS use the undocumented /Y switch for the mouse driver.

Windows mouse doesn't work.
- Be sure DOS mouse is installed and working before installing Windows.
- Use Windows Setup and be sure correct Windows mouse is installed.

Mouse pointer won't move.
- Be sure mouse is plugged in.
- Reboot.
- Use Setup from Main group in Program Manager to check for correct mouse hardware.
- Check interrupts.

Mouse cursor distorted.
- Add Mouse Soft/nit=false to [386] section of SYSTEM.INI.

Serial mouse doesn't work.
- Check for correct driver version for Windows and DOS.
- Use COM1 or COM2.
- Set BUFFERS to 20 in CONFIG.SYS.
- USE IRQ4 or IRQ3.

Mouse movement erratic.
- Clean mouse.
- Load mouse after starting Windows.
- Adjust desktop Granularity.
- Check for interrupt conflict.

Mouse leaves trail.
- Use Mouse Option in Control Panel to turn Trails off.

Windows jump.
- Adjust desktop Granularity.

Double-clicks don't work.
- Use Control Panel mouse and adjust double-click speed.

Bus mouse doesn't work.
- Check for correct mouse driver version.
- Be sure driver installed for Windows and DOS.
- Check interrupt conflicts.

Mouse won't work with DOS applications in Windows.
- Run application full-screen.

Mouse won't work with DOS applications.
- Check for missing/defective mouse driver.

Help! I have mouse problems.

The system uses two mouse drivers. The DOS mouse driver is installed as part of AUTOEXEC.BAT or CONFIG.SYS. The Windows mouse driver is specified in the [boot] section of SYSTEM.INI and installed on starting Windows. DOS applications use the DOS mouse driver, even when running under Windows. Windows applications use the Windows mouse driver. Be sure that you first identify the mouse driver (DOS or Windows) giving the problem.

Identify the version of each driver. The Windows mouse driver version is displayed from the Setup program (choose Setup from the Main group and then Change System Configuration). The DOS driver version is displayed on booting.

First, if you have just installed the mouse hardware or other hardware, check the mouse driver card. Be sure the mouse is using the right interrupt. On an XT, interrupt 2 is normally used. On an AT or later, avoid 2. Use 5 if possible. The interrupt is set by a switch on the mouse card. No other device (card) should be using this interrupt.

Second, isolate the problem to the DOS mouse driver used by DOS applications in the C:\ directory or the mouse driver used by Windows in the \WINDOWS\SYSTEM directory; that is, is the problem with a Windows application or a DOS application?

Third, if using EGA.SYS, the mouse driver should be loaded after EGA.SYS.

If running in the 386 enhanced mode with a serial mouse, select the 386 Enhanced icon from the Control Panel and be sure that the port you are using for the mouse is set to Never Warn. Don't use COM3 or COM4 with a serial mouse.

I have DOS mouse problems.

For DOS mouse problems, try these possibilities:

- ☐ Check for interrupt conflicts.

- ☐ Be sure you are using the proper version of the mouse driver. The DOS mouse driver version number is displayed on booting. Sometimes using an older mouse version is best. For a Microsoft mouse, use version 7.04 or later. For a Logitech mouse, use version 6.0 or later.

- ☐ Try reducing the number of buffers in CONFIG.SYS by editing that file with a text editor or EDLIN.

- ☐ Be sure two copies of the DOS mouse driver aren't loaded, such as one on boot and another from a batch file.

- ☐ For the Microsoft mouse, using the undocumented /y switch with the line that loads the mouse driver in CONFIG.SYS changes the icon for the mouse in text mode. This may or may not work with Windows when switching between applications.

I have Windows mouse problems.

- ☐ Be sure the mouse works in DOS. The DOS mouse must be installed before installing Windows.

- ☐ Run Setup from the Main group and be sure Windows is set for the type of mouse you are using. Check the \WINDOWS\SYSTEM directory. The file for the mouse driver will have a DRV extension. Although a COM file, it's really a dynamic link library and designed to work specifically with Windows. Try replacing the file in the \WINDOWS\SYSTEM directory. If necessary, use the EXPAND program with Windows or DOS 5 to expand the MOUSE.SY$ or MOUSE.COM files to the proper directory. The MOUSE.COM file on the Windows disk is not the MOUSE.COM driver; it must be expanded first, as follows:

```
EXPAND A:\MOUSE.COM C:\WINDOWS\SYSTEM\MOUSE.COM
```

The mouse pointer is displayed but won't move.

☐ Be sure the mouse is plugged into the computer.

☐ Reboot the computer and start Windows again.

☐ If the pointer still doesn't move, use Setup from the Main group in Program Manager and be sure the mouse hardware is selected correctly.

☐ Check to see if another device is using the mouse interrupt.

The mouse cursor is distorted.

☐ Add `MouseSoftInit=false` to the [386] section of SYSTEM.INI (see Appendix G).

The mouse movement leaves a trail on the screen.

☐ If you don't want the trail, use the Mouse option of Control Panel and turn off the Mouse **T**rails check box.

The serial mouse doesn't work right.

☐ Be sure you are using the right driver version and that the driver is installed to both Windows and DOS. For Logitech, you will need version 6.0 or later.

☐ Be sure you are using COM1 or COM2. COM3 and COM4 don't work.

☐ Be sure the buffers setting in CONFIG.SYS is 20 or less (see Appendix G). If higher, you may have problems.

☐ The serial mouse generally uses IRQ 4 (if COM1) or IRQ 3 (if COM2). This is set by a switch on the adapter card. No other device should use this interrupt (see Appendix C).

The windows jump when you move them with the mouse.

☐ Adjust the Granularity setting by choosing the Desktop icon after you choose the Control Panel icon. The jumping windows aren't really a mouse problem. The desktop is set to use an invisible grid, and the windows move to follow the grid lines. You can use the Desktop option of Control Panel to stop this alignment by setting Granularity to 0 in the Desktop dialog box.

The mouse pointer is jumpy or erratic.

☐ Clean the mouse, following the directions in your mouse documentation. If it's a mechanical mouse (roller ball), remove the cover on the bottom and take the ball out. Use a rag or cotton swab with electrical contact cleaner or isopropyl alcohol. Clean all metal rollers and contacts. Wipe off any excess fluid and then replace the ball and cover.

☐ Instead of loading the mouse before starting Windows, load the mouse after starting Windows, using a batch file for the application under Windows.

☐ Adjust the Granularity setting by choosing the Desktop icon after you choose the Control Panel icon and then by setting **G**ranularity in the Desktop dialog box.

☐ Check to see if there is a mouse interrupt conflict. The interrupt is set by a switch on the mouse adapter card. No two adapters should use the same interrupt (see Appendix C).

The bus mouse doesn't work right.

☐ Be sure you are using the mouse driver version that came with Windows.

☐ Be sure the mouse driver is installed to Windows and DOS.

☐ Check for an interrupt conflict. The interrupt is set from a jumper on the mouse card. For AT-class machines, use interrupt 5 if no other card is using it. Otherwise, use interrupt 3 or 4. These, however, are often used by COM ports (see Appendix C).

Sometimes, I can't get double-clicks with the mouse to work.

☐ Choose the Control Panel icon and then the Mouse icon to display the Mouse dialog box. This dialog box enables you to set the mouse for a slower double-click speed, as shown in Figure 3.6. You can test the double-click speed in this dialog box by double-clicking the test area.

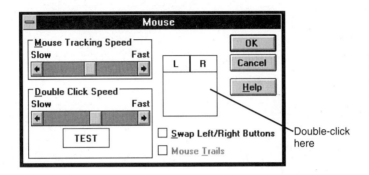

Figure 3.6
Setting the mouse double-click speed.

The mouse won't work with DOS applications outside of Windows but does work with Windows applications.

■ There is no DOS mouse driver or there is a defective DOS driver. Since the driver is loaded during bootup, reboot the computer and watch for error messages during boot about the mouse driver. Watch for a message that the driver is installed and watch to see which version is installed.

The mouse won't work with DOS applications inside Windows, but does with Windows DOS applications before Windows is started.

■ The DOS mouse won't work with DOS applications under Windows 3.0 when the application is running in a window. Upgrade to Windows 3.1 or use Alt+Enter to run the

Help! I have mouse problems.

application full screen. Some display drivers may not support the DOS mouse in 3.1 when the application is running in a window. Try changing the mouse driver (perhaps to an older version with the Microsoft mouse). With an IBM mouse, you can't use version 1.0 of the driver.

Help! How can I change the shell program, which defaults to Program Manager?

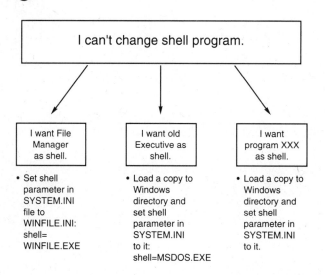

```
┌─────────────────────────────────────────────┐
│        I can't change shell program.         │
└─────────────────────────────────────────────┘
```

I want File Manager as shell.	I want old Executive as shell.	I want program XXX as shell.
• Set shell parameter in SYSTEM.INI file to WINFILE.INI: shell= WINFILE.EXE	• Load a copy to Windows directory and set shell parameter in SYSTEM.INI to it: shell=MSDOS.EXE	• Load a copy to Windows directory and set shell parameter in SYSTEM.INI to it.

Windows starts with the Program Manager application. This is the shell application from which other applications are launched. You can change this shell application by modifying the `shell=` parameter of the `[boot]` section of SYSTEM.INI (see Appendix G). One word of warning, however. In creating custom shells, the run and load parameters of WIN.INI will often not work with other shells. That is, you can't load programs as icons or as windows on startup. A few shells may read these two parameters, but most won't.

How can I use File Manager as the shell?

To use File Manager as the startup shell, change the `shell=` parameter of SYSTEM.INI (see Appendix G) to:

```
shell=WINFILE.EXE
```

and restart Windows.

How can I use the old MS-DOS Executive as the shell?

If you are more comfortable with the MS-DOS Executive program that was part of the older versions of Windows, it is still provided with Windows 3.0 and is available for use. Simply edit the shell parameter in SYSTEM.INI (see Appendix G) to:

```
shell=MSDOS.EXE
```

You might think that using Executive is a step backward in time, but there are situations when you might want to use it (even when it's not a shell). You can run multiple copies of Executive, and it's fast. It's no longer provided with Windows 3.1.

How can I use commercial shells or application programs as shells?

In the early days of Windows, Microsoft marketed a run-time version of Windows for using single applications in the Windows environment. This version is no longer sold, but you can create your own by using the application program as a shell. To do this, edit SYSTEM.INI (see Appendix G) so that the shell= parameter points to the desired application program. Several commercial shells are available for use with Windows. If you find one of these is more useful as your startup shell, edit the shell parameter to point to it.

Many Windows applications have an extensive macro facility that permits using this language to create custom menus. This can be used to create shells from the application program. For example, if you have some less experienced users in your company and wish to control which programs they can access, you could boot the system into

Windows and use the `shell=` parameter to define the application. The application, in turn, should have a custom menu. Assuming you were using Microsoft Excel, the following macro would start Microsoft Windows (DOS version) from Excel:

```
RUN WORD
=EXEC("WORD.PIF")
=RETURN()
```

For information on creating the custom menu, see the Excel documentation or other books about Excel. Most Windows applications will not have this facility, however, because they are not intended to be used as shells.

Help! I can't quit Windows.

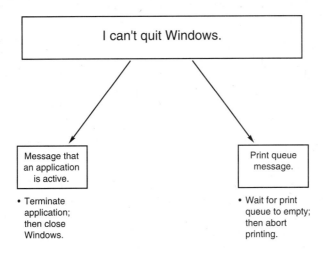

Quitting Program Manager will terminate Windows and remove Windows from memory.

Note: For Windows 3.1, if you wish to save the current window and icon organization when you quit, be sure that **S**ave Settings on Exit is checked on the **O**ptions menu of Program Manager. For Windows 3.0, check the check box on the exit to save the settings.

To quit Program Manager, use any of these methods:

- Select E**x**it Windows from the **F**ile menu.
- Double-click Program Manager's Control-menu box.
- Select **C**lose from the Control menu.
- Press Alt+F4.
- Press Alt,Spacebar,C.

In all cases, you will get a confirmation box asking if you wish to exit. Select Yes or Cancel. In Windows 3.0, there is a check box that you can mark if you want to save changes to the Desktop when you exit. To save changes in Windows 3.1, you must select the **S**ave Changes on Exit command from the **O**ptions menu before you try to exit.

Performance Tip: The quickest way to exit Windows is often without the mouse. Press Alt+Tab to get the Program Manager; then press Alt+F4 and Enter.

Caution: Always exit Windows to the DOS prompt before shutting down the computer. Some of the changes you make are not saved until you actually exit Windows. Failure to do this can cause the loss of groups or program items within groups or, even worse, file corruption. As a safety precaution, keep backups of all INI and GRP files.

Secrets and Surprises: There is an animation scene built into Windows. To see it, choose **A**bout Program Manager from the **H**elp menu of Program Manager. Hold down the Ctrl and Shift keys and double-click the icon in this dialog box. Nothing apparently happens the first time. Choose OK to close the dialog box and try the same step again. This time you should see a small flag with a message. Choose OK again, and repeat the step a third time. You should now get the animation, with the credits scrolling by and one of the famous Microsoft leaders pointing to the list.

I try to terminate Windows and get a message that an application is still active.

First, be sure that you have quit all DOS applications and that their files are saved. Each runs in a virtual machine, and all of these must be terminated before you can terminate Windows. This also includes the DOS command prompt. If you have a DOS command prompt minimized at the bottom of the screen, its virtual machine is still active. Activate the prompt, type **EXIT**, and then close Windows. (In standard mode, you can close Windows with the command prompt minimized, because there is no virtual machine.)

I tried to quit Windows, and it says the print queue is still active. It asks whether it should save the queue.

 Print Manager prints in the background and normally appears as a minimized icon on the screen during a print. If you try to quit while this program is printing, Windows will sense this and query. Normally you will wish to wait until the queue has finished printing. You can double-click the Print Manager icon and verify the printing status.

Note: Terminating Print Manager or Windows clears the print queue, eliminating all waiting print jobs. When you are through using Print Manager as an active program, minimize it again unless you wish to clear the queue.

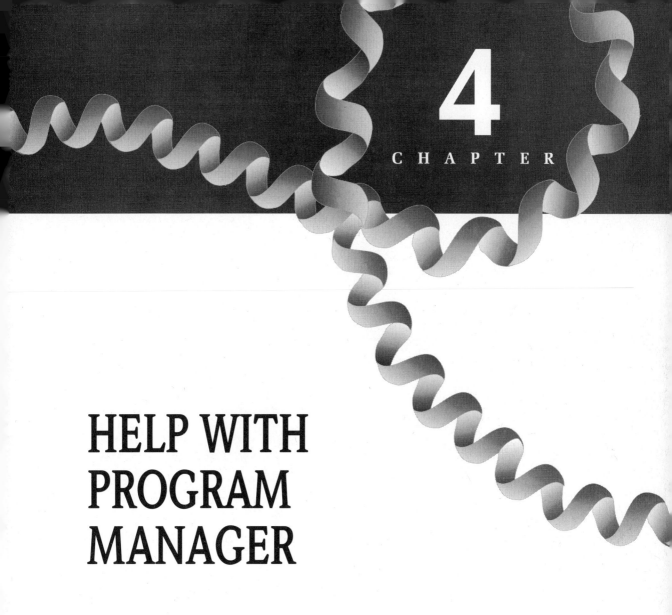

4
C H A P T E R

HELP WITH PROGRAM MANAGER

This chapter gives some general troubleshooting guidelines for using Program Manager. Program Manager is used to launch the application of other programs. It will start each time you start Windows, unless you install Windows otherwise. If you start Windows with another application (such as Excel with the command WIN EXCEL), Program Manager still loads, but it is minimized as an icon at the bottom of the desktop.

General Information About Program Manager

To simplify management of program execution, Program Manager partitions programs into logical groups, with each group managed from its own group window. Each group window is a document window to Program Manager. When you start Windows the first time, some of the group windows are opened, with other groups represented as document icons (group icons) at the bottom of the Program Manager application window (see Figure 3.1 in Chapter 3). All the group icons are identical except for their labels. In the group window, application programs are represented by program-item icons. You launch (start) programs from the program-item icons.

The grouping of programs has no relationship to how your hard disk or your directories are organized. Programs in a group can be on different directories, and the same program may be on a disk once but launched from several group windows.

The document (group) icons can be moved within the application window, but not outside of it to the desktop. If you try to move a group icon into a group window, it may appear to be in the window. In reality, however, it is still on the underlying application window. If you make the group window active, the document icon underneath will be hidden.

The program-item icons can be moved within the group window. You can define the groups you wish to use and the programs for each group. You can add or delete groups (including the initial installation groups), and add or delete programs within the groups. It is not necessary for a program to be in a group to start it from Windows. The Program Manager only

Help with Program Manager

makes it easier to start the program. Program-item icons can be used to start Windows applications, DOS applications, and batch files.

Help! I can't get the system status.

```
┌──────────────────────────────────────────────────┐
│               I can't get system status.           │
└──────────────────────────────────────────────────┘
                          │
                          ▼
```

- Use About Program Manager on Help menu.
- Use MSD program with Windows.
- Use MEM program with DOS.
- Use FREEMEM shareware utility.

Program Manager is also useful for getting information about your Windows system: the mode in which it is running, memory allocations, and the status of system resources. Use this feature of Windows occasionally to make sure that Windows is really running the way you want it to.

To find out more about your Windows configuration, choose **A**bout Program Manager from Program Manager's **H**elp menu. This will give you a small message box with some critical information about your system. The box will list the current Windows mode (standard or 386 enhanced), memory-use statistics, and the percent of system resources used. Also, you can check to see if a

Help! I can't get the system status.

115

permanent swap file is being used and what its size is by opening Control Panel and choosing the 386 Enhanced icon. You can find the information on your virtual memory (swap file) from this option.

□ Use the MSD program with Windows to get an analysis of your system: interrupt maps, DMAs in use, memory addresses in use, and more. This program is on the fifth Windows disk and is installed to the Windows directory when Windows is installed. It is not compressed.

□ Use the MEM program with DOS to monitor how memory is being used. Many memory managers and competitive products have similar products. The command MEM /d, for example, shows which drivers are really in upper memory (see Appendix A). Unfortunately, these programs are generally no more intelligent than Windows in detecting what memory is really being used. A disk controller routine in the UMB area, for example, can go completely undetected. Use these programs for working with memory conflict problems in the UMB area.

□ Use a FREEMEM shareware program to monitor memory use by Windows dynamically. There are several of these programs around, and they all load as icons and display available memory as other programs execute.

Help! I can't define and edit groups.

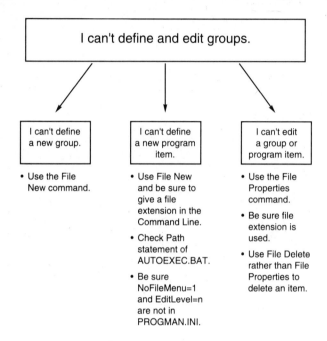

I can't define and edit groups.

I can't define a new group.	I can't define a new program item.	I can't edit a group or program item.
• Use the File New command.	• Use File New and be sure to give a file extension in the Command Line. • Check Path statement of AUTOEXEC.BAT. • Be sure NoFileMenu=1 and EditLevel=n are not in PROGMAN.INI.	• Use the File Properties command. • Be sure file extension is used. • Use File Delete rather than File Properties to delete an item.

To define groups, use the **N**ew command of the **F**ile menu. To edit groups, use the **P**roperties command of the **F**ile menu. Here are some performance tips for using groups:

■ Keep the description short so that it fits under the icon neatly. Windows 3.1 automatically wraps long descriptions to two or more lines, but you should try to keep descriptions as short as possible and yet uniquely define the icon.

■ Don't use the full path name if the file is in the current directory or in the path defined by AUTOEXEC.BAT.

Help! I can't define and edit groups.

117

When defining a new item in a group, be sure to add the file extension to the filename in the Command Line text box.

If the associations are defined correctly (in File Manager), you can start a program with a data file by entering the data filename and its extension in the Command Line text box after the path and filename of the program itself.

When using the **B**rowse option on the Properties dialog box, define the directory in the Command Line text box before selecting the command. You will then see the contents of that directory.

Many programs, such as Program Manager, have multiple icons. You can use Change **I**con to define the icon you wish to use. In thc Change Icon dialog box, you can enter as an icon file any file with an ICO, EXE, or DLL extension. Program Manager will use the icon you choose for the program.

To change the default icon spacing, start Control Panel and choose the Desktop icon. Change **S**pacing to control the icon spacing.

Save frequently any files in the Windows directory having the INI and GRP extensions. Windows is not too kind about saving these under certain error conditions, such as low disk space. The GRP and INI files can become scrambled. Save backup versions with GRK and INK extensions in the Windows directory.

Make groups read-only when you wish to protect them from changes. To make a group read-only, use File Manager. Select the GRP file that corresponds and then choose **P**roperties from the **F**ile menu. Turn the **R**ead-only check box on and click OK.

Once your groups are defined (or if you change them), use the **T**ile option of the **W**indows menu (or Shift+F4) to tile the windows. Then save the settings when you exit. You can do a save without exiting by holding down Shift and clicking **F**ile E**x**it Windows.

You can put programs in several groups. Putting a program in multiple groups doesn't mean the program is on the disk several times. Programs in multiple groups use very little additional disk space. Deleting a program from a group does not delete it from the disk. Here are basic organizational strategies you can use:

Organize your groups in a logical manner that meets your needs. For example, if you do desktop publishing, you may wish to put a paint program, word processor, and desktop publishing program in the same group. You can put the same program in multiple groups if you wish. This doesn't mean that multiple copies of the program are on the disk; it means only that the program can be launched from several groups. You can also mix Windows and non-Windows applications in a group. Keep no more than 12 programs in a group so that you can see all the program-item icons when the window is opened. If several users share the system, you might want to set up special groups for each user.

Group applications together in their own group windows. PageMaker, CoralDRAW, Excel, and many others install as two or more programs in a single group. You may wish to keep these groups, but keep them normally closed. Copy to working groups any primary applications from these groups that you use frequently. Another variation of this might be a group containing the program file and several data files, such as several word processing files in a group with a word processor.

Help! I can't define and edit groups.

119

■ Group applications together by category. Using this approach, all spreadsheets are in one group, all word processors in another, and database managers in another. DOS and Windows applications are mixed in groups.

■ Group applications together by project. For preparation of a budget, you might use a word processor, a spreadsheet, a presentation program, and several data files. All of these could be in a single group.

Whichever organizational strategy you use, follow these guidelines when using groups:

■ Minimize the number of open groups. Choose program items you use and keep them in a small number of open groups. For example, the DOS prompt on the Main group might be used frequently along with Control Panel, but others here can be kept in a closed group. Why not create a small group with just those containing the few accessories you use and keep the others out of the way?

■ Keep the Program Manager window small enough that you can see the minimized applications easily for starting them. Otherwise, you are constantly resizing the Program Manager window or starting second copies of applications. This is a good reason for keeping only a few good groups open.

■ Define groups in a way that relates to your work style. Keep unused program items out of the way. Groups that you don't use often should be kept closed.

■ In Windows 3.0, groups and icons can use up system resources quickly. Monitor this with the **A**bout option of the **H**elp menu. Even making a group window an icon doesn't reclaim these resources once the window has been opened. Keep windows and icons to a minimum. This is

not as much of a problem in Windows 3.1 because resources are managed better. The problem is still there,
however. Monitor resources from the **H**elp menu.

☐ When leaving Windows, save the configuration by selecting **S**ave Settings on Exit from the **O**ptions menu before
you terminate Windows. When you restart, turn this
setting off until you reorganize your groups again.

I can't define a new group in Program Manager.

☐ To define a new group, choose **N**ew on the **F**ile menu.
This opens a dialog box from which you can define a
group or program item. Choose to define a group, as
shown in Figure 4.1. Enter the group name (no group
filename is needed) and click OK.

	Program Group Properties	
Description:	Desktop Publishing	OK
Group File:		Cancel
		Help

Figure 4.1
*Defining a new
group.*

I can't define a new program
item in an existing group.

☐ To define a new program item for an existing group,
choose **N**ew from the **F**ile menu. A dialog box appears
from which you can define a group or program item.
Choose to define a program item. When defining a new
program item, you can define the **D**escription for the icon,

Help! I can't define and edit groups.

121

the **C**ommand Line (use the full path and file extension), the **W**orking Directory, and a **S**hortcut Key to start the program, as shown in Figure 4.2. Click OK. Be sure to use the file extension in defining the command line.

■ Make sure the program path is included in the PATH command of AUTOEXEC.BAT (see Appendix G).

■ Make sure that `NoFileMenu=1` and `EditLevel=`*n* (where *n* is 1–4) are not in the PROGMAN.INI file.

Performance Tip: The fastest way to add a program item to a group is to drag the file (program, PIF, BAT, data, etc.) from File Manager to the group.

Figure 4.2
*Defining a
program item.*

Program Item Properties		
Description:	Oilcap game	**OK**
Command Line:	L:\test\oilcap.exe	**Cancel**
Working Directory:	L:\test	
Shortcut Key:	None	**B**rowse...
☐ **R**un Minimized		**Change Icon...**
		Help

I can't edit an existing group or program item.

■ To edit an item, select the item and **P**roperties from the **F**ile menu. Edit the desired parameters and click OK.

■ Check to make sure a file extension is used for the **C**ommand Line of program items.

▢ To delete a program item, choose the item and **D**elete from the **F**ile menu. If all program items are deleted, choosing the group and **D**elete will delete the group.

Performance Tip: For quick Properties editing, hold down the Alt key and double-click the item.

Help! I'm having trouble starting a program in Program Manager.

```
┌─────────────────────────────────────────┐
│     I'm having trouble starting a program. │
└─────────────────────────────────────────┘
```

Double-clicking doesn't start the program.	I can't start a program minimized.	I can't start DOS prompt.	Data file icon won't start program.

- Check properties of icon — be sure file extension is specified.
- Check to make sure the program is installed.
- If DOS program, check PIF file.
- Check PATH statement of AUTOEXEC.BAT.

- Hold down Shift key and double-click icon.

- System can't find COMMAND.COM. Verify path with File Properties.

- Use File Manager to define association.
- Use File Properties to check command line.
- Use appropriate startup convention for the DOS application.

Help! I'm having trouble starting a program in Program Manager.

123

If you can't start a program in Program Manager, the program is probably not installed correctly as a program item. There are a few other things that can go wrong, as well. The advice given in the following sections should help you get your programs started with Windows.

Double-clicking a program-item icon doesn't start the program.

▢ Select the icon and **P**roperties from the **F**ile menu. Check the **C**ommand Line. Be sure that the full path and the program filename extension are specified. To start a program in a directory other than the program's native directory, enter the startup directory as the Working Directory in the Program Item Properties dialog box.

▢ Check to see that the program is installed.

▢ If using a batch, data, or PIF file with the program, verify the file. To verify a batch file, use an editor such as Notepad. To verify a data file, use the program that created it. To verify a PIF file, use the PIF Editor with Windows.

▢ Be sure the AUTOEXEC.BAT PATH command includes the path for the program file (see Appendix G).

How can I start a program as an icon (minimized) without running it?

□ If you hold down the Shift key when starting an application, the application will load as an icon without executing.

The DOS icon in the Main group doesn't work.

□ This generally means that the system can't find the COMMAND.COM file. In the default mode, when you drop to DOS from Windows the system will try to find COMMAND.COM from the root directory of the C drive. The root directory of the C drive (C:\) should be almost the first entry of the PATH command in the AUTOEXEC.BAT file (see Appendix G), for example, PATH C:\WIN; C:\; C:\MW5.

If COMMAND.COM is somewhere else, the DOS icon will not work. Some users place COMMAND.COM elsewhere to give it better protection from viruses. The solution is quite simple: select the DOS icon; then use the **P**roperties command of the **F**ile menu to indicate where COMMAND.COM is stored. For example, if COMMAND.COM is stored in the \START directory of the C drive, enter C:\START\COMMAND.COM as the command line.

Help! I'm having trouble starting a program in Program Manager.

125

An icon is assigned to a data file, but selecting the data file doesn't start the program with it. I get a message that no association exists.

Most Windows applications automatically set up all proper associations when they are installed. You should, however, use this assumption with caution and check after installation to be sure all proper extensions are added to the WIN.INI file. Verify by using the **A**ssociate command of the **F**ile menu of File Manager, or check the [extensions] section of WIN.INI (see Appendix G).

In Program Manager, use the **P**roperties command of the **F**ile menu to check the program's **C**ommand Line to be sure it's properly specified.

Every DOS application has its own convention for starting a program with a data file. When starting programs with data files, you must always follow this convention. For example, to start a Lotus 1-2-3 program with a data file, you might use in the PIF file:

```
C:\LOTUS\123.EXE  -wC:\BUDGET\YEAREND.WK1
```

See Chapter 10 for more information.

Performance Tip: Remember that if you have several program items for different data files and the same program, each item will start another copy of the program. For better memory management, you may wish to start one copy of the program and load data files as needed.

Help! I can't manage icons.

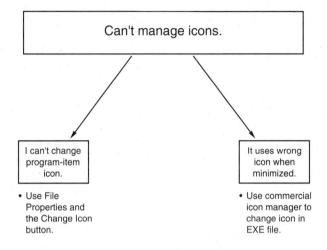

Can't manage icons.

I can't change program-item icon.
- Use File Properties and the Change Icon button.

It uses wrong icon when minimized.
- Use commercial icon manager to change icon in EXE file.

Icons are used to represent programs or actions. In Program Manager, icons represent actions. Clicking an icon can start a program, execute a batch file, or initiate an action by following a sequence of keystrokes created with the Recorder. When you minimize a program that is executing, it remains in memory and is quickly available as a minimized icon on the desktop.

I can't change the icon for a program item.

To change the icon, choose the Change **I**con button on the Program Item Properties dialog box that appears after you select the icon and choose **F**ile **P**roperties. Enter the name of the file containing the icon and then choose the icon from that file, as shown in Figure 4.3. Click OK. The selection defaults to the program filename, but you can

enter the name of any EXE file that contains icons or you can use any of the variety of DLL or ICO files available on bulletin boards or commercially. Program Manager alone has 45 icons from which you can choose. Be sure to use the full path name and file extension in defining this file.

Secrets and Surprises: You can find a collection of icons with Windows 3.1 in the file MORICONS.DLL in the \WINDOWS directory. Enter this filename in the Change Icon dialog box and choose the desired icon.

Figure 4.3

Changing the icon.

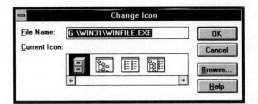

When minimized, the program uses its default icon instead of the one I assigned in Program Manager.

Even though an icon is defined in Program Manager, it is only used in the group to represent the program. When the program is minimized, the default icon in the program's EXE file will be used. Windows 3.1 permits some freedom from this if the software developer takes advantage of it. Some commercial icon managers (such as hDC's) also permit you to change the icon in the EXE file.

■ To change this, use an icon manager that can change the icon in the EXE file.

Help! I can't customize Windows to start with another program.

```
┌─────────────────────────────────────┐
│      I can't customize starting.     │
└─────────────────────────────────────┘
                    │
                    ▼
        • Use shell=
          parameter of
          SYSTEM.INI
          to define startup
          program.
```

■ Windows can be customized to start in many ways. For example, you could start Windows with the File Manager or your own application instead of Program Manager. Edit the shell= parameter line in SYSTEM.INI (see Appendix G) to point to the startup program. In the default mode, this will be shell=progman.exe.

Use caution in changing the shell. If you have a third-party program manager, you may have trouble installing new programs to it. In many installations, once the application is installed it tries to set up a new group in Program Manager. If Program Manager isn't there, it won't complete the installation.

Help! I can't customize Windows to start with another program.

129

Help! How can I save the current configuration without quitting?

I can't save configuration without quitting.

• Start any DOS application. Be sure Save Settings on Exit is on; then try to quit.

With Windows 3.1, to save changes without exiting, hold down Shift and click **E**xit on the **F**ile menu. Nothing apparently happens, but if Windows is reloaded you will find that the previous configuration was saved. To use this trick, Save Changes on Exit does not have to be turned on.

Starting Programs with Windows

Any programs you place in the Startup group will start with Windows. You can use the **F**ile **P**roperties command to set the program to start minimized.

Performance Tip: Put Program Manager in the Startup group and assign it a shortcut key.

Help with Program Manager

Two people use a computer and Windows. How can each user have a personal Startup group and Program Manager configuration?

Create a PROGRAM.INI file for each user, with no duplicate group names in the file. In the [Settings] section, place a **Startup=xxxx** line in each file to define the Startup group name for each user:

```
Startup="Charlie's Startup Group"
```

Now create a batch file for each user that copies the appropriate file to PROGRAM.INI and starts Windows.

I have a startup program defined in the Startup Group, but it runs when Windows starts instead of being minimized (or starts minimized when I want it to run).

Select the icon in Program Manager and then choose **P**roperties from the **F**ile menu. Be sure Run Minimized is turned on to start the program minimized on or is off to start it executing with Windows.

The Startup programs start with Windows. How can I start Windows without the Startup programs starting?

When starting Windows, hold down the Shift key after the startup logo is on the screen.

5

HELP WITH USING WINDOWS FILE MANAGER AND APPLETS

Included with Windows are a number of Windows applications. Learning how to use these applications effectively is a good introduction to managing more complex Windows

applications. This chapter will cover two major Windows applications, File Manager and Program Manager. It will also cover the Windows accessory applications known as *applets*. These include Notebook, Sysedit, Write, Paintbrush, and WinHelp.

General Information About File Manager

File Manager is an important Windows application program that is used for file and disk management. When you work with File Manager, the windows are automatically updated as you add, delete, or rename directories and files. Figure 5.1 shows a directory display in File Manager. Each time you quit File Manager, the current configuration is saved.

Here are a few of the things you can do with File Manager:

- View the directory tree or files in one or more directories.
- Initiate program execution.
- Name and rename files and directories.
- Create and delete directories.
- Search for files and directories.
- Move and copy files and directories.
- Print files.
- Modify file attributes.

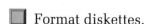 Format diskettes.

 Make system diskettes.

 Copy diskettes.

 Label diskettes.

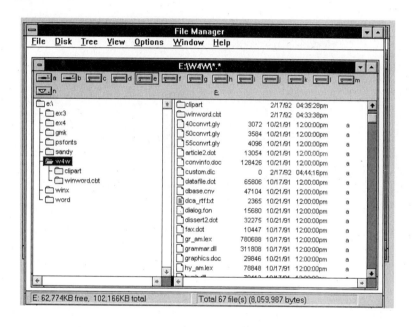

Figure 5.1
*File Manager
with a directory
display.*

File Manager uses directory windows to display a specified directory and the files on that directory. Directory windows behave like any document windows. Only one directory
window can be active (have the keyboard focus) at a time.
Windows can be minimized to an icon to get the windows
temporarily out of the way. Clicking the icon displays a Control menu, and selecting **R**estore returns the directory display.

You can also double-click the directory icon to restore. Directory windows can be maximized to get a larger view. Clicking the Restore button returns the window to its normal size.

Directory windows can be closed with one exception: you cannot close the last directory window. Close windows from their Control menu by selecting **C**lose or by double-clicking the Control-menu box. You can use the **W**indow menu to cascade or tile open directory windows. From a directory window, you can create, edit, move, and delete directories, as well as select directories for file viewing.

Tips for Using File Manager

The following tips will help you use File Manager effectively:

▢ Open only the directory windows that you need. Keep unused directory windows minimized. Open the same window on another directory instead of opening a new window.

▢ If you are not using File Manager as the shell, keep it closed as an icon at the bottom of the screen. You will use it often.

▢ Use the Recorder feature in the Accessories group to automate repetitive File Manager operations by creating batch files. Use macros to do backups and automate copy operations that you perform often.

▢ Use Ctrl+F6 to cycle through open directory windows.

▢ Build associations to simplify starting programs with data files.

■ Keep the display of hidden and system files turned off unless you need to view them. This will prevent their accidental deletion.

■ Reduce visual clutter. Use the **V**iew menu to display only the files of interest. Expand only directories of interest.

■ Verify disk space by using the status bar before copying or moving.

■ Set the attributes of important files you wish to keep (such as COMMAND.COM) as read-only. This prevents them from being accidentally erased or altered by a virus.

■ Put File Manager in the Startup group. This will force it to start on loading and will cause it to be displayed as an icon. This way, you are only a click away from any file management chores.

Help! I updated some files, but the display doesn't show the update.

```
┌─────────────────────────────────────┐
│  I updated some files, but the screen │
│       doesn't show the update.        │
└─────────────────────────────────────┘
                   │
                   ▼
          • Choose Window
            Refresh or
            press F5 to
            update display.
```

Help! I updated some files, but the display doesn't show the update.

137

As you use File Manager with other windows open on the screen, the File Manager windows should automatically change to reflect the status of displayed drives and directories.

Sometimes a command may not update the display to reflect a change. If you need to update the display, choose **R**efresh from the **W**indow menu or press F5.

Help! I can't move/copy a directory or file.

```
┌─────────────────────────────────────────────┐
│                                             │
│   I can't move or copy a directory or file. │
│                                             │
└─────────────────────────────────────────────┘
                      │
                      ▼
```

• To move, hold down Alt and drag the file or directory icon. To copy, hold down Ctrl and drag the icon.

You can copy and move directories and files from one location (the *source*) to another location (the *destination*) by dragging icons, by using shortcut keys, or by using the **File** menu. When copying or moving, the source can be a file or a directory. The destination can be a directory or a disk drive.

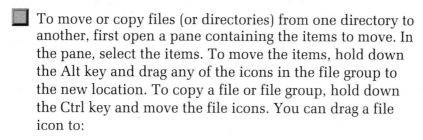 To move or copy files (or directories) from one directory to another, first open a pane containing the items to move. In the pane, select the items. To move the items, hold down the Alt key and drag any of the icons in the file group to the new location. To copy a file or file group, hold down the Ctrl key and move the file icons. You can drag a file icon to:

A directory in a directory tree.

A disk icon.

A directory icon in a pane opened from the directory tree.

A minimized directory window.

If you move files to a drive icon, File Manager will move the current selection to the last directory that was used on that drive. You can move directories in the same way. Multiple files or directories can be moved in one operation.

To use the keyboard to move or copy a file, a group of files, or directories from one directory to another, first open the directory window for the files (directories) to move or copy. Select the items. Choose **M**ove or **C**opy from the **F**ile menu. Enter the destination directory and click OK. File Manager will move or copy the files to the destination directory. As a short-cut, you can use F7 for a move and F8 for a copy. Figure 5.2 shows the dialog box for copying.

Secrets and Surprises: Dragging without pressing any key will initiate a copy if the destination is a different drive and will initiate a move if the files are on the same drive. It's a shortcut, but it can be confusing. Here's a neat trick

continues

Help! I can't move/copy a directory or file.

continued

to help you remember whether you are copying or moving. Click the source icon and drag it to the destination. Don't release the mouse button. Press Ctrl and then Alt, and watch the source icon in the file window. The icon will show whether the file remains at the source. If the source icon is still there, it will be a copy. If not, it's a move. No transfer takes place until you release the mouse button. If you decide to cancel, drag the icon where it won't initiate any action and release the mouse.

Another way to tell if files are being moved or copied is to look at the icon attached to the mouse pointer. If the files are being copied, a plus sign (+) will appear on the icon at the pointer. If the files are being moved, the icon will be blank.

Figure 5.2

Copying a file.

Copy
Current Directory: E:\W4W
From: 55CONVRT.GLY
To: ⦿
○ Copy to Clipboard

OK Cancel Help

Using the keyboard for copying has one advantage. You can use the **C**opy command to rename and copy a file at the same time. Use the **F**ile **C**opy command as before and then specify the new name in the **T**o: text box.

With Windows 3.0, if you are moving or copying a group of files with related names, use the Searc**h** command of the **F**ile menu to locate all matching files. These are placed in a Search

Results box. You can then initiate a move or copy from this box just as you would from a directory window; that is, you can drag the icons.

With Windows 3.1, use the **S**elect Files command of the **F**ile menu to select the type of files to move or copy. For example, to back up all DOC files in a directory to a diskette, use **F**ile **S**elect Files and enter `*.DOC` as the template for **F**ile(s):. Choose **S**elect and **C**lose. Then use F8 to initiate the copy. (The **C**lose button is available only after making a selection or deselection.)

Help! I can't remember where a file or directory is located.

```
┌─────────────────────────────────────┐
│   I can't remember where a file or   │
│        directory is located.         │
└─────────────────────────────────────┘
                  │
                  ▼
```

• Use Search command on File menu. Results are displayed in the Search Results window.

You can search a particular drive for a directory or file.

▢ Select the drive and, if desired, the directory to search. Choose Searc**h** from the **F**ile menu. In the dialog box that is displayed, enter the directory or filename. You can use wildcard characters, such as asterisks or question marks,

Help! I can't remember where a file or directory is located.

141

in the specification. Toggle the Search Entire Disk (Windows 3.0) or Search All Subdirectories (Windows 3.1) on or off, as appropriate, and select OK. The result is displayed in a Search Results window.

The Search Results window does not behave like a directory window. In general, you would not move or copy files into the window. You can, however, select within the Search Results window and move, copy, or print from it by using the commands on the File menu. You can also copy a file from a directory pane to a directory on the Search Results window.

Secrets and Surprises: If you have large disks with many directories and can't remember how you spelled a directory, the Search Results window is one way to find a list of possibilities.

Help! I have problems selecting files or directories.

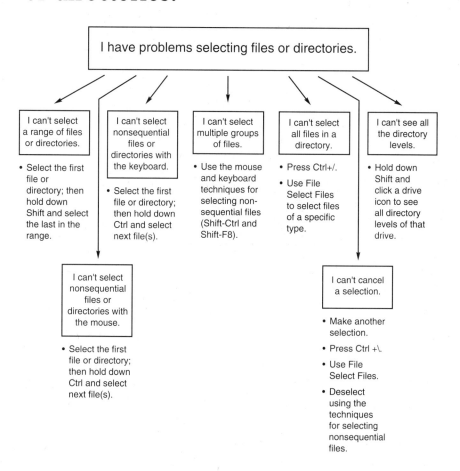

You can work with multiple directories at the same time, moving and copying files between them. Each directory is displayed in its own document window. Each has two panes,

Help! I have problems selecting files or directories.

143

and each split bar can be positioned as desired. If you click another drive icon in the window, all you do is change the displayed directory in the current window. That's because the drive icons are in the directory window, and clicking one changes only the display for that window. To open multiple directory windows, double-click the drive icon or choose **N**ew Window from the **W**indow menu. This will open a second directory window, the same as the first. Now use the icons in it to change to another drive or change the directory.

You can quickly switch between all open directory windows by selecting the window name from the **W**indow menu or by using Ctrl+F6.

To perform a file operation from a directory window, select the files on which to perform an action and then select the action. You can select a single file, a range of files, or files that are not adjacent in a file list. You can also select multiple groups of files. Making multiple file selections is called *extending a selection.*

I can't select a range of files or directories.

To select a range of files, open the directory window for the file and, with the mouse, click the first file in the range to highlight it. Hold down the Shift key and click the last file in the range. The entire range will be highlighted. To do it from the keyboard, use the direction keys to highlight the first file in the range. Hold down the Shift key and extend the range with the direction keys.

I can't select nonsequential files or directories with the mouse.

☐ To select files or directories that are not in sequence, open the directory if necessary and, with the mouse, click the first filename. Then hold down the Ctrl key and click each additional filename.

I can't select nonsequential files or directories with the keyboard.

☐ From the keyboard, you can select nonsequential files and directories. Select the first file or directory. Press Shift+F8, and the selection cursor will begin to blink. Use the direction keys to move the cursor to each file and press the Spacebar. When the selection is complete, press Shift+F8 again.

Note: The files selected can be from multiple directory windows.

I can't select multiple groups of files.

☐ To select multiple groups with the mouse, click the first file of the first group. Hold down the Shift key and click the last file of the group. The first group is now

Help! I have problems selecting files or directories.

145

highlighted. Hold down the Ctrl key and click the first file of the next group. Hold down the Shift+Ctrl keys and click the last file of the second group. Continue with as many groups as desired.

You can also select multiple groups of files from the keyboard. Select the first group by holding down the Shift key as you move the highlight over the group. Then press Shift+F8. Use the direction keys to select the first item of the second group. Press the Spacebar. Hold down the Shift key and use the direction keys to select all of the second group. Press Shift+F8 when finished.

I can't select all the files in a directory.

☐ To select all the files in a directory, press Ctrl+/.

☐ To select all files of a specific type (or all directory files from the menu), choose **S**elect Files from the **F**ile menu. Enter a template for the selection, using wildcards in **F**ile(s):, such as *.DOC. You can use the default *.* to select all files. Choose **S**elect and then **C**lose. The **C**lose button is available only after making a selection or deselection. (With Windows 3.0, choose **S**elect All from the **F**ile menu. There is no dialog box.)

Secrets and Surprises: When you select a group of files, the amount of disk space required by the files is at the bottom of the display window. This is useful for planning file moves to other directories or for backing up files. For example, to back up all DOC files in a directory, you could select them and then see if the combined file space listed at the bottom of the window will fit on the backup diskette.

I can't cancel a selection.

To cancel a selection, you can use any of four methods:

■ Make another selection. If you reselect, it will cancel the first.

■ Press Ctrl+\. This will clear all selections.

■ Choose **S**elect Files from the **F**ile menu. Define the template, select **D**eselect, and then **C**lose.

■ Deselect individual filenames from an extended list by holding down the Ctrl key and clicking the individual filename. From the keyboard, you can do this by pressing Shift+F8 and using the direction keys to move the cursor to the file to deselect. Press the Spacebar and then Shift+F8 again.

I can't see all the directory levels.

■ Hold down the Shift key and click a disk drive to see all directory levels of that drive. Another way to accomplish the same thing is to press Ctrl-* (press Ctrl and then press * on the numeric keypad).

Help! I have problems selecting files or directories.

5

C H A P T E R

Help! I have problems renaming and deleting files or directories.

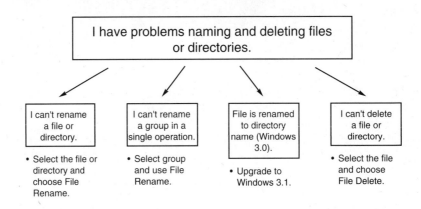

File Manager enables you to rename files and directories without returning to DOS. The rules for naming and renaming files are the same as those for naming a directory. You can use letters or numbers as well as any of these symbols:

' ~ ! @ # $ % ^ & ( ) _ - { }

Avoid the use of periods, asterisks, question marks, and other special characters. The following names are reserved by the system and cannot be used for files: CON, AUX, COM1, COM2, COM3, COM4, LPT1, LPT2, LPT3, PRN, and NUL.

Besides its filename, a file or directory can have a suffix, or *extension*, to define its type. To rename a file with an extension, you must specify the extension name. The extension can be from one to three characters in length, and is preceded by a period, for example, RESOURCES.DBF.

I can't rename a file or directory.

☐ To rename files (or directories), first select the files (or directories) to rename. Choose Re**n**ame from the **F**ile menu. Enter the new name and select OK. With the **F**ile **C**opy command, you can both rename and copy a file at the same time.

Caution: Use caution in renaming the Windows directory or files in it. Group and INI files may refer to this directory or to files in it.

Note: Renaming a directory or file does not alter or move files but only changes the directory entry in the disk directory. If you rename a directory, all the files will be in the directory with the new name.

I can't rename a group of files with a single operation.

☐ To rename a group of files, select the group and use the Re**n**ame command on the **F**ile menu. To rename all files with the WP extension to the MS extension, for example, select the files with the WP extension, choose **F**ile Re**n**ame and then enter `*.MP` in the **T**o: box. Click OK.

Help! I have problems renaming and deleting files or directories.

149

Performance Tip: You can rename multiple files with a single command by using wildcard characters. Use caution, however. The results may not be what you expect. For example, in Figure 5.3 if the **To:** box contained `win?.doc`, you would have a problem. However, `win???.doc` works.

Figure 5.3
*Using
wildcards to
rename a file.*

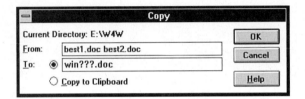

I tried to rename a file, and it was renamed to the directory the file was in.

◻ With Windows 3.0, if you press Enter or click **R**ename without entering a new name, the file will be renamed to the name of the directory containing the file. For example, if you have a file named `CHAP1.DOC` in the \WP directory and try to rename it without entering a new name, the file will be renamed `WP` (without an extension). With Windows 3.1, this is fixed. Trying to rename to a blank name results in no action.

I can't delete a file or directory.

▢ To delete files, select the file or files to be deleted and choose **D**elete from the **F**ile menu. You can use the Del key as a shortcut.

With Windows 3.0, if you are deleting a group of files with related names, use the Searc**h** command of the **F**ile menu to locate all matching files. These are placed in a Search Results box. You can then press the Del key to delete the files from the directory.

With Windows 3.1, you can delete a group of files of the same type by using the **S**elect Files command of the **F**ile menu. For example, to delete all BAK files on a directory choose **F**ile **S**elect Files. Enter `*.BAK` as the template in the **F**iles(s): box. Choose **S**elect and **C**lose; then press Del.

Performance Tip: You can delete multiple directories with a single command. You can't do this from the pane with the directory tree, but you can from a pane that displays the contents of a directory. First, from the parent directory, open a pane containing the directories to delete. In the new directory window, select the subdirectories to delete (see the earlier section "Help! I have problems selecting files or directories."). Then choose **D**elete from the **F**ile menu. Use caution because this action will delete the directories and the files in them.

Help! I have problems renaming and deleting files or directories.

151

> **Note:** Use caution in deleting directories. When deleting a directory with files, the directory and files are physically removed from the disk. Unlike deleting with DOS, deleting a directory in Windows will delete the files in it and (depending on the confirmation level set) may not give you any warnings.

Help! I accidentally erased a file I needed.

```
I accidentally erased a file I needed.
```

• Use a
Windows-based
commercial file
recovery program.
(It must already
be installed.)

If you accidentally delete the wrong file or group of files, you may be able to recover the file if you attempt the recovery immediately. Don't try to write to any other file until the file is recovered.

If you have a commercial Windows undelete utility, use it immediately. If using a commercial DOS utility or DOS 5 to undelete, reboot without exiting Windows (assuming all open files are saved), and then use the utility. A normal Windows exit can update certain files and make the file recovery impossible on the Windows drive.

Performance Tip: Sooner or later everybody accidentally erases a file. Be prepared, and invest in a file recovery program that can be run from Windows.

Help! I have printing problems in File Manager.

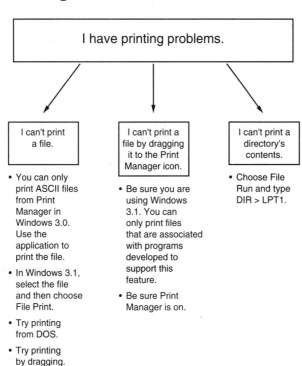

I have printing problems.

I can't print a file.

- You can only print ASCII files from Print Manager in Windows 3.0. Use the application to print the file.
- In Windows 3.1, select the file and then choose File Print.
- Try printing from DOS.
- Try printing by dragging.

I can't print a file by dragging it to the Print Manager icon.

- Be sure you are using Windows 3.1. You can only print files that are associated with programs developed to support this feature.
- Be sure Print Manager is on.

I can't print a directory's contents.

- Choose File Run and type DIR > LPT1.

Help! I have printing problems in File Manager.

153

Windows includes a Print Manager program that is automatically invoked on any print request from a Windows application. The application "prints" to the Print Manager, and the Print Manager queues all print requests and then prints in the background while you are doing other work (see Chapter 9).

You can print files directly from File Manager. Select the file to print and choose **P**rint from the **F**ile menu or (with Windows 3.1) drag the file icon to the Print Manager icon.

I can't print a file.

With Windows 3.0, you can print only ASCII files, that is, files containing text characters (such as the TXT files of Notepad).

With Windows 3.1, the print option is greatly enhanced and supports OLE. For example, try printing a BMP file. You can find one in the Windows directory. When you select **F**ile **P**rint, Windows automatically loads Paintbrush briefly and executes the printing from that application program and then returns to File Manager. If you click a WRI file, Write will load briefly and print the file. In other words, Windows "knows" the application program that created the file and will execute the print from it automatically.

- If you have trouble with printing, return to DOS and try to print from DOS, for example using the command **DIR *.* > LPT1**. If this fails, the problem is in the printer or the printer connection. For more information see Chapter 8.

- With Windows 3.1, you can print by dragging. Start the Print Manager from the Main group and then minimize it to an icon. Drag a TXT file to the Print Manager icon, and it will print. In the same way, you can drag a BMP or WRI file to Print Manager and it will print. In other words, if the Print Manager is minimized to an icon, you can print a file by dragging the file to it.

I dragged a file to the Print Manager icon and it didn't print.

- Make sure you are using Windows 3.1. In 3.1, dragging the filename to the Print Manager icon is the same as using **File Print** in that program with the selected file. This also assumes that Windows knows which application is associated with that particular file extension as defined in the [extensions] section of WIN.INI. This technique should work with the applets (accessory applications) such as Write and Paintbrush.

  But dragging doesn't work with all applications. It depends on whether the application program developer included the proper "hooks" for doing it, and whether the program is registered. File Manager has to be aware of what to do when a file is selected, and the application program has to know what to do when it is handed a file. This is known as the *drag and drop* feature of Windows

Help! I have printing problems in File Manager.

155

3.1. At the present time, File Manager is the only program that can act as the source; that is, only File Manager can pass a file to another program for printing or other action.

■ Be sure that Print Manager is on (Control Panel Printers).

I can't print a directory's contents.

■ Unfortunately, the **P**rint command on the **F**ile menu doesn't support printing a directory or directory tree. To print a directory list or tree, you must use DOS. The easiest method is to open a window containing the file to print, select **F**ile **R**un from the **F**ile menu, and then type a command like `DIR > LPT1` or `DIR > PRN`. Press Enter or click OK.

Help! I can't change the file attributes.

```
┌─────────────────────────────────────────┐
│      I can't change file attributes.     │
└─────────────────────────────────────────┘
                      │
                      ▼
```

• Select the file and choose File Properties. Select the desired attributes and click OK.

Each file directory entry has four attribute bits associated with it. Each bit can be either on or off. Table 5.1 lists the bits and their purpose.

Bit	Description
A	*Archive.* If on, the file has not been backed up since it was last edited.
H	*Hidden.* The file will not show up on an MS-DOS DIR listing.
R	*Read only.* If on, the file cannot be deleted or edited.
S	*System.* One of the MS-DOS system files. The file does not show up on an MS-DOS DIR listing.

Table 5.1
Attribute Bits for File Directory Entries

In the default Windows display, the file attributes are not shown, and hidden or system files are not displayed in a directory window. You can see the current attributes for the files in a directory window by choosing **F**ile Details (Windows 3.0) or **A**ll File Details (Windows 3.1) from the **V**iew menu. In Windows 3.0, if you wish to see the hidden or system files, choose In**c**lude from the **V**iew menu and toggle on Show **H**idden/System Files. In Windows 3.1, choose By File **T**ype from the **V**iew menu and select Show Hidden/**S**ystem Files in the dialog box.

You can alter the file attributes for any file or group of files. To change a file's attribute, select the file and then choose Change Attributes (Windows 3.0) or **P**roperties (Windows 3.1) from the **F**ile menu. A Change Attributes or Properties dialog box is displayed. Toggle the desired attributes on or off, and then select OK or press Enter. Figure 5.4 shows a Properties dialog box.

Figure 5.4

Changing a file's attributes.

```
┌─────────────────────────────────────────────────┐
│ ▬         Properties for COMMAND.COM              │
│                                                   │
│  File Name:    COMMAND.COM          ┌──────────┐  │
│  Size:         47,845 bytes         │    OK    │  │
│  Last Change:  7/16/91  12:00:00PM  └──────────┘  │
│  Path:         C:\DOS               ┌──────────┐  │
│                                     │  Cancel  │  │
│  ┌Attributes─────────────────────┐ └──────────┘  │
│  │ ⊠ Read Only   □ Hidden         │ ┌──────────┐  │
│  │ ⊠ Archive     □ System         │ │   Help   │  │
│  └───────────────────────────────┘ └──────────┘  │
└─────────────────────────────────────────────────┘
```

Note: To protect against viruses, it's a good idea to set the attributes of COMMAND.COM and the DOS system files to read-only. In this way, they can't be altered by any other program or user unless the bit is first turned off again.

Secrets and Surprises: To set properties, hold down the Alt key and double-click the filename. Then choose the desired attributes.

File Manager has an advantage over the older versions of DOS here. The DOS ATTRIB command can change only the read-only and archive bits in older versions of DOS. In DOS 5, ATTRIB can change any of the bits.

Help! I accidentally formatted a diskette.

> I accidentally formatted a diskette.

- If the disk was formatted with DOS 5, use DOS to recover it.

Formatting a diskette is the process of preparing a disk for use with DOS. The tracks and sectors are defined, and an empty directory is placed at the beginning of the disk. You can format a disk by using the **F**ormat Disk command on the **D**isk menu.

Formatting erases all data from a diskette. As a general rule, you cannot recover files from a formatted diskette. If the disk was formatted using DOS 5, you can do some level of recovery by using the DOS UNFORMAT command. For information on diskette recovery under DOS 5, read the DOS manual.

Help! I'm having problems copying diskettes.

> I have problems copying disks.

- Make sure the disk isn't write-protected or the wrong type.
- Be sure the disk is correctly and completely in the drive.

The Windows copy procedure does a sector and bit copy from the source to destination diskette. You can use this procedure only if both diskettes have the same capacity and are of the same type.

If you need to copy one diskette to another, it's quicker to copy the diskette than to copy files. To copy a diskette with Windows 3.1, use the following procedure:

1. Place the source diskette in the drive you wish to copy from.

2. Select the disk drive icon for this drive. The source drive icon should be highlighted.

3. Select Copy Disk from the Disk menu.

4. Select the source and destination drives in the next dialog box. Choose OK.

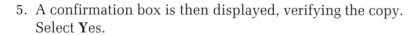

5. A confirmation box is then displayed, verifying the copy. Select **Yes**.

6. You will then see a box requesting the insertion of the source diskette. Select OK.

As the copy proceeds, File Manager will prompt you as necessary for the changing of diskettes if you have only one drive.

Note: All previous data on the destination diskette will be destroyed. If you wish to keep data already on the destination diskette, copy the files.

Secrets and Surprises: If you are using the Copy Disk command, you do not need to format the diskette before copying onto it.

Caution: Don't try to copy a low-capacity disk in a low-capacity drive to a low-capacity diskette in a high-capacity drive. It may seem to work, but reading the resulting diskette will be marginal. Instead, use the single low-capacity drive and use it as both the source and the destination drive. File Manager will prompt you when to change diskettes.

If for some reason Windows does not let you continue the copy procedure, check for the following:

■ Make sure the disk isn't write-protected or of the wrong type (that is, double-density versus high-density, etc.).

■ Be sure the disk is correctly and completely in the drive.

Help! I get a message from File Manager.

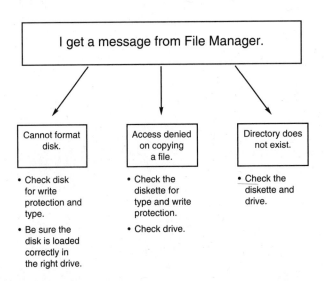

If File Manager has a problem, you will generally get a message box describing the problem. You can then take appropriate action based on the message.

I get the message "Cannot format a disk."

Figure 5.5 shows what this error message looks like. If you get this message, try the following:

- Be sure that the disk isn't write-protected (that is, no tab or tape over the notch) and that it is the right type.

- Check to see that the disk is in the right drive and is properly loaded.

Figure 5.5

The error message that appears when Windows can't format a diskette.

I get the message "Cannot Replace *xxxxx:* Access Denied."

Figure 5.6 shows this error message. You tried to copy a file to a write-protected diskette or to the destination drive and the diskette is not ready. Try the following:

- Be sure that the disk isn't write-protected (that is, no tab or tape over the notch) and that it is the right type.

- Check to see that the disk is in the right drive and properly loaded.

Help! I get a message from File Manager.

163

Figure 5.6

The error message that appears when Windows can't replace a file.

I get the message "Directory x: does not exist. Create it?"

This message, shown in Figure 5.7, means that you tried to rename a file on a write-protected disk or on a drive that isn't ready. Try the following:

■ Be sure that the disk isn't write-protected (that is, no tab or tape over the notch) and that it is the right type.

■ Check to see that the disk is in the right drive and is properly loaded.

Figure 5.7

The error message that appears when Windows can't rename a file.

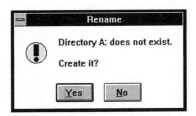

Changing File Manager's Menus

Windows supports modification of the menus in File Manager, and even adding new ones, but much of this involves programming skills that are beyond the skills of the average user. However, with Wilson WindowWare's two shareware programs, File Commander and WinBatch, making modifications is simple.

Performance Tip: Use File Commander to add a menu for launching commonly used applications from File Manager.

Changing File Manager's Font or Font Size

To change the font, select **F**ont from the File Manager **O**ptions menu. Choose the new font and size (see Figure 5.8) and then click OK.

Performance Tip: On a VGA or Super VGA screen, you will find that you can get more on a screen and it's still readable by using the Small Fonts font and choosing a 6-point or 7-point size.

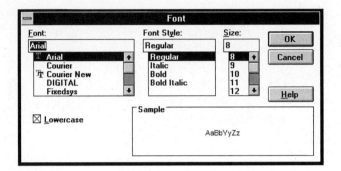

Figure 5.8
Changing the File Manager's font.

Help! I have problems using the accessories Notepad or Sysedit.

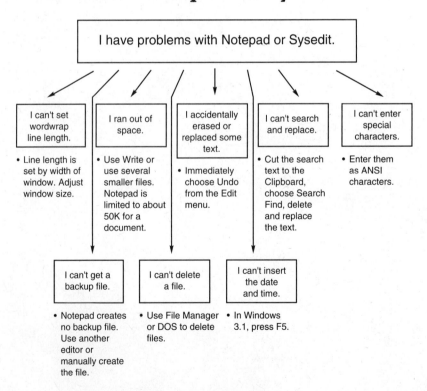

Help with Using Windows File Manager and Applets

Windows contains a number of accessory applications, or *applets*, including Notepad and Sysedit. *Notepad* is a useful editor in the Accessories group for editing ASCII files. You can use it to track telephone calls, edit memos for electronic mail and consultations, and make general notes. Unlike Write, it does not support formatting and has only a primitive wordwrap option. All text is kept in memory, which limits Notepad to documents of about 50,000 characters or less. Use the Help option to monitor memory with long documents. The default file extension is TXT.

If you want a better Windows editor, try WinEdit from Wilson WindowWare. WinEdit uses all of memory to support larger files. It supports multiple document interface, and prints correctly in wordwrap mode.

Sysedit is a useful program that is included with Windows. It is loaded automatically on installation to the WINDOWS\SYSTEM directory. The user must add it to the Main group in Progam Manager. When started, it automatically opens WIN.INI, SYSTEM.INI, AUTOEXEC.BAT, and CONFIG.SYS. Otherwise, it works like Notepad.

Performance Tip: Add Sysedit to the Main group to make it easily accessible.

Help! I have problems using the accessories Notepad or Sysedit.

167

I can't set the line length for wordwrap.

Unlike Windows Write and most other word processors, the length of the line with wordwrap on is determined by the width of the window. Resize the window to get the desired width.

When you save a file with wordwrap on, the lines are saved in their full length (no wordwrap). This makes it hard to read the text when you are using it with another editor or even in Notepad without wordwrap. Even more disconcerting is that if you try to print a word-wrapped file, the wordwraps aren't there and you end up with lines of text too long to print. At least with Notepad, you will probably wish to avoid the wordwrap feature. Also, wordwrap is not the default mode. If you need wordwrap for a file, you must turn it on each time you load the file.

Secrets and Surprises: To edit large blocks of text with the mouse, first click the beginning of the block to move the insertion point there. Then press and hold the Shift key and click the mouse at the end of the block. With the keyboard, you can use Shift+Home to select to the beginning of the line, and Shift+End to select text to the end of the line.

> **Performance Tip:** If you find yourself using Notepad frequently, place it in the Startup group. This will start Notepad as an icon with Windows.

I can't create a backup file.

☐ Unlike many word processors, Notepad does not create an automatic backup of the original file when it saves a file. If you think that you might need the original file again, save the new version of the document under a different name.

I ran out of space with Notepad.

☐ Notepad is limited to editing files of about 50,000 characters. If you find yourself running out of space in Notepad, break the file into two files or import the file to Windows Write.

I can't delete a file from Notepad.

☐ Notepad provides no command for deleting files from the disk. If you need to delete a file, use the File Manager or return to the DOS prompt and delete the file.

Help! I have problems using the accessories Notepad or Sysedit.

169

I accidentally replaced or erased text.

■ If you hit a key while text is selected, the text will be replaced by the key you have hit. If you do inadvertently erase some text, immediately use **E**dit **U**ndo to recover it.

I can't insert the date and time.

■ F5 inserts only the date in Windows 3.0. This is a bug. In Windows 3.1, F5 inserts the date and time.

I can't search and replace.

■ Notepad doesn't have a replace command, but here is a method of doing a search and replace. You can use Recorder to automate the process and do the entire replacement from a macro.

1. Enter the replacement string at the beginning of the document.

2. Highlight this string and use Ctrl+X to cut it to the Clipboard.

3. Use the **F**ind command of the **S**earch menu to locate the string to replace. The specified string will be highlighted.

4. Press Del to delete it and then Ctrl+V to replace it with the Clipboard contents.

5. Press F3, repeating until you reach the end.

Secrets and Surprises: You can use Ctrl+Home as a shortcut for placing the insertion point at the beginning of the document before a search.

Secrets and Surprises: If you put .LOG as the first line of the file, each time the file is opened a time and date stamp will be inserted.

I can't enter special characters.

Notepad supports the entry into the document of any special characters from the extended ANSI set. First, be sure the Num Lock key is on. To enter an extended ANSI character, hold down the Alt key and (with the keyboard in numeric mode) press zero (0) and the numeric value for the special character. The special character will appear on the screen. To enter IBM PC extended ANSI characters, hold down the Alt key and enter the number without the zero prefix. See Appendix E for key codes.

Help! I have problems using the accessories Notepad or Sysedit.

171

Help! I have problems with Calculator.

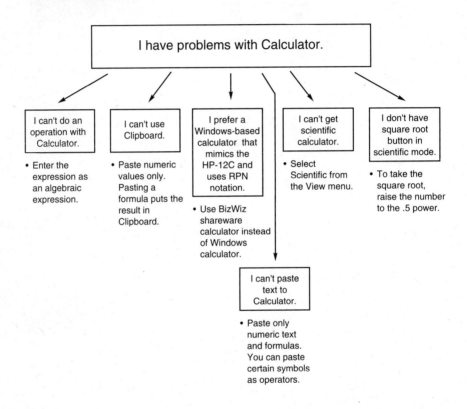

I have problems with Calculator.

I can't do an operation with Calculator.

• Enter the expression as an algebraic expression.

I can't use Clipboard.

• Paste numeric values only. Pasting a formula puts the result in Clipboard.

I prefer a Windows-based calculator that mimics the HP-12C and uses RPN notation.

• Use BizWiz shareware calculator instead of Windows calculator.

I can't get scientific calculator.

• Select Scientific from the View menu.

I don't have square root button in scientific mode.

• To take the square root, raise the number to the .5 power.

I can't paste text to Calculator.

• Paste only numeric text and formulas. You can paste certain symbols as operators.

Calculator is a useful applet for quick calculations. The Calculator contains a single memory location that can be used to store temporary results.

I can't do an operation with Calculator.

◻ Enter the expression as an algebraic expression. To add 5 and 3, for example, enter **5 + 3 =**. The answer will appear in the display.

I can't use the Clipboard with Calculator.

◻ Paste numeric values only. Use the **C**opy command to copy Calculator results in the display window to the Clipboard for pasting to another program.

I prefer a Windows-based calculator that mimics the Hewlett-Packard HP-12C and uses RPN notation.

◻ Use the BizWiz shareware calculator instead of the standard calculator included with Windows.

I can't paste text to Calculator.

◻ When pasting text to Calculator, you should generally paste only numeric text. Several alphabetic characters can be interpreted as commands and may initiate actions. For example, a *q* will clear the Calculator. Table 5.2 lists the characters that initiate actions when pasted.

Table 5.2

Characters
That Initiate
Action in
Calculator

Character	Action
C	Ctrl+C (clears memory).
E	Scientific notation in decimal mode, the value E in hexadecimal.
M	Ctrl+M (store the current value in memory).
P	Ctrl+P (add the value to the value in memory).
Q	Esc (clear the current calculation).
R	Ctrl+R (display value in memory).
:	Ctrl if before letter, function key letter if before number. For example, :P is Ctrl+P, :3 is F3.
\	Data key.

I can't get to the scientific calculator.

If you are a programmer or businessperson, you may wish to use Calculator in an advanced mode—as a scientific calculator. In this mode, you can convert values between number systems, use mathematical functions (such as the trigonometric functions), and do statistical calculations. Switching modes does not affect a displayed value. The Scientific mode always starts in Decimal mode with the same displayed value of the Standard mode.

To switch to the Scientific mode of Calculator, select **S**cientific from the **V**iew menu. To switch back, select **S**tandard from this same menu. Calculator remembers its last mode, so if you restart Calculator later it will return to the last mode used.

I don't have a square root button in Scientific mode.

When switched to the Scientific mode, you no longer have a square root button. You can obtain a square root in this mode by raising a number to the power of .5. Enter the number, press "x to the power of y," enter **.5** and then press =.

Help! I have problems with Windows Write.

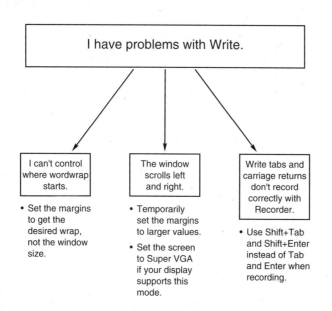

Write is a good accessory application, or applet, for adding formatting to your ASCII files. For example, suppose you download a text file from CompuServe. You can use Write to add a proportional font and give the text file a more polished look when you print it. You can also use it for letters, notes, and other documents. You can paste in graphics through the Clipboard and with OLE, so the program is quite a versatile application.

Here are some tips for using Write productively:

- Write doesn't support working with multiple documents, but you can open multiple copies of Write. Each can have a different document open. Use this technique with the Clipboard to copy and move text and graphics between documents.

- Cutting and deleting text are different actions. When you cut something (Ctrl+X), it is moved from the current document to the Clipboard. When you delete it (Del), it is removed from the document but the Clipboard is unaltered.

- With Clipboard, you can paste pictures to a Write document. You can then use the **P**aragraph menu to align the picture left, right, or center. You can also paste text from a DOS application to a Write document.

- When you paste text through the Clipboard, all formatting is lost. When the Clipboard contents are pasted, the text will take the format of the place where the text is pasted.

- To select the entire document for formatting, hold down the Ctrl key and click in the selection bar located to the left of the text.

- When you are creating documents, save your work frequently. The document that you see on the screen is saved only in computer memory and is not saved on disk. If a

Help with Using Windows File Manager and Applets

power glitch occurs or someone steps on the power cord and disconnects it, your work will be lost unless you have saved it. A good rule of thumb is to save your work every 15 to 20 minutes. Always save your work before printing. This ensures that your letter is saved if the computer should hang up during the print operation.

■ Keep your files short. If you are working with a long document, you will probably find it helpful to break the document into several files.

I can't change the point where the wordwrap starts.

■ Unlike Notepad, wordwrap is based on the current margins. Set the margins to give the desired width.

The window scrolls left and right when I enter text.

When you are working with a small window that can't accommodate a full line of text, the window will scroll left and right as you enter text, and this can be annoying.

■ To prevent the scrolling, use a larger window (maximize Write) or change the margins (decrease the values) until the entire line will fit in a window. Remember the default values. Before printing, return the margins to these default values (or the values you wish to use).

■ An alternative is to switch to Super VGA if your video adapter supports it. This will permit more characters on a line.

Write tabs and carriage returns don't record correctly with Recorder.

■ If tabs aren't inserted correctly on playback or if Enter keys appear as page breaks, use Shift+Tab and Shift+Enter instead of the Tab and Enter keys when recording.

I need to port (transfer) a Windows file with formatting (TrueType fonts) and graphics to another system.

■ If they both use the same word processor, move the data file.

■ If not, use Write. Write is the only "free" word processor that can create documents complete with TrueType fonts and graphics. This makes the WRI file format a *de facto* standard for transferring documents with TrueType fonts and graphics across bulletin boards and data services.

Help! I'm having problems with Windows Paintbrush.

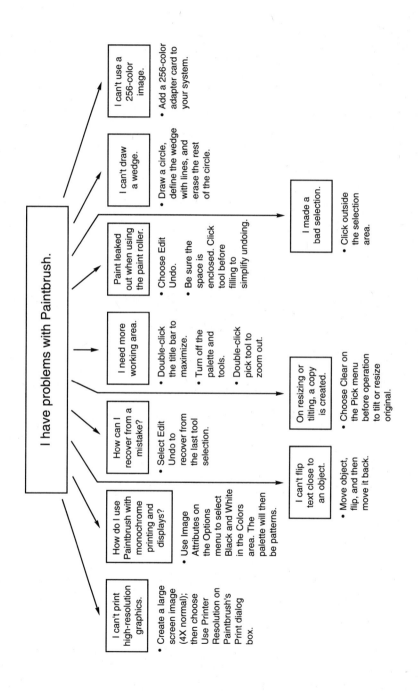

I have problems with Paintbrush.

I can't print high-resolution graphics.
- Create a large screen image (4X normal); then choose Use Printer Resolution on Paintbrush's Print dialog box.

How do I use Paintbrush with monochrome printing and displays?
- Use Image Attributes on the Options menu to select Black and White in the Colors area. The palette will then be patterns.

How can I recover from a mistake?
- Select Edit Undo to recover from the last tool selection.

I need more working area.
- Double-click the title bar to maximize.
- Turn off the palette and tools.
- Double-click pick tool to zoom out.

Paint leaked out when using the paint roller.
- Choose Edit Undo.
- Be sure the space is enclosed. Click tool before filling to simplify undoing.

I can't draw a wedge.
- Draw a circle, define the wedge with lines, and erase the rest of the circle.

I can't use a 256-color image.
- Add a 256-color adapter card to your system.

I can't flip text close to an object.
- Move object, flip, and then move it back.

On resizing or tilting, a copy is created.
- Choose Clear on the Pick menu before operation to tilt or resize original.

I made a bad selection.
- Click outside the selection area.

Help! I'm having problems with Windows Paintbrush.

Paintbrush is a Windows application that permits you to create freehand sketches and charts. These can be pasted into Windows Write documents or desktop publishing programs (such as PageMaker), or they can be printed directly from Windows Paintbrush. Using Paintbrush, you can create graphic images with the following effects:

- Lines of various shades, widths, and colors.

- Brush strokes using a variety of styles, widths, shades, and colors.

- Airbrush effects of various widths, colors, shades, and densities.

- Shapes that are unfilled, or filled with selected shades or colors.

- Text in any Windows-supported font in various styles, sizes, and colors.

- Special effects such as tilting, rotating, and inverting.

Pictures are an important part of communications today. You can use Paintbrush to add clip art to newsletters, memos, presentations, and letters. You can also edit existing clip art or create your own to build a library that you can use with all of your communications.

If you need a more sophisticated paint program, try Publisher's Paintbrush from ZSoft Corporation. They wrote the Windows Paintbrush program. Also you will find several special paint programs that can do specific paint tasks (such as editing color scans) very well.

Here are a few tips for using the drawing tools in Paintbrush:

- To make a borderless object, make the foreground and background colors or patterns the same.

- To draw squares or rounded squares, hold down the Shift key while using the box or rounded box tool. To draw circles, hold down the Shift key while using the ellipse tool.

- To draw straight or vertical edges, hold down the Shift key while using the polygon or line tool.

The following problems are ones that you may encounter while using Paintbrush. All have easy solutions.

I can't create and print high-resolution graphics.

- Windows Paintbrush is a painting program; that is, it uses bit-mapped graphics. Graphics can be created only in the screen resolution: approximately 75 to 90 dpi (dots per inch). This doesn't mean that you can't create high-resolution print images. You can create large images on the screen (75 dpi) that would print using perhaps six pages. Then you can print the large image with the command **U**se Printer Resolution on Paintbrush's Print dialog box. This technique reduces it to one page and 300 dpi.

Help! I'm having problems with Windows Paintbrush.

181

Paintbrush has a color palette. How can I switch it to work with my monochrome printer to a pattern palette?

With a color monitor, Windows defaults to a palette for selecting colors. If you are using a laser printer, you may wish to change this default to monochrome and work with patterns. To change the display so that you can select patterns, select **I**mage Attributes from the **O**ptions menu and select **B**lack and White in the Colors area. Then reset the display by selecting **N**ew from the **F**ile menu. On a monochrome monitor, Paintbrush defaults to a patterns palette.

I can't flip text close to an object.

If you need to flip text that is close to other objects, you may not be able to use the pick tool to select it. The solution is to select the text with the scissors and then move it to another location in the drawing. Flip it with the **P**ick menu and then move it back to its normal position.

How can I recover from a mistake?

When you are drawing, save your work frequently—much more frequently than when you are using a word processor. You can use the **U**ndo command of the **E**dit menu to clear a mistake. It will undo to the last tool selection.

Secrets and Surprises: To protect your work when drawing multiple objects with the same tool, click the tool between each object that you create. When the result for each object is satisfactory, select the tool again so that a subsequent action will not clear your finished work.When undoing, Paintbrush clears only to the last tool selection.

When I tried to tilt or resize an object, I tilted or resized only a copy of the object.

Tilting or resizing affects only a copy of the original object anywhere in the drawing, leaving the original object unchanged. If you want the original object cleared on tilting or resizing, choose **C**lear on the **P**ick menu before the operation.

Performance Tip: Create a graphics library of the objects you use frequently. Use it as your own clip art library, keeping all the objects in a single document. To use this clip art, open two copies of Paintbrush. With one copy of Paintbrush, open your library file. The other copy of Paintbrush contains your working document. When you need an object from the library, select it and copy it to the Clipboard. Then paste it from the Clipboard to your working document. Another alternative is to create a clip art library by using Cardfile or Scrapbook (a commercial utility).

Help! I'm having problems with Windows Paintbrush.

183

I don't have enough working area.

- Painting programs work best maximized. Double-click the title bar to maximize.

- Turn off the palette and tool display.

- To zoom the image to a full screen, double-click the pick tool. Press Esc or click on the screen to restore the image.

I tried to use the paint roller, but the "paint" leaked out and filled the entire screen.

- Immediately choose Undo from the Edit menu and then zoom in to see where the hole occurs in the enclosed shape.

- When you are using the paint roller, be sure that the space is really enclosed. If the shape has even a single pixel open, the fill will leak out and cover the entire workspace. Click the paint roller before each fill to make undoing easier.

I made a bad selection.

- If you make a mistake with either of the selection tools, click the mouse outside of the selection area. This will clear the selection and permit you to select again.

I can't draw a wedge.

Although there is no tool for drawing wedges, you can use the circle/ellipse and line tools to create a wedge. First, mark the circle center with a small dot. Then use the circle/ellipse tool to define the outer circle. From the center of the circle, draw lines to define the straight edges of the wedge. Finally, use the eraser tool to erase the unneeded portions of the circle.

I can't use a 256-color image with Paintbrush.

If you load a 256-color image to Paintbrush but your adapter card is only a 16-color, you can save the file only as a 16-bit color image. This is true even if you choose to save it as 256 colors. To get 256 colors with Paintbrush, you must have a 256-color video adapter card.

Using WinHelp

WinHelp is another applet included with Windows. It is used to support the Help function of Windows applications. However, you can use it to create your own hypertext documents with hot words and *hot spots* (spots you can click for pop-up text).

To create your own hypertext documents, you will need additional software. The text files are created in RTF format and then compiled to the HLP format. You need the Windows SDK or a Help file compiler for this.

5

CHAPTER

Secrets and Surprises: You can change the colors of the Help file components by adding the following to the WIN.INI file:

```
[Windows Help]
Jumpcolor=red green blue
Popupcolor=red green blue
```

where red, green, and blue are the values for each of these colors (see Chapter 7). Jumpcolor defines the color for the hypertext words. Setting green to 255 and other values to 0 will make the color of the hypertext words green.

You can force WinHelp to load automatically from File Manager with any Help file by adding this line to the WIN.INI [extensions] section:

```
hlp=winhelp^.hlp
```

One word of caution. Some programs, such as Excel 2.1, have their own help engine. Clicking the respective Help file in this case won't work.

HELP USING WINDOWS APPLICATIONS

A *Windows application*, or *WinApp,* is an application program that is designed specifically to execute under Windows. This chapter covers problems that you may encounter when you are using Windows applications and offers troubleshooting advice. It discusses installation and startup problems, error messages from Windows or the application, and problems related to specific Windows applications.

General Information About Windows Applications

A Windows application (WinApp) is developed in C or Pascal by using the Windows SDK kit or using any of the various development tools specifically designed for Windows application development. A WinApp requires that Windows be active before it can be run. If you try to run a WinApp from DOS, the program will not start and you will get a message that Windows must be started first. Examples of WinApps are Microsoft Excel and Aldus PageMaker.

All Windows applications have the same type of user interface and share similar features. (WinApp developers should follow the *Common User Access Advance Interface Design Guide* that is published with the Microsoft SDK.) Because all commercially developed Windows applications have a common set of features, it is easy to learn a new Windows application after you have had a little Windows experience.

Windows is an *object-processing* environment. Applications, then, are tools for working with objects. Objects are the focus of the user's attention and can have *sub-objects*. Actions should modify the properties of an object or manipulate the object in some way. You select the object, then the action. Menu items, keyboard actions, and the mouse initiate actions.

Let's look at two examples of how this object-oriented concept works in applications:

In a word processing program, the document is the object. The sub-objects are paragraphs, sentences, words, and characters. The Format menu should be designed for formatting a document, paragraph, or character in some way. The Word for Windows program is a classic example of how menu design should be done. In fact, this object-oriented concept is very apparent even in the DOS version of Word.

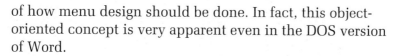 In a spreadsheet program, the spreadsheet is the object. The sub-objects are rows, columns, a range of cells, or a single cell. You can modify the properties of an object or sub-object, such as the width of a column or the format of a cell.

Any good Windows program should support this object-processing concept. It is similar to the way the human brain processes information, and is therefore more natural. Windows supports two types of objects, the *application objects* (such as a basic spreadsheet form) and the *user objects* (such as the spreadsheet data). In a spreadsheet program, the underlying spreadsheet form is the application object. Information is put in the form and becomes the user object. The user can modify the properties of either type of object.

In addition, Windows programs are essentially modeless. Early word processors required that you enter data in one mode, edit it in a second mode, and then switch to a third mode for formatting the document. Even now, some major desktop publishing programs use multiple modes, making it confusing to remember which mode you are using. A good Windows program should have a single mode, with all actions available in that mode.

Running Windows applications gives you the advantages of an easy-to-use graphical interface, device independence, improved memory management, object-oriented environment, data transfer standards (Clipboard, OLE, DDE), and font management independence. Many companies are already insisting that their employees purchase only Windows-based applications. Some of these applications are excellent; others are poorly designed and reflect a bad user interface. When buying a Windows application, it's important to distinguish the better products and why they are better. Features aren't everything. Using the product must be natural and easy. The mechanics of using the program shouldn't get in the way of accomplishing the desired task.

The following sections offer advice on using Windows applications and solving common problems that arise during use.

Help! I can't install a Windows application.

I can't install the application

- Avoid installing to the Windows directory.

- Audit changes to WIN.INI to aid in deinstalling.

- Delete DLL and INI files for applications you no longer use.

- The installation program probably doesn't recognize the shell. Complete the installation by adding the new program manually to your shell.

Windows applications install using the directions provided with the application. The better Windows applications install using a graphical installation procedure and automatically update the WIN.INI file and add the proper icons to Program Manager. Here are a few installation tips:

- Never install a Windows application to the Windows directory. Be sure it is installed in a separate directory. If you install it to the Windows directory, you will never be able to tell whether a file belongs to your new program or to Windows. For Adobe Type Manager, this means moving all files from the Windows' directories (see Chapter 8).

- Save a copy of WIN.INI under a new name (such as WIN2.INI) before installing, and compare the version after installation with the original. Check the [extensions] section, the [embedding] section, and any new sections. Most programs have no deinstallation program. It's up to you to monitor the changes made in case you wish to remove the program later.

- When installing new programs, files may be installed to the Windows directory. The most typical examples are the INI files and DLL files. An *INI file* is an initialization file, specifying program-specific parameters, and all INI files must be in the Windows directory. A *DLL file* is a library file, and can be shared by more than one program. DLL libraries extend the application programming interface for Windows. For example, both pen and multimedia extensions to Windows are added through the use of DLL files. Be sure that you track INI and DLL files as you add to Windows and delete those files you no longer use.

Help! I can't install a Windows application.

191

Many installation programs try to create a group for the new program and install the proper program items. If you are using another program as a shell, the installation program may have trouble at this point. You may have to manually add the program items to the shell.

Help! A Windows application won't start after installing.

The Windows application won't start after installing.

The application won't start at all.

- Make sure you are running Windows.

- If you tried to start from Program Manager, use File Properties command to verify that the entries are correct.

- If you tried to start from File Manager, check for wrong filename or missing program.

I can't start an older application.

- Run it with the version of Windows it's written for.

- Update to a more recent version.

I get "Out of Memory" messages at startup.

- Clean up the screen, close unused applications, and be sure swap disk space is sufficient.

- Be sure disk space is available for swap files or create a permanent swap file.

Even though Windows applications are designed to run under Windows, it is still possible to experience problems. The following sections discuss typical problems and their solutions.

The application won't start at all.

■ If you get a message that the program must run under Windows, you tried to start the program from the DOS prompt. Windows applications must be run from Windows.

■ If you tried to start the program from Program Manager, examine the properties of the icon by using the **File Properties** command. Be sure the entries are correct.

■ If you tried to start the program from File Manager, you are clicking the wrong filename or a part of the program is missing.

I can't run an older Windows application.

■ Windows 3.1 cannot run older (pre-Windows 3.0) applications at all. If you have a pre-Windows 3.0 version of an application, you must run it under Windows 2.x or the real mode of Windows 3.0. The best alternative is to contact the manufacturer and get an update of the program. This will give you a version of the program that can support the new features, such as the extensive virtual memory of the new Windows.

■ Some Windows 3.0 applications will not run under Windows 3.1 unless they have been updated for this new version. You will also find that some applications that

Help! A Windows application won't start after installing.

have been updated to take advantage of the features of Windows 3.1 will not run under Windows 3.0. If you have trouble running an application under Windows 3.1, contact the manufacturer for an update.

I have extended memory but still get "Out of Memory" messages. Windows reports that I have free memory.

Windows creates two buffer areas called USER and GDI local heaps. Each of these is limited to 64K. Using About Program Manager on the Help menu, you should see that although memory is available the percent of "Free System Resources" is low. The best solution is to clean up the screen, reducing the number of objects and closing un-used applications. If the problem happens only with a particular application, contact the application vendor. It's probably using poor management of data objects. First, close other applications, including TSRs. Minimize Windows applications to icons. Clear or save the Clipboard contents. Use the Control Panel Desktop option to set the wallpaper to <None>. Be sure you do not inadvertently have expanded memory or do not have a RAMDisk in-stalled that's using more memory than you expect (use About Program Manager from the Help menu to check this).

Be sure disk space is adequate for the swap files you are using. Use a permanent swap file if possible. (See Appendix B.)

Windows 3.1 has solved some of this problem through better resource management, but it is still possible to run out of resources. In fact, the numbers may look good on the About dialog box for resources, yet you still can be low. That's because memory pointers are not included in the percentage calculation.

Help! I get a message from Windows when I try to run an application.

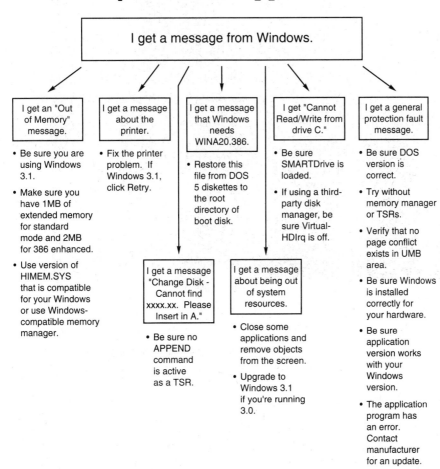

I get a message from Windows.

I get an "Out of Memory" message.

- Be sure you are using Windows 3.1.
- Make sure you have 1MB of extended memory for standard mode and 2MB for 386 enhanced.
- Use version of HIMEM.SYS that is compatible for your Windows or use Windows-compatible memory manager.

I get a message about the printer.

- Fix the printer problem. If Windows 3.1, click Retry.

I get a message that Windows needs WINA20.386.

- Restore this file from DOS 5 diskettes to the root directory of boot disk.

I get "Cannot Read/Write from drive C."

- Be sure SMARTDrive is loaded.
- If using a third-party disk manager, be sure Virtual-HDIrq is off.

I get a general protection fault message.

- Be sure DOS version is correct.
- Try without memory manager or TSRs.
- Verify that no page conflict exists in UMB area.
- Be sure Windows is installed correctly for your hardware.
- Be sure application version works with your Windows version.
- The application program has an error. Contact manufacturer for an update.

I get a message "Change Disk - Cannot find xxxx.xx. Please Insert in A."

- Be sure no APPEND command is active as a TSR.

I get a message about being out of system resources.

- Close some applications and remove objects from the screen.
- Upgrade to Windows 3.1 if you're running 3.0.

Help! I get a message from Windows when I try to run an application.

195

The message may be from Windows or from the application. Application messages are specific to the application. Follow the directions of the message. Use the Help feature of the application, if necessary, to help identify the problem. Messages from Windows are more general in nature, such as an out-of-memory message.

I get an "Out of Memory" message.

■ Be sure you are using Windows 3.1, which can manage resources better.

■ Be sure the physical memory of the computer is at least 1MB of extended memory for standard mode and 2MB for the 386 enhanced mode.

■ Make sure that the drivers, particularly SMARTDrive and RAMDisk, are not taking too much memory.

■ Be sure you are using the HIMEM.SYS that came with your Windows or a Windows-compatible memory manager.

I get a message about the printer.

■ If the printer runs out of paper or jams, you will get a message describing the problem. Fix the problem and retry printing. To terminate, start the Print Manager and remove the item from the queue (see Chapter 9).

When trying to open a file, I get the message "Change Disk - Cannot find *xxxx.xx.* Please insert in drive A."

■ An APPEND command is active. Don't use the DOS APPEND command with Windows. Check the AUTOEXEC.BAT file to be sure no APPEND command is included. (See Appendix G.)

When I try to start in the 386 enhanced mode, I get a message that Windows needs a WINA20.386.

■ Restore the WINA20.386 file to the root directory of the boot disk. This file is provided with DOS 5; it is not on the Windows Setup diskettes. In a compressed form, the file is WINA20.38_. You will need to use the DOS EXPAND utility to decompress this file, entering the following command line:

```
C:\DOS\EXPAND A:\WIN20.38_ C:\WINA20.386
```

If you wish to put this file in another directory, add **SWITCHES**=/W to CONFIG.SYS and then insert the following line in the [386enh] section of SYSTEM.INI:

```
DEVICE=C:\DOS\WINA20.386
```

where the path defines the location of the file. (See Appendix G for information on editing CONFIG.SYS and SYSTEM.INI.)

Help! I get a message from Windows when I try to run an application.

197

Windows tells me it can't run a program because it's out of system resources.

■ Resources are data objects: icons, bit-mapped images, dialog boxes, accelerator key tables, some fonts, and more. When a resource is used, the program registers it with Windows. This helps Windows manage it, and that way the same object isn't loaded twice by different programs. When you get this message, the common area used in memory for these objects is full. When this area is full, you are at a deadend, no matter how much extended memory you have. Use **A**bout Program Manager on the **H**elp menu to see the percent of resource space left. Your best bet is to close some applications and clean up data objects you aren't using any more. Remove unused icons from Program Manager's groups.

■ If you're using Windows 3.0, upgrading to Windows 3.1 will significantly decrease the frequency with which you receive these messages.

I get intermittent disk problems or the message "Cannot read/write from drive C."

■ If you are using an SCSI drive, be sure that SMARTDrive is loaded. If you are using an Adaptec disk controller with an SCSI drive, use the /b parameter with SMARTDRV.EXE in the CONFIG.SYS file.

■ If you are not using SCSI but are using third-party disk managers (Disk Manager, SpeedStor, Innerspace, or Vfeatures), be sure that VirtualHDIrq in SYSTEM.INI is off (see Appendix G). If you are using Windows 3.00a or later, Windows can detect if one of these disk managers is in use and will turn SMARTDrive off. Avoid using a permanent swap file if VirtualHDIrq is off.

I get a general protection fault message.

The old UAE (Unrecoverable Application Error) message of Windows 3.0 is now a general protection fault message in Windows 3.1. The advantage with Windows 3.1, however, is that Windows is probably still stable and you stand a chance of recovering.

The message indicates that an application tried to write to a memory area where it didn't have access. When you see this message, the message box will provide information about the application causing the error and where the error occurred. Windows will also provide you with a message on how to recover.

The causes of this error are the same as for the UAE message of Windows 3.0:

■ You have the wrong version of DOS. Type **VER** at the DOS prompt to see the DOS version number. Update the DOS version to 3.1 or later.

Help! I get a message from Windows when I try to run an application.

199

An incompatible TSR or memory manager is installed. Try removing various TSRs and memory managers and see if the problem clears up.

You may have a page-mapping conflict in the UMB area (see Chapter 7 and Appendix A). Start Windows using **WIN** **/3** **/d:x**. If the application runs now, suspect a UMB conflict.

Windows installed for the wrong hardware. Use a custom install.

You are running an application designed for Windows 2.x. Windows 3.1 does not support running these applications. Contact the manufacturer for an update.

The application program has an error. Contact the manufacturer for a possible update.

If Dr. Watson is in the Startup group, it will automatically start on the general protection fault and will log relevant information for tracing the problem.

Help! I have other problems when I run an application.

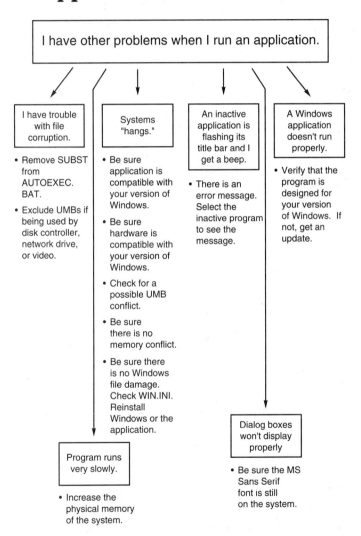

I have other problems when I run an application.

I have trouble with file corruption.

- Remove SUBST from AUTOEXEC.BAT.
- Exclude UMBs if being used by disk controller, network drive, or video.

Systems "hangs."

- Be sure application is compatible with your version of Windows.
- Be sure hardware is compatible with your version of Windows.
- Check for a possible UMB conflict.
- Be sure there is no memory conflict.
- Be sure there is no Windows file damage. Check WIN.INI. Reinstall Windows or the application.

Program runs very slowly.

- Increase the physical memory of the system.

An inactive application is flashing its title bar and I get a beep.

- There is an error message. Select the inactive program to see the message.

Dialog boxes won't display properly

- Be sure the MS Sans Serif font is still on the system.

A Windows application doesn't run properly.

- Verify that the program is designed for your version of Windows. If not, get an update.

Help! I have other problems when I run an application.

201

Other typical problems include the program hanging up, slow execution, and disk I/O error messages. Solutions to these problems follow.

I have trouble with file corruption.

☐ Check to see if SUBST is installed as a TSR in AUTOEXEC.BAT. If so, remove it (see Appendix G). You may also have memory conflicts in the UMB area (see Chapter 7 and Appendix A).

☐ Check to see if the disk controller, network driver, or video is using a UMB area and exclude that area (see Chapter 7).

The program runs very slowly.

☐ A slow-running program generally means that you are low on memory and that Windows is swapping too much out to disk. If this is happening, you should see a lot of disk light flashing. Buy more memory or try some of the ideas already mentioned to solve memory problems (see the earlier section "I have extended memory but get 'Out of Memory' messages. Windows reports that I have free memory.")

Windows "hangs"—the system locks up. System was NOT printing.

☐ First, be sure the application is compatible with the version of Windows you are using. Windows 2.x applications cannot run under Windows 3.1.

■ Be sure the hardware is compatible with Windows. Try using Setup to change the hardware designation.

■ Possibly there are UMB conflicts (see Appendix A).

■ Assuming compatible hardware and application, a hanging system generally indicates a memory conflict that Windows cannot resolve. To find the problem, first remove all TSRs. The easiest way is to create a boot floppy disk. Remove all TSRs from the boot diskette by editing both CONFIG.SYS and AUTOEXEC.BAT. Boot from the diskette and try whatever hung the system again. If the system does not hang, there is a TSR problem. If the problem still occurs, look within Windows. Be sure the EMMExclude option in the SYSTEM.INI file specifically excludes any extended memory used for video or network drivers. (See Appendix G for information on viewing and editing SYSTEM.INI.) Windows is supposed to be intelligent enough to automatically exclude this memory, but it doesn't hurt to be sure that it is indeed excluded. Try to repeat the problem in standard or real mode, that is, using a more stable Windows mode. If this succeeds, examine the parameters for the problem mode in SYSTEM.INI.

■ Check to see if any of the INI files are damaged. Reinstall Windows or the application if necessary.

An inactive application is flashing its icon or title bar and I get a beep.

■ The inactive application has a status or error message. Select the application to see the message.

I can't get dialog boxes to display correctly.

☐ Be sure you haven't removed the MS Sans Serif font from the system (or Helv with Windows 3.0). This font is used for the dialog boxes.

The application just doesn't run properly.

☐ Verify that the program is designed for your version of Windows. If not, get an upgrade.

Help! I have a problem with a specific application.

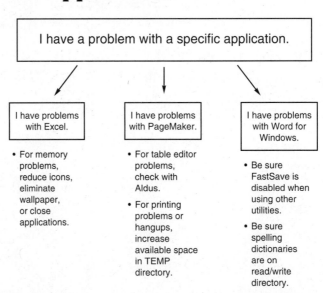

I have a problem with a specific application.

I have problems with Excel.	I have problems with PageMaker.	I have problems with Word for Windows.
• For memory problems, reduce icons, eliminate wallpaper, or close applications.	• For table editor problems, check with Aldus. • For printing problems or hangups, increase available space in TEMP directory.	• Be sure FastSave is disabled when using other utilities. • Be sure spelling dictionaries are on read/write directory.

If you have an application problem using Windows 3.1, check with the application manufacturer. Some applications are designed specifically for Windows 3.1 and use new function calls that were added with this version.

Windows applications vary widely in their efficiency in reading and writing files. NBI's Legacy is a real slowpoke, since it transfers only 512 bytes at a time. Excel is a little better, transferring 2048 bytes at a time. Excel's Setup program, however, installs 60,000 bytes at a time and can quickly install over 4 megabytes of files. Windows 3.1 uses its own file manager (FastDisk), which can improve file transfers dramatically when it's installed.

I have problems with Excel.

■ If you have too many objects on a worksheet, there won't be enough memory. Reduce icons, eliminate wallpaper, or close applications.

I have problems with PageMaker 4.0.

■ PageMaker 4.0 has problems printing to a non-PostScript printer if the document contains more than a single table editor file on a page. The first table will print at each location. A fix is available from Aldus and is also on CompuServe.

■ Printing large files can cause Windows to hang or you may get an error message about a generic printer error. Use a smaller document or increase the size of the \TEMP directory area.

Help! I have a problem with a specific application.

205

I have problems with Word for Windows.

◻ If you have data corruption problems with Grammatik or other utilities, check to be sure that Word for Windows' FastSave is disabled. Don't use FastSave when using utilities. Update information is placed at the end of the file, so the file doesn't have a normal linear flow. To disable FastSave, edit the `FileSaveAs` macro in NORMAL.DOT to include the line:

```
dig.FastSave=0
```

◻ If Word for Windows won't spell-check on a network, it's probably because the program needs to write to the dictionary files, and the network directory with the files is read-only. Copy the LEX-AM.DAT, LEX-AM.DLL, and STDUSER.DIC files to your personal user directory. (Use COPY if the STDUSER.DIC is zero length.) Then modify your WIN.INI file as:

```
[Microsoft Word]
util-path=c:\zz
```

to point to the new directory (`c:\zz` in this example). See Appendix G for more on editing WIN.INI.

Secrets and Surprises: If you have Word for Windows, you can find the WordPerfect monster. Turn the paragraph marks on (**T**ools **O**ptions Paragraph **M**arks) and click OK. Select **M**acro from **T**ools and enter `Spiff`. Click **E**dit. Delete everything in the Edit window except the middle paragraph marker. Click **C**lose on the **F**ile menu and answer **Y**es to the prompt. Now bring up the About box and click on the Word for Windows icon. Tiny people will run across the box and line up. A WordPerfect monster then appears and chases them all. The Word for Windows icon slides down and crushes the monster, and all the little people leap for joy. Then there's the list of credits. It's a good 3-minute animation. Wonder what the WordPerfect people will come up with?

7

C H A P T E R

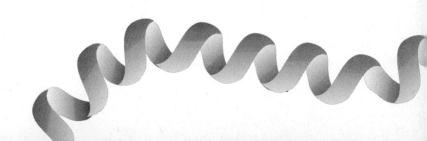

HELP WITH
DISPLAY PROBLEMS

This chapter offers troubleshooting advice for display problems. These include problems with VGA, Super VGA, and EGA displays as well as color problems and other common display problems. You will also find information about the display system, graphic standards, and ways to improve video performance.

General Information About the Display System

The display system consists of three components: the display, or the monitor; the video adapter; and the video driver. The *display*, or the monitor, is hardware. The display shows the data from the computer. The *video adapter* is a card that is installed within the computer or on the computer's motherboard. This card is used for interfacing the video digital information to the display. The display must support the same video standard as the video adapter. The *video driver* is the software that is installed to the computer and is used to drive the video adapter and display. All Windows applications always use the same video driver, which is specific to your system and installed as part of Windows during Setup.

When using Windows, you can choose from a wide variety of video displays and adapters. The video mode that is used determines the exact resolution of the screen and the number of colors available. For maximum quality, you want a resolution of 640 x 480 pixels or more and 16 or more colors.

Windows includes generic drivers for most displays, including VGA and Super VGA. Many display adapters furnish their own drivers for Windows. Taking full advantage of the Windows display is another issue, however. The display, adapter, and adapter software may support 16 million colors, but if the application can't manage this many or if the computer doesn't have enough speed, all those pixels and colors won't do you much good.

Choosing a Graphic Standard

The screen resolution is measured in *pixels*. Each addressable dot on the screen is a single pixel. When using an EGA standard, the typical resolution is 640 x 350, that is, 640 horizontal pixels by 350 vertical. This is a total of 224,000 pixels. The more pixels on the screen, the higher the resolution but the slower the display. Also, the more colors, the slower the display because (again) more data must be processed for the screen display. Some video adapter cards contain an accelerator or coprocessor to process the video data, relieving the main computer processor of much of the display work overhead. These adapters are faster, but more expensive.

For Windows, you won't lose much speed going from VGA to Super VGA, but you will see a dramatic speed loss if you go higher and don't use a board with its own accelerator or processor. You will also see some speed loss going to 256 colors or more. Windows itself uses only 16 colors. You don't need more colors unless the applications demand it, such as an editor for color scans.

First, let's look at the basic standards supported by the current drivers and displays. Table 7.1 lists the various graphic standards and their characteristics.

Standard	Resolution	Colors	Windows Support
CGA	320 x 200	4	No
	640 x 200	2	Yes
Hercules	720 x 348	2	Yes
EGA	640 x 350	16	Yes

Table 7.1
PC Graphic Standards

continues

Table 7.1
continued

Standard	Resolution	Colors	Windows Support
MCGA	640 x 480	2	Yes
	320 x 200	256	No
VGA	320 x 200	256	No
	640 x 480	16	Yes
Super VGA	800 x 600**	16	Yes
	800 x 600**	256	Yes*
8514/A	1024 x 768	16	Yes
	1024 x 768	256	Yes
XGA	1024 x 768	256	Yes*
TIGA	1024 x 768	16	Yes
	1024 x 768	256	Yes

*with third-party driver
**No real standard exists for this mode.

IBM has yet to support Super VGA (S-VGA), and as a result this standard for video mode has been difficult to achieve. The most common resolution is 800 x 600. Now that VESA has defined a Super VGA BIOS, most of the newer manufacturers use this to ensure a high level of compatibility.

One way to determine whether a VGA installed as VGA or Super VGA is to check the Word for Windows display. If Windows is installed as VGA, there are only 6 horizontal inches of viewing space and you must scroll to see an entire 8½-inch page. With Super VGA, there are 8 inches on a line and you don't have to scroll. The Super VGA is now a standard and is generally the minimum working resolution for users. Most multiscan monitors can support Super VGA. If you have a Super VGA display and adapter and the screen is VGA, you can use Windows Setup to switch the screen to Super VGA.

Another way to check display resolution is to examine the setting in the Windows Setup dialog box. Third-party drivers are especially likely to give the resolution at which they operate as part of the description of the driver.

Performance Tip: If you use Word for Windows for word processing, you will probably wish to use a Super VGA adapter or better so that you don't have to horizontally scroll.

The adapter paints the picture on the screen from top to bottom, one frame at a time. The *horizontal frequency* defines how fast the beam moves across the screen. The *vertical frequency* defines how fast the beam moves down the screen. If the beam doesn't move fast enough, the eye perceives a flicker. Also, room lighting affects the perception of flicker. Fluorescent lights are notorious for increasing flicker. Flicker also increases with white backgrounds, the most common wallpaper used by Windows. Larger monitors need higher vertical frequencies to eliminate flicker.

Every adapter has specific horizontal and vertical frequencies. The video monitor has to be matched to the frequencies of the video adapter. Some monitors are called multisync monitors and can match a wide variety of adapter boards automatically.

The vertical frequency at which flicker is apparent varies with the individual, but for most people a vertical frequency of 60 cycles per second (cps) or more is flicker-free. Super VGA uses 56 cps, which may introduce flicker in some cases. Most monitors today should use a vertical frequency of 74 cps or more. Some of the older monitors (such as the IBM mono-chrome monitor for the original XT) used a lower-persistence screen so that a phosphor pixel, once hit with the beam, stayed lit for a while. This enabled it to work with low vertical frequencies but made it a poor choice for animation and graphics work, since ghosts tend to follow objects on the screen (such as the mouse cursor) as they are moved.

Improving Video Performance

The following guidelines will help you improve your video performance:

▪ Go VGA or Super VGA if possible. For higher resolution standards, use a video adapter with an accelerator or coprocessor. VGA does have an advantage over EGA. When you are using a pull-down menu with VGA, Windows saves a bit map of the screen and can restore it when the menu is closed. Windows can't do this with EGA.

▪ When purchasing high-resolution video boards or using 256 colors, be sure the board has an accelerator or coprocessor. High resolutions and more colors mean that you need more processing power on the video board.

▪ VGA boards should be 16-bit. Don't use 8-bit VGA boards. They are too slow.

Not all Windows video drivers are created equal. Some are better and faster than others. Explore different drivers for your video adapter. Check with your adapter manufacturer.

Using 256 colors may be nice, but the performance penalty can be big. To get 256 colors, the speed penalty is 3 to 10 times longer.

Flicker perception varies with the individual, environment, and the display. In terms of the display, at a vertical frequency of 53 Hz, flicker is usually noticeable. A few people can perceive flicker at 56 Hz—the common frequency for Super VGA today. At 70 Hz, the flicker is generally gone. Flicker is more perceptible under fluorescent lights or against a white screen. Windows likes to use a white screen.

For best results, test-drive the display. A display that works for someone else may not work for you.

Display systems also use the technique of *interlacing* to minimize flicker. With an interlaced screen, alternate lines are displayed on each vertical scan. It takes two vertical scans to display the entire screen. A noninterlacing screen draws the entire screen with a single pass. Interlacing reduces flicker but can create a horizontal jiggling effect with thin horizontal lines, which are popular with Windows. IBM's 8514/A and the XGA standards use interlaced screens. It is not a requirement, however, for either standard. Some adapter boards have a switch to use either mode. Try both. High resolution noninterlaced boards are expensive.

Use shadowing if your computer supports it, but be sure to read the section about EMMExclude in the SYSINI.WRI file with Windows.

■ Run Windows in the lowest level of video that meets your needs.

■ Try to keep the number of colors to a minimum. Windows uses only 16 colors, and most programs need only that many. You need only 256 colors for graphic image editing, such as the creation of presentations or color scan editing. Using more than 16 colors decreases speed significantly unless coprocessors are used.

■ Using a wallpaper slows performance some, but not much.

■ Some video adapter cards use *antialiasing* to make screen fonts look better, particularly at low resolutions. These fonts can slow video performance. On slower machines, you will have to make a tradeoff between smoother fonts and video display speed. In some cases, using a higher resolution may be better than trying to get quality fonts with antialiasing.

■ Some third-party software is available for improving video speed, such as Panacea's WinSpeed (Panacea, Inc., Post Office Square #4, 24 Orchard View Drive, Londonderry, NH 03053, Phone: 603 437-5022).

Video adapter boards come in three types: dumb, accelerator, and coprocessor. With both accelerator and coprocessor boards, the board has some processing power for the Windows

GDI functions that enables it to process data faster. As a benchmark, assume that a 16-color dumb card is 1, and use Table 7.2 to check speed guidelines.

Board	Colors	Speed Factor
Dumb	16	1
Dumb	256	0.3–0.8
Accelerator	16	1–2
Accelerator	256	4
Coprocessor	16	1–3
Coprocessor	256	3–5

Table 7.2

Color and Speed Factors for Video Adapter Boards

Accelerator boards are similar to the coprocessor boards, but are lower in cost. Accelerator boards have fixed integrated circuits to implement their graphic functions, and the board cannot be modified for future graphic enhancements. *Coprocessor boards* have a true processor, and the graphic functions can be reprogrammed by changing a ROM or the video driver. They are a little more expensive but have more flexibility.

Help! My display doesn't work with Windows.

My display doesn't work with Windows.

- Try exiting to DOS and restarting Windows.

- Be sure you're using the latest version of the video driver for your adapter card.

- Disable screen saver and restart Windows.

- Check to be sure the correct screen "grabber" is installed.

- If you can't change the screen font, see Chapter 8 for more information.

Windows interfaces with the display by using a driver. This driver can be changed by using the Windows Setup program in the Main group. Windows contains several internal drivers for various displays. You can also find drivers for downloading from CompuServe. When you purchase a new display adapter, it may contain its own driver designed specifically for Windows. Read the README.WRI file in the Windows directory. This contains the latest information on display adapters and drivers. Also try the following fixes:

In many cases with a display problem, you haven't lost the computer, but Windows has simply lost the ability to restore the screen. Recover using the keyboard—try to use Alt+F4 and then press Enter to exit Windows and return to the DOS prompt.

Be sure you are using the latest version of the video driver for the adapter card you are using. Contact the manufacturer of the display adapter you are using and be sure the driver does, indeed, work with your Windows version. Some display drivers may need to be updated.

If you have a screen saver installed, it may be the source of the problem. In some cases, the problem may show up as a garbaged screen after leaving an application in normal fashion, such as exiting Cardfile. To test this hypothesis, exit Windows and remove the loading line for the screen saver after the `load=` parameter in the WIN.INI file (see Appendix G). Then restart Windows.

Another potential source of display problems is using the wrong screen grabber. Suspect this problem if you lose the screen when you switch between applications. The *grabber* is the Windows component that saves and restores the screen when you switch between applications. Several grabbers come with Windows, and Setup should install the correct one for your mode and display. A scan of the SYSTEM.INI filenames (see Appendix G) will give you plenty of clues about which grabber you are using. You shouldn't use an EGA grabber, for example, with a VGA display.

If you try to change a font size or style and the screen doesn't change to match, it probably means the installed font doesn't support the size or style with the current screen fonts. See Chapter 8.

Help! My display doesn't work with Windows.

219

7
CHAPTER

Help! I have problems with a VGA display.

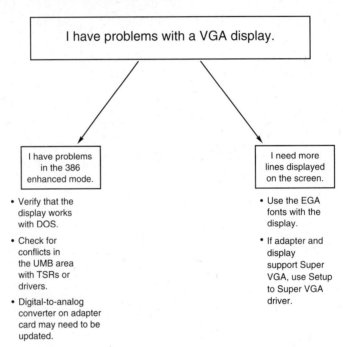

I have problems with a VGA display.

I have problems in the 386 enhanced mode.

- Verify that the display works with DOS.
- Check for conflicts in the UMB area with TSRs or drivers.
- Digital-to-analog converter on adapter card may need to be updated.

I need more lines displayed on the screen.

- Use the EGA fonts with the display.
- If adapter and display support Super VGA, use Setup to Super VGA driver.

A potential source of video problems is video contention in the upper memory block area (UMB) when Windows is using the 386 enhanced mode. You can test for this problem by starting Windows in the 386 enhanced mode using `/d:x`. If Windows works now, you have a UMB conflict. To solve this, add the parameter `EMMExclude=` in the `[386]` section of the SYSTEM.INI file (see Appendix G). For example, here is a good starter:

```
EMMExclude=A000-FFFF
```

This line is the same as using the /d:x parameter in starting Windows. Then work it down until you get as much UMB as possible. Sometimes you may have to experiment, excluding certain UMB areas until you get the video to work. You can use utility programs such as MEM (with DOS 5), MSD with the Windows Resource Kit, Manifest, or QEMM.COM to determine which areas of the UMB are being used. The problem is that most utilities are no smarter than Windows, and won't recognize the sly problems any better than Windows.

Table 7.3 is a general map of the UMB area as used by video adapters (that is, these are the numbers you should use with the EMMExclude= line in SYSTEM.INI).

Memory Location	Description
A000–AFFF	VGA and EGA.
B000–BFFF	Hercules and CGA, or the text mode of EGA or VGA.
C000–CFFF	VGA adapters place their ROM BIOS here.
D000–DFFF	EMS page frame is often placed in this area.
E000–EFFF	IBM PS/2 have extra ROM here.
F000–FFFF	System ROM.

Table 7.3
Map of the UMB Area

Network adapter cards and other adapters may also use space in the UMB area. If you are using the QEMM386.SYS driver, the problem may be in the WINHIRAM.VXD driver that Microsoft provides to memory manager vendors. Make sure

Help! I have problems with a VGA display.

221

that this file is in the same directory as QEMM386.SYS and that it is identical to the one provided on the QEMM-386 distribution disks.

On ATI Wonder cards, turn DIP switch #8 off if running in VGA. Refer to the manual that comes with the cards to obtain more information about setting DIP switches.

> **Note:** Windows 3.0 does not support resolutions any higher than the VGA 640 x 480 for DOS applications in the 386 enhanced mode.

The next sections provide more information about troubleshooting VGA display problems.

I have problems with a VGA display driver in the 386 enhanced mode.

☐ Be sure the display is working as a VGA display under DOS. Test it with a DOS program or with a test program that came with the display adapter.

☐ There is probably a memory conflict in the UMB area. Windows is supposed to be smart enough to detect this and to avoid memory used by the display cards, but sometimes this detection fails. To test, start Windows in the 386 enhanced mode by using the /d:x switch, which excludes the UMB area. If the display driver works now, suspect memory conflicts. See the introduction to this section for strategies for configuring. This situation is most likely to occur if you have both a VGA and an 8514 display adapter or if you have a VGA adapter that Windows does not recognize.

Another possibility is that the digital-to-analog converter on the adapter needs to be updated. Contact the adapter manufacturer for more information.

I have a VGA display and need more lines on the screen.

If you have a VGA display, you may wish to use the Windows EGA fonts. This will give you more lines on the screen; Notepad will have 42 lines. To do this, first expand the EGA fonts from the Windows disks:

```
EXPAND A:\EGA*.FON C:\WINDOWS\SYSTEM
```

Now edit the SYSTEM.INI file (see Appendix G) to point to the new fonts by changing these parameters:

```
fixfon.fon=egafix.fon
oemfonts.fon=egaoem.fon
fonts.fon=egasys.fon
```

Now restart Windows. Your display will show the smaller screen fonts. There will also be some other changes, such as the aspect ratio of the dialog boxes. You may or may not like the changes.

If the adapter and display support Super VGA, use Windows Setup to switch to the Super VGA driver.

Help! I have problems with a VGA display.

223

Performance Tip: If you constantly switch between display modes, here is another method to make switching easier. First, use Setup to install each video mode that you wish to use. Run Windows Setup from within Windows and choose **C**hange System Settings from the **O**ptions menu. Insert diskettes as requested, and on the final dialog box choose **R**estart Windows each time. Once all the files are in place, you can use Setup to switch between the modes without using the diskettes again. You can now even use the Recorder and create a macro to do the switching from an icon. All of this assumes that you are using standard Microsoft display drivers. If you are using third-party drivers, modify the SETUP.INF file first (see Appendix A).

Help! I have problems with a Super VGA display.

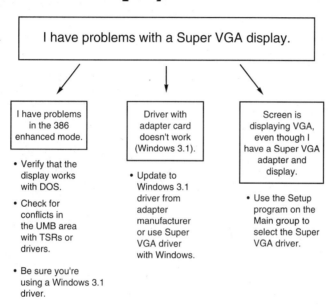

Super VGA is the preferred mode for most people if your video adapter and monitor support this mode. You will get more lines on the screen, and word processors are more likely to display an entire print line on the screen. Following are some solutions to problems with Super VGA.

I have problems in the 386 enhanced mode.

Be sure the display is working as a Super VGA display under DOS. Test it with a DOS program or with a test program that came with the display adapter.

Help! I have problems with a Super VGA display.

225

■ Check for conflicts with TSRs or drivers in the UMB area (see the introduction to the preceding section).

■ The display driver needs to be updated to a Windows 3.1 driver, or use the generic Super VGA display driver with Windows.

The Super VGA driver that came with my video adapter card doesn't work with Windows 3.1.

■ If using Super VGA with Windows 3.1, you may find that the Super VGA display driver you have been using doesn't work. Upgrade to a Windows 3.1 compatible driver or the Super VGA driver with Windows. If using a TIGA or DGIS display adapter, use the Windows 3.1 drivers for these displays.

I have a Super VGA monitor and adapter, but the screen is displaying in VGA.

You can easily tell that you're having this problem with certain applications. For example, Word for Windows shows only 6 inches horizontally in VGA display instead of 8 inches.

■ Windows Setup is probably displaying VGA instead of Super VGA after installation. Use Setup and **C**hange System Settings on the **O**ptions menu to switch Windows to Super VGA. You may have to contact the adapter manufacturer and get a video driver that supports Super VGA. Use 16 colors (instead of 256) unless you need the 256 and have a fast enough system.

Help! I have problems with an EGA display.

```
┌──────────────────────────────────────────────┐
│                                                │
│    I have problems with an EGA display.        │
│                                                │
└──────────────────────────────────────────────┘
                        │
                        ▼
```

- Be sure
  EGA.SYS is
  installed from
  CONFIG.SYS.

- Try adding
  local = EGA$ in
  the [386enh] section
  of SYSTEM.INI.

■ With an EGA display, you must use the EGA.SYS driver, and Setup must be configured for this. Reinstall the driver using Setup and be sure the driver is placed in the CONFIG.SYS file.

■ If you have trouble with a screen when running more than one DOS application under Windows with an EGA monitor in the 386 enhanced mode, try adding `local=EGA$` in the `[386enh]` section of SYSTEM.INI (see Appendix G).

Help! I have problems with an EGA display.

227

Help! I have color problems.

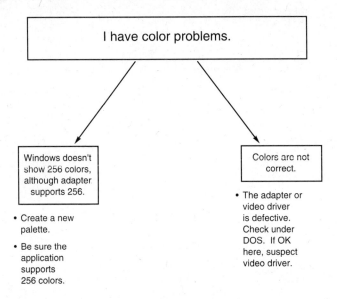

Upgrading your system to support more colors enhances its usefulness, particularly if you're involved in any desktop publishing activities. But you can quickly become frustrated when something goes wrong with your color display in Windows. Following are the problems that might occur and their solutions.

Windows doesn't show 256 colors, although my color adapter supports 256 (or 32,000 or a million) colors.

The Super VGA drivers in Windows can support four levels of color: 16, 256, 2,048, and 32,768. The last is often called 24-bit color because the color information is carried in three 8-bit words. To support the last two, adapter vendors use special RAMDAC's (random-access memory digital to analog converters).

The important point to realize, though, is that Windows itself does not support more than 20 pure colors. The Setup screen may show that you are running a driver that supports 256 colors, but when you bring up the Color option of Control Panel and set the colors, you can find only 20 pure colors. Forty-eight colors are displayed in a scheme, each color created from the 20 basic colors supported by Windows. You can alter the scheme and save it, but the 20 basic colors remain the same. Other colors are supported through a process of *dithering;* that is, mixing dots of different colors on the screen to effect a new color. Applications may use the extra pure colors supported by the driver (if written to do this), but Windows can't and Control Panel can't.

■ To create a custom palette if you have Super VGA, choose Color from Control Panel. Choose Color **P**alette and then **D**efine Custom Colors. Figure 7.1 shows the Custom Color Selector dialog box that will appear. Using the large square and the Color|**So**lid box, you can generate almost any color. All but 20 of these will be dithered. Notice that the Color|Solid box changes as you adjust the colors. The left side of the box shows the current color as a dithered color; that is, dots of different colors are combined to approximate the color. At the right of the box is the closest pure color. Click on **A**dd Color when you have the right shade. Choose **C**lose and **Sa**ve Scheme to save a color palette.

■ Only a few programs can support 256 simultaneous colors. These include CorelDRAW, PowerPoint, and PageMaker (version 4.0). The list is growing, but be sure the program you are using supports 256 colors. You will also need enough memory on the adapter card. For Super VGA or 8514/a, you need 1 megabyte of display memory. For VGA, you need 512K of display memory.

Figure 7.1
Exploring color options with Control Panel.

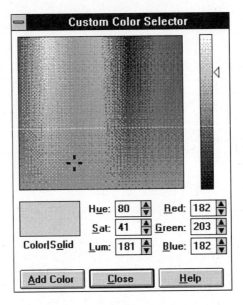

The display colors aren't correct.

The adapter or video driver is defective. Check the colors in a DOS application. If they're OK under DOS, suspect the video driver and replace it.

Help! The screen update is too slow.

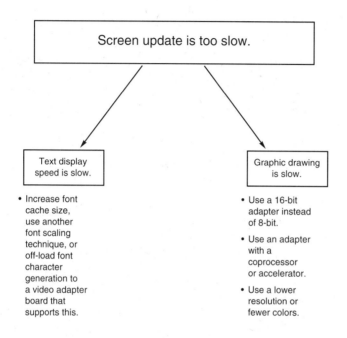

Screen update is too slow.

Text display speed is slow.

- Increase font cache size, use another font scaling technique, or off-load font character generation to a video adapter board that supports this.

Graphic drawing is slow.

- Use a 16-bit adapter instead of 8-bit.
- Use an adapter with a coprocessor or accelerator.
- Use a lower resolution or fewer colors.

System speed is of the essence these days. Don't let the video display slow down your system when you're working with Windows. The following sections discuss some common problems and solutions.

The text display speed is slow.

If you are using scalable fonts, you lose some time in creating the fonts. You can improve display speed some-what with ATM by increasing the font cache size. Use the ATM Control Panel on the Control menu to do this. You might also try a video adapter card that off-loads screen font character generation from the CPU, such as the ATI Graphics Vantage.

Graphic drawing is slow.

■ Screen speed can vary greatly with the video driver used. Contact the video adapter manufacturer and get the fastest driver available that supports the mode and Windows version you wish to use. Be sure the adapter switches are set for 16-bit mode. Change the adapter if it doesn't support 16-bit mode. Check with the adapter manual to see which modes are supported.

■ The display will be slow when using Super VGA 256 color adapters if the adapter doesn't have an accelerator or coprocessor. Change to a video driver that does.

■ Try using a lower resolution or fewer colors.

Help! I have other display problems.

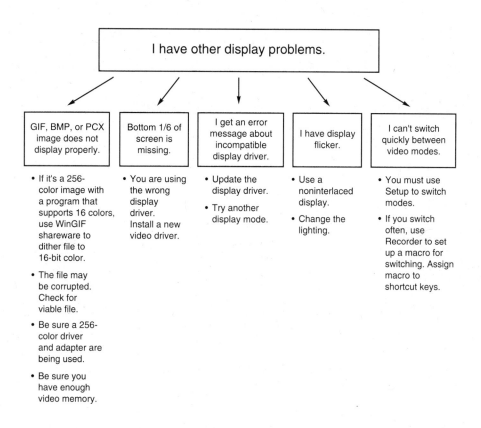

I have other display problems.

GIF, BMP, or PCX image does not display properly.

- If it's a 256-color image with a program that supports 16 colors, use WinGIF shareware to dither file to 16-bit color.
- The file may be corrupted. Check for viable file.
- Be sure a 256-color driver and adapter are being used.
- Be sure you have enough video memory.

Bottom 1/6 of screen is missing.

- You are using the wrong display driver. Install a new video driver.

I get an error message about incompatible display driver.

- Update the display driver.
- Try another display mode.

I have display flicker.

- Use a noninterlaced display.
- Change the lighting.

I can't switch quickly between video modes.

- You must use Setup to switch modes.
- If you switch often, use Recorder to set up a macro for switching. Assign macro to shortcut keys.

A number of miscellaneous problems can occur with the display when you're running Windows. Following are some of the other problems you may encounter, and practical advice for resolving them.

A GIF, BMP, or PCX file image does not display properly.

The images are probably 256-color images that you are trying to display on a 16-color system or on a 256-color system with too little memory in the video adapter. Use the WinGIF shareware program to dither BMP or GIF images to 16-color. (See the disk order form at the back of the book.)

The file may be corrupted. Read it to Paintbrush and verify that it is readable. Verify the pixel resolution used for the image.

You are trying to display 256 colors with a 16-color driver or adapter. Make sure you're using a 256-color driver and adapter. See the information that came with your adapter card, and check Windows Setup to be sure the correct driver is installed.

You don't have enough memory (RAM) on the video adapter board. A 640 x 480 display will need 320K, an 800 x 600 card will need 512K, and a 1024 x 768 card will need 768K. Check the information that came with your system to confirm how much video memory you have. If it's not enough, contact the video board manufacturer to find out how you can upgrade your video memory.

The bottom sixth of the screen is missing.

You are using the wrong display driver, such as a VGA driver used with an AT&T display adapter. Use Setup to select a display driver specifically for your display.

I get an error message about an incompatible display driver.

The display adapter is not supported by Windows, or the display driver files are not complete for your display. Verify the display installation with Setup.

□ Try another mode, such as VGA instead of Super VGA. To change the mode, start Windows Setup and choose **C**hange System Settings from the **O**ptions menu.

I have display flicker.

□ Display flicker can be a problem with Windows because of the white background. Use a noninterlaced display screen and a high horizontal scan frequency (48 kHz or better for Super VGA) to minimize flicker. Some video adapter boards have a switch to set for interlaced or noninterlaced. Others use a software program to switch the card. Use the appropriate method to switch to a noninterlaced mode.

□ Change the lighting near your computer to alleviate the impact of flicker.

I can't switch quickly between video modes.

□ To switch modes, you must use the Windows Setup program.

□ If you use different modes often, use the Recorder to set up a macro to switch modes. Then assign the macro to a shortcut key. Here are the basic steps:

1. Start Recorder and choose Re**c**ord from the **M**acro menu. Enter the macro name to the dialog box (such as Startup). Enter a shortcut key, such as Shift+F12. Select Ignore Mouse in the Record **M**ouse area. Choose **S**tart.

2. Use the keyboard to enter the steps needed to switch the video mode. Don't use the mouse (press Alt+F, then R; then enter **Setup**; press Alt+O, C, etc.).

3. Press Ctrl+Break to terminate recording and then choose **S**ave Macro in the dialog box. Make the Recorder window active and use **F**ile **S**ave As to save your macro. Use the name **Start**.

4. Exit Windows and edit WIN.INI (see Appendix G) so that the `load` parameter loads Recorder and the file:

   ```
   load=recorder.exe start.rec
   ```

   Be sure to use the file extensions.

5. Restart Windows and press the shortcut key to switch the modes.

Performance Tip: For most users, the Recorder is the most underutilized utility. With it, you can add shortcut keys for doing other tasks, such as changing the display color scheme. Use keystrokes instead of mouse actions, starting programs by using Task Manager (Ctrl+Esc) and pressing the first letter of the program name. To start a macro on loading, use the /h parameter and the shortcut key that is assigned:

```
WIN RECORDER.EXE -H<shortcut keys> <macro filename>
```

For example, the command
```
WIN RECORDER.EXE -H^L LETTER.REC
```
loads Windows and then executes the macro in the file assigned to the Ctrl+L keystroke. Use ^ for Ctrl, + for Shift, and % for Alt keys.

You can also set up icons that start macros by entering a command line to the Properties dialog box, such as:
```
RECORDER.EXE -H<shortcut keys> <macro filename>
```

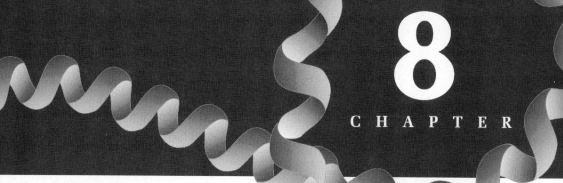

8

C H A P T E R

HELP WITH FONT MANAGEMENT

For the purpose of Windows, Microsoft defines a *font* as a set of symbol designs. The set includes all the letters of the alphabet, the numerals, and any special characters desired. Times Roman, Helvetica, and Futura are examples of font names. A *type manager* is a program for installing, managing, and using fonts. TrueType is a font manager that is internal to Windows. ATM, from Adobe, is an example of an external font manager.

This chapter discusses problems with fonts and offers solutions for fixing them. It covers problems with specific fonts such as TrueType fonts, with font managers such as ATM, and with certain types of printers such as PostScript and HP LaserJet. In addition, you will find general information about choosing fonts and about the basic types of fonts—raster, vector, and scalable.

Choosing a Font

Before you can choose a font, you need to know a few of the basic typesetting terms used in discussing characters and fonts. All the characters in a given font have a particular size and style. *Size* refers to the vertical height of the font in points. A *point* is $^1/_{72}$ of an inch. The height is measured from the bottom of a lowercase descender to the top of the capital letter. Using this definition means, then, that you can't measure the height of a single capital letter to obtain its point size. For a good approximation, measure from the top of the *f* to the bottom of the *g*. These are the tallest and lowest of the characters because their curved lines force an illusion that necessitates them being taller and lower.

Style refers to a specific variation of the general font design. The standard style is often called Regular. Other common styles include Bold, Italic, and Bold Italic.

To choose a font, use the **F**ont command of the application. This command may be on a Forma**t** menu. Figure 8.1 shows a Font dialog box from which you select a font.

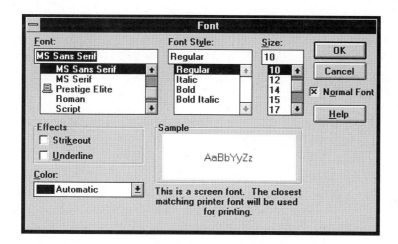

Figure 8.1
Choosing a font.

Fonts are of three basic types: serif, sans serif, and decorative. *Serif fonts* have small horizontal lines in the letters as part of the design. Historically, serifs originated in the letters that Roman builders used to carve inscriptions in Roman arches. The serifs added an ornamental touch to the letter design. Theoretically, serifs improve reading speed by guiding the eye along the horizontal type line. This may or may not be true, but in America most of us learn to read with serif font publications. These fonts, such as Times Roman, are good for body text. The text you are reading now is a serif font. Notice how the strokes of each letter vary in width.

Sans serif fonts do not have horizontal guide lines. Helvetica is a typical sans serif font. These fonts are good for headlines and section headings. Some sans serif fonts (Helvetica is one) are very readable, and you can use them even in body text. The name *Helvetica* refers to the Celtic people who inhabited western Switzerland during the Roman era. The strokes of this font are of uniform width.

Decorative fonts are used for brochures, posters, and occasionally headlines. They attract attention and add an element of design. Most are difficult to read, however, and they shouldn't be used for long sections of text.

Fonts can be fixed (or monospaced) or proportional. In a *fixed-space font,* each letter is the same width. An *m* takes as much space as an *i*. Courier and Prestige are examples of fixed-space fonts. (Courier is supplied with Windows 3.1.) In a *proportional font* (such as Helvetica), the width of the letter varies with the character. Dot-matrix printers generally support only fixed-space fonts. Laser printers can support both.

The font that you use becomes part of your message. Century Old Style, Century Schoolbook, and Bookman are designed for legibility and are good choices for body text in books. Helvetica is a sans serif font with a more serious look that is useful for headlines, captions, forms, and catalogs. It's also very readable. Palatino is often chosen for poetry and art publications. Garamond is a rounded serif font and is characterized as warm and informal. Baskerville is a formal serif font, and is a favorite with bankers and professionals. Futura has a modern look associated with simplicity, integrity, and precision.

Some fonts are designed specifically for the limited (300 dpi) resolution of the laser printer. These include Bitstream's Charter and Adobe's Caslon and Lithos. Certain fonts, such as Times Roman, are designed to make better use of space to reduce cost while maintaining legibility. Some of the products available now let you design your own personal font.

Line spacing refers to the amount of space from the baseline of one line to the baseline of the next. It is typically about 20 percent more than the character height. The term *leading* (pronounced "ledding") refers to the number of points

Help with Font Management

between the bottom of the characters of one line and the top of the characters of the line below. Thus, a 10-point character has a normal line spacing of about 12 points, including 2 points of leading.

Applying Certain Font Effects

Font effects are supported by the individual application and vary with the application. Typical effects include underlining, strikeout, and color.

If you are having problems achieving specific font effects, follow these steps:

- If you're unable to achieve an effect in the Fonts dialog box of the application, check with the application manufacturer.

- To achieve an effect that is not listed on the Fonts dialog box, you must purchase a font designed with the special effect and install it.

Using Certain Fonts with Certain Applications

Certain Windows applications can work only with certain types of fonts. The basic font types are raster, vector, and scalable. The following sections will explain each type.

Remember that fonts you install to Windows are available to all programs running under Windows. You may have already noticed, however, that certain fonts are not always available in some programs. The MS Sans Serif and MS Serif (Windows 3.1) or Helv and Tms Rmn (Windows 3.0) are available to Paintbrush, but not to Windows Write. Have you wondered why this is so? Are all fonts really always available? It depends on how the font is stored.

Raster vs Vector Fonts

There are various methods for storing fonts in a system. Each method, however, is a variation of one of two basic formats: raster or vector.

Raster fonts are really bit-mapped images (images created out of a series of dots). Each symbol in the set is stored as a bit map, and there must be a bit map for each size of the font. This means that a lot of disk space is required to store all sizes and styles of a particular typeface. In addition, there must be a file for both the display and the printer character sets. Finally, there must be separate font sets for portrait and landscape orientation.

To minimize file size, raster fonts are resized by means of integer values. Windows can resize the raster fonts provided with it. Windows can also *synthesize* (create from the basic font) italic, bold, and bold italic for the raster fonts provided with it.

Vector fonts are stored as mathematical descriptions. They can be resized, which means that you need to store only a single "outline." You can create any size from the outline. Windows (3.0 and 3.1) provides three vector fonts: Roman, Script, and Modern. You might want to experiment with these fonts (if you haven't already) to see the difference. Vector fonts take less space but lack body in larger sizes. They are primarily useful for large spreadsheets where you need tiny letters that are very readable. For example, try 6-point Modern for a large spreadsheet that you want to fit on a single page. In larger font sizes, vector fonts are good replacements for raster fonts having jagged edges.

Windows 3.0 has Helv and Times Roman raster fonts available as display fonts. Windows 3.1 has these same fonts and sizes available as MS Serif and MS Sans Serif. You can purchase additional raster fonts from many vendors. Table 8.1 lists the fonts included with Windows.

Font	Type	Description
Helv/MS	Sans serif, raster	A Helvectica typeface. A proportional sans serif font.
Tms Rmn/MS	Serif, raster	A proportional Times Roman typeface with serifs.
Courier	Serif, raster	A fixed-pitch (monospaced) font with serifs.
Symbol	Raster	A proportional font for math-ematical symbols.

Table 8.1
Fonts Supplied with Windows

continues

Table 8.1

continued

Font	Type	Description
Roman	Serif, vector	A proportional roman font with serifs.
Modern	Sans serif, vector	A proportional modern font without serifs.
Script	Vector	A proportional script font.

Note: The raster fonts provided with Windows are display fonts only. You can't print them with a laser printer. Avoid using them except with raster image programs, such as Paintbrush. Use the TrueType or ATM fonts instead. Some dot-matrix printers can use raster fonts.

Now let's see what happens when you try to print with a printer raster font for which there is no matching display raster font. Suppose, for example, you try to print text that is New Century Schoolbook Italic 40 point. The printer font is there, but no matching screen font is available. The application sends a call to the GDI program (see Appendix A), requesting a screen font that doesn't exist. The GDI, in turn, calls on the video device driver. It informs Windows that the screen font is missing. The device driver also tells Windows which fonts are available and in which sizes. The closest font that Windows can find is Times Roman (Windows 3.0) or MS Serif (Windows

3.1) in 18 points, which doubles to 36 points. The resulting display font is the wrong typeface and the wrong size, and is slanted to make it look italic. The letters look quite jagged.

Raster fonts are good quality, but trying to put many sizes, styles, and orientations on a computer disk can take too much disk space. Besides occupying disk space, these fonts often have jagged edges at larger sizes (the "jaggies"). Finally, you don't get true WYSIWYG with raster fonts, since the screen and the device fonts are two separate files. Sometimes, as with the LaserJet cartridge fonts, there is no screen font and Windows can only approximate the print image on the display.

Some application programs, such as PageMaker, automatically switch to vector fonts when trying to display a raster font image in larger sizes. In PageMaker, you can choose the point size at which this switch takes effect.

Scalable Outline Fonts

To solve the font problem, users are switching to *scalable outline fonts*. With this technique, the font is stored as an outline. The type manager intercepts Windows' calls to the printer and screen. The font is scaled from the outline for the display or printer to the desired size and then rasterized for the desired output device. The process of scaling and rasterizing is called *rendering*. The font is almost infinitely scalable, and there are no jaggies. The resulting fonts are very attractive, and you save disk space.

A very simple document with raster fonts may take 10-point New Century Schoolbook for body text, 14-point Helvetica Bold for a main head, and 12-point Helvetica Bold for a subhead. The headline might be 24-point Helvetica Bold.

That's four fonts, with the larger 24-point font taking the most disk space. With scalable fonts, you need only two small outline fonts: Helvetica Bold and New Century Schoolbook Normal.

Font scaling systems can work on the fly or not. If the software creates fonts *on the fly*, the fonts are created automatically on demand for both the display and the printer. If not, the font manager creates raster fonts for the desired size and style from the outline and saves them on the disk for use later. Scaling fonts on the fly is slower, but it simplifies type management and saves disk space.

Scaling fonts to disk files is faster for the print and display cycle and provides more flexibility (multiple character sets, outline fonts, pattern files, editable fonts, etc.) but can quickly take a large amount of disk space. Zsoft's SoftType, Hewlett-Packard's Type Directory, and Adobe's Font Foundry are examples of font generators that can produce bit-mapped (raster) fonts as files from outlines. Some of these products can also produce outlines (such as Type 1) for on-the-fly rendering.

Now let's see what happens when a request is made with on-the-fly formatting to display text in 24-point Helvetica Bold. The font manager intercepts the request to the video device driver for the font. The font manager appends its own list of fonts that currently exist only as outlines. If Helvetica Bold is on the list, the video driver is told to produce the bit map. The font manager again intercepts the call, creates a scaled outline to 24 points, and then rasterizes the outline for the particular display. The rasterizing is done by overlaying the character on an imaginary grid that represents the pixels of the output device (screen, printer, etc.). The pixels that fall within the outline are turned on to create the character bit map. Some hints are applied, as necessary, to clean up the resulting font.

Help with Font Management

For example, some pixels are bordered only partially by the outline. *Hinting* defines which pixels to turn on. The font manager then returns the bit map to the video driver and issues the display request.

PostScript, a programming language that describes how to print a page, was the first successful implementation of the scalable font concept. The fonts are stored as outlines—Bezier outlines of 1000-point characters. When a particular point size is requested, the Bezier curve is factored by .001 and returns a 1-point font. The font is then scaled by the interpreter to the desired size. The PostScript device driver sends the final page to the printer by using a PostScript PDL (high-level Page Description Language). The PostScript engine in the printer interprets the PDL and rasterizes the fonts as necessary to create the page. Most of the intelligence is in the PostScript interpreter residing in the printer.

Because the printer must rasterize the page as well as print it, PostScript printing is slow. The print quality is very high, however. Future versions of the PostScript interpreters will use faster processors to improve print speed.

PostScript is fine for Apple computers where the installed PostScript base is high. Most PC users have a non-PostScript LaserJet printer, however. To give PC users PostScript fonts, Adobe (who owns PostScript) introduced the Adobe Type Manager (ATM). It uses the same scalable font outlines that PostScript uses for fonts (Type 1 outlines), and ATM rasterizes the font for the screen and printer. ATM will rasterize fonts for almost any type of printer: laser, dot-matrix, ink-jet, and PaintJet.

Type Managers and Hinted Fonts

Many problems with fonts can often be solved in advance by installing a type manager. A *type manager* is a program for installing, managing, and using fonts. The TrueType font manager is internal to Windows and is accessible by choosing Fonts from Control Panel. ATM, if installed, is an external font manager. It is controlled from the ATM Font Manager in the Main group of Program Manager.

Any good type manager must be capable of reading some type of hinting format. Basically, *hinting* involves the ability to change the appearance of the font with size. Think of the font as being rendered to fit a grid. For a laser, the typical grid is 300 points to the inch horizontally and vertically. The final font won't align perfectly with the grid, and hinting defines how to change the character to fit the grid. Details that add personality to a large font clutter the same font at a smaller size and make it less readable. Parts of the character may be moved left, right, up, or down. It is important, however, to maintain the details that give the font its distinctive characteristics.

Hinting is accomplished by including, in the font file, information about how the font changes with size. Adobe pioneered the concept with PostScript but kept their hinting techniques proprietary for years. When Microsoft and Apple decided to develop their own TrueType hinting technique, Adobe opened the hinting code of PostScript, making it more available and affordable. Adobe also released the Adobe Type Manager (ATM), making it possible to use their extensive library with non-PostScript printers. PostScript fonts that include hinting are called Type 1 fonts. PostScript Type 3 fonts are those without hinting.

Help with Font Management

Caution: Avoid using unhinted Type 1 fonts below 18 points. With Intellifont fonts, you can go somewhat lower using unhinted fonts.

ATM is not alone in the world of type managers. Other vendors, recognizing this need, have introduced their own scalable outline technology. Unfortunately, the font formats are not compatible, and you can't mix fonts from the various vendors. Bitstream introduced Speedo fonts and their Facelift type manager. Atech introduced Publisher's PowerPak, and MicroLogic introduced MoreFonts. All use different font formats. Here is a brief review of each font/type manager product:

ATM/Type 1 (Adobe). The ATM fonts are the only ones that work with both a PostScript printer and a non-PostScript printer. These fonts (along with TrueType) are recognized as being the highest in quality. Adobe provides the largest font selection (over 1,000). The cost of ATM fonts is high but is dropping as a result of competition. Most printers are supported: ink-jet, PaintJet, dot-matrix, and others. ATM will work with most Windows applications and printers, but you may have trouble with some printers. For example, I had to update my PaintJet printer driver to use ATM with that printer. I'll have to update both drivers (again) and update ATM to use ATM with Windows 3.1.

ATM is one of the fastest type managers. Because of its consistent and tighter spacing (than FaceLift), the text has a typeset quality. You must quit Windows and restart to deactivate ATM. There are no non-Latin typefaces outside of Japan. Avoid the early Adobe fonts (number 60 or lower) which have less hinting. You can get Type 1 fonts

from a wide base of suppliers, including (free) from some local BBS systems.

FaceLift/Speedo (Bitstream). The quality is good, with 1,100 well-designed typefaces. Bitstream can also supply fonts in Type 1 or TrueType. Almost any type of printer can be used if supported by Windows: ink-jet, dot-matrix, and laser. However, you may experience problems with some printer drivers. FaceLift supports PostScript printers, but you must use Bitstream Type 1 fonts, which are unhinted. With a PostScript printer, you may wish to turn Facelift off for the printer and use Type 1 fonts directly, leaving FaceLift on only for the screen. Another option with Hewlett-Packard Series III printers is to use FaceLift for the screen and use a printer-resident scalable font for printing.

FaceLift comes with 13 fonts. It is supposed to work with all Windows applications, though it may appear jumpy or unusably slow with some applications. In some cases, you may have spacing problems with italicized type. Unlike ATM, you can use Facelift to create soft fonts for a laser printer. Speedo (unlike Adobe's fonts) is still a proprietary format. You can't buy fonts of this format from anyone else, which limits you to Bitstream's library. Bitstream's Fontware utility will convert fonts to unhinted scalable outlines for LaserJet III or unhinted PostScript outlines. If you want quality, choose Bitstream's Type 1 or TrueType format instead of the Speedo format.

Publisher's PowerPak (Atech Software). This product is for those who are economy minded but who need lots of fonts. The cost is low, but so is the quality. PowerPak quality will work for flyers, but it's not advisable for standard text printing. Effects supported include thin, wide, expanded, and hollowed-out letters. Leading is small in some applications.

PowerPak uses its own screen driver, and screen fonts do not support some displays, such as enhanced VGA. PowerPak replaces existing printer drivers. It works with most printers (but not PostScript or LaserMaster). Font styles are synthesized instead of being stored as separate fonts. You can purchase a converter to convert Type 1 fonts to PowerPak format.

PowerPak offers more styles than competitors do, but there is no symbol typeface in the basic package as there is with others. You can purchase PowerPak for Windows, (DOS) Microsoft Word, (DOS) WordPerfect, the GEM version of Ventura, and other word processors. Fonts can be shared between the versions. PowerPak supports Cyrillic, Greek, Hebrew, and four variations of Korean and Thai characters.

MoreFonts (MicroLogic Software). This is another low-cost alternative. MoreFonts supports special effects (special fills, outline weights, shadows, and reverse) and has the capability to create fonts for (DOS) Microsoft Word and (DOS) WordPerfect as well as Windows. The latest font releases are hinted.

MoreFonts uses its own screen and printer drivers. It is the only program that can convert its fonts to LaserJet III format to let the printer do the scaling. Font quality is moderate.

SuperPrint/Nimbus/SuperQue (Zenographics). This product is in a class by itself. SuperPrint will work with almost any font format: Adobe Type 1, TrueType, Bitstream Fontware (older version of Speedo), and others.

This is truly amazing. A special SuperQue utility with SuperPrint improves print management dramatically. SuperQue replaces the print drivers and Print Manager of Windows. Printing is done in the background, with control returned to the user much faster than with Windows' Print Manager. Print jobs are sent to the printer line by line, and resident or cartridge printer fonts are lost. This means slow printing of straight text. Fortunately, it is easy to turn SuperPrint off when you want fast text printing, by using the standard Windows print driver. Fonts are saved to disk after creation, which can mean a heavy loss of disk space unless you create them each time. The advantage is that there's not much loss of RAM to the manager.

This product has the best graphic quality, and you will see a dramatic improvement over the standard Windows drivers when you are doing graphics with programs like CorelDRAW. SuperPrint supports 9- and 24-pin dot-matrix, DeskJet, PaintJet, and LaserJet. Fonts are moderate in quality, but you can use high-quality Type 1 or TrueType fonts with SuperPrint.

Intellifont for Windows/Intellifonts (Hewlett-Packard). This product is a font scaling program and font format for LaserJet Series III printers only. One big advantage here is speed—this font manager is fast. The Intellifont fonts are supported by these printers and this scaling program only (see next section). Approximately 200 typefaces are available, some of only moderate quality, however.

Since all of these products modify standard Windows functions to some extent, their reliability can vary with Windows versions and applications. They may or may not work with Windows 3.1, or you may need an update. Check with the company to be sure the product has been updated, if necessary,

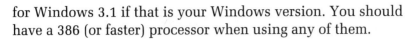

for Windows 3.1 if that is your Windows version. You should have a 386 (or faster) processor when using any of them.

You can use multiple products, but use caution. You can even mix fonts of different formats from different scalers on the same page. This issue becomes more and more of a problem because some applications include their own font manager program. When using two or more font managers, you can get memory conflicts. Both ATM and PowerPak, for example, load to the same memory address. This can corrupt the WIN.INI file, among other things. The solution is to deinstall both programs and then install PowerPak first. Then install ATM, which is smarter and will allocate itself to whatever memory is left.

Most of the products use extensive memory. The program itself requires memory, and then you need memory for the cache that holds the fonts. ATM requires a 96K cache. FaceLift works with 16K but works best with 256K. PowerPak uses only 2K but supports only a few monitors (CGA, EGA, VGA, MCGA, Hercules, 8514, and a few more). SuperPrint stores fonts to disk, so the memory required is small.

Note: With Windows 3.0, font files are limited to 64K maximum. This means you may have problems displaying large fonts that require large files (such as SuperPrint). This is an anomaly of Windows 3.0, which may be fixed in Windows 3.1.

Display Fonts

The font files supplied with Windows are display files. They have the extension FON and are stored in the \WINDOWS\SYSTEM directory. Table 8.2 shows an example of what you should find there. You should also find the TrueType FON files (four each) for the Arial, Courier, and Times New Roman typefaces.

Table 8.2

Font Files for Windows

WINDOWS 3.0	WINDOWS 3.1	Description
ROMAN.FON	ROMAN.FON	Roman vector font
MODERN.FON	MODERN.FON	Modern vector font
SCRIPT.FON	SCRIPT.FON	Script vector font
HELVx.FON	SSERIFx.FON	Helvetica or MS Sans
TMSRx.FON	SERIFx.FON	Tms Rmn or MS Serif
SYMBOLx.FON	SYMBOLx.FON	Symbol
COURx.FON	COURx.FON	Courier

The raster fonts have a suffix code (*x* in Table 8.2) that indicates the resolution and aspect ratio—the factors that define the font set. The suffix code is necessary because each display has a different resolution and aspect ratio, and Windows must install a display-specific raster font for your display. Also, some printers can print raster fonts. Thus, to support that printer, you must install the raster font for that device. Table 8.3 shows the resolution and aspect ratio.

Table 8.3

Windows Raster Fonts

Font Set	Display	Horizontal Resolution	Vertical Resolution	Aspect Ratio (H:V)
A	CGA	96 dpi	48 dpi	2:1
B	EGA	96 dpi	72 dpi	1.33:1
C	N/A	60 dpi	72 dpi	1:.83
D	N/A	120 dpi	72 dpi	1.67:1
E	VGA	96 dpi	96 dpi	1:1
F	8514/A	120 dpi	120 dpi	1:1

Fonts are graphic images, and the font characters can either be stored as vector graphics or raster images. Windows contains a sample of both types of fonts.

Tips for Font Management

Here are a few tips for managing your fonts efficiently:

- Type 1 fonts are considered the highest quality fonts for Windows 3.0. For Windows 3.1, TrueType and Type 1 are the highest quality.

■ When you are using a laser printer with a font manager, install plenty of memory in the printer. A 512K memory is too small. Two megabytes is a good memory size to use.

■ After you have installed a new ATM font, restart Windows before using the font.

■ Fonts take disk space, and trying to support various formats and techniques can turn font management into a real challenge. Plan well before purchasing or installing fonts.

Help! The fonts are displayed with jagged edges.

The fonts are displayed with jagged edges.

• Use a scalable font; use TrueType or ATM, instead of raster.

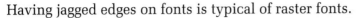

Having jagged edges on fonts is typical of raster fonts.

■ Use a scalable outline font, such as an ATM font or a TrueType font.

Help! The font display and printed output are different.

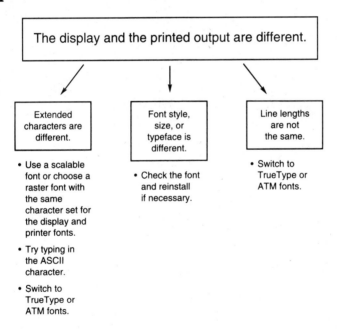

The display and the printed output are different.

Extended characters are different.

- Use a scalable font or choose a raster font with the same character set for the display and printer fonts.
- Try typing in the ASCII character.
- Switch to TrueType or ATM fonts.

Font style, size, or typeface is different.

- Check the font and reinstall if necessary.

Line lengths are not the same.

- Switch to TrueType or ATM fonts.

In this case, what you see isn't what you get. Try the following suggestions to resolve this problem.

Help! The font display and printed output are different.

257

The printed character sets are different only for the extended characters.

When you install Windows to your system, two files are required for each raster font that is installed: a screen or display font file and a device or printer font file. The character sets of each should match. If not, the printed character set won't match the displayed characters for those characters having ASCII codes above 128, such as opening and closing quotation marks, copyright symbols, and other special characters.

The printer will print from the device (or printer) character set, and the screen shows the display character set. If these character sets are not identical, the printer output won't match the display.

- If you are using a cartridge or a soft font with the printer, try using a different character set. Often the same font is stored in the cartridge (or as a soft font) using multiple character sets.

- Use the manuals with your printer or printer cartridges to see what ASCII value is needed for a particular symbol. Then hold down the Alt key and enter that number. The displayed symbol may not be correct, but it will print correctly.

- Switch to the TrueType or ATM fonts. With scalable fonts, the display and printer fonts are always from the same character set.

A certain style, font, or font size doesn't appear the same on both the printer and the display.

- The font isn't installed correctly, or the installed font doesn't support that size or style. Verify that both the screen and printer fonts are installed for that font, size, and style. Verify that the printer supports this font. Be sure the printer is configured correctly and is set to the correct resolution. Reinstall the font if necessary.

The line lengths are not the same, and characters on the screen use widths different from what the printer uses.

With raster fonts, the character widths are controlled from a character width table. If you are using cartridge or resident fonts, the character width table for the display fonts should define the same widths as the fonts installed to the printer. The table is a part of the printer driver. Switch to ATM or TrueType fonts. With Truetype fonts, the same width table is used for both display and printer fonts, and there is no problem.

Help! I have problems with TrueType scalable fonts.

259

Help! I have problems with TrueType scalable fonts.

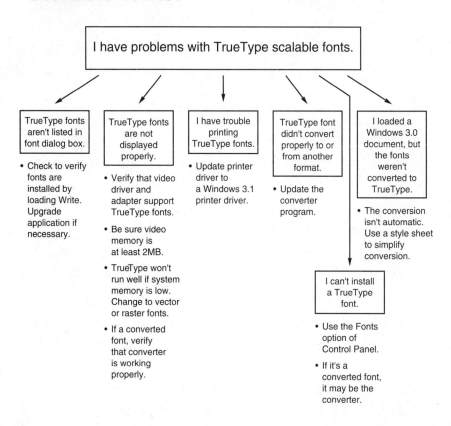

I have problems with TrueType scalable fonts.

TrueType fonts aren't listed in font dialog box.

• Check to verify fonts are installed by loading Write. Upgrade application if necessary.

TrueType fonts are not displayed properly.

• Verify that video driver and adapter support TrueType fonts.

• Be sure video memory is at least 2MB.

• TrueType won't run well if system memory is low. Change to vector or raster fonts.

• If a converted font, verify that converter is working properly.

I have trouble printing TrueType fonts.

• Update printer driver to a Windows 3.1 printer driver.

TrueType font didn't convert properly to or from another format.

• Update the converter program.

I loaded a Windows 3.0 document, but the fonts weren't converted to TrueType.

• The conversion isn't automatic. Use a style sheet to simplify conversion.

I can't install a TrueType font.

• Use the Fonts option of Control Panel.

• If it's a converted font, it may be the converter.

Windows 3.1 includes the TrueType Arial, Times New Roman, and Courier fonts in a variety of styles. (Windows 3.0 doesn't support TrueType fonts.) These fonts were designed by

Monotype. (Note that Windows 3.1 includes both a raster Courier font and a TrueType Courier font.) The following problems are ones that you may experience in using TrueType fonts.

TrueType fonts aren't listed in the Font dialog box.

- The fonts should be installed and available in applications such as Write. If available in Write but not in the desired application, contact the company that sells the application for an update.

I have trouble displaying TrueType fonts.

- Some display drivers cannot display TrueType fonts correctly. Such drivers include those that cache unused fonts in memory. If you have problems, contact the display adapter manufacturer and update the display adapter driver or use a generic driver in Windows 3.1. Windows 3.0 display drivers won't work with TrueType.

- Verify that you have at least 2 megabytes of video memory. Check the video adapter card and its manual.

- TrueType will not function well in systems with low system memory. If you must run with low memory, use vector or raster fonts.

- If the font is a converted font, the converter may not be working properly. Contact the converter manufacturer.

I have trouble printing TrueType fonts.

Most printer drivers developed for Windows 3.0 do not support TrueType fonts. With some printer drivers, you can choose Help from the Printer Setup dialog box to get the driver version number. Use a generic printer driver in Windows or contact the printer manufacturer for an updated driver.

I have trouble converting TrueType fonts to or from other formats.

Various converters, such as FontMonger, are available for converting Type 1 fonts to TrueType fonts. This is useful if you don't have ATM but do have access to an Adobe Type 1 font library.

Some font converters are not completely compatible with TrueType. Contact the manufacturer for an updated converter.

I can't install a TrueType font.

Use the Fonts option of Control Panel to install TrueType fonts. Figure 8.2 shows a Fonts dialog box.

If you still have trouble and the font is a converted font, you may have a defective converter.

Help with Font Management

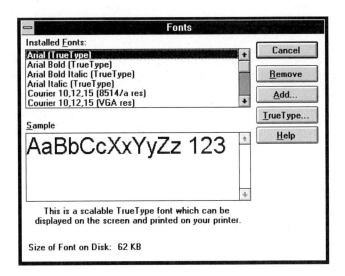

Figure 8.2
Installing TrueType fonts.

I loaded a document from Windows 3.0, but the fonts weren't converted to TrueType.

Windows does not automatically convert the older fonts to the new font technology. You must manually convert the fonts after the document is loaded under Windows 3.1. With word processors, style sheets can simplify your task. Update the style sheet to 3.1 fonts, and all documents using that style sheet are converted.

Performance Tip: You can speed up the screen display with TrueType by creating a document that has a sample of all the characters in all the sizes you will use and then storing it. Next load the word processor from that document. This will force the TrueType manager to create all the characters and save them, speeding up the font display as you create your new document.

Help! I'm having problems with ATM and Windows.

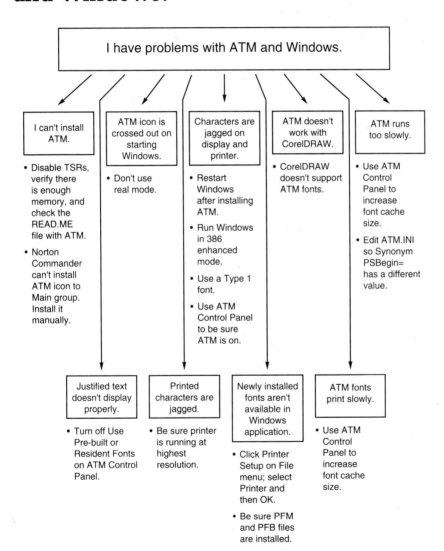

I have problems with ATM and Windows.

I can't install ATM.

- Disable TSRs, verify there is enough memory, and check the READ.ME file with ATM.
- Norton Commander can't install ATM icon to Main group. Install it manually.

ATM icon is crossed out on starting Windows.

- Don't use real mode.

Characters are jagged on display and printer.

- Restart Windows after installing ATM.
- Run Windows in 386 enhanced mode.
- Use a Type 1 font.
- Use ATM Control Panel to be sure ATM is on.

ATM doesn't work with CorelDRAW.

- CorelDRAW doesn't support ATM fonts.

ATM runs too slowly.

- Use ATM Control Panel to increase font cache size.
- Edit ATM.INI so Synonym PSBegin= has a different value.

Justified text doesn't display properly.

- Turn off Use Pre-built or Resident Fonts on ATM Control Panel.

Printed characters are jagged.

- Be sure printer is running at highest resolution.

Newly installed fonts aren't available in Windows application.

- Click Printer Setup on File menu; select Printer and then OK.
- Be sure PFM and PFB files are installed.

ATM fonts print slowly.

- Use ATM Control Panel to increase font cache size.

Help! I'm having problems with ATM and Windows.

265

To avoid most problems between ATM and Windows, be sure you have upgraded to ATM version 2.0 or later. Reconfigure your current ATM before upgrading to Windows 3.1 so that ATM is less dependent on the location of Windows. This means moving these files from the \WINDOWS or \WINDOWS\SYSTEM directory to an ATM directory such as D:\ATM: ATMCTRL.EXE, ATM.DLL, or ATMSYS.DRV. ATM requires the ATM.INI file to be in the same directory as WIN.COM, so it must be in the Windows directory. Other ATM files, however, can be moved. Make sure that any relevant pointers in the WIN.INI file are modified (see Appendix G). The line in the SYSTEM.INI [boot] section specifying the directory for the ATM driver must be changed to point to the new location:

```
system.drv=d:\atm\atmsys.drv
atm.system.drv=system.drv
```

The D:\ATM directory must also be in the system path. This gives the ATM protection, enabling it to be moved to new versions of Windows quickly. Once you've installed a new version of Windows, you install ATM as if it were a new install. To install a new version of ATM, save the old ATM directory (rename it) and create a new ATM directory with the new version.

I can't install ATM. The system hangs during installation.

Make sure that all TSRs are disabled (see Chapters 1 and 2) and that there is enough memory on your system (type MEM at the DOS prompt, or use About on the Windows Help menu). Two megabytes is recommended. Read the READ.ME file on the ATM disk. Be sure you have 1 megabyte of hard disk space.

The ATM installation program tries to create the proper program groups and program items for Program Manager. If you have Norton Desktop for Windows on your system, it does not use the same structure as Program Manager. Therefore, the ATM icon will not be properly installed to the Main group. You must add it manually. All the proper files are copied, however.

Justified text extends beyond the right margin on the screen, but it prints correctly.

Try turning off the Use Pre-built or Resident fonts option in the ATM Control Panel. If this solves the problem, it was caused by Windows using a screen font for a font of different size.

On starting Windows, the ATM icon is crossed out.

■ Be sure that ATM is installed properly and that the system is running in standard or 386 enhanced mode. Don't use real mode. Open the ATM dialog box and make sure that ATM is on.

Printed characters are jagged but appear fine on the screen.

■ Be sure the printer is set to its highest resolution.

Characters appear jagged on the screen and the printer.

■ Make sure that you restarted Windows after installing ATM.

■ Windows must be running in standard or 386 enhanced mode.

■ You must be using a standard PostScript language Type 1 font. Try other fonts to see if the problem is isolated to a single font.

■ Be sure ATM is turned on. The ATM Control Panel should show ATM as active.

I installed some new ATM fonts, but they aren't available in a Windows application.

◻ Select Print Setup from the File menu of Word for Windows. Verify that the correct printer is selected and choose OK. This will cause Word for Windows to recheck its list of available fonts. Word for Windows communicates with the printer driver to determine which fonts are available. Since this procedure is time consuming, Word doesn't do it every time—only when Word thinks that the font list may have changed. This trick foxes Word for Windows into thinking you may have changed printers, and it rereads the font list.

◻ Be sure the PFM and PFB files are installed for the font by checking the directory defined for them in WIN.INI. The PFM files are the font metric files (width tables). The PFB files define the outline.

CorelDRAW! doesn't work right with ATM.

◻ CorelDRAW! version 2.0 does not work with ATM fonts.

Printing is slow with ATM fonts.

◻ Increase the size of the font cache by using the ATM Control Panel. The default is 96K. For graphic art, use 128K or larger.

ATM runs too slowly.

▢ Try using the ATM Control Panel to change the cache size.

▢ You can also edit the ATM.INI file (see Appendix G) in the \WINDOWS directory. You should find a parameter `SynonymPSBegin=9` in the `[Settings]` section. This parameter controls the font size at which the fonts listed in the `[Synonyms]` section begin scaling. Set this size to 12, 14, or another value. The next time you start Windows, ATM will use only the screen fonts installed and loaded to memory for font sizes below the specified value.

Help! I'm having problems with fonts on a PostScript printer.

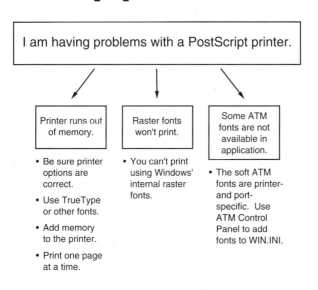

I am having problems with a PostScript printer.

Printer runs out of memory.	Raster fonts won't print.	Some ATM fonts are not available in application.
• Be sure printer options are correct. • Use TrueType or other fonts. • Add memory to the printer. • Print one page at a time.	• You can't print using Windows' internal raster fonts.	• The soft ATM fonts are printer- and port-specific. Use ATM Control Panel to add fonts to WIN.INI.

Help! I'm having problems with fonts on a PostScript printer.

271

With PostScript printers, the TrueType outlines are converted on the fly to PostScript Type 1 fonts by using a C language routine developed by the Mathematics department of the University of Calgary. The faces are then downloaded to the printer. As with LaserJet printers, only the characters needed for the document are downloaded to reduce downloading time. There is not much speed penalty in the conversion.

PostScript printers use a special Postscript language. The Postscript driver sends the page to the printer in this special language. The Postscript "engine" in the printer interprets the language and creates the page, which is then printed. As with a LaserJet printer, there must be enough memory in the printer to hold the entire page image for printer. The following problems are ones that you may encounter.

The printer runs out of memory.

☐ Try changing the printer options. From the Printer Setup dialog box (using Control Panel Printers), choose **O**ptions. Choose Ad**v**anced. In the **S**end To Printer As, be sure that Adobe Type 1 is selected. Be sure C**l**ear Memory Per Page and Use Substitution **T**able are selected. Use Help or F1 as necessary in setting the options.

☐ Try using TrueType or printer fonts instead. Do this by specifying them in the document.

☐ Add more physical memory to the printer. Contact the manufacturer or the company that sold you the printer for information on doing so.

☐ Try printing a document one page at a time.

I can't print a Windows raster font on my PostScript printer.

There's no problem. PostScript printers cannot print the Windows raster fonts.

Some fonts on the ATM Control Panel don't appear in the font panel of an application when I'm using the PostScript driver.

The soft font entries are missing for this printer and port in the WIN.INI file. Soft fonts are printer-and port-specific. If you change either, the font is no longer available. Add the missing fonts by using the ATM Control Panel or edit WIN.INI. ATM does not have to be active when you are printing with a PostScript printer, since no fonts are rasterized.

To add fonts to ATM, choose the ATM Control program from the Main group. Choose **A**dd. Insert the disk with the fonts. In the Add ATM Fonts dialog box, choose the input drive and directory (normally A). Choose the desired fonts to add from the list and **A**dd. You will then need to restart Windows for the new fonts to be available.

Help! I'm having problems with fonts on a PostScript printer.

273

Help! I'm having problems with fonts on a PCL (LaserJet) printer.

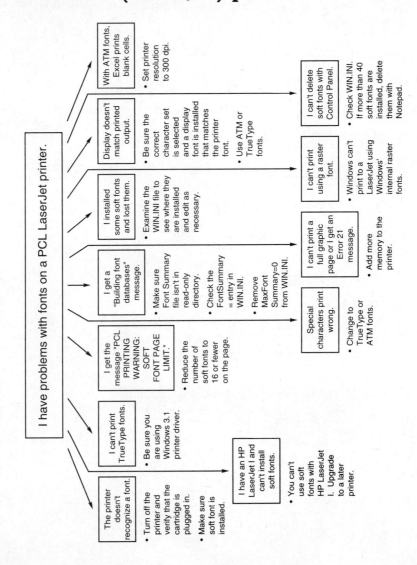

I have problems with fonts on a PCL LaserJet printer.

With ATM fonts, Excel prints blank cells.
- Set printer resolution to 300 dpi.

Display doesn't match printed output.
- Be sure the correct character set is selected and a display font is installed that matches the printer font.
- Use ATM or TrueType fonts.

I installed some soft fonts and lost them.
- Examine the WIN.INI file to see where they are installed and edit as necessary.

I get a "Building font databases" message.
- Make sure Font Summary file isn't in read-only directory.
- Check the FontSummary = entry in WIN.INI.
- Remove MaxFont Summary=0 from WIN.INI.

I get the message "PCL PRINTING WARNING: SOFT FONT PAGE LIMIT."
- Reduce the number of soft fonts to 16 or fewer on the page.

I can't print TrueType fonts.
- Be sure you are using Windows 3.1 printer driver.

The printer doesn't recognize a font.
- Turn off the printer and verify that the cartridge is plugged in.
- Make sure soft font is installed.

I have an HP LaserJet I and can't install soft fonts.
- You can't use soft fonts with HP LaserJet I. Upgrade to a later printer.

I can't delete soft fonts with Control Panel.
- Check WIN.INI. If more than 40 soft fonts are installed, delete them with Notepad.

I can't print using a raster font.
- Windows can't print to a LaserJet using Windows' internal raster fonts.

I can't print a full graphic page or I get an Error 21 message.
- Add more memory to the printer.

Special characters print wrong.
- Change to TrueType or ATM fonts.

Hewlett-Packard LaserJet Series printers support a *PCL page description language*. The language is constantly changing, and the new Series III printers support a PCL level 5 language (with internal scalable fonts). With PCL, control codes are sent to the printer through the use of specified escape sequences. To print text in Times Roman from a cartridge font, for example, you send a control code to the printer that switches the printer to that font. Then the ASCII characters are sent to the printer as with any other character printer. Some level of graphic control is also available from the PCL language. You can send a control code to the printer to switch it to graphic mode and then send lines and basic shapes to the printer. Fonts internal to the printer (in the printer's ROM) are called *resident fonts*.

When using Hewlett-Packard LaserJet compatible printers, you are using a printer driver that is included with Windows or is supplied by the printer manufacturer. You can then purchase *cartridges* with various fonts either from Hewlett-Packard or from third-party manufacturers, such as Pacific Data Products. The cartridges have the fonts stored as raster images. Since proportional fonts have varying widths, the printer driver must contain cartridge information. If you add a cartridge that is not defined in the driver, you must add additional Printer Cartridge Metric files just as if you were adding a soft font. Once installed, you'll see the new cartridge in the driver Setup dialog box.

Help! I'm having problems with fonts on a PCL (LaserJet) printer.

275

To add a metric file, choose **F**onts from the Printers Setup dialog box. Choose **A**dd Fonts on the Font Installer dialog box. Insert the disk with the files. You will then need to select the files to add and choose **M**ove.

With LaserJet Series II and III printers, TrueType fonts are treated as downloadable soft fonts in PCL4 format.

Cartridge fonts are fast and don't require any computer disk space. Another plus is that some companies will create custom cartridges for you, making your favorite font readily available. There are some disadvantages, however. If there is no screen font file installed to Windows, you won't get true WYSIWYG. Windows will do the best it can to match the printer font to one of its internal raster fonts, but it's not a true match. In addition, it's difficult to find large fonts in a cartridge because they require so much of the cartridge memory. LaserJet III Series printers can use scalable font cartridges, although the standard printer driver with Windows 3.0 does not support them.

Another alternative is to use *soft, or downloadable, fonts.* Soft fonts are sold by Hewlett-Packard and other vendors and are stored on the computer hard disk. They are installed from the printer driver by using the Printers option of Control Panel or from a third-party installation program. With soft fonts, you can use any size fonts and have a larger selection, but you will need disk space. This also permits the installation of screen fonts with the printer fonts to get true WYSIWYG printing. (In fact, you should make sure you install both when installing soft fonts.)

Soft fonts are raster fonts that are resident on the computer and are downloaded to the printer as they are needed. In the default mode, they are downloaded on a temporary basis; that is, Windows automatically downloads the fonts it needs

from the computer to the printer as it needs them. This slows printing by the amount of time it takes to download the fonts. With permanent downloading, the fonts are downloaded to the printer's memory when the computer is booted and remain ready to be used whenever a document requires them. The disadvantage of permanent downloading is that the soft fonts are always using the printer's memory, and turning off the printer means that they must be reloaded when the printer is turned back on. The advantage of permanent downloading, however, is speed.

The big disadvantage of soft fonts is their requirement for large amounts of disk space. Since they are raster fonts, large font sizes mean a large font file. Also, screen and printer files must be kept for each font, and each style and size is a separate file. Trying to manage your fonts (by taking them off and putting them on the disk as needed) becomes very inconvenient.

Soft fonts are always installed for a particular printer and port and from the printer driver. Install both the screen and the printer fonts when installing raster fonts. Use this basic procedure:

1. Select Printers from Control Panel.

2. Select the printer, and be sure its connection is defined the way you wish it. Soft fonts are always installed for a particular printer and port (connection).

3. Choose **S**elect, then **F**onts.

4. Select **A**dd Fonts on the Font Installer dialog box. Enter the disk with the soft fonts and click OK.

5. The disk fonts are listed in the right dialog box. Hold down Shift and select each font you wish to add.

Help! I'm having problems with fonts on a PCL (LaserJet) printer.

277

8

CHAPTER

Figure 8.3 shows this dialog box. The destination printer and port are displayed in the upper left.

6. Click **A**dd.

7. Enter the destination directory in the Add Fonts dialog box. Click OK.

8. The fonts will be transferred and moved to the left list box. Click E**x**it, OK, and **C**lose to back out from the dialog boxes.

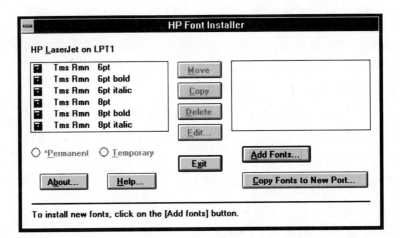

Figure 8.3
Installing soft fonts for a laser printer.

If you are using Windows 3.1, be sure you are using the PCL driver with this version instead of a Windows 3.0 printer driver or a third-party driver not designed for Windows 3.1. Then, if you encounter problems, use the following strategies to solve them.

Help with Font Management

The printer doesn't recognize a particular font.

- [ ] If you are using a cartridge for the font, turn off the printer and verify that the cartridge is plugged in all the way. (Don't check this with the printer on.)

- [ ] If you are using a soft font, make sure that it is properly installed. (See the preceding guidelines for using Control Panel to install soft fonts.)

I have an HP LaserJet and can't install soft fonts.

- [ ] Only the HP LaserJet Series II, HP LaserJet+, HP LaserJet II, LaserJet III, HP LaserJet 2000 and later models support soft fonts. The HP LaserJet does not. Select the right printer from the setup.

I can't print TrueType fonts on my laser printer.

- [ ] You must be using Windows 3.1 or later and have a Windows 3.1 printer driver. Update the printer driver if necessary.

   To update the printer driver, choose Printers from Control Panel and Install. Select the desired printer and then follow the displayed dialog boxes and directions.

Help! I'm having problems with fonts on a PCL (LaserJet) printer.

279

I get the message "PCL PRINTING WARNING: SOFT FONT PAGE LIMIT."

■ The HPPCL driver has a limit of 16 soft fonts per page. Reduce the number of soft fonts on the page.

Special characters print wrong.

■ Printers and the display use different characters sets unless TrueType or ATM is used. Change to TrueType or ATM fonts in the document.

I occasionally get the message "Building font database. Please wait."

The HPPCL driver used with laser printers maintains a font database in memory. This database must be rebuilt each time the printer is set up or when fonts are added or connections changed. The database message will also appear each time you change to the printer from another printer when you print. The message should not appear with each print job. However, if you do see it with each print job, check these possibilities:

■ Check to see if the font summary file (specified in WIN.INI) is in a read-only directory. (See Appendix G for information on viewing and editing WIN.INI.)

■ Make sure that the FontSummary= entry is in WIN.INI and that it points to a valid file and path.

■ Be sure MaxFontSummary=0 is not in WIN.INI. If so, remove the entry.

I can't print a full graphic page or I get an "Error 21" message on my LaserJet printers Series II or earlier.

🔲 You can solve the problem by adding additional memory to the printer. Either you don't have enough memory installed in the printer or the installed memory is not recognized by Windows. Reconfigure the printer by using Control Panel. Select the Printers icon, then select the printer, and choose **S**etup (or **C**onfigure and then **S**etup with Windows 3.0). On this dialog box, make sure that the memory specified is the same as the hardware memory installed in the printer. If there is not enough hardware memory installed, use this same dialog box to print at a lower graphics resolution. In the same dialog box, be sure the paper size is correct. Check the printer documentation or contact the company that sold you the printer for information on adding memory.

I installed some soft fonts to my printer but lost them.

🔲 Soft fonts are installed for a specific printer on a specific port. Examine the WIN.INI file (see Appendix G) to see if the fonts are installed and to see which printer and port they are installed to.

Since the fonts are installed to a specific printer and port, you will find that new fonts are unavailable if you are using the printer on another port, such as printing to a file. To add the fonts to an additional port:

Help! I'm having problems with fonts on a PCL (LaserJet) printer.

1. Select the destination printer and port.

2. As before, return to the Font Installer dialog box.

3. Select the fonts to "transfer" and click **C**opy Fonts to a New Port.

4. Select the destination port and **M**ove.

5. Select **E**nd Copy Fonts to a New Port and back out of the dialog boxes.

   The fonts are not physically moved with these steps. The steps only update the WIN.INI file so that the fonts are recognized on that port.

Secrets and Surprises: If you lost soft fonts, there is an easy and undocumented way to recover them after updating to a new Windows version. The fonts are in a directory on the hard disk, usually C:\PCLFONTS. There is also a PFM file for each font that determines the metrics for the font. The basic strategy is to create a FINSTALL.DIR summary file with your old version of Windows and then use this file to update the new version. Start with the current (older) version of Windows:

1. Use Control Panel and select Printers.
2. From the Setup dialog box, choose **F**onts to display the Font Installer.
3. Hold down the Ctrl and Shift keys and press Enter. A new dialog box appears.
4. Edit the directory and path for the FINSTALL.DIR file, if necessary, and then choose OK.

To reinstall with the new version of Windows:

1. Use Control Panel and select Printers.
2. From the Setup dialog box, choose Fonts to display the Font Installer.
3. Hold down the Ctrl and Shift keys and choose Add Fonts.
4. In the Add Fonts dialog box, enter the drive, directory, and filename for the FINSTALL.DIR file you created.
5. Choose OK.
6. Select the desired fonts and Move.
7. At the prompt for the target directory, specify the current directory of the fonts.

The fonts will appear in the left box and are installed. There is no copy. The procedure simply updates WIN.INI.

I can't print a Windows raster font on my laser printer.

PCL printers cannot print the Windows raster fonts.

Help! I'm having problems with fonts on a PCL (LaserJet) printer.

283

The display doesn't match the printed output. Boxes and lines on the screen print as funny characters on the printout, or the wrong font is printing.

▪ Make sure the correct character set is installed and that you have a display font installed that matches the printer font.

▪ When ATM or TrueType fonts are used in the document, both the printer and screen use the same fonts and the printer and screen should always match.

I can't delete soft fonts by using Control Panel.

▪ Check WIN.INI to see how many soft fonts are installed. Control Panel soft font installer/deinstaller works only if 40 or fewer fonts are installed. If you have more than 40 installed, delete the extra fonts from WIN.INI by using Notepad.

With ATM fonts, Excel prints blank cells instead of characters.

▪ Make sure that the printer resolution is at least 300 dpi. To set the resolution, use Printers from Control Panel and then Setup.

Help! I'm having font problems with a DeskJet printer.

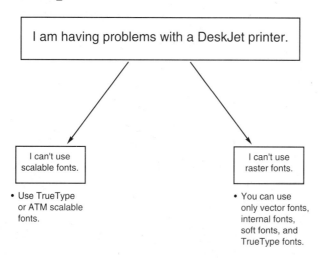

The DeskJet printers offer uneven support of internal landscape and cartridge fonts. If you have a problem, switch to the TrueType fonts, or try one of the following solutions.

I can't use DeskJet scalable fonts.

When Hewlett-Packard introduced the Series III printers, they included a scalable font technology in the printer. The font control was a part of the PCL level 5 language. The basic fonts were from Agfa Corporation's Intellifont format. Intellifont-for-Windows is a free product that creates the matching screen fonts on the fly. A similar product is available for the DeskJet printer. Agfa has a Type Director product for creating fonts from outlines for downloading to a printer. It comes with only 8 outlines and

Help! I'm having font problems with a DeskJet printer.

285

additional fonts are $99 per typeface (family), or $199 for 12. This is an easy (but expensive) way to expand the font selection.

Otherwise, use TrueType or ATM fonts.

I can't print with raster fonts.

The Windows 3.1 DeskJet printer device driver supports Windows vector fonts, DeskJet internal fonts, soft fonts, and Truetype fonts. Printer resolutions are 75, 150, and 300 dpi. Resident fonts are Courier and LinePrinter only. Cartridge can be purchased for other fonts. Soft fonts can be installed with the Font Installer.

Help! I have another printer type, and I'm having font problems.

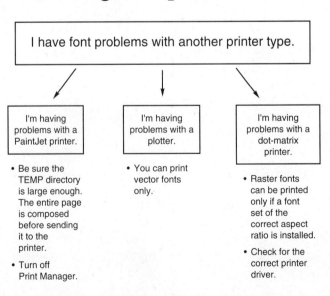

I have font problems with another printer type.

I'm having problems with a PaintJet printer.	I'm having problems with a plotter.	I'm having problems with a dot-matrix printer.
• Be sure the TEMP directory is large enough. The entire page is composed before sending it to the printer. • Turn off Print Manager.	• You can print vector fonts only.	• Raster fonts can be printed only if a font set of the correct aspect ratio is installed. • Check for the correct printer driver.

Help with Font Management

With Windows, you can have problems with the way other types of printers handle fonts. Following is some practical advice for times when you might encounter font and printer problems.

I'm having font problems with my PaintJet.

The Hewlett-Packard PaintJet is a color ink-jet printer. The driver composes a page at a time and then sends it to the printer as a bit map. PaintJet supports PaintJet internal fonts, Windows raster and vector screen fonts, and PaintJet soft fonts. Since the page is composed before sending it to the printer, soft fonts for the PaintJet are not downloadable. They are used internally by the driver. The font itself is never sent to the printer. Windows includes the Courier 12 and Letter Gothic (8- and 12-point) soft fonts for the PaintJet. You can purchase additional fonts from Hewlett-Packard. You can also purchase scalable soft fonts from Hewlett-Packard as the HP Color PrintKit. You can use Type 1 fonts with ATM and the PaintJet.

- Make sure there is adequate space in the TEMP directory. If disk space is inadequate (use the DOS DIR or CHKDSK commands to find out how much room is left), the system may hang with no message.
- Turn off Print Manager.

I'm having font problems with my plotter.

- Plotters are vector devices and can print only vector fonts. You cannot print a bit map to a plotter. For this reason, you can't print raster fonts. Windows' vector screen fonts (Modern, Roman, Script) can be printed on HP plotters. HP Plotters include one internal vector font called Plotter.

Help! I have another printer type, and I'm having font problems.

I'm having font problems with my dot-matrix printer.

☐ Raster fonts can be printed if their resolution and aspect ratio match what is required by the printer. If raster fonts are not in the Fonts dialog box, check the printer resolution and aspect ratio and compare them with Table 8.3 (shown earlier). If there is a match, start Control Panel and select Fonts. Verify that the appropriate font set is installed. The 9-pin printers usually have a 1.67:1 aspect ratio and can therefore support resolutions of 120 x 72 and 240 x 144. The 24-pin printers have resolutions of 120 x 180 at 1:1.5, 180 x 180 at 1:1, and 360 x 180 at 2:1 (Epson, IBM Proprinter). The NEC has a 360 x 360 resolution at 1:1. Some printers support cards or cartridge. These can be used if you have the proper printer driver.

☐ If you still have problems, it could be the printer driver. Make sure the correct driver is installed.

Help! The system hangs after I delete a font.

System hangs after deleting a font.

↓

- Restart Windows and reinstall the screen font.

■ Don't delete a Windows screen font. If you do, exit Windows and restart. Then reinstall the screen font.

Help! I have other font problems.

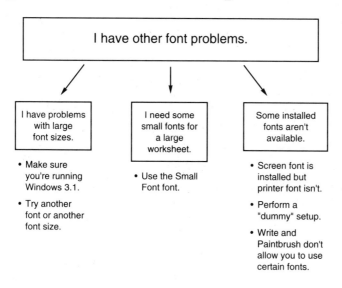

I have other font problems.

I have problems with large font sizes.

- Make sure you're running Windows 3.1.
- Try another font or another font size.

I need some small fonts for a large worksheet.

- Use the Small Font font.

Some installed fonts aren't available.

- Screen font is installed but printer font isn't.
- Perform a "dummy" setup.
- Write and Paintbrush don't allow you to use certain fonts.

I have problems with large font sizes.

■ Make sure you're running Windows 3.1.

■ Windows 3.0 has an anomaly that prohibits using any font file larger than 64K. This is particularly true with SuperPrint, which uses disk-based files. This problem has been recognized by Microsoft, and should be fixed in later versions. Try using another font or font size with a file size of less than 64K.

I need some small fonts (less than 8 points) on the screen for a large worksheet.

☐ Use the Small Font font (select the Small Fonts option in the Fonts dialog box) for sizes under 6 points instead of TrueType. For large font sizes, use scalable fonts (such as TrueType or ATM).

Certain fonts aren't available on the Fonts dialog box, even though they are installed.

☐ The application's font selection dialog box has the option of permitting you to choose from the screen or display fonts. Choosing from the screen fonts (such as Windows' own raster fonts) may mean no corresponding print font is available.

☐ Some applications require you to go through a dummy setup cycle after installing a new font before the font can be used. Choose **P**rint Setup from the **F**ile menu and then **S**etup. Finally, back out and the fonts will be available.

☐ You won't see Windows' raster fonts on the Windows Write selection box (there's no printer font for it), and you won't see Windows' vector fonts with Paintbrush, which is a paint-type program and supports only raster fonts.

9
CHAPTER

HELP WITH PRINTING

This chapter covers printing problems and their solutions. It explains the various error messages that you are likely to encounter if you have a printing problem, typical printer problems, and problems that are specific to certain types of printers.

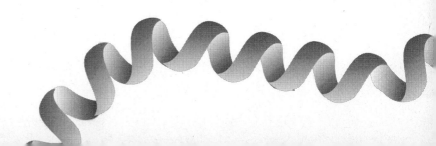

General Information About Printing

The method of printing used by an application running under Windows depends on whether you are using a Windows or a non-Windows application. In both types of programs, you must have some type of printer driver that does the actual printing. The *printer driver* is the software code that directly controls the printer.

When you print from a DOS program running without Windows, you use a printer driver that is part of that program. (DOS) Ventura, (DOS) WordPerfect, and (DOS) Lotus 1-2-3 all have their own printer drivers. Each program has a printer driver installed for every printer that is in use. With a DOS application under Windows, printing is identical to printing from that same application without Windows. If you have an HP LaserJet, each program must have a printer driver for the HP LaserJet. As a result, each software product you purchase must include several disks containing a collection of printer drivers. Moreover, your hard disk becomes cluttered with large application programs, each including its own printer drivers. Finally, each time you purchase a new printer, every application program must be reinstalled for that printer. In addition, many printer-specific fonts must be installed for each application.

Microsoft Windows eliminates this problem by making the printer drivers for your system a part of Windows. You install the drivers for your printers when you install Windows. All drivers are then available for every Windows application that you use. If you purchase a new printer later, you simply add the driver for that printer to Windows by using the Printers option of Control Panel. Once this is done, the new printer is available to every Windows application. All of the fonts that you install for the printer are available for all Windows applications.

Note: Some Windows application programs have their own printer driver.

When you make a print request from a Windows application (by using **F**ile **P**rint), the application loads the Print Manager and sends the printer output to this program. Print Manager automatically loads as a minimized program; that is, it runs in the background. Print Manager creates a print queue of all print requests sent to it, printing them in order as you continue with other work.

Note: Since Windows and DOS programs use different methods of printing, don't try to mix print requests. Avoid multitasking Windows and DOS programs when printing.

Printers are attached to the computer by means of a port. For the fastest printing, you should use a parallel port. The printer should be located within 25 feet of the computer unless a hardware buffer is used.

Installing a Printer with Windows

Printers are generally installed by using the Printers option of Control Panel. For Windows 3.1, click **A**dd>> on the first screen, as shown in Figure 9.1. Select the printer to install from

the List of Printers, as shown in Figure 9.2, and then click Install. Insert the diskette with the driver and follow the directions. After you install the printer, use Connect on the Printers dialog box to assign the proper port to the printer.

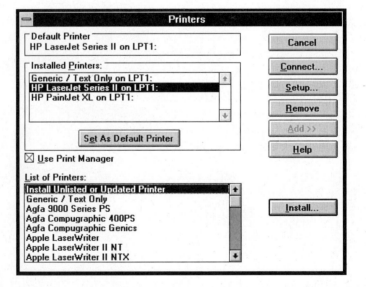

Figure 9.1
Starting the install.

Figure 9.2
Choosing the printer to install.

You must have a software driver for the printer. If you do not have the correct driver on the Windows installation disks, you need to obtain a driver from the printer manufacturer or from a third party (such as downloaded from CompuServe).

If you use both PostScript and non-PostScript printers, install the PostScript printer to LPT2 and the non-PostScript printer to LPT1. This makes it easy to switch between them in application programs.

Help! I get a message while printing.

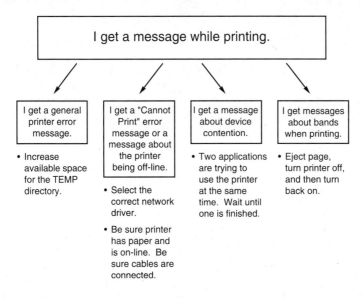

Normally, printer problems will show up when you're actually trying to print. The following messages are ones that may appear at such times. They alert you that there is a printing problem. Try the procedures suggested here to fix the problem.

I get a "general printer error" message when I try to print.

Windows requires some disk space for temporary files when printing, even if the Print Manager is not being used. This space is allocated in the \TEMP directory. With some programs (such as PageMaker), this temporary file can be megabytes in size when the program is printing graphics, particularly color graphics. Locate a drive with plenty of disk space, create a \TEMP directory on it, and use the DOS **SET TEMP** command to set the temporary directory to this new path. Restart Windows and try to print the document again. If this works, edit the TEMP parameter in the AUTOEXEC.BAT file as necessary (see Appendix G).

When trying to print, I get a "Cannot Print" error message or a message that the printer is off-line or not selected.

Figure 9.3 illustrates this kind of message. Try the following procedures to fix the problem.

Figure 9.3

The printer is off-line and cannot print.

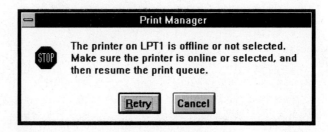

Help with Printing

- If on a network, make sure that you are using the correct Windows network driver. Check with the network administrator to identify the current driver in use.

- Be sure the printer is on-line, the printer is not out of paper, and the printer is not jammed. The printer Ready light should be on. The problem can also be caused by faulty cabling, an incompatible printer device, or a defective hardware buffer or one that isn't installed properly. If using a hardware buffer, try printing without it.

I get a message about device contention or device conflict when I try to print.

- When printing from Windows applications, Windows uses its own printer drivers and there is no conflict or contention. When DOS applications are being run under Windows, the DOS program will use its own printer driver. There may be some conflict, since a DOS and a Windows application program cannot both use the printer at the same time. In the 386 enhanced mode, you do have some control over the contention by using the 386 Enhanced option of Control Panel. In most cases, it is simply a matter of waiting until one program is through with the printer and then trying again.

I get messages about "bands" while I'm printing.

- Graphics are often printed on a laser printer by means of a banding process in which only part of the page at a time is sent to the queue. There is nothing wrong with this kind of displayed message. Terminating a graphic print may mean that part of the page is already printed or in the memory of the printer. To clear the printer with graphic printing, you may have to eject a page or turn the printer off and then back on.

Help! I have a general printer problem.

As a general strategy, begin addressing printer problems by exiting Windows. Then try to print from a non-Windows DOS program or print directly from DOS (using `DIR > LPT1`). If that works, you know the printer is all right. Read on for other ideas about what could be wrong and how to solve the problem. If you can't print under DOS, the problem is in the printer system (bad cable, printer off, paper out, wrong port connection, etc.). Make sure that the printer is correctly connected and on-line. When using a serial printer, make sure that the serial port is set correctly. Under DOS, use the MODE command to set the port (see your DOS manual).

For printers attached to serial ports, the correct port must be selected. The port must be configured for the correct speed, data bits, and parity. Be sure there is no interrupt conflict; no other device should be using the same interrupt. The interrupt is set by a switch on the various adapter cards. Serial ports normally use interrupt 3 or 4 (see Appendix C).

For printing to a network printer, you must be connected to the network printer. Network printers can use parallel ports only.

Help with Printing

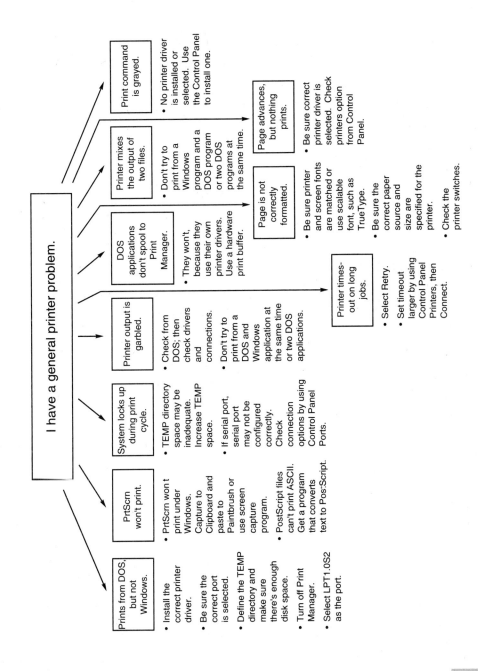

I have a general printer problem.

Prints from DOS, but not Windows.
- Install the correct printer driver.
- Be sure the correct port is selected.
- Define the TEMP directory and make sure there's enough disk space.
- Turn off Print Manager.
- Select LPT1.OS2 as the port.

PrtScrn won't print.
- PrtScrn won't print under Windows. Capture to Clipboard and paste to Paintbrush or use screen capture program.
- PostScript files can't print ASCII. Get a program that converts text to PostScript.

System locks up during print cycle.
- TEMP directory space may be inadequate. Increase TEMP space.
- If serial port, serial port may not be configured correctly. Check connection options by using Control Panel Ports.

Printer output is garbled.
- Check from DOS; then check drivers and connections.
- Don't try to print from a DOS and Windows application at the same time or two DOS applications.

DOS applications don't spool to Print Manager.
- They won't, because they use their own printer drivers. Use a hardware print buffer.

Printer mixes the output of two files.
- Don't try to print from a Windows program and a DOS program or two DOS programs at the same time.

Print command is grayed.
- No printer driver is installed or selected. Use the Control Panel to install one.

Printer times-out on long jobs.
- Select Retry.
- Set timeout larger by using Control Panel Printers, then Connect.

Page is not correctly formatted.
- Be sure printer and screen fonts are matched or use scalable font, such as TrueType.
- Be sure the correct paper source and size are specified for the printer.
- Check the printer switches.

Page advances, but nothing prints.
- Be sure correct printer driver is selected. Check printers option from Control Panel.

assumes that the printer is on when you boot the computer and that it remains on. If you turn the printer off and back on, the header file must be downloaded to the printer again. To set up the header file for downloading at bootup, follow these steps:

1. Create the header file by choosing Control Panel Printers, then **S**etup and **O**ptions. Choose **S**end Header on the dialog box, as shown in Figure 9.4.

2. Select the **D**ownload button on the next dialog box and click OK.

3. Enter the filename you wish to use on the next dialog box and click OK. Assume the name PSHEAD.HDR.

Figure 9.4

Setting up to download a PostScript header.

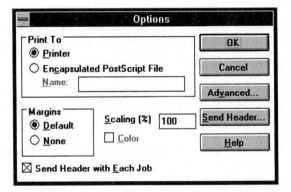

4. Reinstall the printer by selecting the printer and choosing **S**etup, **O**ptions, and Send Header with **E**ach Job.

5. Modify the AUTOEXEC.BAT file to include the line:

```
COPY PSHEAD.HDR LPT1
```

Help with Printing

Help! I can't print to a file.

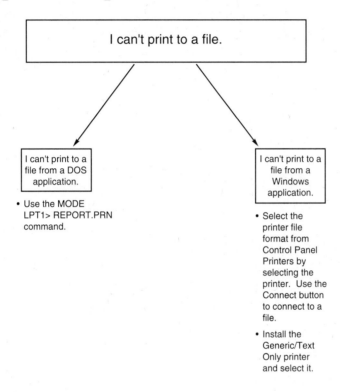

Printing to a file is useful at times for a variety of purposes. Most word processors (such as Word for Windows) save documents in a special format. Suppose you need to save a document in simple ASCII for printing with Notepad or for sending to someone on a BBS. You can do so by printing the document to a file with Windows' generic ASCII printer. (Another way to do this is to copy and paste the text through the Clipboard. Formatting is lost in the Clipboard, however.)

Help! I can't print to a file.

307

In another application, you might be doing electronic publishing and wish to deliver a document in electronic form to a commerical printing service. Check with the printing service first, but many of these companies can do high quality printing if you give them the document in electronic PostScript form. To do this, you must print the document to a file using the PostScript printer driver. Be sure that it is installed (even if you don't have a PostScript printer) and select the PostScript printer for printing. Then print the document to a file. Send the file to the printing service electronically by using a modem or by delivering it on disk. For large files, compress them first or break them down into multiple documents. Some electronic publishers use a Bernoulli disk to deliver large documents to a publisher.

Read on for solutions to problems with printing to a file.

I can't print to a file from a DOS application.

DOS applications have their own printer driver. To print to a file from a DOS application under Windows, you must first redirect the output to a file by using the MODE command:

```
MODE LPT1:> REPORT.PRN
```

Select the proper printer type within the application and then select to print. The output will be redirected to a file.

I can't print to a file from a Windows application.

■ With Windows applications, there are three methods of printing to a file. In any case, be sure you have selected the printer type first. To select the printer, use the Print Setup option of the File menu. If you are creating a PostScript file, for example, select the PostScript printer. You may need to install the printer driver first, even if you don't have the hardware. For example, you may not have a PostScript printer, but you plan to deliver an electronic document to a printing service as a PostScript file. You then need to install the PostScript driver. Once the printer driver in installed, you can print to a file. In the Control Panel's Printers Configure dialog box, choose the printer and, when connecting, select the FILE: option. Now if you try to print the file, you will get a dialog box. Enter the filename to use and click OK.

■ For generic print files (no format characters), install the Generic/Text Only printer and select this printer. Use Connect, as before, to select the FILE: printing option. If this print driver is not used for anything else, you may wish to leave it hooked to a file. That way, you can select it from the application's File menu by using Print Setup.

Help! I can't print to a file.

309

Caution: Don't try to print justified text with the generic printer.

If you capture the output to a file by using the generic print driver, you may wish to print it later. To print this data, use the DOS COPY command. For example, if the file is OUTPUT.PRN, use this command at the DOS prompt:

```
COPY OUTPUT.PRN LPT1: /b
```

The /b switch forces the entire file to print. Without this switch, printing would stop at the first Ctrl+Z in the file.

Help! I have problems with a PCL (LaserJet) printer.

I have problems with a PCL (LaserJet) printer.

I have problems with a PostScript cartridge in the printer.

- Be sure you have installed the driver for that cartridge. The drivers should be compatible with your Windows version.

The printed image doesn't match the displayed image.

- Be sure you are using matching screen and printer font files, or use TrueType fonts.

I lost my soft fonts when I changed the printer to another port.

- Soft fonts are installed to a particular printer and port. Edit the WIN.INI file to move the fonts to the new port.

I received an "Error 20" message on the printer.

- Too many fonts were downloaded. Use fewer fonts or add more memory to the printer.

I can't print large graphics or the printer times-out.

- Increase the Transmission Retry Time.

I changed printer font cartridges in the printer, but the new fonts are not available.

- Be sure the cartridge is fully seated (with printer off).
- Use Printers option of Control Panel, select the printer, and use Setup. Define cartridges in use.
- Check WIN.INI and remove excess soft fonts.

Driver always reports 75 dpi on the Options dialog box and scalable fonts don't print.

- Add the line prtresfac=0 in the [<printer>,<port>] section of WIN.INI.

Edge of paper doesn't print or printer overlaps to the next page.

- Reset the margins. Laser printers must have at least a 1/4" margin.

Help! I have problems with a PCL (LaserJet) printer.

311

With Windows 3.1, make sure that you are using the LaserJet generic printer driver provided with Windows instead of a Windows 3.0 printer driver. If using a third-party printer driver, make sure that it is Windows 3.1 compatible.

Use Control Panel, select Printers, and then highlight the printer name. Check to see that the connection options are correct. You can use **C**onnect to change these. Check the printer options by choosing **S**etup. The dialog box here will vary with the printer. Figure 9.5 shows the dialog box for a Hewlett-Packard Series II LaserJet. Verify that the memory, orientation, and cartridge settings are correct.

Figure 9.5

Checking the options.

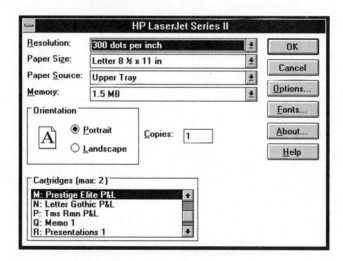

Help with Printing

I'm having trouble with a PostScript cartridge in a printer.

☐ If you are using a PostScript cartridge with a LaserJet printer, you will need the PostScript driver for that cartridge. It should be installed like any other driver by using the procedures described at the beginning of this section. If you are using Windows 3.1, the driver should be compatible with that version.

The printed image doesn't match the displayed image on-screen (line breaks, etc.).

☐ With certain printer fonts (such as a cartridge font with a LaserJet), there is no corresponding screen font file. Windows does the best it can, but you won't get WYSIWYG. Be sure that both the screen and the device fonts are installed if you are using soft fonts. Try using TrueType or ATM scalable fonts.

I changed printer font cartridges in my HP LaserJet printer, but the new fonts are not available.

☐ Make sure the new cartridges are firmly seated (do this with the printer off).

☐ Use the Printers option of Control Panel, select the printer, and get the Setup dialog box. Then select the cartridges. Choose OK.

Help! I have problems with a PCL (LaserJet) printer.

313

You may have too many soft fonts. Most drivers recognize a maximum of about 250. The size of the WIN.INI file also limits the number, since this file has a maximum size of 64K. Check WIN.INI, and delete extra soft font lines, if necessary (see Appendix G).

I changed my printer to a different port, and the soft fonts disappeared.

Soft fonts are installed to a particular device and port. Use the soft font installer and copy the soft fonts to a different port or edit the WIN.INI file (see Appendix G).

The current driver for a LaserJet always reports 75 dpi, and scalable fonts don't print.

Add the line `prtresfac=0` in the [<printer>,<port>] section of WIN.INI (see Appendix G).

I received an "Error 20" message on a Hewlett-Packard LaserJet printer when printing.

You downloaded too many fonts or you printed a graphic and ran out of printer memory. Add more memory to the printer or use fewer fonts. Check with the printer manufacturer.

The edge of the printed page won't print, or I get overlapping with the first lines of the page.

■ Most laser printers will not print within the ¼-inch margin of the page. Change the margins of the document to avoid printing in this area.

I can't print large graphic images, or the printer times-out when printing.

■ Use the Printers option of Control Panel. Choose **C**onnect and increase the Transmission Retry time in the Printers Configure dialog box.

Help! I'm having trouble with a PostScript printer.

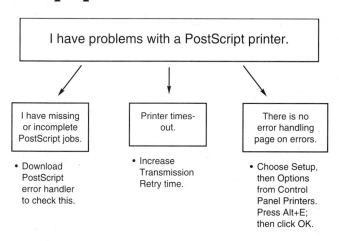

Help! I'm having trouble with a PostScript printer.

315

With Windows 3.1, be sure you are using the PostScript printer driver provided with Windows instead of a Windows 3.0 printer driver. If using a third-party printer driver, be sure it is Windows 3.1 compatible. Then, use the following trouble-shooting techniques.

I have missing or incomplete PostScript jobs.

Download the PostScript error handler to check this, as follows:

1. Choose Printers from the Control Panel. Then choose the PostScript driver and **S**etup.

2. Select **O**ptions on the dialog box.

3. Press Alt+E to get the Error Handler dialog box (this is undocumented).

4. Choose to send the Error Handler to the printer.

5. Repeat the print request that caused the problem. Check for a PostScript error message.

The printer times-out when printing.

Use the Printers option of Control Panel. Select **C**onnect and increase the Transmission Retry time in the Printers Configure dialog box as described in the preceding section.

There's no error-handling page on errors.

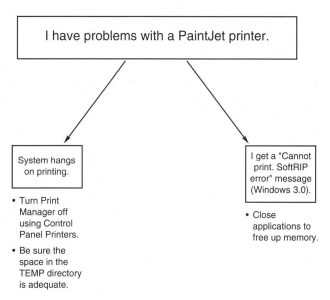 Choose Printers from Control Panel and select **S**etup and **O**ptions. Press Alt+E and choose to send Error Handler to the printer.

Help! I have problems with a PaintJet printer.

```
┌─────────────────────────────────────────────┐
│   I have problems with a PaintJet printer.   │
└─────────────────────────────────────────────┘
              ↙                      ↘
┌──────────────────┐      ┌──────────────────────┐
│  System hangs    │      │ I get a "Cannot      │
│  on printing.    │      │ print. SoftRIP       │
└──────────────────┘      │ error" message       │
                          │ (Windows 3.0).       │
                          └──────────────────────┘
• Turn Print
  Manager off             • Close
  using Control             applications to
  Panel Printers.           free up memory.

• Be sure the
  space in the
  TEMP directory
  is adequate.
```

The PaintJet driver creates the entire bit-mapped page before printing. Turn off the Print Manager for this printer so that queue space is minimized. Make sure that the \TEMP directory has enough space (using the DOS DIR command and then deleting excess files as necessary), since this directory is used

Help! I have problems with a PaintJet printer.

317

even with the Print Manager off. For additional safety, save the file before printing. Use the following techniqes when problems occur.

The system hangs on printing.

- Turn off the Print Manager.
- Be sure that the \TEMP directory has enough megabytes of space to save the image.

I get the message "Cannot print. SoftRIP error."

- Close some windows and remove objects to free up memory (system resource memory area). This problem can happen when you are using a printer that forms a bit map in memory before sending the page to the printer, as with the Hewlett-Packard PaintJet. This problem is solved in Windows 3.1.

Help! I have trouble controlling the queue.

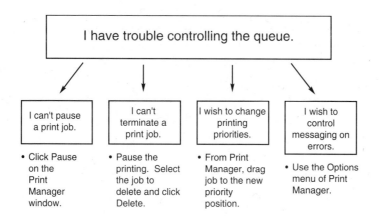

The printing queue is controlled from the Print Manager. You can double-click the Print Manager icon to make the Print Manager active in the foreground, as shown in Figure 9.6.

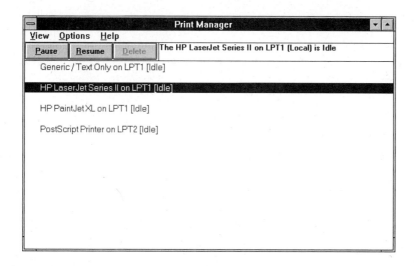

The work area shows each installed printer, its connection, the printer status, any active print jobs in the queue for

that printer, and the status of each job. Each print job is identified by the program that initiated the print and by the status of the file. Print Manager prints from the top down. The topmost job is the one currently printing. At the top right of the window, a message box displays the current status of the Print Manager. To the left of the message box are three buttons to control the printing. As with most applications, there is also a menu bar with three options: **V**iew, **O**ptions, and **H**elp.

Tip: You can also load the Print Manager manually by selecting the Print Manager icon in the Program Manager's Main group window. This will make the Print Manager active immediately.

Secrets and Surprises: As another trick, you can batch print jobs by selecting the Print Manager on the Main group window and using **P**ause to suspend the printing. Then load the queue. Once you are ready to start the printing, select **R**esume from the Queue menu.

How do I pause a print job?

Double-click the Print Manager icon to make the Print Manager active. Click **P**ause to stop the printing. To continue, press **R**esume.

Note: If you are using an external hardware buffer, pausing the printer will not stop the printer until the external buffer is cleared.

How do I terminate a print job?

Double-click the Print Manager icon to make the Print Manager active. Click **P**ause to stop the printing. Select the print job to stop and click **D**elete.

Secrets and Surprises: If the printer jams, your first reaction is probably to run to the printer. The proper reaction is to terminate or pause the print job—then run to the printer.

How do I change printing priorities?

To change printing priorities, make the Print Manager active by double-clicking the Print Manager icon. The Print Manager program will then display an active window. Drag the queued file that you wish to change to the new position in the queue. Alternatively, use the direction keys to select the file to change, then hold down Ctrl, and move the file to the new position.

How can I control the messaging on errors?

The second section of Print Manager's **O**ptions menu defines how the Print Manager's messages are displayed. You can select any of three modes: **A**lert Always, **F**lash if Inactive, and **I**gnore if Inactive. Table 9.1 describes the modes.

Table 9.1

Modes for Print Manager's Messages

Mode	Action
Alert Always	Always display messages in a dialog box.
Flash if Inactive	If Print Manager is inactive, flash icon. User must then make the Print Manager active to read the message. This is the default mode.
Ignore if Inactive	If Print Manager is inactive, ignore error messages.

HELP WITH DOS APPLICATIONS

This chapter covers problems that occur when you are using
Windows with DOS applications. These include installation
and startup problems, error messages, problems when switching between applications, PIF files, display problems when a
DOS application is running, and memory problems.

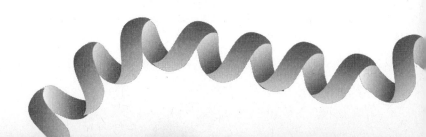

10

General Information About DOS Applications

DOS applications would seem, at first, to be totally hostile or incompatible with the Windows environment. When a DOS application runs, it takes total control of the computer. DOS gives control of the computer resources to the DOS application (memory, printer, CPU, etc.). When the program terminates, a part of DOS is reloaded and control is returned to DOS. If the program crashes, DOS is never reloaded and you must reboot. DOS applications are totally unaware of Windows presence. DOS programs use memory in a physical way, taking what they need and using it as they wish. DOS programs have their own video and printer drivers, never caring that these drivers exist redundantly in Windows and could be used from it.

Given this type of operation, it is surprising that Microsoft or anyone could get DOS programs and Window applications to work together in any type of multitasking environment. Yet Windows can run a DOS application and Windows applications together in the standard mode, and can even multitask DOS applications in the 386 enhanced mode.

To do this, Windows makes certain assumptions about how the DOS application behaves: how it uses memory and how it manages the video. You can change these assumptions for a DOS program through the use of a PIF file.

A *PIF file* describes the name and location of a DOS program, its memory requirements, and the way that certain system resources are used. A PIF file is not needed for a Windows application, nor can you use one with a Windows application. PIF files are used only for DOS applications. The PIF file often has the same filename as the program but has a file extension of PIF. For example, if the program filename is

WP.EXE, the PIF filename is WP.PIF. In some cases, you may wish to have multiple PIF files for the same program, each PIF file having a different name and each starting the application in a different way. You can start a DOS program by selecting its PIF file from File Manager or by clicking an icon in Program Manager installed to the PIF file.

Microsoft Windows provides you with a collection of PIF files for many popular commercial programs. These are generally automatically installed for the programs you have when you set up Windows. The programs will appear as icons in the Applications group of Program Manager. Generally, you will want to keep the PIF files you use in the directory containing the application program files.

You will also find that many application products that you purchase contain their own PIF files. Using the PIF Editor provided with Windows, you can modify existing PIF files or create new ones.

Caution: Although most DOS programs can run under Windows, there are certain programs that should not be run this way. In general, you should avoid running under Windows any programs that use certain special physical areas of memory, that depend on specific aspects of system timing, or that access specific physical areas of the disk. Examples of programs that shouldn't be run include the DOS CHKDSK program, compression utilities, and DOS backup programs. Also, you will find that some programs that use certain undocumented DOS features will not run under Windows. DOS 5 adds protection if you try to run CHKDSK, but a better rule is to avoid running such programs under Windows.

Why should I use Windows with a DOS program?

There are two basic reasons for using Windows with a DOS program: Clipboard editing and fast context switching. DOS applications running in Windows can access the Clipboard for transferring data between applications. In the standard mode, Clipboard usage is very limited (full-screen captures only), but in the 386 enhanced mode true cuts and pastes are possible.

Context switching is the ability to move quickly between applications. With the Windows environment, you can have several applications (both Windows and non-Windows) in memory at once. Switching between them is a matter of only a few keystrokes.

Using Windows also has some disadvantages. DOS applications run slower under Windows, particularly when placed in a window. In some cases, the only way to get sufficient speed is to run the application from a DOS prompt within Windows or to exit Windows. You can often get enough speed, however, by editing the PIF file for faster DOS execution. The default PIFs assume certain worst-case conditions.

When you run a DOS application under Windows, you will have better control if you create a PIF file for the application. You can obtain or create the PIF files in any one of five ways:

- A collection of PIF files for many popular programs comes with Windows. When you install Windows, these files are put in the Windows directory.

- Commercial programs often include a PIF file for the corresponding program. For example, if you purchase Microsoft Word version 5.5 (or update an earlier version),

Help with DOS Applications

the installation disks include a new WORD.PIF file that should be copied to the WORD directory. (The next section shows how you can create or edit your own PIF files.)

- You can create a PIF file for a DOS application by using the Windows Setup program.

- You can use Program Manager to create a PIF file when you add a DOS application to a group.

- You can use the PIF Editor included with Windows to create a PIF file.

How do I create or edit a PIF file with the PIF Editor?

To create a PIF file for an application, start the PIF Editor from the Main group of Program Manager. The Editor, shown in Figure 10.1, can be used to set the PIF parameters for either the standard mode or the 386 enhanced mode. The PIF parameter window that is displayed is the one for the current mode. If you are defining parameters for an alternative mode, use the Mode menu to select that mode. Fill in the window.

Many parameters (such as the program filename) are the same for both the real/standard and 386 enhanced modes; that is, if you enter them in one mode they will also be the same for the alternative mode. Other values, such as the **O**ptional Parameters setting, will vary with mode. Enter any desired startup options for the program in the **O**ptional Parameters area of the PIF dialog box. For example, you can enter /**l** with Microsoft Word to start Word with the last document. Note that if you start the program with the **R**un command on the **F**ile menu in Program Manager, any parameters specified in that dialog box will override those in the PIF file.

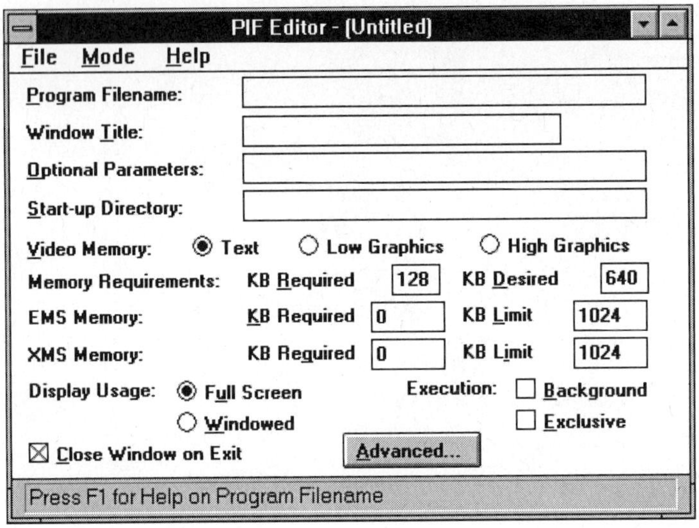

Figure 10.1

*Editing the PIF
file with the
PIF Editor.*

```
┌─────────────────────────────────────────────────────────┐
│ ─              PIF Editor - (Untitled)              ▼ ▲  │
│  File   Mode   Help                                        │
│                                                            │
│  Program Filename:   [                              ]     │
│  Window Title:       [                            ]       │
│  Optional Parameters: [                             ]     │
│  Start-up Directory:  [                             ]     │
│                                                            │
│  Video Memory:    ● Text   ○ Low Graphics   ○ High Graphics│
│  Memory Requirements:   KB Required [128]  KB Desired [640]│
│  EMS Memory:       KB Required [0]    KB Limit  [1024]     │
│  XMS Memory:       KB Required [0]    KB Limit  [1024]     │
│  Display Usage:  ● Full Screen    Execution: ☐ Background  │
│                  ○ Windowed                  ☐ Exclusive   │
│  ☒ Close Window on Exit      [ Advanced... ]              │
│ Press F1 for Help on Program Filename                      │
└─────────────────────────────────────────────────────────┘
```

Once you've defined the parameters, save the file by using
the Save **A**s option of the **F**ile menu. Terminate the Editor
either by double-clicking the Control-menu box icon, by selecting **C**lose from the Control menu, or by using Alt+F4.

Should the PIF Exclusive and Background options be on or off?

Normally you should leave **B**ackground turned off unless you
are installing a communications program or using a program
that requires background processing, such as WordPerfect
Office. Turning off **B**ackground keeps Windows' speed up
and reduces memory requirements. If you need background
processing on a temporary basis, run the application in a
window (Alt+Enter if necessary), open the Control menu

(Alt+Spacebar), and set the background processing from the Settings menu.

In most cases, **E**xclusive should be left off. Run **E**xclusive applications full-screen because in this mode Windows will release the resources that it needs for running other programs.

How do I create a PIF file with the Setup program?

When you run Windows Setup from the Main group, you can choose to install applications from it. Select **S**et Up Applications from the **O**ptions menu. From the dialog box, choose Search for Applications or Ask You to Specify an Application. Choose the drive to search. You can also choose to select all drives. Windows will search for the available applications. In the next Setup Applications window, highlight each desired application and click **A**dd>> for each. This will move the name to the right list box. When all the desired applications have been selected, click OK. Windows will create a PIF file for each DOS program that you have selected to install.

How do I create the PIF file with Program Manager?

When you define a new program item for a DOS application, the Program Manager tries to find a corresponding PIF file to use. If it finds one, they are set up to run together. If this fails, the Program Manager makes some assumptions from an internal table and then displays a dialog box for verification. If you choose Yes on this dialog box, Windows creates the PIF file. If Windows has no information in its internal table for the application, Windows will use the default _DEFAULT.PIF file.

Why should I use Windows with a DOS program?

Will PIF files from an earlier version of Windows work with Windows 3.1?

PIF files created for earlier versions of Windows will probably work in Windows 3.1. Load the files into the PIF Editor and then resave them so that they will be in the new PIF format.

What's the advantage of using the 386 enhanced mode with DOS applications instead of standard mode?

Here are some of the new features available from the PIF file in the 386 enhanced mode:

- You can control, or limit, the amount of memory used by the DOS application.

- You can run the DOS application in a window.

- You can allocate extended memory to an application if it supports the DPMI standard. You can control the amount of extended memory allocated.

- You can control application priority and the way that the processor is shared between applications.

- Windows can simulate expanded memory for the application, and you can control how much expanded memory is allocated.

- You can control whether or not the application uses the high memory area (HMA).

Running DOS Programs Under Windows

The following is a list of programs and commands that should not be used with Windows because you risk losing data, if not the entire disk contents. However, if you exit Windows before running utilities, disk optimizers, and backup software, the software will run fine. Do not run them from an icon in Windows.

- Third-party disk-caching programs, unless specifically designed to work with the version of Windows you are using.

- Hard-disk optimizing programs that are non-Windows (DOS). Examples include The (DOS) Norton Utilities, Speed Disk, Steve Gibson's Sprinrite II, (DOS) PC Tools Compress, and Golden Bow Systems Vopt.

- Hard-disk test and repair programs such as Mace Utilities REMEDY.

- DOS-based disk backup utilities such as Fastback Plus, COREfast, or SYTOS software, unless specifically designed for Windows.

- The DOS FORMAT command (when formatting a hard disk).

- The DOS CHKDSK, APPEND, JOIN, and SUBST commands.

Here are some general rules:

1. Use caution when you are installing disk-caching programs of any type, except for the disk-caching program supplied with Windows. Some products may work with your version of Windows 3 but not as effectively as they would otherwise, some may work perfectly, and some can destroy your disk contents. Check with the manufacturer.

2. Do not run (DOS) PC Tools Compress and other disk-optimizing programs under Windows.

3. Do not run any program under Windows that physically modifies the disk directly unless specifically designed as a Windows application. This includes DOS undeletion or disk repair programs.

4. Do not run disk backup utilities under Windows unless the backup utility is a Windows application.

Besides the programs already mentioned, there are still other programs that you would be wise to avoid. These programs will not do any damage to your disk, but they may hang up, not work as they should, or not run at all. These programs fall into the following categories:

- Programs that are simply too large to run under Windows. So much of Windows would be swapped out that there would be no advantage in using Windows.

- Programs that use special programming tricks (nonstandard DOS conventions) incompatible with Windows.

- Some memory-resident programs. Certain of these programs cannot run with Windows. The memory-resident concept is really not a DOS standard, and how each product interfaces with DOS varies in quality.

- With Windows 3.1, you can no longer run Windows applications designed for Windows 2.x or earlier.

Help! I'm having trouble installing a DOS application.

I'm having trouble installing a DOS application.

- Install like any DOS application; then create the PIF file and place it in the program's directory.

DOS applications can be installed to run under Windows, and will even run in a window with Windows 3.1 in the 386 enhanced mode.

Install DOS applications in the same way you would install them without Windows. Follow the directions that came with the DOS program. Then follow these three additional steps:

1. Add the program's PIF file to the directory with the application's program files. Use the PIF file with Windows, use the one with the DOS program, or create your own.

2. Put the application subdirectory name in the PATH name of the AUTOEXEC.BAT file (see Appendix G).

3. Edit the PIF file to indicate the subdirectory of the application program.

4. Assign an icon to the program in Program Manager.

Help! I'm having trouble installing a DOS application.

333

Help! I'm having trouble starting a DOS application under Windows.

I have trouble starting a DOS application under Windows.

I get an error message on starting that there isn't enough memory.

- Edit the Memory Requirements: KB Required in the PIF file.

I can't start a DOS program with a data file or parameters.

- Edit the Optional Parameters field of the PIF file to specify the data file or parameters.
- Use the data filename for Program Filename in the PIF file.

I can't start the program in a particular directory.

- Specify the directory as the Start-up Directory in the PIF dialog box.

I can't start a DOS application from a batch file.

- Define a BAT file that starts the program. Then specify it as the command in the PIF file.

An application doesn't load when I click the PIF file in File Manager.

- Be sure the WIN.INI file identifies the PIF extension for the programs= parameter.

I get a message about insufficient memory.

- Close applications, clear unused icons, and edit PIF file.
- Add memory to your system.
- Edit the KB Required in the PIF file and make other adjustments.

I get an "incorrect system version" error message on starting the program.

- The grabber and video display driver have mismatched versions. Check SYSTEM.INI.

DOS applications can be started with a mouse or from the keyboard in the same way that you start a Windows application. Before starting, you will probably want to add the application to one of the Program Manager's group windows. Use the **File** **N**ew command of Program Manager to do this.

If the DOS program won't start, make sure that the PIF file is correct. If you try to load a DOS application for which there is no PIF file, Windows will try to run the program by using the _DEFAULT.PIF file. If the PIF file is included with Windows or the application, you can use that file when installing the application to Windows. If not, create the file.

When I start the application, I get an error message that there's not enough memory to load.

☐ Adjust the Memory Requirements: KB **R**equired in the PIF file. (See Figure 10.1 shown earlier and also see the earlier section on creating and editing PIF files.) The default 128K is too low for many DOS applications, particularly if many Windows applications are loaded at the same time. Adjust it higher. See the manual for the amount of memory the application uses.

Help! I'm having trouble starting a DOS application under Windows.

335

I can't start a DOS program with a data file.

◻ In the **O**ptional Parameters area of the dialog box, you can specify a data file to be opened when the program starts. Specify the full path for the data file, and include the extension. For example, if you specify CH1.DOC as the data file for Microsoft Word, the PIF Editor will start Word with CH1.DOC open.

◻ Another alternative is to use the data filename for **P**rogram Filename in the PIF file. Then use the File **A**ssociate command of File Manager to associate the file extension with that program name. For example, you could enter CHAP1.DOC for **P**rogram Filename and then use the **A**ssociate command to associate all DOC files with Microsoft Word. Figure 10.2 shows the Associate dialog box.

Figure 10.2
Using the Associate command.

Secrets and Surprises: If you start the application by specifying the PIF file from a File **R**un command, any parameters entered in the Run dialog box will override those specified in the PIF file.

At startup, I get a message about "insufficient memory to run the application."

■ Close other applications. Run full-screen instead of in a window (use Alt+Enter to switch). Minimize Windows applications to icons. Clear or save the Clipboard contents. Set the wallpaper to <None> (using Control Panel Desktop).

■ Add memory to your system.

■ Edit the PIF file with the PIF Editor (see the instructions given earlier in this chapter). Increase the Memory Requirements: KB **R**equired that is specified in the PIF file. In standard mode, select Prevent Program S**w**itch. With this on, you will have to quit the application to return to Windows. You can also turn on No Screen E**x**change. Reduce the **V**ideo Mode. With 386 enhanced options, set Display Usage to F**u**ll Screen, Execution to **E**xclusive, and **V**ideo Memory to as low a mode as possible.

How can I start the DOS program in a particular directory?

■ Specify the directory as the **S**tart-up Directory in the PIF dialog box. (See the section earlier in this chapter on creating and editing PIF files.) Use this entry to define the initial directory that the program should be in when starting. If the program needs overlay or configuration files, use this option to specify the directory for those files.

Help! I'm having trouble starting a DOS application under Windows.

337

> **Note:** When no directory is specified, the default directory is that of the PIF file if the program is started from selecting its PIF file. If the program is started from an EXE, COM, or BAT file (even if the PIF exists), the PIF file is still used but the default directory is that of the EXE, COM, or BAT file. This holds true for all methods of starting DOS applications under Windows.

When working with a collection of data files in a directory (for example, a collection of DOC files with Word), enter the data path here and be sure that the program can be started from a path entry in the AUTOEXEC.BAT file. Using this method, you can assign an icon for each directory for which you use an application.

When I start a DOS application in Windows, I get an error message about incorrect system version.

The virtual display driver and the grabber have mismatched versions. Both are defined in the SYSTEM.INI file (see Appendix G). The grabber is defined in the [boot] section and the virtual display driver in the [386enh] section. If the grabber file is part of the video driver file, the first character of the driver filename will be an asterisk. Reload the video driver.

I can't start a DOS application under Windows from a batch file.

When launching a batch file from Windows, always use a PIF file. Although the batch file may launch a series of programs, the settings should match the largest and most video-intensive application started. For example, if the batch file starts a mouse program (MOUSE.COM) and Lotus 1-2-3, the settings should be those for Lotus 1-2-3. Also, you must realize that you will need to reserve more memory than you would ordinarily use for the largest program because it is launched from the batch program and, in this example, both the mouse driver and Lotus 1-2-3 will be in memory.

■ You can start programs from batch files by defining a PIF file (see the section earlier in this chapter on creating and editing a PIF file) that starts the BAT file and by creating an icon for the PIF file in Program Manager. Be sure to include the BAT extension in the **P**rogram Filename line. Remember that the PIF file for a batch file must define enough memory for both the program and the batch file. PIF files can be used to control the execution of EXE, COM, and BAT files. When a PIF file is used to launch a batch file in the 386 enhanced mode, the batch file starts a virtual machine. You must use the PIF to set the parameters for that virtual machine instead of those for the DOS application started with the batch file. For example, if the batch file loads the mouse driver and Microsoft Word, you must use the PIF file to allocate memory for both the driver and Word.

An application doesn't load when I click the PIF file for it.

■ If no DOS program loads when you click the corresponding PIF file, make sure that the programs= parameter in the WIN.INI [extensions] section (see Appendix G) includes PIF, as follows:

Help! I'm having trouble starting a DOS application under Windows.

339

```
Programs=com exe bat pif
```

If the problem is just one program, the PIF file for that program is incorrect. Check the program name to see that it is spelled correctly and that it designates the correct path and extension.

Help! I have general DOS problems with all DOS applications.

```
┌─────────────────────────────────┐
│  I have general problems with all │
│       DOS applications            │
└─────────────────────────────────┘
```

DOS applications run slowly.	DOS applications crash.	I hear a beep when I press a key.	I can run only one DOS application at a time.	I can't scroll in a DOS application.
• Expect a 20% speed penalty when running a DOS application under Windows. • If running in 386 enhanced mode, edit the PIF file. • Add physical memory. • Add FileSys Change=off to SYSTEM.INI.	• Use Alt+Tab or Alt+F4; then exit and reboot to recover for testing. • There may be a memory conflict. Be sure the software doesn't use the VPCI standard. Edit the PIF file.	• The application may be suspended or there may be an error condition. Press Alt+Enter.	• The swap file or \TEMP directory isn't large enough. Increase this space.	• Run the application in a window rather than full-screen. • Select the Scroll command from the Control menu.

If you have a general DOS problem with all DOS applications, the most likely cause is an error in the PIF file, particularly _DEFAULT.PIF.

DOS applications run slowly.

This is normal under Windows. Expect about a 20-percent performance penalty for running DOS applications under Windows. The only solution is to use faster processors when you run DOS applications under Windows. If that's your goal, purchase hardware with increased performance in mind. Otherwise, run DOS applications outside of Windows. DOS applications will run even slower in a windowed mode.

Windows includes a default PIf file that is used to define the values for the DOS execution when a named PIF is not found. This file is called _DEFAULT.PIF. In the 386 enhanced mode, it defines the default virtual machine values. Unfortunately, however, Microsoft uses values in this file that are worst-case; that is, these are conservative values that will work for most DOS applications. You will get much better DOS performance if you edit the _DEFAULT.PIF file for less-conservative values. You can then use it as a template file for starting other DOS applications. For the 386 enhanced mode, set the following values in the PIF file:

Help! I have general DOS problems with all DOS applications.

341

1. If you aren't running background tasks, set Execution to **E**xclusive.

2. Set Expanded and Extended Memory Requirements (EMS Memory and XMS Memory) to zero. If a DOS program needs either, it should have its own PIF.

3. Set the **V**ideo Memory option to Text. If a graphics program is started in this mode, the system will switch to graphics.

4. With Windows 3.1, you can select under Display Usage either **F**ull Screen or **W**indowed. Programs run faster using full-screen mode. With Windows 3.0, select **F**ull Screen for VGA systems. In Windows 3.0, you can run only character-based DOS programs in the windowed mode.

Now click **A**dvanced and set these values:

1. Set the Multitasking Options: **F**oreground Priority to 10000. If you have background tasks that can't function with this value, reduce it some.

2. Turn all Memory Options off. For example, **U**ses High Memory Area should be off. This is required if using DOS 5 and DOS is in the HMA (DOS=HIGH).

3. Under Display Options, turn off all the Monitor Ports options. They are there for poorly behaved EGA applications. For VGA, they really hurt the performance.

4. Under Display Options, be sure **E**mulate Text Mode is on. This allows Windows to use the faster text-mode calls.

   Be sure to save the new PIF by using **S**ave from the **F**ile menu. If you need help on any option, select the option in the dialog box and press F1.

- If there is too much disk activity, the problem is not enough memory. Add more physical memory.

- Be sure that **FileSysChange=off** in the [386enh] section of SYSTEM.INI (see Appendix G) to prevent file change messages from being sent to File Manager.

DOS applications crash.

- Use Alt+Esc, Alt+Tab, or Ctrl+Esc to return to Windows. Another possibility is Alt+F4, which closes Windows. Save all documents that are open. Then return to the DOS application and use **T**erminate from the **S**ettings option of the Control menu to kill the DOS application. Then exit Windows and reboot.

- If the applications are using extended memory and the VCPI standard, they can conflict with each other. Examples of applications that can do this are Lotus 1-2-3 version 3.0 and QEMM-386 version 5 or earlier. Certain DOS software may use the first part of extended memory (HMA). Examples include DOS 5 and QEMM-386. When using this software, be sure that in the PIF files for applications and in _DEFAULT.PIF you set the application so that it does not use the HMA.

I hear a beep when I press a certain key.

- The application may be suspended. For example, you may have tried to run a DOS application in a window when it won't run in a window. Try pressing Alt+Enter in this case to return to full screen. A beep is also an error response if you have pressed a wrong key. For example, you

Help! I have general DOS problems with all DOS applications.

343

will hear a beep if you try to enter inappropriate information in a dialog box, such as a value when a Yes/No response is called for.

I can run one DOS application in real or standard mode, but when I try to start a second application I must close it before returning to Windows.

The swap file or \TEMP directory isn't large enough to hold the data for swapping (see Appendix B). Each DOS program that is context-switched will need a megabyte of space. A 1MB swap file, for example, can support only a single DOS application for context-switching. The actual data is kept in the swap file, but the \TEMP directory has to hold some temporary data for the swap. Check the swapdisk parameter in SYSTEM.INI (not in WIN.INI) and be sure you have enough space in the specified directory. Also check the current \TEMP directory, deleting all files there and opening up several megabytes of disk space. Try putting the \TEMP directory on other drives if they have more space. In real mode, you can't use the /e parameter for setting the swapdisk parameter to use expanded memory. It was mentioned as possible for pre-Windows 3 versions, but it didn't work.

I can't scroll in a DOS application.

Some DOS applications support scrolling. You will find that scrolling works best in the window mode (press Alt+Enter to switch to a window). If you have a mouse and are in the window mode, you can use the scroll bars just as you do with a Windows application.

To scroll with the keyboard, select the **S**croll command from the Control menu (press Alt+Spacebar to open it). Then use the direction keys to scroll. To turn off scrolling, select the command again.

Help! I get a message when I try to run a DOS application.

I get a message when trying to run DOS applications.

I get the message "Application Execution Error; Unexpected DOS Error #11."	I get the message "Insufficient File Handles, Increase Files in CONFIG.SYS."	I get an "out of environment" message.	I get a message no association exists for the file.	I get a message I can't run this application while other applications are running full-screen.
• Try loading grabber and swapper files from Windows disks and expanding them.	• Add PerVMFiles=15 to [386enh] section of SYSTEM.INI.	• Use Program Manager's File Properties command to set a larger environment space for COMMAND.COM. • Use PIF Editor to increase the environment space. • Set a DUMMY variable.	• Be sure the programs= parameter in WIN.INI includes PIF. • Use File Associate in File Manager to assign the data file extension to the program.	• Run the application in text mode or upgrade to Windows 3.1.

Help! I get a message when I try to run a DOS application.

345

When you are are running a DOS application, Windows releases the system resources to DOS. Messages will generally come from DOS.

I get the message "Application Execution Error: Unexpected DOS Error #11."

Windows found an error in its own DOS-handling files in the WINDOWS\SYSTEM directory. Try loading the grabber and swapper files from the Windows disks and expanding them. These will vary with the installation but could include VGA.GR3 or WINOA386.MOD.

I get the message "Insufficient File Handles, Increase Files in CONFIG.SYS."

Add `PerVMFiles=15` to the `[386enh]` section of SYSTEM.INI (see Appendix G). Increasing `FILES=` in CONFIG.SYS will not make the message go away.

I get an "out of environment" message.

The *environment* is a global memory area in DOS that is used to hold some variables used by all DOS applications. The variables are set with the DOS SET command (see the DOS manual). When you start a DOS session under Windows, any existing environment is collapsed to less than 16 bytes of free environment (actually, 224 bytes) or the space required to hold the current environment, whichever is larger. If the DOS session needs more (for example, to set a variable in a batch file), it isn't available. There are several ways to fix this problem:

- Select the program-item icon for the DOS prompt and choose File Properties. Edit the Command line to read `COMMAND.COM /e:512 /c`. For starting DOS applications, edit the line to `COMMAND.COM /e:512 /c XXX.BAT`, where *XXX*.BAT is the batch file for starting the application.

- Create a PIF file and do the same trick; that is, use the `/e:nnn` option with the program filename for COMMAND.COM.

- Specify a dummy variable, such as `SET DUMMY1=xxxx` at the DOS prompt, before starting Windows. Then start each DOS session by using `SET DUMMY1=`. to reclaim the space for other variables. When you get the message "out of environment" with batch files, the batch file probably sets some environmental values (`SET=`). Extra environmental space assigned from booting is not available for virtual DOS machines under Windows. Use the preceding tips or avoid the SET commands.

I get a message that no association exists for the file.

- If the file is a PIF file, check WIN.INI (see Appendix G) and make sure that the PIF extension is included in the `programs=` line:

```
programs=com exe bat pif
```

Help! I get a message when I try to run a DOS application.

■ If the file is not a PIF file, use the File Manager's **F**ile
Associate command to associate the extension with a
program. You can also do this by including the association
in the [extensions] section of WIN.INI.

I get a message that I can't run this application while other applications are running full-screen.

■ This is a common message in Windows 3.0 when you are
trying to run DOS applications in a window using a VGA
or higher-resolution screen. Run the application in text
mode or upgrade to Windows 3.1.

Help! I'm having trouble switching between applications.

```
┌─────────────────────────────────────────────────────────────┐
│ I have problems switching between applications.               │
└─────────────────────────────────────────────────────────────┘
```

I can't switch from the DOS application back to Windows.

- Check PIF file to be sure shortcut keys are not reserved.
- Be sure PIF file Prevent Program Switch is not on.
- Be sure Video Mode is set to Graphics/Multiple text.
- Be sure Directly Modifies is off.
- Check for suffcient disk space. If EGA, be sure EGA.SYS is installed.

I can't switch to full-screen from window.

- Be sure you haven't started a Clipboard operation.

When switching between graphic applications, the screen is not restored properly.

- Check PIF file settings. Use high graphic settings and make sure Monitor Ports is on.
- Be sure the video driver is correct.

I can't switch from a DOS application.

- Check PIF settings.
- If running in standard mode with an EGA display, make sure the EGA driver is installed in CONFIG.SYS.

Help! I'm having trouble switching between applications.

349

The Windows environment makes it easy to switch between applications. This is known as *context switching*. In real and standard modes, you can switch between a single DOS application and one or more Windows applications. In the 386 enhanced mode, you can switch between multiple DOS and Windows applications. Only one window can be active at a time, but several programs can be in memory at the same time, ready to use.

To use context switching with DOS applications, hold down the Alt key and press and release Tab until the title bar of the desired application is displayed. Release the Alt key. The new application will now be active. The Alt+Tab combination is much like a preview mode, enabling you to scan through all programs that are loaded, including programs that are minimized or represented by icons.

Here is an example that uses Microsoft Word, but the directions are the same for WordPerfect or whatever you are using. Before starting:

1. Make sure that the PIF file exists in the program's directory for the word processor version you are using.

2. Make sure that the word processor is installed to a Program Manager group so that it starts from a PIF file. You can verify this by using Program Manager, selecting the program's icon, and then choosing **P**roperties from the **F**ile menu.

Start Windows and then start the word processor from Program Manager. The word processor should load and take the full screen. Now press Alt+Tab and release; the Program Manager is active. Press Alt+Tab again, and you are back in the word processor.

Another method of changing applications is to press Alt+Esc. One way to look at this is that Alt+Esc always makes the next application in the chain active, and Shift+Alt+Esc goes backward through the loading chain. For only two applications, this technique is probably better than Alt+Tab, but if you have several applications loaded, it can be time-consuming to sequentially activate each program to get to the one you want. Alt+Tab is a preview mode, showing each title bar as the Tab key is pressed, without loading the application. When you get to the application you want, releasing the Alt key makes the application active. Shift+Alt+Tab goes backward through the applications.

A third method of changing applications is to press Ctrl+Esc to access the Task List. Then choose the program that you want to be active.

Note: The Alt+Tab, Alt+Esc, and Ctrl+Esc keystrokes are disabled from any use they may have had in the application program.

Occasionally, you may have problems with context switching. Following are some of the situations that may occur and how you can correct them.

Help! I'm having trouble switching between applications.

351

I can't switch from the DOS application back to Windows.

■ Check the PIF file (see the section earlier in this chapter) and be sure you are not reserving some of the Windows shortcut keys (Alt+Esc, Alt+Tab).

■ Be sure the Prevent Program Switch checkbox in the PIF file (standard mode) is not on.

■ Make sure the Video Mode setting in the PIF file is set to Graphics/Multiple Text (standard mode).

■ Turn off any Directly Modifies options (standard mode). If any are on, you won't be able to switch away from the DOS application while the application is running.

■ If you are running in real or standard mode, the problem may be a lack of disk space. If this is true, you may get a message about insufficient disk space (there may be no message if there is no disk space at all). To solve this problem, clear more space on the hard disk. If you are using an EGA display, be sure the Windows device driver for the display is loaded by CONFIG.SYS (DEVICE=C:\WINDOWS\EGA.SYS).

Note: If you select Text as the Video Memory for a graphics application, you may not be able to switch from the application back to Windows.

I can't switch to a full-screen display from a window.

■ If you've started using the Clipboard (the word "Select" or "Mark" in the title bar), you can't switch away until the operation is completed. Press Esc or the right mouse button to clear the operation first. If you've selected Edit Scroll from the Control menu, you won't be able to switch away.

When I switch between graphics applications, the screen is not restored properly.

■ If you are running in real or standard mode, make sure that the Video Mode of the PIF file is set to Graphics/ Multiple Text. In the 386 enhanced mode, access the advanced options to make sure that the Video Memory is set to High Graphics and that in the advanced options the High Graphics option of Monitor Ports is on.

■ Reinstall the video driver. You may have a problem with the grabber file.

I can't switch from a DOS application.

■ Make sure that the shortcut keys you need are not re-served by the PIF file. (See the section earlier in this chapter on creating and editing PIF files.) Check for the correct video mode in the PIF file. Check the PIF file for other options that might prevent switching, such as the Prevent Program Switch option.

■ If you are running in real or standard mode with an EGA display, make sure that the EGA display driver is installed in CONFIG.SYS. This driver is called EGA.SYS. Specify the full path for the driver:

```
DEVICE=C:\WIN3\EGA.SYS
```

Help! I'm having trouble switching between applications.

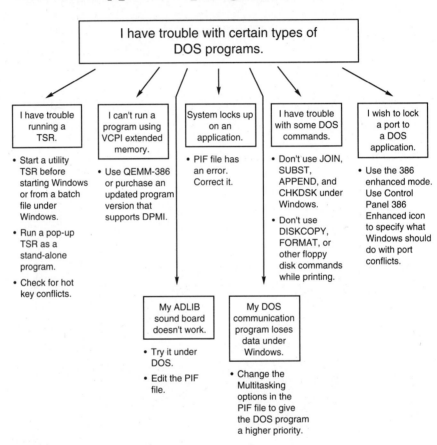

Help! I'm having problems running certain types of programs.

10
CHAPTER

I have trouble with certain types of
DOS programs.

I have trouble running a TSR.

- Start a utility TSR before starting Windows or from a batch file under Windows.
- Run a pop-up TSR as a stand-alone program.
- Check for hot key conflicts.

I can't run a program using VCPI extended memory.

- Use QEMM-386 or purchase an updated program version that supports DPMI.

System locks up on an application.

- PIF file has an error. Correct it.

I have trouble with some DOS commands.

- Don't use JOIN, SUBST, APPEND, and CHKDSK under Windows.
- Don't use DISKCOPY, FORMAT, or other floppy disk commands while printing.

I wish to lock a port to a DOS application.

- Use the 386 enhanced mode. Use Control Panel 386 Enhanced icon to specify what Windows should do with port conflicts.

My ADLIB sound board doesn't work.

- Try it under DOS.
- Edit the PIF file.

My DOS communication program loses data under Windows.

- Change the Multitasking options in the PIF file to give the DOS program a higher priority.

Help with DOS Applications

Certain types of DOS programs cannot be run under Windows—or will run under Windows with reservations. These include TSRs (including some DOS commands), programs that use VCPI extended memory, communication programs, and programs that violate basic DOS programming constraints.

I have trouble running memory-resident applications (TSRs) in Windows.

There are two types of memory-resident programs: utility software and pop-up programs. *Utility software* includes mouse drivers, disk caches, and delete tracking utilities (they keep an audit in case you want to undelete files that have already been deleted). These programs are virtually invisible when running and have no keyboard interface. They are often called *device drivers*.

Pop-up programs are programs that remain inactive until a certain *hot key* (a predefined key sequence) is pressed. The program then becomes active and suspends all other programs until it is finished. An example is Borland's Sidekick.

When Windows is running in 386 enhanced mode, any TSR loaded before Windows is started will steal memory from each virtual machine that is started. Each DOS application started after Windows is loaded (such as a TSR running as a DOS application) takes up memory.

Help! I'm having problems running certain types of programs.

355

Note: Certain memory-resident utilities, such as some disk cache products, can destroy information on a hard disk. Check with the manufacturer before using them with Windows.

A DOS pop-up will not be available from within a Windows application. For example, you won't be able to access SideKick from within Microsoft Excel. You can, however, access the pop-up from a DOS application running full-screen under Windows or, in the 386 enhanced mode, from a windowed DOS application.

If you need to use a utility over a broad base of programs (such as the mouse driver), start it before you start Windows. The utility is then available to all Windows programs. The disadvantage is that it is always taking up memory, and this memory will not be available for Windows.

Note: Windows applications use their own mouse driver, which is defined in the SYSTEM.INI file. The Windows mouse driver is normally in the \WINDOWS\SYSTEM path. The DOS mouse driver is normally in the root directory of the C drive.

If you need a memory resident utility for only a few programs that are running under Windows, start the utility from a batch file that loads the utility software and then starts the application. On quitting the application, the batch file should unload the utility. An example would be a TSR program that provides mouse support for dBASE III or IV.

■ Some pop-ups can be run as stand-alone programs, such as PC Tools Desktop and PC Shell utilities. If this can be done, it is the preferred method. Start the pop-up this way and run it as you would any other DOS application. You may need to create a PIF file for it (see the section on creating and editing PIF files earlier in this chapter). You can also define a hot key in the PIF file so that you can quickly switch to the pop-up.

■ If the pop-up can be run only as memory-resident, create a PIF file to run it and create an icon for it in the Program Manager. After you start the program, its hot keys become active. Check to make sure that the hot keys for the pop-up don't conflict with other hot keys. If you use the pop-up with only a few programs, create a batch file that loads the pop-up when one of the programs is started and that removes it from memory on termination.

I can't run protected-mode software or a program using VCPI extended memory under Windows.

Programs that fall into this category include (DOS) Lotus 1-2-3, AutoCAD 386 version 1.1, Interleaf Publisher 1.1, Mathematica 2.0, SQL 2.0/PME 2.1, and Paradox 386 3.5. Versions 1.x, 2.x, and 3.1 of Lotus 1-2-3 run in standard and enhanced modes but don't support many environmental features. Try Excel instead or use the Lotus 1-2-3 for Windows product.

Help! I'm having problems running certain types of programs.

357

All of the programs just mentioned use the VCPI DOS Extender technology, which is not supported under Windows' 386 enhanced mode. You can run them by using QEMM-386 memory manager (see Appendix A) and launching them in standard mode.

I can't run a game using my ADLIB sound board in DOS under Windows.

Note that some games won't run under Windows no matter what you do.

Try running the program under DOS to confirm it's a Windows problem.

First, start the game by using the command line **COMMAND /C GAME.BAT** as **P**rogram Filename in the PIF, where the batch file is the file to start the game. Using standard mode is best. To use 386 enhanced, be sure that KB **R**equired in the PIF file is enough (typically 500). Then set **E**xclusive Execution on. Under the **A**dvanced options, disable monitor ports function, disable **D**etect Idle Time, and disable Allow Fast **P**aste. Be sure High Graphics is on and run full-screen. Disable use of HMA.

The system locks up when I use a particular DOS application.

This situation generally means that the PIF file for the application has an error, particularly if the DOS application is running in a window. With Windows 3.0, many

DOS graphics applications won't run using a VGA display in a window. In the 386 enhanced mode, you can use Alt+Esc to return to Windows. Close any open documents, return to the DOS application, and terminate it from the Control menu by using the Settings Terminate option.

My DOS communications program loses data under Windows.

You probably have a priority problem with the communications program. Run Windows in the 386 enhanced mode. The Multitasking Options of the PIF file (Advanced screen) allow you to change the priority of the application when it is running with other applications. Figure 10.3 shows the Advanced Options dialog box. (See the section earlier in this chapter on creating and editing PIF files.) In the standard and real modes, inactive DOS applications are swapped to disk. With the 386 enhanced mode, you have virtual multiple machines, and several DOS programs can be running at once with Windows.

One of these programs is said to be in the *foreground;* that is, keyboard input is directed to that application and its window is active. Other DOS applications can still run in the background, however. Background programs can be doing a file transfer with a remote system (if it is a communication program), calculating (if it is a large spreadsheet), or (if you are a developer) compiling a program. You can control priorities between the foreground and background programs. All Windows programs are executing in a single virtual machine, and together they have a

Help! I'm having problems running certain types of programs.

359

single priority. All Windows applications, as a unit, are either in the foreground or background.

Figure 10.3

Setting the multitasking options.

```
┌─────────────────────────────────────────────────────────┐
│ ⊟                    Advanced Options                     │
├─────────────────────────────────────────────────────────┤
│ ┌─Multitasking Options──────────────────────┐  ┌───────┐ │
│ │ Background Priority: [50]  Foreground Priority: [100] │  │  OK   │ │
│ │            ⊠ Detect Idle Time              │  ├───────┤ │
│ └────────────────────────────────────────────┘  │Cancel │ │
│ ┌─Memory Options──────────────────────────────┐  └───────┘ │
│ │  ☐ EMS Memory Locked      ☐ XMS Memory Locked        │ │
│ │  ⊠ Uses High Memory Area  ☐ Lock Application Memory  │ │
│ └──────────────────────────────────────────────────────┘ │
│ ┌─Display Options─────────────────────────────────────────┐│
│ │ Monitor Ports:  ☐ Text  ☐ Low Graphics  ☐ High Graphics ││
│ │      ⊠ Emulate Text Mode  ☐ Retain Video Memory         ││
│ └──────────────────────────────────────────────────────────┘│
│ ┌─Other Options────────────────────────────────────────────┐│
│ │ ⊠ Allow Fast Paste            ☐ Allow Close When Active  ││
│ │ Reserve Shortcut Keys:  ☐ Alt+Tab  ☐ Alt+Esc  ☐ Ctrl+Esc ││
│ │                         ☐ PrtSc    ☐ Alt+PrtSc ☐ Alt+Space││
│ │                         ☐ Alt+Enter                      ││
│ │ Application Shortcut Key: [ None              ]          ││
│ └──────────────────────────────────────────────────────────┘│
└──────────────────────────────────────────────────────────────┘
```

Note: The priorities for the Windows virtual machine are set from Control Panel by using the 386 enhanced option. For DOS applications, priorities are set from the PIF file.

Looking at the PIF file, if Execution: **B**ackground is checked on the first screen (see Figure 10.1 shown earlier), you can specify a priority when the application is running in the background and a second value for running in the foreground. The value can be any number from 0 to 10000. The default background priority is 50. The default foreground priority is 100.

To understand how this option works, assume that a background communications program is running at 50 and a foreground Windows program is running at 100. The total is 150. The foreground program gets two clock cycles (100/150 of the time) for every one cycle that the background program gets. You can also change this "on the fly" by using the **S**ettings option of the Control menu. The values have no meaning unless a background process is running. Without a background process, the foreground process gets all the processor resources regardless of the value entered here. Setting the foreground process to 10000 forces the foreground process to have all the processor time, regardless of the background setting.

Now let's take this another level. Assume dBASE IV and Lotus 1-2-3 are running with Windows. Windows has a foreground priority of 100 and a background of 50. The dBASE IV program has a foreground of 150 and a background of 25. Lotus 1-2-3 has a foreground of 200 and a background of 100. All of these values can be set from Control Panel (for Windows priority) or the DOS application PIF file.

With Windows in the foreground, the total is 100 (Windows) plus 25 (dBASE IV in background) plus 100 (Lotus 1-2-3 in background), or 225. Windows gets 100 of this, or almost half. Lotus 1-2-3 gets almost that much time, and dBASE IV gets only $\frac{1}{9}$ ($25 \div 225$).

With dBASE IV in the foreground, however, the picture changes. The total is now 50 (Windows) plus 150 (dBASE IV) plus 100 (Lotus 1-2-3), or 300. The dBASE IV program gets $150 \div 300$, or $\frac{1}{2}$. Windows gets $50 \div 300$, or $\frac{1}{6}$. Lotus 1-2-3 gets what is left.

Help! I'm having problems running certain types of programs.

361

With Lotus 1-2-3 in the foreground, the picture changes again and Lotus 1-2-3 gets 200/275 of the processor time.

In summary, with the 386 enhanced mode you can tune your system to allocate priorities to the various programs as you need them.

If **D**etect Idle Time is checked on the Advanced Options window of the PIF file, the foreground application will give the system's resources to other applications when it is idle, such as when it is waiting for input from you. Leave this option on for most applications. If normal maintenance operation of a foreground process causes a background DOS process to run too slowly, turn the check mark here to off. Turn it off for DOS communications programs, which often run for long periods without keyboard input.

I have trouble running some DOS commands.

▪ Don't use the JOIN, SUBST, and APPEND commands and don't use the CHKDSK command with the /f option. CHKDSK, for example, modifies the FAT, or file allocation table (part of the directory system), on the disk when you use the /f option. For this reason, the command doesn't run properly and may damage the FAT, making it unusable. DOS 5 adds some protection, but the better rule is to avoid all of these commands.

▪ Don't use DISKCOPY, FORMAT, or other floppy disk commands while printing.

How do I lock a port (such as a serial port for communication) to a DOS application so that it can't be used by another program?

Use the 386 enhanced mode. You can use the 386 Enhanced icon in Control Panel to define what Windows should do with port conflicts.

Help! I have trouble using the mouse with DOS applications under Windows.

```
┌─────────────────────────────────────────┐
│  I have trouble with the mouse when using │
│            DOS applications.              │
└─────────────────────────────────────────┘
                    │
                    ▼
```

- DOS application must run full-screen and in text mode (Windows 3.0).
- Be sure the DOS mouse is working (try it outside of Windows).
- To get mouse support under Windows 3.1, you must use the mouse drivers (MOUSE.COM and MOUSE.SYS).

Help! I have trouble using the mouse with DOS applications under Windows.

363

Windows 3.1 supports the use of the mouse with DOS applications. Windows 3.0 does not.

In Windows 3.0, if the DOS application must use a mouse, the application must run in full-screen mode. In addition, the application must run in text mode. When running in a window, Windows owns the mouse and the mouse can be used only for the Clipboard. If you move the mouse into the client area of a windowed application, Windows assumes you are initiating a Clipboard operation: moving, copying, or pasting. With Windows 3.1, this is no longer a problem and you can use the mouse with a DOS application.

Make sure the mouse is working outside Windows. Mouse operations under Windows utilize a mouse driver (MOUSE.DRV) in the \WINDOWS\SYSTEM directory. DOS applications use a separate mouse driver in the C:\ directory. This means you have the option of using two separate mouse drivers if you wish. For example, if you have Microsoft Word and wish to use the MOUSE.SYS that came with Word, place the file in the C:\ directory and use it as a part of CONFIG.SYS (`DEVICE=MOUSE.SYS`). The mouse driver will then be used for all DOS applications, including those under Windows. Alternatively, you could use MOUSE.COM and load it from AUTOEXEC.BAT.

For batch files that start a DOS application, you can load MOUSE.COM from the batch file before starting the DOS application. Leave Windows' own mouse driver in the C:\WINDOWS\SYSTEM directory. It is accessed by name from the SYSTEM.INI file.

Note: If you are using the Microsoft mouse, MOUSE.COM should be run before Windows is started. MOUSE.COM will then be available for all DOS applications running under Windows. If you are using the Logitech mouse, it should always be loaded from a batch file after Windows is started and before the application is started. Do not load the Logitech mouse as a driver from CONFIG.SYS. In addition, when using the Logitech mouse with Windows, use version 4.1 or later.

If a serial mouse does not work after installation, be sure the BUFFERS setting in AUTOEXEC.BAT is 20 (see Appendix G). Using a higher value can cause mouse problems. Don't use COM3 or COM4 for the mouse. If using a bus mouse, be sure there is no interrupt conflict. The interrupt is set from a jumper on the mouse card, and should be set to a value that is not used by any other port in the system. If you are using a bus mouse on an AT-class machine, interrupt 5 is the best alternative unless it is already in use. If it is unavailable, try interrupt 3 or 4. They are normally serial port interrupts, but if a serial port is not in use interrupts 3 and 4 are available. Avoid using interrupt 2 because it has a special purpose on the AT. For more information, see Appendix C.

Help! I have trouble using the mouse with DOS applications under Windows.

365

To get mouse support under Windows, you must use the mouse drivers (MOUSE.COM and MOUSE.SYS) with Windows 3.1).

Help! I have trouble using a PIF file.

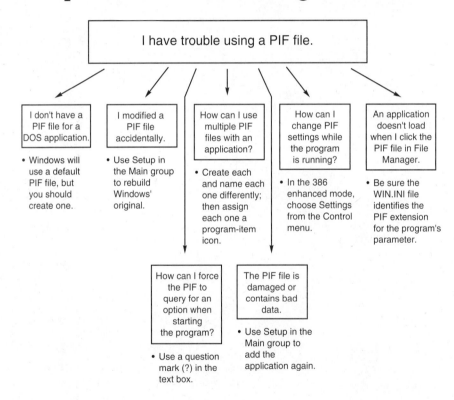

The *PIF file* provides information to Windows for controlling the execution of the DOS application under Windows. There should be a PIF for each DOS application that is installed.

I don't have a PIF file for a DOS application.

■ You can run a DOS program without a PIF file. However, when you do, Windows uses the default _DEFAULT.PIF. This PIF, as defined by Microsoft, assumes certain worst-case conditions about your program. You are better off creating a new PIF, or even modifying the default PIF for your system.

I accidentally modified a PIF file. Can I recover the original?

■ If you inadvertently modify a PIF provided with Windows, you can use the Windows Setup program to restore the PIF's original settings. To do this, first launch Windows Setup. Select Set Up Applications from the Options menu. From the dialog box, choose Search for Applications or Ask You to Specify an Application. Choose the drive to search for DOS applications. You can also choose to select all drives. Highlight each desired application and click Add>> for each. This will move the name to the right list box. When all the desired applications have been selected, click OK. Icons will also be added to Program Manager.

Can I force the PIF Editor to query for an option when starting the program?

■ If you enter a question mark for a control in the PIF Editor, Windows will prompt for that value when starting the application. For example, if you use the same program frequently with different startup parameters, put a ques-

Help! I have trouble using a PIF file.

367

tion mark in the field for **O**ptional Parameters. This will force Windows to prompt you each time for the startup parameters.

How can I use multiple PIF files with a DOS application?

You can use multiple PIF files for the same DOS application. For example, you might wish to have one PIF for running an application full-screen, and another for running in a window. The full-screen mode is faster but not as versatile. Use it when you are running the program by itself. Run the program in the window mode when you are running it with other applications and need to use the Clipboard. Some programs, such as Microsoft Multiplan, are sold with both PIF files.

■ Create each PIF, saving each under an appropriate name. Then create the icons in Program Manager. Label one icon to indicate it is full-screen (such as "MS Word – full scrn") and a second to indicate it is windowed ("MS Word – windowed"). If you use multiple PIF files, always start the program by clicking or selecting the correct PIF filename instead of the program name. In this way, you know which PIF file is being used. If you click the program name, the PIF file that most closely matches the program name will be used.

Can I recover the PIF file if it is damaged or contains bad data?

■ You can recover the original PIF file by using the Windows Setup program and adding that application again.

How do I change the PIF settings while a program is running?

If a program is running with Windows in a 386 enhanced mode, you can change the PIF settings dynamically while the program is running. The new settings will be in effect only while the program is loaded, and the PIF file is not changed. Also, you can alter only a limited number of PIF settings: the display options (window/full-screen), the tasking options (exclusive and background), and the priority. To change these options, select **S**ettings from the Control menu. Windows will display a dialog box similar to the one in Figure 10.4. Select the new settings and choose OK. There is also an emergency **T**erminate command on this dialog box. Use it to terminate an application if the application locks up and won't terminate by the normal means. By using this command, you can get back to Windows and close files in other applications.

Note: Choosing **T**erminate with Windows 3.0 permits you to exit the application to Windows, but using this command leaves Windows and DOS in an unstable condition. Leave Windows as quickly as possible and reboot the system.

An application doesn't load when I click the PIF file in File Manager.

Be sure the WIN.INI file (see Appendix G) identifies the PIF extension for the program's parameters in the [extensions] section.

Help! I have trouble using a PIF file.

369

Figure 10.4
*Changing the
PIF setting
dynamically.*

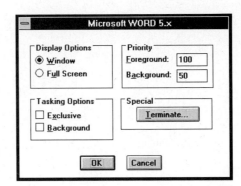

Help! I have display problems with a DOS application when it is running.

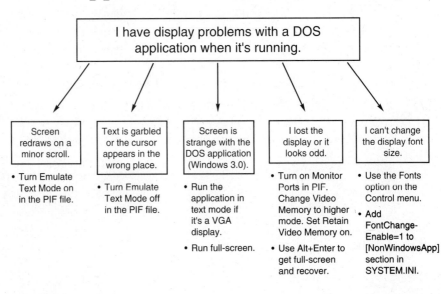

If you have display problems, first read Chapter 7. Be sure that the display is working properly with DOS applications outside of Windows and with Windows applications.

The screen is completely redrawn on a minor scroll, slowing down the display.

In the PIF file, **E**mulate Text Mode on the Advanced Options screen controls the rate at which text is displayed. Turn on this option to scroll text faster. It is most useful for DOS applications in a graphics mode when the application completely redraws the screen for a minor scroll.

Text is garbled or the cursor is displayed at the wrong place.

In the PIF file, **E**mulate Text Mode controls the rate at which text is displayed. Turn it off if the text becomes garbled or if the cursor is displayed at the wrong place.

Help! I have display problems with a DOS application when it is running.

371

The screen is strange when I try to run a DOS application in a window (Windows 3.0).

◻ If running VGA with Windows 3.0, you may have problems running a graphics application in a window, such as Microsoft Word in a graphics mode. Windows has trouble managing VGA DOS graphics screens with this version of Windows. To use in a window, switch the application to text mode. Generally you can do this by starting the program with a command-line parameter, switching the program after starting and exiting in a text mode, or by reinstalling the program.

◻ You can usually recover an application lost in this way by using Alt+Enter to switch to full-screen mode. In Windows 3.0, you can't use the mouse with a DOS application in a window. Windows 3.1 supports graphic DOS applications in a window and supports the mouse. When running in the 386 enhanced mode, you can switch quickly between full-screen and window modes by using Alt+Enter. This is a very important point to remember. If your application hangs in a windowed mode, pressing Alt+Enter will get you to full-screen mode and a functional application.

I lost the display or it looks odd in 386 enhanced mode.

◻ If you are using an EGA display, try turning on one of the Monitor **P**orts options after clicking **A**dvanced from the

PIF file. Another possibility is to change the **V**ideo **M**emory on the first PIF window to a mode that sets aside more memory. Be sure that Retain Video **M**emory is turned on in the Advanced Options.

■ Many graphic programs won't run under Windows in a windowed mode. Use Alt+Enter to return the program to full-screen and use it that way. Then edit the PIF file for a full-screen display.

I can't change the display font size in a DOS application.

■ Font sizes are changed by using the **F**onts option of the Control menu to display the Font Selection dialog box, as shown in Figure 10.5. Run the application in a text mode if you wish to change font sizes. Make sure that you are using the correct video driver.

■ Try adding **FontChangeEnable=1** to the [NonWindowsApp] section of SYSTEM.INI (see Appendix G).

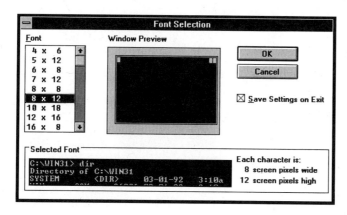

Figure 10.5
Changing the font.

Help! I have display problems with a DOS application when it is running.

373

Help! A certain key combination used by Windows is also used by the DOS application. I want the DOS application to use it.

A key combination is used by Windows. I want the DOS application to use it.

↓

- In the PIF file, use Reserve Shortcut Keys to reserve the combination.

Certain key combinations in Windows are often used by the DOS application as well, so you will need to correct such conflicts.

In the PIF file's Advanced Options screen, the Reserve **S**hortcut Keys option allows Windows to ignore certain key combinations. Use this option if a certain key combination is used by an application program. In the case of Microsoft Word, Alt+Spacebar is used to set the normal type and is used by Windows to display the Control menu. To resolve the conflict, check with Microsoft for a Microsoft Word update or use style sheets to change the keystroke that sets the normal type.

Help! I just updated a DOS application (or my version of Windows), and the application no longer works with Windows.

```
┌─────────────────────────────────────────────┐
│   I updated an old DOS application and it     │
│       no longer works from Windows.           │
└─────────────────────────────────────────────┘
                      │
                      ↓
```

- Create a new
  PIF file.

The old PIF file is probably no longer correct. First, check to see if a new PIF file was provided with the update. If so, copy it to the directory with the program. Alternatively, edit the old PIF file to support the new version. In some cases, you may find that the new version requires so much memory that it will not run under Windows. Also, be certain that you access the correct PIF file. If you are using Windows with a PIF file that supports Microsoft Word version 5, the PIF file won't work if you are using the older version 4.

Help! I just updated a DOS application, and the application no longer works.

375

Help! I have memory problems with DOS applications.

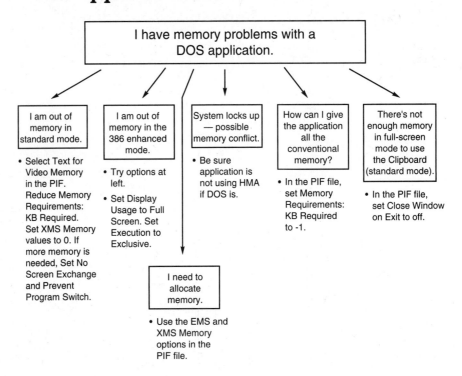

I have memory problems with a DOS application.

I am out of memory in standard mode.

- Select Text for Video Memory in the PIF. Reduce Memory Requirements: KB Required. Set XMS Memory values to 0. If more memory is needed, Set No Screen Exchange and Prevent Program Switch.

I am out of memory in the 386 enhanced mode.

- Try options at left.
- Set Display Usage to Full Screen. Set Execution to Exclusive.

System locks up — possible memory conflict.

- Be sure application is not using HMA if DOS is.

I need to allocate memory.

- Use the EMS and XMS Memory options in the PIF file.

How can I give the application all the conventional memory?

- In the PIF file, set Memory Requirements: KB Required to -1.

There's not enough memory in full-screen mode to use the Clipboard (standard mode).

- In the PIF file, set Close Window on Exit to off.

By changing various options in the PIF file, you can recover memory when DOS applications are being used. Memory problems are generally caused by incorrect settings in the PIF file.

I'm out of memory in standard mode.

▣ Edit the PIF file (see the section earlier in this chapter to learn how to do so). Under **V**ideo Memory, select Text. However, this setting may prevent you from switching away from the application. If you are out of memory on startup, reduce the value of Memory Requirements: KB **R**equired. If you are out of memory after startup when you try to run an application, free more memory before starting Windows. If the application doesn't need extended memory, be sure that both XMS Memory values are 0. Select No Screen E**x**change. If No Screen E**x**change is selected, you won't be able to copy the screen to the Clipboard. Select Prevent Program S**w**itch. With this option selected, you can't switch back to Windows without quitting the application.

I'm out of memory in the 386 enhanced mode.

▣ First, try the solutions suggested for the previous problem.

▣ Under Display Usage in the first PIF file window, set to run the application in F**u**ll Screen. Under Execution in the first PIF file window, set to run the application **E**xclusive.

I need to allocate memory for a DOS application.

▣ Use the 386 enhanced mode. Set the EMS Memory and XMS Memory amounts in the PIF file. Windows (in the 386 enhanced mode) can simulate expanded memory for those applications that need it. Use the EMS Memory options to specify the amount of extended memory to

Help! I have memory problems with DOS applications.

377

reserve for expanded memory simulation. **KB** Required specifies the amount of memory needed to start the application. Leave this setting at 0 unless memory is needed. KB **Limit** specifies the maximum amount to allocate. Set it to 0 if no memory is needed. Use these options to limit the memory available to the application if the application (such as early versions of AutoCAD) gobbles up too much expanded or extended memory. A typical limit setting is 1024 if expanded memory is needed. This memory will be available only to the application if it is needed. It is not automatically allocated.

If the application always needs expanded memory (such as some older versions of Ventura), go ahead and assign it using both **KB** Required and KB **Limit**. If the program only needs it in some cases, leave **KB** Required at 0 and set it from KB Limit unless a memory error message is displayed.

Caution: Don't use EMM386.SYS (Windows 3.0) to simulate expanded memory in the 386 enhanced mode. This driver is only needed for standard mode (unless you are using it with DOS 5 to manage the UMB area for the driver). Using it in 386 enhanced mode will take memory away from Windows. Windows HIMEM.SYS can simulate its own expanded memory in 386 enhanced mode without needing the extra driver.

The system locks up and I think I have a memory conflict with DOS applications.

■ In the PIF file, the Uses High Memory Area toggle defines whether the application can use the first 64K page of extended memory. Keep this option selected for most applications. If you are running DOS 5 and have DOS in HMA (DOS=high in AUTOEXEC.BAT), you would want to keep DOS applications out of this area.

How can I give a DOS application all the conventional memory?

■ In the PIF file, set Memory Requirements: KB **R**equired to -1. This will give the application all conventional memory up to 640K. Set Memory Requirements: KB **D**esired to -1 to give the application as much memory as possible, up to a maximum of 640K.

It is your responsibility, when saving memory, to limit the memory used by a DOS application by setting these values in the PIF file. If you have 4 megabytes of memory or more, the issue isn't that important. If you have less memory or get messages about insufficient memory, you need to start limiting the memory used by the DOS applications.

There's not enough memory in the full-screen mode to use the Clipboard (standard mode).

■ In the PIF file, turn off the **C**lose Window on Exit check box. This option closes the application's window when

Help! I have memory problems with DOS applications.

379

you exit the application. It should normally be toggled on. Leave it untoggled if you are tight on memory in a full-screen mode and need to use the Clipboard. Quitting the application releases the memory, but the window will not be closed. You can then copy to the Clipboard from the window.

Help! I can't terminate a DOS application.

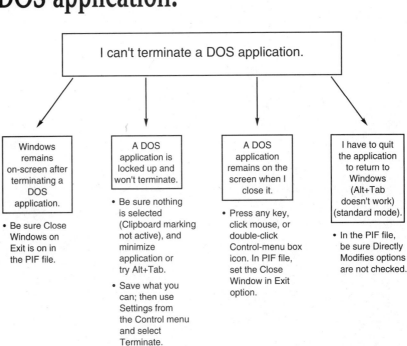

I can't terminate a DOS application.

| Windows remains on-screen after terminating a DOS application. | A DOS application is locked up and won't terminate. | A DOS application remains on the screen when I close it. | I have to quit the application to return to Windows (Alt+Tab doesn't work) (standard mode). |

- Be sure Close Windows on Exit is on in the PIF file.

- Be sure nothing is selected (Clipboard marking not active), and minimize application or try Alt+Tab.

- Save what you can; then use Settings from the Control menu and select Terminate.

- Press any key, click mouse, or double-click Control-menu box icon. In PIF file, set the Close Window in Exit option.

- In the PIF file, be sure Directly Modifies options are not checked.

To terminate a DOS program execution and remove it from memory, you can use the normal program termination procedures. For Multiplan, for example, you would use Esc Q. For Microsoft Word, select **Q**uit from the **F**ile menu. For BASIC, type **SYSTEM**. To temporarily suspend a DOS program and reduce it to an icon, select Mi**n**imize from the Control menu. Remember that for full-screen mode you will have to press Alt+Spacebar first.

If the normal program termination procedures don't work, try using Ctrl+C or Ctrl+Break. In the 386 enhanced mode, place the application in a window (Alt+Enter) and select **S**ettings from the Control menu. Then choose **T**erminate. If this doesn't work, use Alt+Tab to return to Windows. Press Ctrl+Esc to see the Task List. Select the application and **E**nd Task. Reboot the computer.

Another method is to press Alt+Spacebar, if necessary, to get a window. Choose the **S**ettings option of the Control menu. Select **T**erminate on the dialog box. Reboot the computer.

Window remains on-screen after terminating a DOS application.

If a window remains on-screen after the program has been terminated, the PIF file is incorrect. Make sure that the **C**lose Window on Exit option is checked on. You can temporarily close the window by using Alt+F4 or by clicking **C**lose on the Control menu.

A standard (DOS) application is locked up and won't terminate by normal means.

◻ When you are running the application in a window, you won't be able to quit the application if anything is selected (the word "Select" or "Mark" in the title bar). If nothing is selected, try to recover Windows by minimizing the application or by using Alt+Tab, Alt+Esc, or Alt+Enter.

◻ If you can't get out, save what you can and choose **S**ettings from the Control menu. Select **T**erminate on the dialog box. Close any open files in other applications immediately. Then reboot. In the 386 enhanced mode, you can generally first use Alt+Tab or Alt+Enter to return to Windows to save open documents.

A DOS application remains on the screen when I close it.

◻ Press any key, click the mouse, or double-click the Control-menu box icon. The **C**lose Window in Exit option in the PIF file is not set. Edit the PIF file to close the window next time.

I have to quit the application to return to Windows.

◻ Check the Directly Modifies options of the PIF file. Make sure that no options are selected here. This option is not available in the 386 enhanced mode. Windows is smarter in this mode and can detect any conflicts and warn the user. Moreover, you can use the 386 enhanced icon in Control Panel to define what Windows should do with port conflicts.

Displaying 50 Lines on the Screen for a DOS Application

Add the following line to the `[NonWindowsApp]` section of SYSTEM.INI:

```
ScreenLines=50
```

After starting a DOS application, use the Control menu to change the font to a smaller one in order to see the entire window if necessary. Only values of 25, 43, and 50 are supported. You use 47, for example.

Changing the DOS Prompt Under Windows

With Windows 3.1, you can no longer start Windows from a DOS prompt inside of Windows. However, you may still wish to remind the user that he or she is in DOS. You can do this by setting the Windows prompt in AUTOEXEC.BAT. Add the line:

```
SET WINPMT=Enter EXIT to return to Windows.$_$_$P$G
```

For more information on defining this prompt, see the information on the PROMPT command in your DOS manual. Reboot before using the new prompt.

10

CHAPTER

Using Recorder with DOS Applications

DOS keystrokes are not recorded by Recorder. You can start a DOS application with Recorder, but any keystrokes entered while in the DOS application will not be recorded. Use WinBatch (shareware from Wilson WindowWare) or Bridge Batch (from Softbridge, Inc.) for better macro recording.

HELP IN SHARING OBJECTS AND DATA WITH APPLICATIONS

One of the most important features of Windows is that it makes possible the sharing of objects (data) between applications. Applications become tools, acting on objects. Thus, multiple tools can act on documents, and at the same time the integrity of the documents is maintained. An important result of sharing between applications is that one application doesn't have to implement all the functions a user needs. The document becomes a *compound document* with a variety of objects that retain their identity and type.

This chapter discusses problems that arise when data is shared by means of the Clipboard, DDE, and OLE, and it offers troubleshooting suggestions to correct the problems.

The Clipboard

For many users, the *Clipboard* is the easiest method of transferring objects (data) between applications—both Windows and DOS applications. The Clipboard supports text and graphics, and is simple and easy to use. The **E**dit menu is available in most Windows applications to support the Clipboard. In DOS applications, you can use the Control menu.

The Clipboard always contains no more than a single object. When you copy or cut to the Clipboard (with **E**dit Cut or **E**dit **C**opy), anything that is already in the Clipboard is replaced with the new object. You can, however, save the Clipboard contents to a file and reload the contents later. Use **E**dit **P**aste to paste the contents of the Clipboard to the current document.

How can I save the Clipboard to disk?

Occasionally you may want to paste data between two applications that are running under different versions of Windows (Windows 3.0 and 3.1, for example). You can't do a paste directly through the Clipboard. However, you can accomplish a paste indirectly by saving the Clipboard to disk. Use the following techniques:

1. Start the source application containing the data to be pasted.

2. Copy the data to the Clipboard by selecting the data and choosing **C**opy from the **E**dit menu.

3. Start the Clipboard viewer and save its contents as a file.

4. Exit Windows and start it again in the Windows version that supports the destination application.

5. Start the Clipboard and load the data from its file.

6. Load the application and paste the data to it from the Clipboard.

There are other times when saving the Clipboard contents to a file is a good idea. For example, if you often work with a particular image (such as a logo), keep the image as a Clipboard file and then load it to the Clipboard whenever you need it.

What are the Clipboard file formats?

When you copy data to the Clipboard from a Windows application, you may be able to copy it in more than one format. The application developer can choose which formats to use, and often will choose multiple formats to ensure compatibility with a wide base of Windows applications. Here are a few of the available formats supported by the Clipboard:

Text. Null-terminated ASCII text.

OEM Text. Null-terminated text, OEM character set.

Metafile. Vector image graphics. The file contains GDI commands, and is a high-resolution image.

Bit Map. A device-independent bit-mapped format (BMP). The bits correspond to the pixels of the screen. Resolution is not as good as a metafile, but the image is compatible with most painting programs, such as Paintbrush.

Miscellaneous. Other formats such as TIFF can also be used with the Clipboard.

When you paste from the Clipboard, the **P**aste command is available as long as the destination application can accept the file format. The **D**isplay menu of the Clipboard shows the currently available formats. From this menu you can then select to view the contents in any of the other available formats. You can't control which format is used for pasting, but you can view which formats are available. By knowing which formats are available for the current Clipboard image and which formats are supported by a destination application, you can determine whether pasting will be supported.

Note: Text in the Clipboard may appear to be formatted. This is misleading because the formatting is lost or becomes that of the destination when you paste from a text format. For example, suppose that from Windows Write you copy text formatted as Courier to the Clipboard. You then paste it to Word for Windows, which is set for Arial. When the text is pasted, it will appear as Arial.

How can I capture the screen to the Clipboard?

You can capture an entire screen to the Clipboard by using the PrtScrn key (or PrintScreen on some keyboards). If this doesn't work (you hear a beep), the problem is likely due to one of the following:

- The PIF file reserves the PrtScrn key.
- Not enough memory is available. EGA and VGA images need a lot of memory. Make a smaller selection.

You can capture the active window to the Clipboard by using Alt+PrtScrn. You can view the Clipboard contents by starting the Clipboard viewer from the Main group of Program Manager. The viewer permits you to view the file in various formats and to save the Clipboard contents to a file.

Help! I'm having trouble with Clipboard and Windows applications.

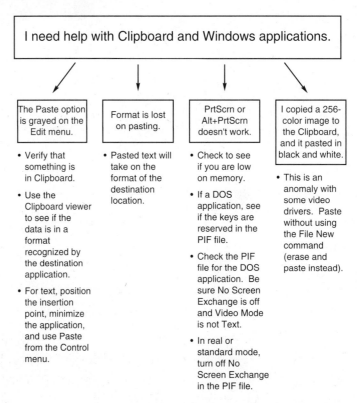

I need help with Clipboard and Windows applications.

The Paste option is grayed on the Edit menu.

- Verify that something is in Clipboard.

- Use the Clipboard viewer to see if the data is in a format recognized by the destination application.

- For text, position the insertion point, minimize the application, and use Paste from the Control menu.

Format is lost on pasting.

- Pasted text will take on the format of the destination location.

PrtScrn or Alt+PrtScrn doesn't work.

- Check to see if you are low on memory.

- If a DOS application, see if the keys are reserved in the PIF file.

- Check the PIF file for the DOS application. Be sure No Screen Exchange is off and Video Mode is not Text.

- In real or standard mode, turn off No Screen Exchange in the PIF file.

I copied a 256-color image to the Clipboard, and it pasted in black and white.

- This is an anomaly with some video drivers. Paste without using the File New command (erase and paste instead).

For Windows applications, you generally use the mouse to select objects for the Clipboard. The technique varies with the application, but in most applications you drag from the upper left to the lower right and choose **E**dit **C**ut (to move) or **E**dit

Copy (to copy). You can then switch to the destination application and choose **E**dit **P**aste to place the Clipboard contents at the cursor. You can also select and copy or move by using the keyboard.

The Paste function on the Edit menu is grayed, but I have something in the Clipboard. Why can't I paste it?

■ First, use the Clipboard viewer to be sure there is really something in the Clipboard.

■ If there is data in the Clipboard, a grayed **P**aste command means that the data is not in the right format for the destination application. For example, you may have copied a metafile image to the Clipboard from the source program, but the destination program may not permit the importing of format.

■ If there is text in the Clipboard and you are in standard or real mode with a DOS application, the **P**aste option might be grayed in some situations. To paste in this case, position the cursor at the insertion point, minimize the application (Alt+Tab), and then try the paste from the icon's Control menu.

Secrets and Surprises: You can use the Clipboard as a file format converter. To convert a TIFF scanned image to bit-mapped format, load it to a graphics program that imports TIFF format and then copy it to the Clipboard. You can

continues

Help! I'm having trouble with the Clipboard and Windows applications.

391

continued

then paste it as a bit-mapped image to another program. Or suppose you wish to send a formatted Word document as electronic mail. Copy the document from Word to the Clipboard, and the Clipboard contents will contain ASCII text. Then paste the text to the communications program when you are ready to send it.

The format is lost when I paste.

This is normal. Pasted text will assume the format of the destination location.

PrtScrn or Alt+PrtScrn doesn't work.

If you can't copy the screen to the Clipboard, check these possibilities:

In the 386 enhanced mode, you may be low on memory. This is unusual, but a graphic VGA Clipboard image can take 150K of memory.

These keys may be reserved shortcut keys in the application's PIF file.

In standard mode, you may have trouble if **V**ideo Memory in the PIF file is set to Text and the program is running in a graphics mode. Change **V**ideo Memory to indicate that the program is running in graphics mode.

In the real or standard mode, these keys won't work if No Screen Exchange is turned on in the PIF file.

I copied a 256-color image to the Clipboard, but it pasted as black and white.

This is an anomaly with Windows for some video drivers. Avoid the Clipboard or try using it without using the **File New** command, which clears the palette. Instead, erase and paste.

Help! I'm having trouble with the Clipboard and DOS applications.

I need help using the Clipboard with DOS applications.

I need help using Clipboard in standard mode.

- You are limited to copying the full screen of a text application to Clipboard. Text is ASCII, and all formatting is lost. To copy, use PrtScrn.

I need help with 386 enhanced, window mode.

- Use the Control menu and select Edit Mark. Hold down Shift and drag to mark. Select Edit Copy. Move to the destination location and choose Edit Paste from the Control menu.

I need help with 386 enhanced, full-screen mode.

- Use Alt+ Spacebar to get the Control menu. Then use the commands as in the windowed mode.

Help! I'm having trouble with the Clipboard and DOS applications.

393

Using the Clipboard with DOS applications is a little more complex. In standard mode, the DOS application must run full-screen. You can copy the entire screen to the Clipboard by using PrtScrn. You will not be able to copy any graphics to the Clipboard.

To view the Clipboard, press Alt+Esc to return to Windows and start the Clipboard viewer program.

I need help using Clipboard in standard mode.

 In standard mode, Clipboard operations are limited to copying the full screen of a text application to the Clipboard. All formatting is lost; that is, the text is copied to the Clipboard as ASCII text. Each line will have a hard carriage return. To copy, display the screen you wish to capture and press PrtScrn. The screen will be placed in the Clipboard as a bit map. Then paste the Clipboard contents.

Note: When pasting to a DOS spreadsheet, paste only a single line at a time.

I need help with Clipboard operations in the window mode (386 enhanced).

If the application is running in a window mode, the title bar is displayed with a Control-menu box in the upper left. Clicking this box opens the Control menu, which has the familiar Control menu commands plus a few new ones for editing with the Clipboard. On the Control menu, select **E**dit and then Mar**k**. A small black rectangle will appear on the screen, and the word Mark will appear in the title bar. Click the mouse to indicate the beginning of the area to copy. Hold down the Shift key and drag to select the area. Click the Control-menu box again to get the Control menu and then select Cop**y** from this menu. The selected area will be copied to the Clipboard. To paste from the Clipboard, first use the Mar**k** command to mark the location for pasting. Then select **E**dit and **P**aste from the Control menu. You can unmark selections by clicking outside of the marked area.

I need help with Clipboard operations in the full-screen mode (386 enhanced)

In the full-screen mode, you can still use the Clipboard. Because the application takes up the full screen, the title bar is not visible. To access the title bar and Control menu, use Alt+Spacebar. To copy and paste, follow the steps described in the preceding problem for using the Control menu.

Help! I'm having trouble with the Clipboard and DOS applications.

395

11

CHAPTER

Secrets and Surprises: Using the Clipboard with DOS applications is a good way of sending text to a remote system. Use your word processor (Word Perfect, Microsoft Word, or whatever) to paste the text to the Clipboard. Then start Terminal, Crosstalk for Windows, or another Windows communication program. Next select the **E**dit **P**aste command in the communications program to send the text to the remote system.

Help! I have problems with some Clipboard techniques.

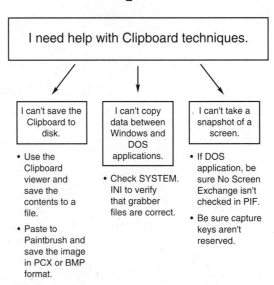

I need help with Clipboard techniques.

| I can't save the Clipboard to disk. | I can't copy data between Windows and DOS applications. | I can't take a snapshot of a screen. |

I can't save the Clipboard to disk.

- Use the Clipboard viewer and save the contents to a file.
- Paste to Paintbrush and save the image in PCX or BMP format.

I can't copy data between Windows and DOS applications.

- Check SYSTEM. INI to verify that grabber files are correct.

I can't take a snapshot of a screen.

- If DOS application, be sure No Screen Exchange isn't checked in PIF.
- Be sure capture keys aren't reserved.

Help in Sharing Objects and Data with Applications

You may have problems saving the Clipboard contents to a file, copying between Windows and DOS applications, or taking a screen snapshot.

I can't save the Clipboard to disk.

▪ Use the Clipboard viewer and save the contents to a file. The basic strategy for saving the Clipboard contents is to start the Clipboard viewer from the Main group of Program Manager. Then choose Save As from the File menu. Enter the filename and OK. The Clipboard contents will be saved in the specified file with a CLP extension.

▪ Paste to Paintbrush and save the image in PCX or BMP format.

I can't copy data between Windows and DOS applications.

▪ Verify that the grabber files are correct. These are defined in the SYSTEM.INI file (see Appendix G). Be sure the name matches the display type you are using. If using third-party grabber files, be sure these are installed correctly.

Help! I have problems with some Clipboard techniques.

397

I can't take a snapshot of the screen.

■ Try both PrtScrn and Alt+PrtScrn. Some keyboards work the PrtScrn keys differently; check with the system manufacturer. If it's a DOS application in standard mode, make sure that No Screen **E**xchange is turned off in the PIF.

■ Make sure that the PrtScrn and Alt+PrtScrn keys aren't reserved for an application. Open the PIF file. Verify that the video mode is correct and that Reserve Short**cu**t Keys is clear. Be sure enough memory is available for the Clipboard image.

Understanding DDE

The Clipboard is quite useful, but it has the disadvantage of being able to hold only a single item at a time. In addition, there must be user intervention for each transfer. DDE permits dynamic transfers without user intervention.

DDE is an abbreviation for *Dynamic Data Exchange*. DDE is available in many Windows application programs and enables several programs to access and use a common pool of commands or objects (data). Excel, Word for Windows, Crosstalk for Windows, and other applications support DDE. Think of DDE as a message system that allows Windows applications to share data or send messages to each other.

As an example of how DDE works, consider a communications program and spreadsheet both loaded to memory. Stock market quotations arrive to the communications program, and are immediately available to the spreadsheet program. You can watch totals and graphs change dynamically in the spreadsheet as the data coming into the communications program updates the stock prices. At the same time, a word processor document can pull up the current data from the spreadsheet each time that it is printed. Here are a few other applications of DDE:

- A Windows application can dynamically access data from medical instruments on a real-time basis and then make the data available immediately to other programs that can process, analyze, or chart it.

- A user can create letters on a network and use DDE to get the addresses from a database without leaving the word processor. Spreadsheets and graphs are pasted in from other applications, again without leaving the word processor. The final documents can then be transmitted as electronic mail from within the same program. The user believes he or she is using a single program.

- Linkages can be created between CAD systems and databases, making the database data available for the CAD work.

- Graphs can be created in a spreadsheet program and used in a word processor. The graph is automatically updated in the word processor whenever the spreadsheet data changes.

- Electronic mail systems can be created between PCs and mainframes, with the data automatically converted to other formats as it flows through the network.

- A spreadsheet program can use an interconnected set of worksheets. For example, all the assumptions could be on a separate worksheet. All dependent worksheets would then automatically be updated whenever the assumptions changed.

An address file created with PackRat can be available to Word for Windows. An option on a Word for Windows menu (created with its macro language) can let the user load an address from the PackRat file without ever leaving Word for Windows.

As you read the next discussion about sharing techniques, you will need to understand certain terms. Here is a brief explanation of those terms:

Object—a piece of data created and edited in a Windows application.

Source document—the original document containing the source.

Destination document—the document in which the object is to be placed.

Client—the application that receives the object.

Server—the application that provides the object.

In a typical application, you might be linking some named Excel spreadsheet cells to a Word for Windows document. The named cells are the object. The source document is the Excel worksheet. The destination document is in Word for Windows. Excel is the Server application, and Word for Windows is the Client application.

DDE was available in pre-3.0 versions of Windows, but because of memory limitations it was not very practical. To use DDE, all the programs sharing the data must be in memory. In earlier versions of Windows without extended memory support, multitasking in this way was impractical. The extended memory support of Windows 3 opened up the full potential of DDE, and applications are now rushing to take advantage of it.

DDE is based on the message-passing system that is an inherent part of Windows. Windows is event-driven (or message-driven). Instead of time-slicing various processing tasks, pressing a key or clicking the mouse, called an *event*, sends a message to a Windows central message-processing loop. This loop then examines the message and dispatches it to the proper application.

How does DDE work?

When you start an application that supports DDE, the application immediately starts sending messages about its name and data files to any other open Windows applications that support DDE. At any time, another Windows application can request that these messages be routed to one of its own data files. Once the communication is established, the relationship is that of a client/server. The application providing the data is the *server*, and the requesting application is the *client*. The communication is referred to as a *conversation*. The client application always starts the communication. The server application simply responds to the request. A given client application may be involved with several conversations with several server applications at the same time. Once the linkage is established by the user, no further user interaction is needed.

For example, suppose you have an Excel graph that you want to display in a Word for Windows document. Further, you want the graph in the Word for Windows document to be automatically updated each time the Excel spreadsheet data changes. Word for Windows is the client application and Excel the server. Therefore, you start from Word for Windows (the client) by telling Word for Windows the name of the application (Excel) and data source. Excel then provides the chart, and the link is established.

The DDE links can be any of three types: cold, warm, and hot. Which of the three types is supported (or all three types may be supported) depends on the application. A *cold link* is much like a snapshot. It is a one-time transfer of data, after which no other transfer occurs. A cold link is similar to a transfer through the Clipboard. With a *hot link*, the data is continually transferred each time the data is updated in the server application. The link is dynamic. With a *warm link*, the data is transferred only at the client's request.

In all cases, there is only a single copy of the object. It is shared by all the applications and stored separately. A copy of the object is displayed in the destination document, but the object is still in the original source document. When you back up the document, all related files must be copied with it.

How do I use DDE?

The next example shows how to link some Excel spreadsheet cells in Word for Windows by creating a hot or a warm link. The principle is similar for other applications. You might try linking a Paintbrush object into Microsoft Write, for example.

Both Word for Windows and Excel utilize DDE linking through the use of the **E**dit menu in the server and the Paste Link command of the client. Here are the basic steps for creating a hot link:

1. Be sure both applications are started and neither is minimized.

2. Open the source worksheet using **File O**pen in Excel.

3. Select the data in the source document (worksheet) and choose **E**dit **C**opy in Excel.

Help in Sharing Objects and Data with Applications

4. Select the Word for Windows document and place the cursor where you wish the object to be. Choose Paste **S**pecial from the **E**dit menu. In the Paste Special dialog box, choose Unformatted Text and Paste **L**ink. Click OK. This will establish a hot link.

With a hot link, the data in the Word for Windows document will always follow the spreadsheet data. Try changing the spreadsheet data and see what happens. With a warm link, the update is not made until the user requests it. To update a warm link in this example, first select the Excel cell or cells to update in the destination document. Choose the Word for Windows window and select the entire data field. Press F9 to update the object. In Word for Windows, F9 updates a warm link.

Remember that the references to the fields in the spreadsheet are absolute references. If you add rows or columns before the named spreadsheet range, the link will no longer be correct. To avoid this problem, use named cell references. To set up a named range, first name the range in Excel. Create the link; then edit the link to use the name. To edit the field codes, use View Field Codes in Word. Edit the line to use the named range.

If you don't have Word for Windows and Excel, you can try a similar experiment with the Windows applications provided with Windows. Create a drawing in Paintbrush, save it (always save before linking), and use **E**dit **C**opy to place it in the Clipboard. Now start Cardfile and choose Paste **S**pecial from the **E**dit menu. Select to link as a Bitmap and then choose Paste **L**ink. Now start Write, choose Paste Sp**e**cial from the **E**dit menu, and then Bitmap and Paste **L**ink again. You have now created linked objects in Cardfile and Write. There is only one real object in the computer memory, and it is shared by all three applications. Edit it in Paintbrush, and all the others will change.

You can also edit a linked drawing from the destination document. For example, open the Cardfile or Write document containing a linked object. Choose Lin**k**s or Lin**k** from the **E**dit menu. In the Links box, select the document to edit. Paintbrush will open with the document. Edit the document and save it. The document in Write or Cardfile is immediately updated if the link was a hot link. You can use **E**dit Lin**k**s to change the type of link.

To do multiple links, copy the object to the Clipboard once and then establish as many links to it as you wish. Most applications also support breaking a link and fixing broken links. These options are available on the linking dialog box (**E**dit Lin**k**s) as Ca**n**cel Link and **C**hange Link.

Note: There are currently no standards on DDE support. DDE options and features will vary with the application. There is a lack of consistency even within Microsoft applications. This situation is changing, however, and you can expect more standardization with future releases.

DDE Tips, Cautions, and Warnings

Although DDE is a powerful feature of Windows and is widely supported by many applications, it does have some limitations and weaknesses in the present version. Here are a few tips and cautions:

- You can link objects from saved documents only. If you create an object for linking, save it first. Then create the link.

- You can use DDE even between documents of the same application. Excel, for example, can be both a server (as in the previous example) and a client. You could create an assumption worksheet for all users to use, and then users could dynamically link to it. As the assumptions changed, all related worksheets would be automatically updated. An individual could break a complex worksheet down into an interconnected group of small worksheets that would be much more manageable. The linking technique would be the same. Use **E**dit **C**opy to place the cells into the Clipboard, then Paste **L**ink at the destination. Remember, however, use named cells for reliability.

- All applications do not support DDE. Some support it only as a client, others only as a server. Write and Cardfile can only be clients. Paintbrush can only be a server. When purchasing software, be sure the level of DDE support is defined before you make the purchase if DDE is important.

- DDE is limited to rather small amounts of data. You certainly should try to link no more than 64K of data. You must use applications to process the raw data and send only the results.

- Remember that Windows is not a true real-time system. For this reason, there are often tricky nuances when you are using certain programs under certain conditions, such as moving real-time data through DDE. Windows is a message-handling system, and if too many messages are moving through the system things can break down. Commercial applications are not always tested in message-intensive environments.

Developers often don't follow the DDE specifications exactly, and this may cause problems with certain applications. Even Microsoft, at times, has violated its own Windows DDE specifications in applications. DDL libraries will be available from Microsoft now that simplify and standardize the DDE interfacing for developers, but that doesn't mean all developers use these libraries.

If you are using networks, you will find that DDE is supported but that the support is accomplished by individual configurators (the system administrator sets up the support system rather than it being internal to the system). When DDE has been implemented, technical support is difficult. Much development work still needs to be done in this area.

There is no DDE between Windows and OS/2 applications. Each runs in its own virtual machine, and there is no method for communication between the machines.

Help! I have problems using DDE.

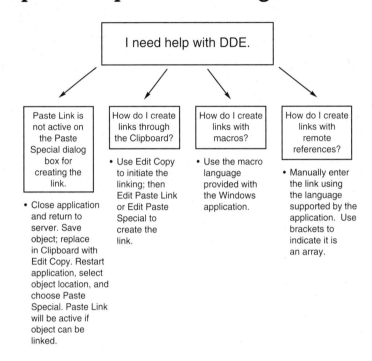

I need help with DDE.

Paste Link is not active on the Paste Special dialog box for creating the link.

- Close application and return to server. Save object; replace in Clipboard with Edit Copy. Restart application, select object location, and choose Paste Special. Paste Link will be active if object can be linked.

How do I create links through the Clipboard?

- Use Edit Copy to initiate the linking; then Edit Paste Link or Edit Paste Special to create the link.

How do I create links with macros?

- Use the macro language provided with the Windows application.

How do I create links with remote references?

- Manually enter the link using the language supported by the application. Use brackets to indicate it is an array.

DDE is available only to Windows applications, and only if the application is specifically designed to support it. It is not available for DOS applications. When purchasing applications, you should verify that the product supports DDE if that is important for your work. In addition, some applications support DDE only as a client (Write, Cardfile) or as a server (Paintbrush). Few are capable of bidirectional support.

There are three ways an application can use DDE: by creating links through the Clipboard, by creating links with macros, or by creating links using remote references.

The Paste Link button is not active on the Paste Special dialog box for creating the link.

Close the client application and return to the server. Save the object and then use **E**dit **C**opy to place it in the Clipboard again. Restart the client application, select the location for the object, and choose Paste **S**pecial again. The Paste **L**ink button should be active if the object can be linked.

How can I create links through the Clipboard?

All Windows applications do not support using the Clipboard for setting up the link. Some applications support one-way use of the Clipboard, either to or from the application. In addition, the standards for DDE are not clearly defined, and therefore the rules and commands vary with the application.

With the Clipboard method, the **E**dit menu is used to create the link between the documents. The **E**dit command of the source application is first used to copy the data to link to the Clipboard. Then the **E**dit Paste **S**pecial Link command in the destination application places the data in the destination document and creates the link. The link is set as hot, warm, or cold by using the dialog box when the link is pasted or it is set from a Lin**k** command on the **E**dit menu of the application.

> **Note:** The Clipboard really has nothing to do with DDE, even though it is often used in setting up the initial link between applications. Many applications use the Clipboard as a temporary storage for transferring information to the client application about the server's application name and data filename.

How can I create links with macros?

Windows applications often support a macro language, and various DDE commands are usually available within this language. Word for Windows, Ami Pro, Crosstalk for Windows, and others support rich macro languages that offer this DDE support.

For example, Crosstalk for Windows supports a script language that includes DDE commands. You essentially write your own "program" using these scripts. Often, sample scripts are available with the product or from bulletin boards (even vendor-supported bulletin boards).

To use the macro language for linking, however, you must be aware of the *protocol*. The protocol is unique to the application but has certain general features. In each case, a three-tiered structure is used to define the data: application, topic, and item. For example, here is a cell

reference in Excel when the reference is pasted to a document:

```
=EXCEL¦STOCKPL¦$A$3
```

The application is Excel, the topic is the worksheet name, and the item is the cell reference. The three tiers are easy to see in a spreadsheet program, but in other applications the tiers may not be as visible. For example, in a stock analysis program the reference may be:

```
=STOCKVW¦NYSE¦IBM
```

If you link some Word for Windows text into an Excel document, you may see something like:

```
{=WINWORD¦'E:\BUDGET\91BGT.DOC'¦DDE_LINK}
```

Some applications may have a complex list of topics and subitems. To extract the data, you must know the available topics and items. IBM's Current is an example of this type of DDE.

How can I create links with remote references?

Some applications permit you to enter a remote reference. To do so, manually enter the link, using the language supported by the application. For an array, use brackets to indicate the array.

With Excel you can enter a remote reference directly into a cell. This is often done when two spreadsheet documents are being linked, such as:

```
92SALES!Total
```

This reference might be a cell entry that links that cell to a cell named Total on a worksheet called 92SALES. The

Help in Sharing Objects and Data with Applications

remote reference can be extended further by adding the application name:

```
=STOCKVW|NYSE|IBM
```

This pastes the IBM quote from a program called STOCKVW to that cell of a worksheet.

Understanding Object Linking and Embedding (OLE)

Windows also supports *object linking and embedding* (OLE) for Windows applications. OLE is a new concept to Windows and is one of the most important concepts or advances supported by the latest Windows releases. In short, it is the cutting edge for object-oriented programming, borrowing from hypertext and multimedia models. It also is not the easiest concept to understand. It can include linking, but it is more than that.

To understand OLE, you need to be aware of the new concepts and definitions it has introduced. With OLE and object-oriented programming, objects are "intelligent"; that is, they carry some computer instructions with them. This is in contrast with the "dumb" data files of most of your current applications. An xBASE file, for example, has a specified format with fields of fixed length. The application program has to know the format to use the file. An intelligent object, in contrast, carries the information within it to interpret its contents.

A *compound document* is a document that can contain many different types of objects, each with the intelligence needed to interpret its contents. The objects could be Excel charts, a database name and address, a picture (PCX-type), a recorded sound track, or any other type of object. With OLE, you are using smart objects. A database address, for example, can be embedded in a Word for Windows document. Double-clicking the address should open up the database program that created the address and permit editing of it.

You can think of your Windows documents as being compound documents. The components for a compound document can reside anywhere on the system. On a networked system, they can reside on any system of the network.

Objects of various types reside in the document. There is no native format for the file. To edit a given object, you simply double-click the object. The user interface becomes very object-oriented. You don't even have to know which application program does what. Just select the object, and the appropriate program is loaded. With object-oriented programming, application programs are no longer programs for creating, editing, and reporting data. Instead, programs become tools for accessing and working with the objects.

The OLE environment must support multitasking, since several applications can be open at once. The environment must support messaging, or IPC (Inter-Process Communication). Programs that are currently running must have the ability to send messages among themselves. Windows meets all of these requirements, and is therefore ideal for supporting OLE.

In OLE, the original object is the *parent object*. Each copy of the object in other documents is called a *child object*, or *instance*. Make a change anywhere, and all OLE-linked changes appear in all documents. Objects can also contain a chunk of the application that created the object. Opening the object may give you enough application tools to do some level of editing. Objects can also be nested within other objects. This is all a very radical concept for those working with computers today, and will eventually change the very nature of the user interface.

Another example will show the real power of OLE. Suppose you wish to create a word processing document about cats. You want the document to have some icon buttons that can initiate various cat sounds. You have another program called Recorder that can record and play back sounds. The word processor knows nothing about the sound format of this program. You use Recorder to record your various cat sounds in several files. You then transfer these files to the word processor document by using OLE. The word processor stores the sounds in the word processing document in two formats: the digitized sound (which it knows nothing about) and a display format (such as some type of cat icon). When you select the icon, Recorder starts (perhaps invisibly) and the word processor passes it the digitized sound, which is then played.

As you can see, OLE permits the creation of complex documents involving various formats, and is really a very powerful concept. Microsoft is developing the OLE technology in cooperation with Aldus, Lotus, and WordPerfect. You won't find OLE in many applications yet because it is still new. With this level of support, however, it is obviously going to be very important in future versions of Windows.

To use OLE, the basic strategy is the same as that for a copy. Select the object and use **E**dit **C**opy to place it in the Clipboard. Then switch to the destination document, mark the insertion point, and use **E**dit Paste Special. To embed a graphics object in a report created with Microsoft Write, you can start from either Write or Paintbrush.

Note: All applications do not support OLE.

Embedding an Object in Write or Cardfile

1. Open the Write document that will contain the embedded drawing.

2. Choose **I**nsert Object from the **E**dit menu. (If using Cardfile, choose Pictur**e** from the **E**dit menu, then **I**nsert Object.)

3. Choose Paintbrush Picture from the Insert New Object dialog box, shown in Figure 11.1. Select OK.

4. Paintbrush opens. Create the drawing. (Or, optionally, open the file or paste from the Clipboard.)

5. Choose **U**pdate from the **F**ile menu.

6. Exit the Paintbrush program (**F**ile E**x**it). Now you can continue working with Write (or Cardfile).

Figure 11.1

Inserting an object.

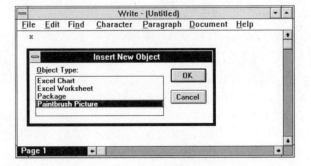

To embed a drawing in Write (or Cardfile) starting from Paintbrush:

1. Start Paintbrush. Create the drawing. (Or, optionally, open the file or paste from the Clipboard.)

2. Select the object.

3. Choose **C**opy from the **E**dit menu.

4. Start the destination application (Write or Cardfile) and open the document.

5. If using Write, place the insertion point and choose **P**aste from the **E**dit menu. If using Cardfile, choose Pictur**e** from the **E**dit menu and then **P**aste.

To edit an embedded object, double-click the object. The source program will start with the object. Edit the object and then choose **U**pdate from the **F**ile menu. Exit the application. For example, to edit a Paintbrush object from Write, double-click the object. Paintbrush opens. Edit the object and then choose **U**pdate from the **F**ile menu. You can also try double-clicking the object to start editing.

Using OLE with Objects from Applications That Don't Have OLE

You've probably already noticed an accessory called *Object Packager* with Windows 3.1 and wondered what it does. Object Packager permits you to package documents with special information that tells other objects or documents that this is really an object and that it contains information about the object's contents. In short, with Object Packager you can turn objects into OLE objects when the application that created them doesn't support OLE.

For example, Object Packager permits you to attach a command line and icon to an object. You can then embed this packaged object in a document. You will see the icon in the document. When you open the object, Windows executes the command line and presents the object to you in its native environment.

One example of packaging is useful if you frequently use Calculator with a document in Write. Package the Calculator and embed it into the Write document. The Calculator is only two clicks away whenever you need it.

Not all applications are OLE-aware yet. But with Object Packager you can add a level of OLE awareness to applications that don't support OLE. For example, you could use Object Packager to embed a CorelDRAW 2.0 graphic in a document.

Creating a Package

To create a package, follow these steps:

1. Open Object Packager from the Accessories group to display it on-screen. Figure 11.2 shows the Object Packager window.

2. Select the Content window by using Tab or clicking with the mouse.

3. Choose Import from the File menu.

4. Select the proper directory and file. Click OK. The filename appears in the Content window, and the icon in the Appearance window.

5. You can change the icon by selecting the Insert Icon button or the label by choosing Label from the Edit menu.

6. Choose Copy Package from the Edit menu.

Help in Sharing Objects and Data with Applications

7. Open the destination document, place the cursor at the insertion point, and choose **P**aste from the **E**dit menu. (Packages are always embedded.)

Figure 11.2
Creating a package.

The package appears in the document. Select the package by double-clicking it or by choosing Packaged Object from the **E**dit menu.

Packaging a Linked or Embedded Document

Packages can contain linked or embedded documents. You can create these packages in any of three ways:

◻ Copy the document through the Clipboard from File Manager to Object Packager.

◻ Copy the document with File Manager through the Clipboard to the destination document and then insert it as a package.

◻ Using the mouse, insert a package containing the embedded or linked document into the destination document.

A given application may not support all three of these methods. Check the application documentation to see which methods will work.

Creating a Package by Using File Manager and Object Packager

This method will work with some applications that support OLE and DDE:

1. Open File Manager and select the document.

2. Choose **C**opy from the **F**ile menu.

3. Select the **C**opy to Clipboard option in the dialog box. Then select OK.

4. Start Object Packager.

5. Choose Paste **L**ink from the **E**dit menu to create a linked document. Choose **P**aste to create an embedded document.

6. Change the icon as desired by using Insert **I**con. Edit the label by choosing La**b**el from the **E**dit menu.

7. Open the destination document.

8. Choose **P**aste from the **E**dit menu. The package will be embedded in the document. (Packages are always embedded.)

Creating a Package by Using File Manager and the Clipboard

Some applications may support this shorter method:

1. Open File Manager and select the document.

2. Choose **C**opy from the **F**ile menu.

3. Select the **C**opy to Clipboard option in the dialog box. Then select OK.

4. Open the destination document.

5. Choose **P**aste from the **E**dit menu.

Creating a Package by Using the Mouse and File Manager

1. Open File Manager and select the document.

2. Open the destination application and document.

3. To create a package containing an embedded document, drag the file's icon from File Manager to the destination document. To create a package containing a linked document, hold down Ctrl+Shift while dragging.

Inserting Part of a Document in a Package

You can create a package containing only part of an object, such as a paragraph of a report. The partial object is called a *subobject*. Here's how to embed or link part of a document in a package:

1. Open the document containing the object from which the subobject will be selected.

2. Select the subobject, and select **C**opy from the **E**dit menu.

3. Open Object Packager. Select the Content window.

4. From the **E**dit menu, choose **P**aste to embed or Paste Link to link.

5. Choose Copy Pac**k**age from the **E**dit menu.

6. Open the destination document and choose **P**aste from the **E**dit menu.

Help! I have problems with OLE.

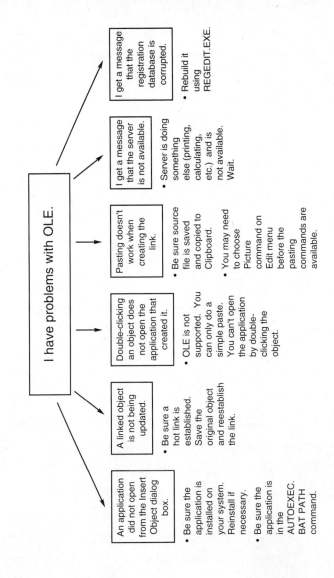

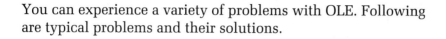

You can experience a variety of problems with OLE. Following are typical problems and their solutions.

An application did not open from the Insert Object dialog box.

■ Be sure the application is installed on your system. Reinstall as necessary.

■ Be sure the application is in the PATH command specified in the AUTOEXEC.BAT file (see Appendix G).

A linked object is not being updated.

■ Make sure you are using a hot link (and not a warm or cold link). Lack of updating may occur in some cases. Save the original document again and then reestablish the link.

Double-clicking an object in a document doesn't open the application that created it.

■ The application that created the object does not support object linking and embedding. When OLE is not supported, the **P**aste command does a simple paste and you cannot edit the object by double-clicking it.

Pasting doesn't work when I create a link.

☐ Be sure the source file has been saved. Save the file before copying it to the Clipboard; you can link information only from a saved file. Be sure the information has been copied to the Clipboard. Use the Clipboard viewer to check this.

☐ In some programs, such as Cardfile, you must choose a Picture command from the Edit menu before the pasting commands are available.

I get a message that the server is not available.

☐ Be sure the server application is available. It will not be available if it is printing, making a calculation, displaying an open dialog box, or otherwise active. Wait for the server to become available and then try again. If a server dialog box is open, close it and try again.

I get a message that the registration database is corrupted.

☐ The registration database is used in linking, embedding, and dragging and dropping to provide information to Windows about an associated program for a file. If this file is corrupted, follow these steps:

1. Quit Windows and delete REG.DAT.

2. Start Windows. Then use File Manager to start REGEDIT.EXE.

3. From the **File** menu, select **M**erge Registration File.

4. Select SETUP.REG as the file.

5. Select each REG file on all system drives.

When should I use OLE, and when should I use DDE?

Use OLE (if the application supports it) over DDE. The most common use of OLE is to insert a spreadsheet range or a graphic in a document. A little creativity will show its true value, however. For example, you could update a return address in a letter and have the address in the database updated automatically. Another use is to launch a spell checker or grammar checker from a document.

You might wonder how OLE differs from DDE, since both support linking. OLE is more robust, with better error checking than DDE. The protocols for OLE are better documented, and there is more standardization. DDE can't launch the application when the object is double-clicked. OLE has far more potential for future developers, so you can expect to see more applications evolving into this from the older DDE. The DDE in Windows 3.1, however, is more reliable than the 3.0 DDE as long as the developer uses the DDE library with Windows 3.1.

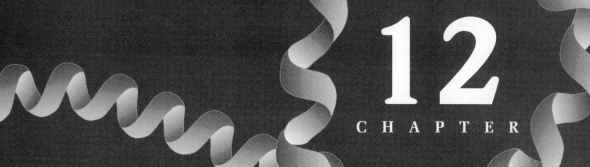

12
CHAPTER

HELP WITH COMMUNICATION PROBLEMS

You can use your computer to access other computers, transferring data to or from your system electronically. This chapter looks at communication problems and offers solutions to fix them.

What do I need for electronic communication?

To use your computer for electronic communication, you will need a modem and a communications program. The *modem* is a hardware device that converts the computer's digital data to an analog form that can be communicated over a telephone link. At the same time, the modem can convert incoming analog signals to a digital form for the computer.

Modems are either internal (it fits in a card slot in the computer) or external (it sits on the desk next to the computer). External modems permit using the same modem with various systems, but they require desk space. They connect to the serial port of the computer, with another connection to the telephone system. Internal modems are not as flexible because they must be used on a single system. However, they create less clutter on the desk. Internal modems don't require the computer's serial port, and they connect to the telephone line with a single cable.

Modems are generally rated for a certain speed, which is called the *baud rate* (the technical term is *bits per second*, bps). The remote computer must also use a modem, and its speed should be compatible. A 2400-baud modem is about the minimum speed considered usable by today's standards. For CompuServe, this means about 220 characters a second can be transferred. For faster transfers, you should purchase a 9600-baud modem. These use a standard V.32 protocol for reliable data transfer across public telephone lines. If the modem supports V.32bis, it can transfer as fast as 14,400 bits per second. Some modems also use a V.42bis data compression to achieve even greater throughput.

Performance Tip: If you are new at computer communications, you might start with local bulletin boards (BBS). These are generally free, and you won't run up a bill while you learn. Check with a local computer user group or a computer store to find the better ones in your area. Some systems stay quite busy. Start with a small BBS to get better access time. A BBS is also an easy way to get answers to questions as you begin.

All modems for PC communications should be Hayes-compatible. *Hayes-compatible* means that the modem uses control codes defined by Hayes Microcomputer Products, Inc. This is not a standard, however, because Hayes is constantly changing the control codes as its products evolve. As a result, all modems marketed as Hayes-compatible are not the same.

For the communications software, you can use any of the available communications products. For simple communications and testing, you can use Terminal with Windows.

Help! I have communication problems.

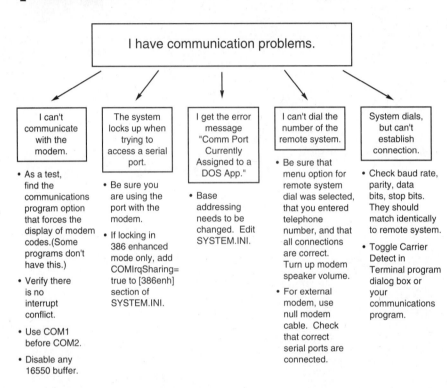

I have communication problems.

I can't communicate with the modem.

- As a test, find the communications program option that forces the display of modem codes.(Some programs don't have this.)
- Verify there is no interrupt conflict.
- Use COM1 before COM2.
- Disable any 16550 buffer.

The system locks up when trying to access a serial port.

- Be sure you are using the port with the modem.
- If locking in 386 enhanced mode only, add COMIrqSharing= true to [386enh] section of SYSTEM.INI.

I get the error message "Comm Port Currently Assigned to a DOS App."

- Base addressing needs to be changed. Edit SYSTEM.INI.

I can't dial the number of the remote system.

- Be sure that menu option for remote system dial was selected, that you entered telephone number, and that all connections are correct. Turn up modem speaker volume.
- For external modem, use null modem cable. Check that correct serial ports are connected.

System dials, but can't establish connection.

- Check baud rate, parity, data bits, stop bits. They should match identically to remote system.
- Toggle Carrier Detect in Terminal program dialog box or your communications program.

If you have a communications problem, try to find out where in the sequence the problem occurs. Are you having a problem accessing the modem? Can you access the modem but have problems dialing a number? Can you dial the number but have a problem synchronizing with the remote system?

I can't communicate with a modem.

☐ As a test, find the communications program option that forces the display of the modem codes (some programs don't have this option). Try to display the modem codes. For an external modem, if you are not accessing the modem the lights on it won't flash.

First, be sure there is no interrupt conflict. The interrupt for each device is set on the adapter card. For an internal modem, the interrupt is set on the modem card. For an external modem, the interrupt is set on the serial communications card, or it may be a fixed part of the computer system. Most systems default to interrupt 4 for COM1 and COM3, and interrupt 3 for COM2 and COM4. If you have recently added a new adapter card set to one of these interrupts (such as a mouse), that may be the problem (see Appendix C).

In general, serial communication problems are often the result of improper settings (baud rate, data bits, etc.). You should also make sure that two programs are not contending for the same port. Device contention is controlled in the 386 enhanced mode from the 386 Enhanced icon in Control Panel. In the 386 enhanced mode, you may not be able to use 9600 baud with DOS applications. (This situation has been improved in 3.1.) Also, if you are having a communication problem with a DOS application in 386 enhanced mode, you might try editing the PIF file to run it in **E**xclusive.

When you are using standard mode and DOS communications programs, be sure that Prevent Program **S**witch is turned on in the PIF file. Switching the program out can cause loss of data because the program will be parked on the disk and will be inactive when it is switched out.

■ Remember to use COM1 before using COM2, and COM2 before using any higher port. Activate lower ports before higher. Check adapter cards and be sure there are no interrupt conflicts.

■ Windows does not support the 16550 and 16550A chips of the PS/2 series in the advanced FIFO mode. Disable the 16550 buffer if it is in use (see your computer manual). Install the computer so that the 16550 chips in these machines emulate the older 8250 UART.

The system locks up when I try to access a serial port.

■ DOS is pretty dumb when it is using the communication ports (COM1 to COM4). There are a lot of problems, and if DOS fails, the system can hang. Adjust the communication parameters (port, baud rate, data bits, etc.) as necessary. Most communications programs use the ports directly, bypassing DOS. For best communications with these ports, use Windows applications. Using Windows applications won't solve everything, but it helps.

■ If the system locks in 386 enhanced mode, try adding `COMIrqSharing=true` to the `[386enh]` section of SYSTEM.INI (see Appendix G).

Some 8514/a display adapters and network adapters may use COM4. Check for a conflict here.

I get the error "Comm Port Currently Assigned to a DOS App."

☐ Base addressing for the communication ports needs to be changed to what Windows is expecting. If you can't do this, change the Com3Base= and Com4Base= parameters in the [386enh] section of SYSTEM.INI (see Appendix G) to the following:

```
[386h]
COM1Base=3F8h
COM2Base=2F8h
COM3Base=3E8h
COM4Base=2E8h
```

Be sure to reboot after changing the parameters. Also, try using the MODE command to set the port at bootup before Windows starts.

I can't dial the number of the remote system.

To initiate the communications, when you request a connection the program should initialize the modem and then dial the number. You should hear the tones from the modem speaker as the program dials the number.

☐ Be sure you have used the menu option for this and entered the number. Verify that all the connections are correct and that the modem is connected to the phone jack.

For the Terminal accessory, start Terminal and then choose **S**ettings from the menu bar and the **C**ommunications option.

Make sure on the Communications dialog box that the correct port is selected. Be sure that a phone number has been entered to the program.

Turn up the modem speaker volume to hear the modem dialing.

If you are connecting an external modem, make sure that you are using a null modem cable (between the modem and the computer) instead of a standard RS-232 cable and that the correct serial ports on both machines are connected.

The system dials but can't establish a connection.

Once the remote system picks up the phone, you should hear the remote modem, and the two systems should synchronize automatically within a few seconds. If this fails, check to see that the baud rate, data bits, parity, and stop bits are correct. They should match the remote system identically. If using the Terminal accessory, try the connection with and without Carrier Detect being toggled on in the dialog box that sets the parameters.

Help! I have problems with ASCII text transfers.

Help with Communication Problems

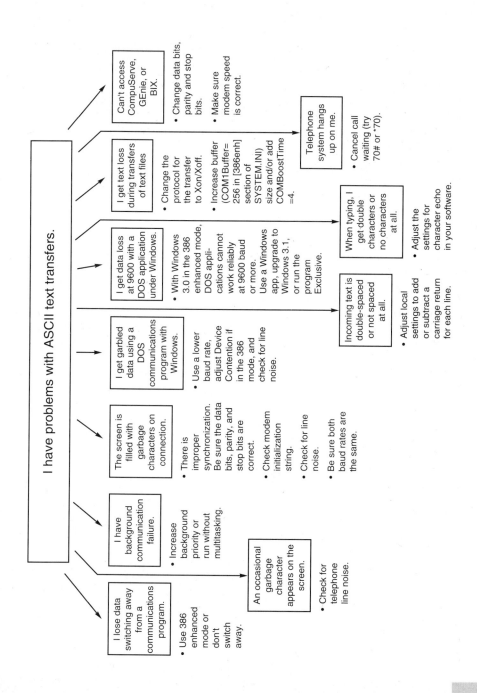

I have problems with ASCII text transfers.

I lose data switching away from a communications program.
- Use 386 enhanced mode or don't switch away.

I have background communication failure.
- Increase background priority or run without multitasking.

An occasional garbage character appears on the screen.
- Check for telephone line noise.

The screen is filled with garbage characters on connection.
- There is improper synchronization. Be sure the data bits, parity, and stop bits are correct.
- Check modem initialization string.
- Check for line noise.
- Be sure both baud rates are the same.

I get garbled data using a DOS communications program with Windows.
- Use a lower baud rate, adjust Device Contention if in the 386 mode, and check for line noise.

I get data loss at 9600 with a DOS application under Windows.
- With Windows 3.0 in the 386 enhanced mode, DOS applications cannot work reliably at 9600 baud or more. Use a Windows app, upgrade to Windows 3.1, or run the program Exclusive.

Incoming text is double-spaced or not spaced at all.
- Adjust local settings to add or subtract a carriage return for each line.

When typing, I get double characters or no characters at all.
- Adjust the settings for character echo in your software.

I get text loss during transfers of text files
- Change the protocol for the transfer to Xon/Xoff.
- Increase buffer (COM1Buffer=256 in [386enh] section of SYSTEM.INI) size and/or add COMBoostTime =4.

Can't access CompuServe, GEnie, or BIX.
- Change data bits, parity and stop bits.
- Make sure modem speed is correct.

Telephone system hangs up on me.
- Cancel call waiting (try 70# or *70).

Help! I have problems with ASCII text transfers.

Once you have established a connection and the two systems synchronize, you should see any characters you type as well as any characters from the remote system.

I lose data switching away from a communications program in Windows real or standard mode.

☐ With Windows 3.0, the program in real or standard mode is swapped to disk and becomes inactive. With Windows 3.1, the program may or may not be switched away. Use the 386 enhanced mode or don't switch away.

An occasional garbage character appears on the screen.

☐ The telephone line has noise. Contact the telephone company and ask them to test the line for noise.

I have a failure of background communication.

☐ Increase the background priority in the system setup or run the communications program without multitasking.

The screen is filled with garbage characters on connection.

- [ ] There is improper synchronization. Be sure the data bits, parity, and stop bits are set correctly.
- [ ] Check the modem initialization string.
- [ ] Be sure the telephone line doesn't have noise.
- [ ] Make sure both baud rates are the same.

I get garbled data when using a DOS communications program with Windows.

- [ ] Try running at a lower baud rate. If you are using 386 enhanced mode, use Control Panel to access the 386 Enhanced icon. Adjust the Device Contention options. Check for telephone line noise.

The incoming text is double-spaced or not spaced at all (the lines are on top of each other).

- [ ] Use Terminal's Terminal **P**references command from the **S**ettings menu to change the CR→CR/ LF option.

Help! I have problems with ASCII text transfers.

I get data loss at 9600 with a DOS application under Windows.

In the 386 enhanced mode, DOS applications cannot work reliably at 9600 baud or faster. Switch to a lower mode or use a Windows-based communications program. Windows 3.1 can handle faster speeds than 3.0. Run the application as **E**xclusive, not as a background.

When typing, I get double characters or no characters at all.

Use Terminal's Terminal **P**references command from the **S**ettings menu to change the Local **E**cho option.

I get text loss when I transfer text files.

Change the protocol used for text transfers. Most systems support the XON/XOFF protocol. Try this first. For back-to-back transfers between computers without a modem, try a hardware protocol.

Try increasing the buffer size used by the communications program. For example, add **COM1Buffer=256** to the [386enh] section of SYSTEM.INI (see Appendix G). You could also try adding **COMBoostTime=4** in the same section if the loss is from a DOS communications program. You may also need to lock memory by setting this option in the Memory Requirements section of the PIF file.

The telephone system hangs up on me.

▢ If you have call waiting, the telephone system may hang up on you if another call interrupts the current call. To solve the problem, use the modem initialization string to cancel call waiting for each call. Check with the local telephone company to find out how to do this. In most cases, this means sending AT70# or AT*70 to the modem.

I can't access CompuServe, GEnie, or BIX.

▢ For CompuServe or BIX, use these settings: `Data bits=7`, `Parity=Even`, `Stop bits =1`. For GEnie, use `Data bits=8`, `Parity=None`, and `Stop bits=1`.

▢ Make sure that your modem speed is correct for the telephone connection to the system you are using. Most services have separate lines for the different modem speeds.

Help! I have problems transferring binary files.

Most communications programs support the transfer of binary files between two systems by using file transfer commands. Typical problems include a system hangup or too many errors.

When I try to download a file, the system hangs.

The system isn't really hung. The remote system is waiting for an acknowledgment. Either you aren't ready or you are using a protocol unrecognized by the remote system.

Downloading refers to transferring binary files from a remote system to your system by using a block method. To work successfully, both systems must be using the same *protocol,* or rules of communication. There are several data communication protocols: X-modem, Y-modem, Z-modem, Compuserve B, and others. You can use any of these as long as the remote system can support the same protocol.

To download, take the following steps:

1. Initiate the download command on the remote system. The remote system requests the file to download from the remote system. Enter the filename.

2. The remote system may then request which protocol to use. Some default to a fixed protocol without any query. Select the protocol if prompted. It must be one supported by your system.

3. The remote system goes into a waiting mode. Switch to your system's command mode, select the protocol you wish to use, and issue a command to receive the binary file. For Windows programs, you generally select the protocol and start receiving the file by using commands on menus.

If the protocols are the same, the two systems should synchronize, and in a few seconds you should see an acknowledgment that the transfer is taking place.

If the system hangs, the protocols are not the same or the receiving system isn't ready. Don't hang up. If you hang up, the

Help with Communication Problems

remote system may keep on billing you for a few minutes. Use your software to send a break to the other system (see your software manual).

I tried to download a file and got too many errors.

You have too much noise on the telephone line. Contact the telephone company and have them test the line.

I can't upload a file.

Uploading refers to transferring binary files from your system to a remote system by using a block method. A failure here indicates that the remote system is not ready or that the protocols are not the same. Get your system ready first and start the upload. Then switch to the command mode of the remote system and start the receiving.

Tips for Using On-line Services

Here are some suggestions for using on-line services:

- Using information services, such as CompuServe, can be expensive. Plan your sessions before dialing and have specific objectives.

- The first time you dial into a new system, find a file list and download it as a capture. Sign off and scan the list at leisure to find the files you wish to download. Then dial in again for the files.

- Prepare electronic mail ahead of time. Then transmit it by pasting from the Clipboard or transferring it as a text file.

- Set up function keys for access to the remote systems you use. This will speed up access and, with systems that charge, reduce on-line costs.

- Monitor your on-line time.

- Keep the local echo off unless necessary. This ensures that the text on your screen is echoed from the remote system, and you can see what you send as the remote system receives it. The result is better accuracy. On most services, you can choose if you wish the remote system to echo. Letting the remote system echo is better.

- Use the Clipboard to convert file formats. For example, compose a letter with Microsoft Word. Copy it to the Clipboard. Now paste it to the communications program when you are ready to send it. The Clipboard converts it to ASCII.

Performance Tip: It is important to log off the remote system properly before disconnecting at your end. This forces the remote system to hang up the phone. If you fail to log off properly, the remote system may remain on the line for a while after you disconnect. If this happens, many data services will continue to bill time to your account for a few minutes. If you drop from a system accidentally, immediately dial back in and continue the session or log off.

Help with Communication Problems

Help! I have problems with local transfers.

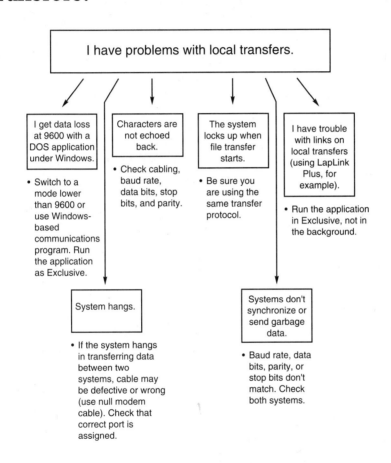

I have problems with local transfers.

I get data loss at 9600 with a DOS application under Windows.

- Switch to a mode lower than 9600 or use Windows-based communications program. Run the application as Exclusive.

Characters are not echoed back.

- Check cabling, baud rate, data bits, stop bits, and parity.

The system locks up when file transfer starts.

- Be sure you are using the same transfer protocol.

I have trouble with links on local transfers (using LapLink Plus, for example).

- Run the application in Exclusive, not in the background.

System hangs.

- If the system hangs in transferring data between two systems, cable may be defective or wrong (use null modem cable). Check that correct port is assigned.

Systems don't synchronize or send garbage data.

- Baud rate, data bits, parity, or stop bits don't match. Check both systems.

With local transfers, the two computers are connected at their serial ports by using a null modem cable. Each system has communications software (no modem), and the transfer is done using the local mode of the software on both systems. Since there is no telephone line or modem limiting the transfer speed, you can go as fast as the serial ports will support. You should select hardware handshaking protocol instead of XON/XOFF.

I get data loss at 9600 with a DOS application under Windows.

In the 386 enhanced mode, DOS applications cannot work reliably at 9600 baud or faster. Switch to a lower mode or use a Windows-based communications program. Windows 3.1 can handle faster speeds than 3.0 can handle. Run the application as **E**xclusive, not as a background.

The system hangs.

DOS is not too kind in recovering from serial port transfers, and generally hangs.

If the system hangs in transferring data between two systems, a defective or wrong cable is probably being used (use a null modem cable), or one of the systems is using the wrong port.

Characters are not echoed back.

■ Once the system is connected, send a few characters to the remote system and let them be echoed back, just as with a modem transfer. If this doesn't work or if the system hangs, check the baud rate, data bits, stop bits, and parity with both systems. Be sure a null modem cable is being used. If the characters are received by the remote station but not echoed back, check for a defective cable or serial card.

The system locks up when the file transfer starts.

■ Be sure you are using the same transfer protocol.

Systems don't synchronize or they send garbage data.

■ If you cannot synchronize two local systems, they are probably not using the same baud rate, number of data bits, parity, or number of stop bits. Check each of these on both systems.

I have problems transferring data on local transfers when I'm using links like Traveling Software's Laplink Plus or White Crane's Brooklyn Bridge.

In a DOS environment these can work to 115,200 bps. Under Windows, you are limited to 19,200 bps. The limitation is Windows' COMM.DRV. If you can find a better one, you might get higher speed. Run the application in Exclusive, not in the background.

13
CHAPTER

HELP WITH MULTIMEDIA

Multimedia is a general term that encompasses full-motion video, hypermedia, interactive video, and other concepts. Intel, IBM, Apple, and Microsoft (as well as other vendors) are all committed to bringing multimedia to the public at a realistic price. It has applications for presentations, education, database management, and home game playing. This chapter will explain the major concepts involved in multimedia and offer troubleshooting suggestions for multimedia systems.

13

Introduction to Multimedia

Microsoft has already released MME (Multimedia Extensions for Windows) version 1.0. This product required over two years of development work and is built on standards developed jointly by Microsoft and the Multimedia PC Marketing Council (MPC), a consortium of many vendors. As you make hardware purchases, you may wish to keep the MPC standards in mind for your long-term plans. In other words, if you purchase a CD-ROM for your system, you should be sure it meets the MPC standards. Windows 3.1 contains a subset of the MME.

Requirements for a Multimedia System

For a minimum multimedia system, you need the following:

- A 25-megahertz (MHz) 386 or faster processor.
- Two megabytes (MB) of RAM (4MB or more for authoring or writing multimedia programs).
- A 16-color 640 x 480 VGA display (256-color Super VGA recommended).
- MIDI synthesizer and ports.
- Sampled output audio at 8 bits: 11.025 kilohertz (kHz) in, 11.025 and 22.05 kHz out.
- A CD-ROM with MSCDEX extensions version 2.2 or later (see text).
- Thirty megabytes or more of disk space (80MB or more recommended).

- A joystick and two-button mouse.

- The Microsoft *Multimedia Extensions Kit* (included with Windows 3.1).

Of all the components listed, the CD-ROM is probably the most expensive to add, but one of the most important because a multimedia system's data storage requirements are large and software (such as the MME) is often delivered on CD-ROM. The CD-ROM drive is read-only. Unlike creating your own floppies with a hard disk drive, creating your own CD-ROMs is expensive. The CD-ROM drive must have a 1-second maximum seek time and a sustained data transfer rate of 150 kilobytes (KB) per second. The average access time should be 380 milliseconds or better. The CD-ROM drive should also have an audio output that can be mixed with the output of the sound card for sending to an amplifier. There is about 600MB of data on a CD-ROM disk, or 300,000 pages of printed material.

Expect the CD-ROM to be much slower than your hard disk. Reading is more than ten times slower than most hard disks today. The volume of data being accessed, though, is very large. If an encyclopedia disk has good indexing software, for example, you can quickly access every article that mentions a given topic.

When you purchase a CD-ROM drive, it can be internal (reside in the computer) or external (on the desk beside it). You will also need the software drivers for the CD-ROM. These should be sold with the drive. Many drives come with a library of CD-ROMs for starting.

Note: Just because a disk drive meets the MPC specifications doesn't mean it will work well with the MME. When you are purchasing a drive, make sure that it will work well with MME. The most critical area is often the use of CD-ROM drives with video and sound synchronization, yet very few products today enable a user to test this. Check magazine reviews before making a decision.

For multimedia support, you will also need a sound card that supports the MPC specifications. There are three basic sources of sound in a multimedia system: waveform audio, CD audio, and MIDI.

Waveform audio is audio that is converted to digital data by a process called *sampling*. A CD-ROM on a stereo system uses 16-bit sampling at 44.1 kHz. The number of bits determines the dynamic range (in this case, 96 decibels), and the sampling rate determines the frequency range. The frequency range is half the sampling rate, or about 20 kHz.

The multimedia input specification calls for 8-bit sampling at 11.025 kHz. This works out to a 48-decibel range for a frequency of 5 kHz. This is adequate for voice, but not for music. With 8-bit sampling, you will definitely hear noise. You could use this specification, for example, to attach voice to electronic mail. The output specification is 8-bit sampling at 11.025 kHz or 22.05 kHz. The latter rate is better for music (supports to 10 kHz). This rate may sound limiting compared with the CD-ROM music on your stereo, but a minute of sound sampled at 11.025 kHz requires 660 KB, and at 22.05 kHz requires 1.3MB. Stereo will double this storage. This is also a lot of data moving through the processor. The sound card should support DMA (direct memory access) or have interrupt-generating FIFO buffers.

CD audio is the audio output from the CD-ROM device. This is mixed with the other sound sources.

The *MIDI sound source* adds a new dimension to producing sound. In video you can use raster and vector graphics. If waveform audio is the "raster" of sound, then MIDI is the "vector." With MIDI, sound is represented as a sequence of computer instructions for producing that sound. MIDI is typically transmitted over a serial cable (MIDI standard) at 31,250 bits per second, or about 3,125 bytes per second. The commands turn a note on, turn a note off, change the volume, etc. The result is that sound commands are stored instead of the sound, and the music is stored much more densely. Most sound equipment today (keyboards, synthesizers, sequencers, etc.) have a MIDI jack. You can connect these devices together so that computer instructions from one device are available to another. A multimedia PC should have both MIDI In and MIDI Out ports. The board must support three simultaneous voices with six-note polyphony each and a percussion channel with five-note polyphony.

Multimedia Products

Multimedia sound boards available today include the Pro AudioSpectrum (Media Vision) and Sound Blaster Pro (Creative Labs). The sound quality of Pro AudioSpectrum is better, but the cost is also higher.

13

CHAPTER

Multimedia systems really hog your hard disk space. Installing the Sony CD-ROM with its laser library (six CD-ROMs) takes about 10MB. Add to this the 10MB for Windows and other application software, and a 30MB disk is hardly sufficient for even starting.

Now add another CD-ROM product like Microsoft's Multimedia Beethoven, and an additional 4.5MB of hard disk space is required. There is no denying the educational experience here. An entire interactive course in music appreciation is on the CD-ROM for only $80. You can explore the biography of Beethoven and the culture in which his Ninth Symphony was written, hear how each instrument sounds, pull the symphony apart to study it in a very nonlinear way to see how the parts add to the whole, or listen to the entire symphony in a linear form. Buttons on each screen let you explore the sound in relationship to the text. Figure 13.1 shows a screen from Multimedia Beethoven.

Figure 13.1
Multimedia Beethoven: The Ninth Symphony screen.

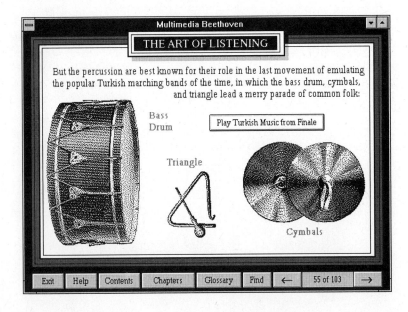

Help with Multimedia

> **Note:** The Windows multimedia extensions are needed for using Multimedia Beethoven. They are included with Windows 3.1.

Now add a few more multimedia products, and you can see the disk problem. When purchasing a hard disk for multimedia work, don't be bashful about purchasing far more space than you think you need. Finally, you may wish to add video products to the system if you are using full-motion video or capturing video screens.

The first version of MME with Windows 3.1 provides the following support for program developers:

- *Audio.* Waveform audio, CD audio, MIDI synthesis, MIDI input/output, hi-res timer services, and MCI support.
- *Animation.* Multimedia movies and player.
- *Media Control Interface (MCI).* Videodisk, scanners, video overlay boards, VCR, and CD player.
- *CD-ROM support.* Streaming data transfer.
- *File formats.* RIFF (Resource Interchange File Format).

At the present time, MME for Windows is primarily an audio and music support system. There are some functions that support the playback of animated movies created with MacroMind Director (for the Macintosh), but there is no version yet for the PC. MME extends the GDI routines some, but not much. There is no support for working with NTSC video (such as from a VCR).

13

CHAPTER

Basic Components of a Multimedia System

Two basic components make up the PC-based multimedia system: the authoring system and delivery platform. The *authoring system* is used to produce the multimedia products, which could be a slide show, business presentation, video database, super-realistic computer games, or whatever. The *delivery system* is what you use to experience the results ("play" the product). Most users will start with a delivery system.

Troubleshooting Multimedia Equipment

In troubleshooting multimedia equipment, remember that the rules are much the same as with printers. Each hardware component must have a driver. DOS multimedia applications have their own drivers for whatever is needed. If you start a DOS multimedia game, it must have its own driver for the sound card you are using. A DOS game generally must be used with a particular type of sound card, and the type needed will be specified on the game box. When Windows is installed for multimedia, it includes its own set of drivers for your sound card and other peripherals that will work with all Windows applications.

Help with Multimedia

Your first task with a multimedia problem, then, is to see if the problem occurs in DOS outside of Windows. If you see the problem in DOS, expect some general problem such as improper settings on an adapter card, missing cable, or improper disk insertion in a CD-ROM. If the problem is only in Windows, there is a problem in the Windows installation for the drivers. Be sure the multimedia extensions are installed. Windows 3.1 includes multimedia extensions, but the drivers for your hardware may not be included. In this case, you will need to get the drivers from the manufacturer of the sound board or the CD-ROM drive. Windows 3.0 includes no multimedia extensions. To use Windows 3.0 with any CD-ROM or sound board, you must obtain multimedia extensions from the sound board manufacturer.

To verify that a driver is installed, start Control Panel. If the option Drivers is not available, the driver is not installed. Choose Drivers. If the driver is shown in the list box, it should be available. If it is not, click the **A**dd button. Then, if your driver is listed as an available driver, select the driver and OK. If not, contact the board or CD-ROM manufacturer for the appropriate driver and then select Unlisted Driver. Insert the OEM diskette in the requested drive. Follow the directions included with the driver. Reboot Windows to try the multimedia again.

Help! I have installation problems. The system won't boot, Windows won't start, or the multimedia options aren't there.

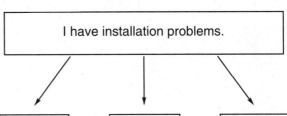

| I have installation problems. |

Computer won't boot after a multimedia installation.

- Check error messages on booting. Be sure CD-ROM is on and cartridge is installed with CD-ROM correctly.
- Check for memory conflicts in UMB area. Try excluding UMB areas.
- Comment out various lines in AUTOEXEC.BAT and CONFIG.SYS and try to boot.

System halts when starting Windows.

- CD-ROM driver or sound card may be causing conflicts in UMB. Use EMMExclude in [386] section of SYSTEM.INI to exclude some of UMB.
- Check for interrupt, DMA, or address conflicts.
- Comment out various lines in AUTOEXEC.BAT and CONFIG.SYS and try to boot.

Multimedia features don't work.

- Check Control Panel and be sure Drivers option is there. If not, reinstall Multimedia Extensions.
- Be sure the correct drivers are installed.

After installing the CD-ROM or sound card, you may find that you have a problem: the computer no longer boots, the computer boots but Windows won't start, or the multimedia options aren't there. Here are possible solutions to these problems.

My computer no longer boots after a multimedia installation.

☐ Be sure the upgrade for multimedia is installed properly. Look at the error messages during the attempt to boot. These may give you a clue if the boot hangs when you are trying to load a driver. The CD-ROM drive may need to be turned on for proper booting, and a CD-ROM disk may need to be in the drive.

☐ Check for a memory conflict in the UMB area (see Appendix A).

☐ Boot from a diskette and try to comment out various lines in AUTOEXEC.BAT and CONFIG.SYS (see Appendix G) until the system boots.

The system halts when starting Windows.

☐ The driver for the CD-ROM or sound card may be causing conflicts in the UMB area. You may need to exclude some of the UMB area by using the EMMExclude parameter in the [386] section of SYSTEM.INI (see Appendix G).

There may be hardware conflicts with the installation of the CD-ROM or audio board. Be sure there are no interrupt, address, or DMA conflicts. The interrupt, address, and DMA are set by jumpers on the audio and CD-ROM controller boards. There should be no duplication with any board in the system.

Try commenting out various lines in AUTOEXEC.BAT and CONFIG.BAT (see Appendix G) and try to boot.

Multimedia features don't work.

Check Control Panel and be sure the Drivers option is there. If not, reinstall Multimedia Extensions. With Windows 3.0, CD-ROM and audio board manufacturers generally supply the multimedia extensions as required. With Windows 3.1, many of these extensions are built in.

Make sure the correct drivers are installed.

Help! I have CD-ROM problems.

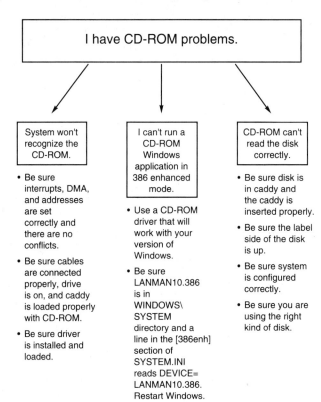

```
+-----------------------------------------------+
|           I have CD-ROM problems.             |
+-----------------------------------------------+
```

System won't recognize the CD-ROM.

- Be sure interrupts, DMA, and addresses are set correctly and there are no conflicts.
- Be sure cables are connected properly, drive is on, and caddy is loaded properly with CD-ROM.
- Be sure driver is installed and loaded.

I can't run a CD-ROM Windows application in 386 enhanced mode.

- Use a CD-ROM driver that will work with your version of Windows.
- Be sure LANMAN10.386 is in WINDOWS\SYSTEM directory and a line in the [386enh] section of SYSTEM.INI reads DEVICE= LANMAN10.386. Restart Windows.

CD-ROM can't read the disk correctly.

- Be sure disk is in caddy and the caddy is inserted properly.
- Be sure the label side of the disk is up.
- Be sure system is configured correctly.
- Be sure you are using the right kind of disk.

Typical CD-ROM problems include not being able to recognize the drive, not being able to use the drive in the 386 enhanced mode, or not being able to read a disk.

The system won't recognize the CD-ROM drive.

■ Make sure that the interrupts, DMA, and addresses are set properly, that there are no conflicts (duplications), and that the software is set to recognize your settings.

■ Be sure cables are connected, the drive is on, and the caddy is loaded properly with the CD-ROM. If the controller card requires a terminator, be sure this is installed.

■ Verify that the driver is installed (see introduction to this section). Make sure that the MSCDEX CD-ROM driver is installed by CONFIG.SYS and that the PATH command in AUTOEXEC.BAT includes the directory that contains this driver.

I can't run CD-ROM Windows application programs in 386 enhanced mode.

■ Make sure that you are using a CD-ROM driver version later than 2.10.

Expand the LANMAN10.386 file off the Windows disks (disk 4 or 5) and add it to the WINDOWS\SYSTEM directory as follows:

```
EXPAND A:\LANMAN10.386 C:WINDOWS\SYSTEM
```

Then modify SYSTEM.INI to include the line:

```
[386enh]
DEVICE=LANMAN10.386
```

Now restart Windows. In some cases, you must enter a DIR command for the CD-ROM drive before starting Windows in order for Windows to work.

The CD-ROM can't read a disk correctly.

Be sure that the disk is in its caddy and that the caddy is inserted correctly.

Be sure the label side of the disk is up.

Check to see that the system is configured correctly.

Be sure you are using the right kind of disk; you can't use File Manager with an audio disk.

Help! I have audio board problems.

I have audio board problems.

A DOS application won't play audio.

- Try running DOS application outside of Windows. If a TSR is needed, start it as part of the application's batch file.
- Check for interrupt, address, and DMA conflicts.
- Be sure speaker is plugged in.
- Check volume setting.

Control Panel's Sound option doesn't work.

- Check volume setting if the test button is not dimmed and DOS applications work.
- Use Control Panel Drivers to verify that right driver is installed. Use Control Panel Sound to check Test button. If dimmed, audio driver is incorrectly installed.
- Check WIN.INI for garbage in sections controlling multimedia.

Sound options quit working under Windows.

- Check WIN.INI file.
- Check for loose speaker cable.

Music box doesn't play a CD or it plays too slow.

- Be sure an audio disk is loaded with caddy, label side up. Check version of MSCDEX.

System hangs on starting Media Player.

- Be sure CD-ROM player is on and disk is in caddy.

Media player doesn't work.

- Verify from Control Panel Drivers that the correct driver is installed.
- Verify that there are no interrupt conflicts and that sound is up.
- For MIDI Sequencer check installation, drivers, and port. Open MIDI Mapper. If no error message, change mode to 1 and try again.
- Make sure speaker volume is up.

Sound Recorder doesn't work.

- Be sure Recorder is set properly.
- Check for address or interrupt conflicts on the sound board. Be sure Multimedia Extensions are installed.

Can I use the PC speaker with multimedia sound?

- Download Microsoft sound driver from CompuServe or obtain from BBS.

If you have been using a sound board, the most common problem is that the volume is set too low or that the speakers are unplugged. The sound level is generally set from a mixer (Windows application). You might also have a garbaged WIN.INI. If the problem is on installation, you probably have the wrong interrupt selected on the card (see Appendix C).

A DOS application won't play audio.

- Try running the application outside of Windows. Some DOS audio applications won't run inside of Windows. If a TSR is required, try running it as part of a batch file in Windows that starts the application.

- Check for interrupt or address conflicts with the settings on the audio board. Be sure the audio software is installed for the settings you are using on the sound board.

- Be sure the speakers are plugged into the right jack. Run any test program provided with the sound card.

- Check volume setting.

The Control Panel's Sound option doesn't work.

- If you can't play test sounds from this option and DOS applications work, check the volume setting for the speakers.

- Use the Drivers option of Control Panel to verify that the right driver is installed. Figure 13.2 shows a typical Drivers dialog box. Then use the Sound option of Control Panel and check the **T**est button (Figure 13.3). If the **T**est button is dimmed, the audio driver isn't correctly installed.

■ Check WIN.INI and be sure it isn't garbaged in the sections controlling multimedia.

Figure 13.2

The Drivers dialog box shows the installed drivers.

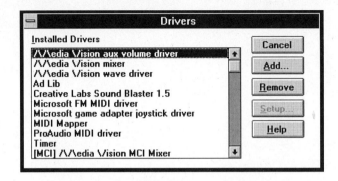

Figure 13.3

The Sound dialog box should show the Test button undimmed.

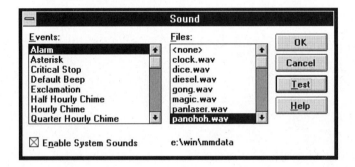

The Music box doesn't play a CD, or it plays slowly.

■ Music box plays an audio disk in the CD-ROM drive. Be sure an audio disk is in the drive, label side up. Use File

Manager to check the CD-ROM drive. If there is a drive
icon displayed for the CD-ROM, you have the wrong kind
of disk in the CD-ROM. Be sure the caddy is used. If
playing is slow, check the version of MSCDEX you are
using. You may need to update it.

Sound options quit working under Windows.

▪ If the sound options still work under DOS, check the
WIN.INI file (see Appendix G). Parameters here may be
scrambled. If so, restore from a backup WIN.INI file or
reinstall the multimedia.

▪ Check for loose speaker cable.

The Media Player doesn't work.

▪ Media Player plays from a file on the CD-ROM or hard
disk. Verify that the proper driver needed is listed under
Drivers on the Control Panel. If not, install the driver (see
introduction to this section). Start Media Player (if not
available, Multimedia Extensions are not installed). Open
the sound file to play (**File O**pen) and then click the Play
button.

▪ If it is a WAV file, check for address or interrupt conflicts
on the sound card. Make sure that the speaker is connected. Start Sound from Control Panel. If Test button is

not selected, install the sound drivers by using the Drivers option of Control Panel (see introduction to this section). If Test button is selected, use Drivers to verify that the correct driver is installed. If not, use the **A**dd button to install the driver. If the correct driver is installed, check for address or interrupt conflict again.

- If it is the CD-ROM player, see the previous question.

- If it is the MIDI Sequencer, check the installation and drivers. Be sure only a single MIDI device is connected. Open MIDI Mapper. If there was no error message, change the mode of the MIDI device to 1 and try again. If there was an error message, troubleshoot based on the error message. Be sure that the correct "port" is used in the MIDI software.

- Verify that the speaker volume is turned up (use the Mixer program).

The system hangs on starting Media Player.

- Be sure the CD-ROM player is on and a disk is loaded in the caddy.

Can I use the PC speaker with the multimedia sound?

- Microsoft developed a sound driver for the PC speaker. Although it worked with most systems, it was not released because it didn't work with all systems. You can download it from CompuServe or obtain it from various bulletin boards. A commercial driver is available for $49 as Wired for Sound from Aristosoft, Inc. Either alternative, however, gives you a tinny sound that lacks body. Your best bet is a sound card that supports the MPC standard.

Sound Recorder doesn't work.

- Be sure the Recorder is set up properly (see the documentation).

- Check for address or interrupt conflicts on the sound board. Be sure Multimedia Extensions are installed. If you get a message on opening the Sound Recorder that no Recording or Playback devices are present, install the sound card driver. If you don't get a message, verify with Drivers (Control Panel) that the correct driver is installed. To install the correct or a new driver, see the introduction to this section. If this doesn't work, check the interrupt and addresses set on the card again for conflicts.

HELP WITH USING WINDOWS ON A NETWORK

Using Windows on a network permits you to share resources such as files, CD-ROM drives, and printers among several users. The primary system on the network is the *server*, and it contains the shared files and resources (such as printers). The server may be a dedicated system. It is generally the fastest system in the network and has the largest amount of disk

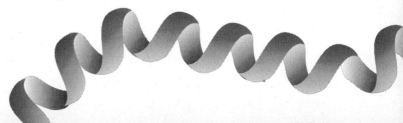

space. The server also handles the background printing. A network has a person who serves as a *system administrator*. The system administrator maintains the network and installs Windows to the server.

Each user has a *workstation* that connects to the server. Objects that you create (clip art, sound files, spreadsheets, style sheets, templates, documents, etc.) can be placed on the server, where they can be shared by all users on the network. Expensive printers or other resources can be installed to the server and shared by all users.

Windows is an ideal environment for applications on a network. Windows applications generally work better on a network than older DOS applications. This is true, however, only if Windows is properly tuned and optimized for the network. This chapter covers typical problems encountered when you are using Windows on a network. In addition, it gives helpful advice for installing and optimizing Windows for a network.

Installing Windows to a Network

Before a Windows installation is started, the network should be operational. The server should be a 386 or 486 system. The hard disk drive should be large, with space for the Windows installation and the shared resources. Access time for the drive should be 18 milliseconds or better.

The server should have 4 to 8 megabytes of RAM disk cache. This means that, 90 to 95 percent of the time, users will be able to get data from RAM instead of from disk—thus ensuring fast access. In technical terms, the *hit rate* when Windows is in use is 90 to 95 percent.

The system administrator should define the type of installation (see next questions) and where resources should be stored. For example, fonts and clip art should normally be kept on the server and available to all users.

Read all the network documentation included with Windows. You should also read all documentation on using Windows that is included with the network software. Be sure you are using the latest update of the network software and that it will work with Windows 3.1.

Finally, define the directory on the server that will be used for Windows.

Windows 3.1 has improved the network support considerably. This chapter is directed specifically to Windows 3.1. If using Windows 3.0 on a network, you should upgrade to 3.1.

Windows can be installed on a network in any one of three ways:

☐ The first way is for each workstation to share a copy of Windows on a server. Almost all of the Windows files, except user-specific files, are on the server and shared by all users. User-specific files are kept on the local workstation. This puts fewer storage requirements on the local workstation but means a little slower access speed. The shared copy of Windows on the server will need about 16 megabytes. The workstations will need only about 300 kilobytes.

■ The second method applies for diskless workstations. In this case, each workstation shares a copy of Windows, and user-specific files are kept in the user's personal Windows directory on the server. This is the slowest method, but it is the only alternative when a diskless workstation is used.

■ The third method is to install Windows locally on each workstation. All Windows files are on your personal workstation. You can, however, access network resources. This is the fastest method, but it means a lot of file redundancy and local disk storage space. You will need about 10 megabytes for the Windows files on each workstation.

Using Windows with any of these methods is similar, but the installation is different. With a network, the login script establishes all the necessary connections, and in each case Windows comes up recognizing those connections. When File Manager is active, you will see all the drives that are connected, and all these drives are available for application programs and documents.

Note: With shared copies of Windows, you must log onto the network before starting Windows, and you can't log off the network while using Windows. With local copies of Windows, you may or may not be able to log on or off the network after Windows is started. It depends on the network type. It is not a good idea, however, to log off the network with Windows running.

Installing Workstations to Share a Copy on the Server

The first method of installing Windows on a network involves setting up the network so that users are sharing a copy of Windows on the server.

 To use this method, the system administrator must first install Windows to the server by using **SETUP** **/A**. Once this is done, user-specific files can be installed on the local workstations.

To install user-specific Windows files to a local workstation, first log onto the network directory containing Windows. Once on this directory, enter **SETUP** **/N**. The Setup program will then take you through the setup process. You will need to specify a directory on your local hard disk to store the Windows-related files for your workstation. Only those files necessary for supporting your local workstation will be copied to this directory. The rest of the files will remain on the server and will be shared with other workstations. During the installation, you will be asked for the type of equipment you are using, the network type, as well as the type of printer. Install the printer that is used by the network server.

> **Note:** When using **SETUP** **/N**, do not attempt to run Setup from the diskettes. Log onto the directory on the server containing the Windows files and execute Setup from it.

Installing for a Diskless Workstation

In the second method of installing Windows on a network, there is no hard disk on the workstation and all files must be stored on the server. This installation is similar to installing for a shared copy on the server.

■ First have the system administrator install the server copy of Windows. At the workstation, then switch to the network directory containing the Windows files. Finally, use **SETUP** /N to install the user-specific files. When prompted for where to place the user-specific files, enter the name of your personal directory on the hard disk.

Installing a Local Copy of Windows

The third method of installing Windows on a network is to install Windows completely on a local workstation, and it will recognize the network resources.

■ Use **SETUP** /A, as before, to install Windows on the server. Then be sure you are on the network directory of the server and type **SETUP** on the local workstation. Do NOT use the /N. Windows will include the network as part of the normal installation procedure. If you use the express install, Windows should automatically recognize your network and install for it.

■ If the proper version of Windows is already installed on the local workstation (non-networked) and you wish to start using the system in a network, start the Windows Setup program from the Main group of Program Manager. Select **C**hange System Settings from the **O**ptions menu.

Open the **N**etwork dropdown box and select the network type, as shown in Figure 14.1. Then choose OK. Setup will prompt for any diskette it needs to install the network driver and will modify WIN.INI and SYSTEM.INI files as necessary. You will then need to restart Windows.

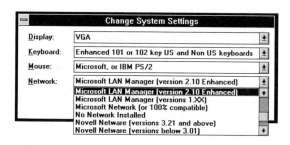

Figure 14.1

Installing an existing Windows to a network.

Strategies for Network Troubleshooting

Early versions of Windows 3.0 had network problems. Be sure you are using a Windows 3.1 and a network software version that supports Windows 3.1. Check with the network software manufacturer for any patches available for supporting Windows. Windows must be version 3.00a or later. Make sure you are using a network that is a Microsoft "tested" network. If using QEMM-386, be sure that you are using the right version of this product.

Help! Windows won't start.

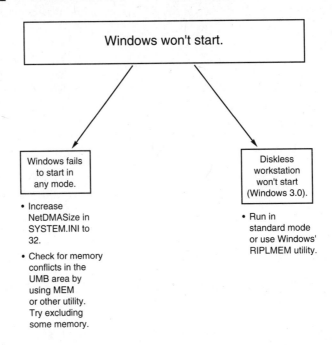

Windows won't start.

Windows fails to start in any mode.

- Increase NetDMASize in SYSTEM.INI to 32.
- Check for memory conflicts in the UMB area by using MEM or other utility. Try excluding some memory.

Diskless workstation won't start (Windows 3.0).

- Run in standard mode or use Windows' RIPLMEM utility.

If Windows won't start after installing to a network, review Chapter 3 for basic problems that might exist. This section will look at some network-specific problems that you might encounter.

Windows fails to start in any mode.

☐ The networked Windows may not be installed for this mode. Another possibility is that Windows needs a larger DMA buffer. Edit the `NetDMASize` in the SYSTEM.INI file (see Appendix G) for a larger size. The default is 16. Try changing the size to 32.

☐ Check for memory conflicts in the UMB area by using MEM or another utility. Use the `EMMExclude` parameter in the `[386enh]` section of SYSTEM.INI to exclude memory already in use.

My diskless workstation won't start (Windows 3.0).

☐ With Windows 3.0, you can run diskless workstations in standard or real mode only. You can't multitask DOS programs. To solve the problem, you must have at least 1MB of extended memory. Then load Microsoft's RIPLMEM utility (free by calling Microsoft at (800) 426-9400). Start Windows using `WIN /3`.

Help! I can't use network resources.

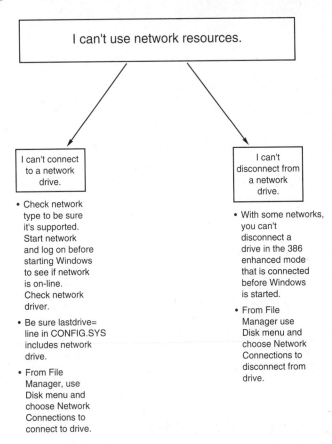

I can't use network resources.

I can't connect to a network drive.

- Check network type to be sure it's supported. Start network and log on before starting Windows to see if network is on-line. Check network driver.
- Be sure lastdrive= line in CONFIG.SYS includes network drive.
- From File Manager, use Disk menu and choose Network Connections to connect to drive.

I can't disconnect from a network drive.

- With some networks, you can't disconnect a drive in the 386 enhanced mode that is connected before Windows is started.
- From File Manager use Disk menu and choose Network Connections to disconnect from drive.

Normally when you log into a network, a login script runs that connects you to the network and sets up the logical connections for the network drives, printer, and other resources. These are then available for the DOS user. When you start

Windows, these same resources will automatically be available under Windows. You can, however, connect to desired resources after starting Windows by using File Manager.

When you start File Manager, the disk drive icons for all available drives are at the top of the directory window. If you are already connected to network drives, the network drives will be included in the drive icon list at the top. To connect additional drives, choose **N**etwork Connections from the **D**isk menu. In the dialog box, the next disk drive available is displayed, as shown in Figure 14.2. Change this, if necessary, by using the **D**rive dropdown list box. In the **N**etwork Path text box, enter the DOS command line to link to the shared directory, such as \\pr\droot. Enter the password in the Pass**w**ord text box if one is required. Then choose **C**onnect. Windows will create the link and display the new icon in the File Manager directory window.

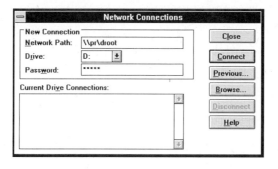

Figure 14.2
Connecting to a disk drive.

Windows automatically remembers previous link commands for recall. Clicking the **P**revious button will display all previous network path commands in a dialog box. You can select and choose **D**elete to remove a line, or select a line and choose **S**elect to move the line to the Connect Network Drive dialog box.

Note: Always use the same logical drive to connect to a given directory. Items in Program Manager are dependent upon a particular path.

On some networks, you can browse shared directories and choose the one to which you wish to connect. To do this, select **B**rowse from the Connect Network Drive dialog box. Choose the volume and then the directory. Then click OK. This enters the path to the Network Path box.

Note: If you have trouble linking, check the `lastdrive=` statement in the CONFIG.SYS file (see Appendix G). Be sure you have allowed enough drives here.

You can disconnect from a network drive from within Windows. To disconnect, choose **N**etwork Connections from the File Manager's **D**isk menu. Select the network drive letter, as shown in Figure 14.3, and **D**isconnect.

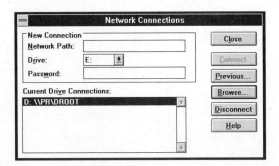

I can't connect to a network drive.

☐ If you have trouble connecting, be sure you are using a network type that is supported. Start the network and log in before you start Windows. Be sure the network is on-line. Be sure the network driver is correct (this is set from Windows Setup).

Figure 14.3
Disconnecting from a drive.

☐ Check the `lastdrive=` line of CONFIG.SYS (see Appendix G) and be sure it has enough drives to allow for the new drive. For example, if the `lastdrive` parameter specifies drive G, you won't be able to connect to drive I.

☐ Use the **D**isk menu of File Manager and choose **N**etwork Connections to connect to the drive.

I can't disconnect from a network drive.

☐ On some networks, you can't disconnect from a drive in the 386 enhanced mode. This is true only for connections made before starting Windows.

☐ Use the **D**isk menu of File Manager and choose **N**etwork Connections to disconnect from the drive.

Help! I have problems running applications on a network.

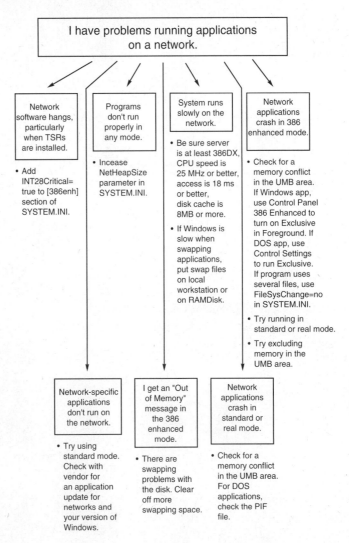

I have problems running applications on a network.

Network software hangs, particularly when TSRs are installed.

• Add INT28Critical= true to [386enh] section of SYSTEM.INI.

Programs don't run properly in any mode.

• Incease NetHeapSize parameter in SYSTEM.INI.

System runs slowly on the network.

• Be sure server is at least 386DX, CPU speed is 25 MHz or better, access is 18 ms or better, disk cache is 8MB or more.

• If Windows is slow when swapping applications, put swap files on local workstation or on RAMDisk.

Network applications crash in 386 enhanced mode.

• Check for a memory conflict in the UMB area. If Windows app, use Control Panel 386 Enhanced to turn on Exclusive in Foreground. If DOS app, use Control Settings to run Exclusive. If program uses several files, use FileSysChange=no in SYSTEM.INI.

• Try running in standard or real mode.

• Try excluding memory in the UMB area.

Network-specific applications don't run on the network.

• Try using standard mode. Check with vendor for an application update for networks and your version of Windows.

I get an "Out of Memory" message in the 386 enhanced mode.

• There are swapping problems with the disk. Clear off more swapping space.

Network applications crash in standard or real mode.

• Check for a memory conflict in the UMB area. For DOS applications, check the PIF file.

To run applications on a network, make sure that you are using a network-compatible version of the application.

The network software hangs, particularly when TSRs are installed.

◻ Network TSR may be using INT28h. Add the line **INT28Critical=true** to the [386enh] section of SYSTEM.INI (see Appendix G).

Network-specific applications don't run on the network.

◻ Try running the application in standard mode. Also contact the application vendor to see if there is a special version of the application for networks and Windows. If the problem occurs on program switching, adjust the PIF file to prevent program switching and run in exclusive mode. If the network software is in the HMA or UMB area, try running it in conventional memory.

Programs don't run properly in any mode.

◻ Increase the NetHeapSize parameter in the [standard] or [386enh] sections of SYSTEM.INI (see Appendix G). The default is 8. You might try 16.

Help! I have problems running applications on a network.

481

I get an "Out of Memory" message in the 386 enhanced mode.

⬚ Windows has a problem swapping applications to disk. Clear off more disk space on the disk that contains the swap files.

The system runs slow on the network.

⬚ If the entire operation is slow, first be sure the server processor is a 386DX or later and running 25 MHz or faster. Be sure the hard disk access is 18 milliseconds or better. Be sure the disk cache is 6 to 8 megabytes or more.

If slowdown is sudden and occurs during swapping when swap speed has previously been adequate, the disk space for the swap files may be tight and Windows may be having trouble managing the swap files under this condition. Clear off some disk space.

⬚ If Windows always runs slow when swapping applications, the swap files may be on the server with a very large disk. For maximum speed, temporary or permanent swap files should be on the local workstation. If using swap files on the server, edit the SYSTEM.INI file (see Appendix G) as:

```
[386enh]
PagingDrive=x
MaxPaging FileSize=1024
```

where *x* is the drive for paging. Files will be placed in the root directory of this drive. Another idea is to put the swap files on a RAMDisk.

If you have a diskless workstation, place the swap files on a RAMDisk.

Network applications crash in standard or real mode.

The problem is probably caused by a memory or file management conflict in the UMB area. If the program is a Windows application, avoid program switching in this mode. If it's a DOS application, edit the PIF file so that Prevent Program S**w**itch is on. If running in standard mode, try the real mode (Windows 3.0).

Network applications crash in 386 enhanced mode.

The problem is probably caused by a memory or file management conflict in the UMB area. If the program is a Windows application, disable background tasks by using Control Panel 386 Enhanced and turning on **E**xclusive in Foreground. If it's a DOS application, use Control Settings to run it Exclusive. If the program uses several files and you suspect file management conflicts, edit the line `FileSysChange=yes` in the `[386enh]` section of SYSTEM.INI (see Appendix G) to **`FileSysChange=no`**.

Try running the application in standard or real mode.

Additionally, try excluding memory in the UMB area, since there may be conflicts here. For example, add **`EMMExclude=C000-C7FF`** to the `[386enh]` section of SYSTEM.INI. See Chapter 7 for information on doing this.

Help! I have problems running applications on a network.

483

Help! I have printing problems on a network.

I have printing problems on a network.

I can't connect to a printer.

- Connect printer before starting Windows so that printer will be available under Windows. Your local workstation must be aware of the printer on the network.
- To connect to network printer under Windows, use Control Panel Printers. Select Connect and Network to display all available network printers. Choose the new printer and fill in the path and port.

Printing is slow.

- Turn off Windows' Print Manager.

I have printer problems on Netware.

- Run Netware's PRINTCON utility and verify print job configurations.

I need help managing network printer queue.

- Print Manager is disabled. Manage the queue on the network server. Open Print Manager from the Main group and choose Selected Net Queue from the View menu.

I get random UAEs or printing problems (Windows 3.0).

- Check for correct Network shell version or an interrupt conflict.

I have inconsistent printing problems.

- Check network installation and printer driver.

Printer times-out on the network.

- Select Control Panel Printers and Connect. Increase Device Not Selected and Transmission Retry times.

With a network, printers can be installed to the server and are available to each workstation on the network. Workstation printers, however, are not available to other workstations.

I can't connect to a printer.

■ Before you can use a network printer, you must link your PC to the printer; that is, you must make your system aware of the resource (printer) on the network. If this linkage is established before starting Windows, Windows will automatically be aware of the resource. If not, you will need to make Windows aware of the resource.

Note: With DOS applications, you must exit the application before the printed output is released to the network printer.

■ To link to a network printer from within Windows (if not already linked before starting), choose Printers from Control Panel. Select **C**onnect. If you are connected to a network, you will see a **N**etwork button at the right of the Connect dialog box, as shown in Figure 14.4. Select this button to display the Printers-Network Connections dialog box shown in Figure 14.5. The new dialog box will show

Help! I have printing problems on a network.

485

all current network printer connections. To connect to a new printer, choose the printer by filling in the path and port, adding the password if necessary. In the Path text box, specify the command you would normally use to connect the network printer, such as \\server\laserjet (3Com 3+Share), \\svr1299\prt91299 (Lan Manager), or myserver/printq_1 (Netware). Enter a password, if necessary, in the Password text box. Choose Connect to connect the printer.

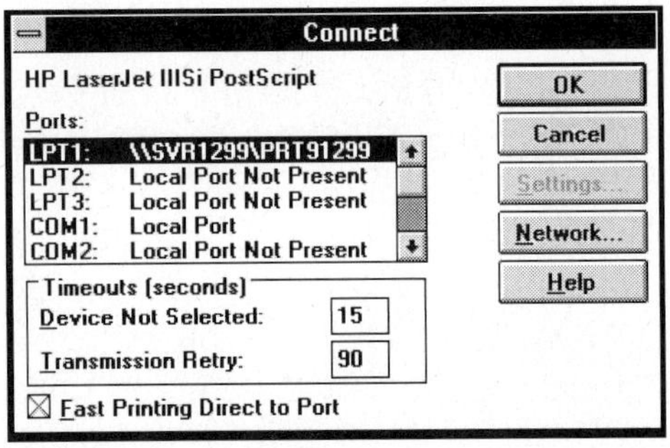

Figure 14.4

Starting the network connection.

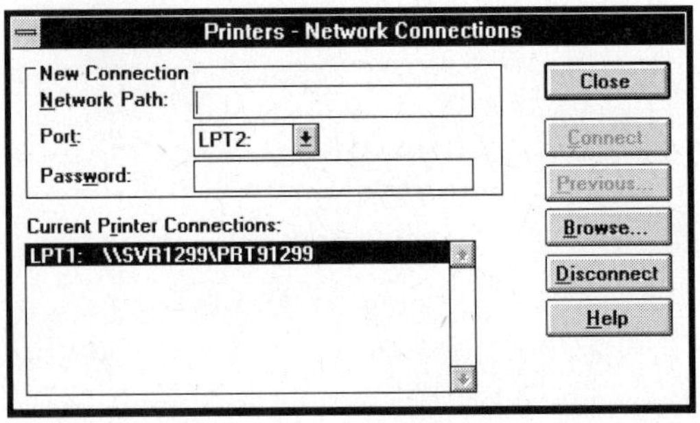

Figure 14.5

Selecting the printer to connect.

Some networks allow you to browse the list of available printers for connection. If this is available on your network, a Browse button will be active on the

Help with Using Windows on a Network

Printers-Network Connections dialog box. Choosing the button will display the available printers for connection. You can then select from this list and click OK. The printer will return you to the Printers-Network Connections dialog box and show the new printer connection listed in the Path text box. You can then click **C**onnect to connect the printer.

To disconnect a printer, select the printer and then choose **D**isconnect in the Printers-Network Connections dialog box. The selected printer is then disconnected.

To print using a network printer, you must first be sure the connection is established. Once this is done, you can print from an application by selecting the network printer from the Print Setup dialog box of that application. For example, to print from Write, choose **P**rint Setup from the **F**ile menu. Verify that the selected printer matches the exact printer (make and model) on the network, as shown in Figure 14.6. Be sure the port selection is correct. Then choose OK. Choose **P**rint from the **F**ile menu, then OK. Some networks may display additional confirmation boxes when the print job is processed.

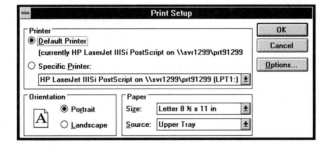

Figure 14.6

Setting up a network printer from an application.

Help! I have printing problems on a network.

487

Printing is too slow.

▢ Turn off Windows' Print Manager (use Control Panel Printers).

I have inconsistent printing problems.

▢ The network may not be installed properly. Use Windows Setup to check the network installation and printer driver.

I have printer problems on Netware.

▢ Run Netware's PRINTCON utility and verify that all print job configurations have Auto Endcap and Enable Timeout set to No. Set Suppress Form Feed to Yes. Turn off the Windows' Print Manager.

The printer times-out on the network.

▢ Use the Printers option of Control Panel, select **C**onnect, and increase the **D**evice Not Selected and **T**ransmission Retry times.

I need help managing the network printer queue.

▢ When you're using a network printer, Windows' Print Manager is disabled and the network print manager is used instead. This manager will have a queue for each printer connected to the network. The print management, then, is done from the network server instead of from Windows. Manage the queue on the network server.

Most network queue managers permit you to view the print queue in order to see the print jobs that are being processed and where your job is relative to others in the queue. For a network with heavy print traffic, your job may take a while. Your computer, however, is returned to your control and (unlike with a local printer) does not have to share its processor with the print manager. In some cases, you can browse the print queues for the various printers and select a printer that is underutilized or not being used.

You can also view the print queue from within Windows. To do this, open Print Manager by double-clicking its icon from Program Manager's Main group window, shown in Figure 14.7. Select **S**elected Net Queue from the **V**iew menu. The window will then show the contents of the queue to which you are currently connected (Figure 14.8). The type of information displayed depends on the network driver you are using. To return to Print Manager, choose **C**lose. To view other queues, select **O**ther Net Queue from the **V**iew menu (Figure 14.9). Enter the name of the queue to view and choose **V**iew. Choose E**x**it to return to Print Manager. Not all networks support this option. If not supported, the option will be grayed.

Windows automatically checks the status of the queues periodically. If the network print traffic is heavy, you may wish to turn this feature off. To turn off the queue monitoring, start Print Manager and choose **N**etwork Settings from the **O**ptions menu. You will see the Network Options dialog box shown in Figure 14.10. Turn off **U**pdate Network Display. Choose OK. To reenable this checking, turn back on **U**pdate Network Display.

Figure 14.7
*Print Manager
on a network.*

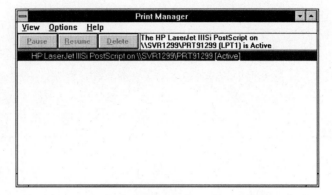

Figure 14.8
*Viewing the
current queue.*

Figure 14.9
*Viewing other
queues.*

Help with Using Windows on a Network

Figure 14.10
Turning off the Network Display Update.

In the default mode, Windows will not use Print Manager when installed to a network except as a queue monitor. Using it to buffer print output would only delay printing more. You can, however, enable the Print Manager's buffering by using the **O**ptions menu. Select **N**etwork Settings and then toggle **P**rint Jobs Direct off. Choose OK. The extent to which Print Manager can be enabled depends on the network. For example, the **P**ause, **R**esume, and **D**elete buttons may or may not be enabled.

I get random UAEs or printing problems (Windows 3.0).

This problem generally indicates an incorrect shell version or interrupt conflicts. Be sure the network driver is not using an interrupt needed by another peripheral.

Help! How do I control network features from Windows?

When you are in Windows, most networks provide support for logging in, logging off, and changing the password.

Help! How do I control network features from Windows?

491

You can control the features of a network by using the Network option of Control Panel. The dialog box and available features will vary with the network. With the Netware network, for example, you will see a list of network utilities available. The items on the list are those determined by the network administrator. With most networks, you should expect to see utilities here for logging on or off the network, changing the network password, or sending a message to another user. Figure 14.11 shows an example screen for Lan Manager.

Figure 14.11
Control Panel's Lan Manager Network option.

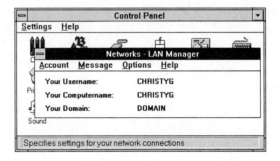

Help! I have problems with Program Manager.

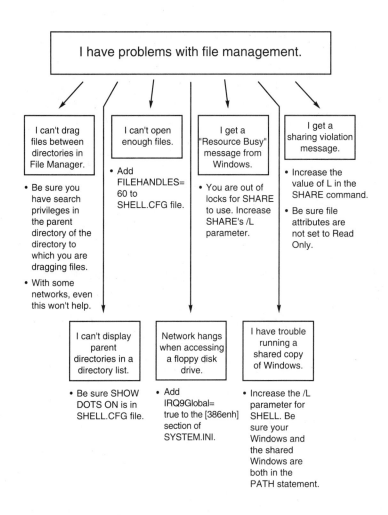

I have problems with file management.

I can't drag files between directories in File Manager.

- Be sure you have search privileges in the parent directory of the directory to which you are dragging files.
- With some networks, even this won't help.

I can't open enough files.

- Add FILEHANDLES=60 to SHELL.CFG file.

I get a "Resource Busy" message from Windows.

- You are out of locks for SHARE to use. Increase SHARE's /L parameter.

I get a sharing violation message.

- Increase the value of L in the SHARE command.
- Be sure file attributes are not set to Read Only.

I can't display parent directories in a directory list.

- Be sure SHOW DOTS ON is in SHELL.CFG file.

Network hangs when accessing a floppy disk drive.

- Add IRQ9Global=true to the [386enh] section of SYSTEM.INI.

I have trouble running a shared copy of Windows.

- Increase the /L parameter for SHELL. Be sure your Windows and the shared Windows are both in the PATH statement.

With a network, Program Manager works the same as it does with a non-networked system. Icons, however, may have properties that enable them to start programs or access icons from networked drives.

■ If the program items don't work correctly, make sure you are always using the same logical drive for the same directory each time you connect. Program items will specify a particular path, and it must remain the same.

Help! I have problems with file management.

With a network, File Manager works the same as it does with a non-networked system. The network drives should be available on the line showing the drives, and you can select directories and files from these drives.

I can't drag files between directories in File Manager.

■ Be sure you have search privileges in the parent directory of the directory to which you are dragging files.

■ With some networks, even this won't help if the destination is a network drive.

I can't display parent directories in a directory list.

■ Be sure SHOW DOTS ON is included in the SHELL.CFG file (see Appendix G). You can temporarily bypass the display of directories by typing double dots (..) as a filename and clicking OK.

I can't open enough files.

▢ The Netware default is a maximum of 40 files open at a time. This is often not enough on a network. Increase this to 60 by using **FILEHANDLES=60** in the SHELL.CFG file (see Appendix G).

Network software hangs when a floppy disk drive is being accessed.

▢ Add **IRQ9Global=true** to the [386enh] section of SYSTEM.INI (see Appendix G).

I get a "Resource Busy" message from Windows.

▢ You've run out of locks for SHARE to use. Increase the value for the L parameter by using **SHARE.EXE /L:500**.

I have trouble running a shared copy of Windows.

▢ If a sharing violation message appears, see the solutions given for the next problem, "I get a 'Sharing Violation' message." Be sure the paths for both your personal Windows directory and the shared Windows directory are in the PATH statement, with your personal path first.

I get a "Sharing Violation" message.

☐ Two applications are trying to access the same file. Increase the value for the L parameter by using **SHARE.EXE /L:500**.

☐ Check to see that the file attributes are not set to Read Only.

Help! I have problems with DOS applications under Windows on the network.

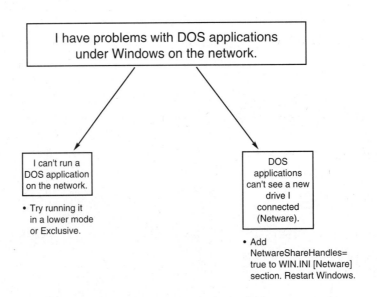

I have problems with DOS applications under Windows on the network.

I can't run a DOS application on the network.

• Try running it in a lower mode or Exclusive.

DOS applications can't see a new drive I connected (Netware).

• Add NetwareShareHandles= true to WIN.INI [Netware] section. Restart Windows.

DOS applications can be run under Windows on a network, just as they can on a non-networked system. Network drives are available for programs and data files under Windows.

I can't run DOS applications on the network.

▪ If running in the 386 enhanced mode, try running the application in standard mode or run it exclusive (set the PIF file to **E**xclusive).

DOS applications can't see the new driver I connected (Netware).

▪ Locate the [NetWare] section of WIN.INI and add the line **NetwareShareHandles=true** (see Appendix G). Restart Windows.

Help! I need to add a Netware utility.

```
┌─────────────────────────────────────────┐
│  I need to add a Netware utility (Netware).│
└─────────────────────────────────────────┘
                    │
                    ▼
            • Add a reference
              in the
              NETWARE.INI
              file.
```

With Netware, when you double-click the Network icon from Control Panel, you will see a list of the available Network utilities. You may wish to add other utilities to the list.

▪ To add a utility, open NETWARE.INI (see Appendix G) and locate the [MSW31-Utils] section. Add new utilities using the form:

```
menu title=program command
```

Help! I need to add a Netware utility.

497

For example, to add SYSCON, enter the line:

`System Configuration=syscon.exe`

You can also reference a PIF file.

To use the utility after modifying the INI file, double-click the Network icon from Control Panel. Then click the scroll button to the right of the field that is below Start Selected Network Utility.

Help! I get a message to increase heap size settings.

```
I get a message to increase the heap size.
```

• Add
NetHeapSize=48
to SYSTEM.INI.

The message about heap size settings refers to a memory area used to manage the network.

■ Add the line `NetHeapSize=48` in SYSTEM.INI (see Appendix G) in the appropriate section.

How can I optimize network performance?

Windows should be tuned for network performance, just as you would tune it for a single-user system. One of the most critical issues on a network in the 386 enhanced mode is where the swap files are kept. Performance is best when they are kept on the (user's) local hard drive.

To check the location of the swap files, be sure the following lines are in the SYSTEM.INI file (see Appendix G):

```
[386enh]
PagingDrive=x
MaxPaging FileSize=1024
```

where x is the drive (without the colon) for the swap files. Windows always uses the root directory of this drive for the swap files. Specifying the maximum size ensures that Windows doesn't have to search the entire drive (which can be large on a network) to calculate the maximum size. This file must be at least 512K in size to enable virtual memory.

Microsoft's basic network strategy is to use the SYSTEM.INI file to define hardware-specific parameters and the WIN.INI file to define user-specific features. A user should be able to log in and use a personal WIN.INI file from any workstation. The SYSTEM.INI file, in contrast, is workstation-specific and stays with the Windows version on that workstation. Unfortunately, this isn't an exact design. The WIN.INI file contains information about display type, keyboard, and mouse—all hardware-dependent aspects. You must have a separate WIN.INI file to change any of these. SYSTEM.INI contains some user-specific information. You may need to create network batch files to do the appropriate switching of these files for users.

MANAGING MEMORY FOR SPEED AND PERFORMANCE

One of the most important ways to improve Windows' speed and operation is to use as much memory as possible and to configure it correctly. The configuration method for your system depends on your processor, the mode in which Windows is running, and the type of applications that you are using. This appendix will review the basic memory management concepts of Windows.

Types of Memory

The 8086 and 8088 processors used in the early XT-compatible machines were limited to addressing a maximum of 1 megabyte (1024K) of memory. The initial IBM design reserved approximately 360K of this amount, leaving a maximum of 640K of memory for applications. Much of this original memory management design is still a part of all PC systems today, since almost all PC systems still use the Microsoft DOS, which was designed specifically for these processors. The 80386 and 80486 systems of today build on this memory management design.

Conventional and Reserved Memory

On all PC systems, the lower 640K of memory is known as *conventional memory*. Approximately 90K of the first part of this conventional memory is used for DOS, leaving about 550K for application programs. You can check this from your system by entering CHKDSK at the DOS prompt. The last line displayed will show the amount of conventional memory that is still available on your system. Figure A.1 shows a typical memory map of these systems.

The space between the upper 640K limit and the end of the 1MB space is called *reserved I/O memory*, or *high memory*. This reserved I/O memory is used by video cards, network cards, and the BIOS. The reserved I/O memory is partitioned into 64K *upper memory blocks* (UMBs).

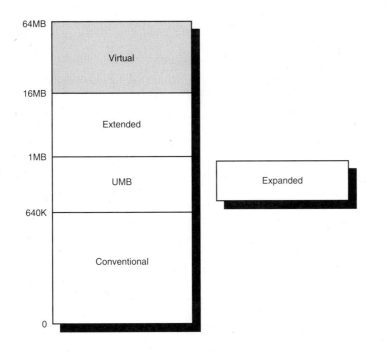

Figure A.1
Computer memory map in the PC architecture.

Expanded Memory

As programs became larger, program developers sought a method of getting more memory for applications. To break the 1MB limit, they developed a memory extension method known as *expanded memory*. The standards for this method were developed jointly by Intel, Lotus, and Microsoft and released in 1984. The advantage of expanded memory is that it can be used by almost any type of PC-compatible computer, including the XT. The early expanded memory (EMS) specification was known as EMS 3.2, and included a hardware and software specification.

Expanded memory is viewed by the system as partitioned into 16K segments called *pages*. The expanded memory driver manages these pages by making the computer think they are in lower memory; that is, the manager "moves" each upper page into a conventional memory area as it is needed. The data is never moved (or swapped); it is just that the upper memory page is addressed as if it were a lower memory page. A free 64K memory area (UMB) in the lower DOS 360K area is used for the alternate addressing. This UMB is called a *page frame*. Although each page is 16K, the expanded memory manager must have four contiguous pages (64K) in reserved I/O memory. The expanded memory manager locates and uses this area automatically.

The EMS 3.2 specification was limited to 8MB, and could really be used only for storing data, such as a spreadsheet or a hyphenation dictionary. You could use a short program in it if it was less than 64K in size. You couldn't use expanded memory for multitasking DOS programs.

Later, AST, Ashton-Tate, and Quarterdeck developed an enhanced expanded memory specification known as *EEMS 3.2*. This version enabled the entire address space (1MB) of the 8088 to be "banked" to expanded memory. This permitted DOS multitasking. DESQview from Quarterdeck was the first program to use EEMS 3.2 for DOS multitasking. Older expanded memory systems that were limited to the 64K page frame were now called *small-frame EMS*. The newer systems were known as *large-frame EMS*. The page frame was still there, but you could now put several DOS programs in expanded memory (without starting Windows) and switch between them quickly in a process called *backfilling*.

In 1987, Lotus, Intel, and Microsoft expanded the 3.2 specification again to include the 1-megabyte access, backfilling, and support for 32 megabytes of expanded memory. The new specification is known as *EMS 4.0* (or LIM 4.0, after the initials of the companies that developed it). This is currently the latest version of the expanded memory specification.

An interesting fact about EMS is that it is possible to implement the hardware part of the specification with software. When this is done, the system is said to be using an *expanded memory emulator*. The early emulators were disk-based and not too efficient. Pages were allocated to a swap file on the disk. A more recent type of expanded memory emulator stores the pages in extended memory (see next section). Emulating to extended memory with an 80286 processor was not too efficient, though, and never caught on. With the 80386 processor or later, the concept is quite practical, however. In fact, you will find an expanded memory emulator with Windows (EMM386.SYS) that will work with an 80386 or 80486 system.

Windows and Windows applications do not use expanded memory. For DOS applications, the following rules apply:

- If Windows is running in 386 enhanced mode, Windows can simulate expanded memory for any DOS application that needs it if the EMM386.SYS driver is installed with the RAM switch (see Appendix B). The key issue here is that Windows must have 64K of contiguous memory for the page frame in the upper memory area. Some memory managers support expanded memory by using four 16K pages that are not contiguous.

- If Windows is running in standard mode, you can use expanded memory for DOS applications with Windows 3.1 if you are using a physical expanded memory board such as AST RamPage! or Intel Above Board.

Note: The only time you should install or use EMM386.SYS with Windows 3.1 is when you have a 386/486 system and either of these are true:

☐ You need the expanded memory for DOS applications outside of Windows and you are not using a third-party memory manager that supports expanded memory.

☐ You are using DOS 5 with Windows without a third-party memory manager. The EMM386.SYS driver permits you to store the drivers specified in CONFIG.SYS (mouse, ANSI, etc.) as well as TSRs in the free area between 640K and 1MB.

Memory allocated with EMM386.SYS is not available to Windows programs using extended memory in other modes; that is, if you install the EMM386.SYS driver and allocate expanded memory, you will have less memory for a 386 enhanced mode.

You can also find third-party products, such as 386MAX from Qualitas and QEMM-386 from Quarterdeck, that emulate expanded memory in systems very efficiently. You can use certain versions of these programs with Windows instead of Windows' own HIMEM.SYS (see the upcoming discussion of this topic).

Extended Memory

When Intel released the 80286 processor in 1984, it supported two modes (or methods) for memory addressing. In the *real mode*, the 80286 was exactly compatible with the older 8088 and 8086 and was limited to addressing 1 megabyte of memory. The 80286 also was capable of supporting a new protected mode that could address 16 megabytes of memory. This new processor mode was known as *16-bit protected mode*, and memory using this addressing method was known as *extended memory*.

In protected mode, several programs can be loaded to memory at the same time and each executed by swapping the processor between them. The memory used by each is pro-tected from being used by other programs in memory. If Lotus 1-2-3 is in memory, for example, nothing else executing in memory can alter data for that program. There is nothing clumsy or tricky about using extended memory—it is a clean solution.

Unfortunately, DOS (including DOS 5) does not support extended memory or the 16-bit protected mode. DOS was written for real mode execution only. DOS programs, then, cannot execute in protected mode or take advantage of ex-tended memory. Some DOS application developers have found a way to get around this problem and use extended memory. They do this by switching to protected mode for memory addressing and then doing the rest of their execution in real mode. These products are used by DOS program developers in their programs to take advantage of extended memory and are known as *DOS extenders*.

Various DOS extender products have been developed to enable DOS programs to take advantage of extended memory. In essence, each product is a type of environment that enables the program to exit DOS to complete its memory addressing, after which the program returns to DOS. We'll return to this issue later in this section.

Also, the 80286 processor was crippled in the sense that it could not switch easily between the two processor modes (real and 16-bit protected) without the computer being rebooted. The proper support of extended memory was not available until Intel released the 80386 processor in 1986. The 80386 supported protected mode and could address 4 gigabytes of memory. For the first time, users could take advantage of extended memory practically. There was no operating system, however, that could run the current DOS applications with the 80386's extended memory. Program developers could do this only by using a DOS extender.

OS/2 was the vision of Microsoft and IBM of an operating system that could take full advantage of extended memory and the 80386. However, Microsoft and IBM were slow to develop OS/2, and users grew impatient. In addition, users were not willing to throw away their extensive investment in DOS application software. Also, IBM and Microsoft hindered OS/2 development by designing the early OS/2 to support both the 80286 processor and the 80386.

Microsoft took a different approach beginning with Windows 3.0. If you have an 80386 or 80486 processor and are running Windows applications in the standard mode, the Windows 3.0 environment converts the computer to an extended memory system. Windows, in this mode, runs in protected mode for Windows applications. Windows applications can run together under DOS, limited only by the amount of physical memory that you have. With the introduction of Windows 3.0, program developers at last could write large programs for the DOS environment as long as the programs were Windows applications. Microsoft also realized that this virtual memory would bring many software developers into the Windows fold (new Windows applications) as well as build a bridge to the eventual protected-mode operating system that could run DOS and Windows applications. This extended memory support made Windows 3.0 stand out from any previous release.

To make extended memory work with DOS and Windows, Microsoft again joined with Intel, Lotus, and AST Research to define the Extended Memory Specification (XMS). The specification details the management of three memory areas:

■ *Upper memory blocks* (UMBs) in the lower 1 megabyte above 640K.

■ A special *high memory area* (HMA) between 1024K and 1088k.

■ *Extended memory blocks* (EMBs) above 1088K.

The HIMEM.SYS included with Windows is the extended memory manager based on this specification that arbitrates the use of all three of these areas.

The HMA, or first part of extended memory, is particularly interesting. In 1987 Microsoft announced a way to use the first 64K of extended memory as if it were part of conventional memory. This trick was used in Windows/286 to provide more conventional memory for Windows applications. This HMA is a small area and most useful for TSRs and device drivers. However, if it is free, it is allocated by Windows on a first-come first-served basis.

Tip: If you know that an application uses the HMA area or that it is already in use, turn off the use of the HMA area for DOS applications. To do this, define a DOS PIF that

continues

continued

turns off the Uses **H**igh Memory Area check box in the
application's PIF file. For example, if DOS 5 is installed to
the HMA area (DOS=HIGH), be sure that the PIF file for
each application does not permit any application to use
this area. Be sure _DEFAULT.PIF is set the same way.

Now let's look at how application programs can access
extended memory. Windows applications can easily address
extended memory with the rules defined by Microsoft for
Windows developers, but what about DOS developers? DOS
developers realized that extended memory was a far better
alternative than expanded memory for applications written for
the 80386, yet DOS did not support extended memory. The
solution was to use a DOS extender, a type of DOS shell that
provides the programming support for extended memory. The
program runs in real mode. For memory addressing, the program switches to protected mode. For file handling and other
I/O, real mode is used and control is passed to DOS. You will
find these DOS extenders now in many popular products such
as Paradox 386, AutoCad 386, and Lotus 1-2-3 version 3.

DOS extenders, such as Quarterdeck's QEMM-386, had
a problem, however, when they were used as an expanded
memory emulator at the same time that extended memory was
being used. The result was that Quarterdeck and others came
together and defined a DOS extender specification known as
Virtual Control Program Interface (or *VCPI*). QEMM-386 version 5.0 or earlier and Lotus 1-2-3 version 3.0 used this VCPI.

Unfortunately, VCPI was not the final solution. It is
designed for 386 and 486 systems and won't work with 286

systems. Also, VCPI uses expanded memory, whereas Windows demands extended memory. As a single-tasking system, VCPI doesn't support multitasking. A VCPI application can access all of extended memory, and there is no protection for multitasking. Further, any VCPI DOS application running under Windows must run as full-screen. Windows is designed with a graphic user interface, and VCPI doesn't support any graphic user interface. Finally, VCPI assumes that the program starts in real mode, which is not true of Windows in the 386 enhanced mode.

Windows does not use the VCPI. Therefore the only time the issue is important is when you are using a DOS application that uses VCPI under Windows. The following DOS applications use VCPI technology:

Company	Product
Autodesk	AutoCAD 386 1.1
IBM	Interleaf Publisher 1.1
Lotus	Lotus 1-2-3 3.0
Wolfram Research	Mathematica 2.0
Oracle	SQL 2.0/PME 2.1
Borland	Paradox 386 3.5

These applications cannot be run at all with Windows 3.0 and can be run only in standard mode with Windows 3.1.

To run these DOS applications in 386 enhanced mode, use a memory manager that supports both expanded and extended memory, such as Quarterdeck's QEMM-386 6.0 or 386MAX 5.1. Then run the DOS application outside of Windows

APPENDIX

A

or in Exclusive mode. *Exclusive* implies that the program has the entire resources of the computer and that there are no other programs running.

To circumvent the extended memory management problem with Windows, Microsoft designed an extended memory DOS extender known as the *DPMI* (DOS Protected Mode Interface). The goal was the support of 16 megabytes of extended memory and a graphic user interface for DOS applications using it under Windows; that is, DOS applications should run as a windowed application. The application should also run on a 286, 386, or 486 processor. As this is written, the only DOS program to support DPMI is Lotus 1-2-3 release 3.1. Other DOS applications that need extended memory using other DOS extenders must run under Windows in standard mode or use the QEMM-386 memory manager.

Memory Management in Windows

Now let's look at each of the two basic Windows modes and see how memory is managed in each. Remember that you can always use the **A**bout command from the **H**elp menu of Program Manager or File Manager to see which mode Windows is currently using. Having two modes means that Windows is really two separate products. Each time you start Windows, a small WIN.COM program first reads your configuration (and startup parameters)and then pulls the parts together to build the Windows program for that mode. You will see how that's done in this section.

Windows 3.1 is essentially an operating system in itself. You boot the computer from DOS, which then hands the

512

resources (memory, printer, processor, etc.) of the system to Windows, just as when starting any DOS application. Windows then owns the processor, memory, printer, and other resources. About the only part of DOS used by Windows 3.0 is the file management system. In many systems with Windows 3.1, you can install the FastDisk option and bypass DOS's file management system. Windows can be started from DOS in either of two modes: standard or 386 enhanced.

Windows always has several components in memory (Figure A.2). At the lowest level is the device independent layer. This layer interacts directly with peripheral devices (hardware), and contains the physical drivers for the printer, video, keyboard, mouse, disk, and other devices. When you change your hardware, it is necessary to change only the drivers in this layer.

Above this is the Windows core. The core contains the kernel, user, and GDK routines:

Kernel—schedules tasks, manages memory, controls I/O, and interfaces with DOS.

User—manages the user interface. Draws windows, menus, icons, and dialog boxes.

GDI (Graphics Device Interface)—draws graphic primitives such as lines and rectangles. Interfaces with the device independent layer.

The kernel, user, and GDI areas each consist of EXE files, but the filename may vary with the mode in which Windows is running. Above these layers are the Windows applications.

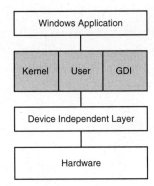

Figure A.2
*The basic
Windows
memory
components.*

Standard Mode

With Windows 3.0, the standard mode is generally the fastest
and most stable mode of Windows for any computer because
Windows does not have to manage virtual memory. You can
run standard mode on a 286 or later PC computer, and you will
need at least 1 megabyte or more of expanded or extended
memory. Even if you have a 386 or 486 machine with the
memory to run enhanced 386 mode, you may still wish to use
standard mode with Windows 3.0 for its speed and stability.

With Windows 3.1, the standard mode does not necessar-
ily provide the most speed and stability. In the 386 enhanced
mode, Windows can bypass DOS for file management with a
32-bit virtual file manager (FastDisk) with some disk controllers. The result is that the 386 enhanced mode is now the mode
of choice if you have a 386/486 machine and a disk controller
that supports FastDisk.

If your default installation is for 386 enhanced mode, you
can run Windows in the standard mode by starting it with the
/s option:

```
WIN /S
```

Tip: With a 386/486 machine, standard mode is useful with Windows 3.0 when you are not using DOS applications. Your Windows applications will run about 20 percent faster. With Windows 3.1, you may or may not notice much difference.

In standard mode, Windows can take advantage of the protected-mode capabilities of the 286 and 386 processor, providing access to a maximum of 16 megabytes of memory (if physically installed). The extra memory means you can support the larger Windows applications. Windows runs in protected mode, switching to DOS for file I/O and other DOS operations. Here are the important characteristics of Windows in the standard mode:

- Windows kernel runs in the 16-bit protected mode.
- Windows programs run in 16-bit protected mode.
- DOS programs run in a real mode.
- DOS applications are task- or context-switched. There is no DOS multitasking.
- The Windows DOS Protected Mode Interface (DPMI) is available to Windows applications.
- Most of Windows is swapped out when a DOS application is running.
- DOS applications must run full-screen.
- DOS applications can use extended memory if using DPMI.

■ DOS and Windows applications can use expanded memory.

■ Clipboard is available for text transfers.

For DOS applications in standard mode, only a single DOS application can be active at a time. To switch to another DOS application, you must return to Windows first. Inactive DOS applications are suspended to the disk by using a swap file. This is called *context-switching*—in contrast to the true multi-tasking of the 386 enhanced mode. Context-switching can mean trouble for any DOS applications using real-time I/O, such as a communications program. When a DOS application is running, Windows swaps itself out to disk. Only a small footprint is left for reloading.

DOS programs, like Windows programs, can break the 640K barrier by using the *DOS Protected Mode Interface* (DPMI). Most DOS programs using extended memory, however, haven't yet been updated to DPMI.

In the standard mode, Windows accesses extended memory directly. The HIMEM.SYS driver is used to allocate all extended memory that is available to Windows. The three memory areas (see the opening discussion "Types of Memory") are conventional memory, extended memory, and high memory (HMA). Up to 15 megabytes of extended memory is supported (or 16 megabytes total with conventional memory).

Figure A.3 shows the memory map in standard mode. To the left is the memory map when Windows applications are running. To the right is the memory map when a DOS application is running. The memory allocation for the DOS application is based on the PIF file parameters. DOSX manages extended memory, and Switcher permits using hot keys to switch between the DOS application and Windows (or other DOS applications). DOSX and Switcher together take about 45K of conventional memory.

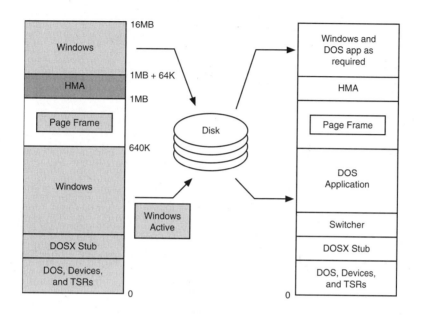

Figure A.3
Memory map for the standard mode.

When Windows is started, it takes all available memory. This memory is assigned to a *global heap*. When you start an application, Windows assigns to the application memory segments from the global heap in 64K chunks. Normally a program uses at least two segments, one for the program and one for the program's data (or *local heap,* as it is called). Memory becomes tighter as more and more applications are loaded, and then Windows has to try to recover whatever memory it can.

Memory in the global heap is either classified as movable, discardable, or fixed. *Movable* means that Windows can move the contents around as necessary to make room for other data. *Discardable* memory is used for programs and other data that can easily be reloaded from the disk. *Fixed* means that Windows is not permitted to move the contents to any other location. Programmers should avoid using fixed memory because using it can cause a dramatic slowdown of execution.

When applications need memory for data, they can generally get it from their own local heap. If a large amount of memory is needed (as for a bit map), however, it just isn't there. In this case, the program can get the memory from the global heap. It is the responsibility of the program to release this global heap block when it is no longer used, freeing up memory space in the global heap.

In the standard mode, fixed and discardable segments are loaded from the bottom up, starting just above the DOS area. Discardable code segments are loaded from the top down. When you load a new application, Windows relocates movable and discardable segments to place the application as low as possible in memory. When you quit an application, Windows defragments memory by moving the movable segments down in memory. If fixed memory is used, this defragmentation can take much longer.

Note that there is no distinction between conventional and extended memory for the Windows applications. Windows has up to a 16-megabyte address space, and it is all treated as a single global heap. Fixed and movable memory is loaded from the bottom up. Discardable memory is loaded from the top down.

Note: If SMARTDrive is installed, it will take some of the extended memory area, and DOS 5 can allocate drivers, TSRs, and some of itself to the upper memory blocks. This means that less extended memory is available to Windows.

If the high memory area (HMA) is available, it is added to the global heap. HMA is generally available because few DOS programs use it. (DOS 5 can use it, however.)

When Windows is run in standard mode, all calls to DOS involve switching to the real mode and then back to protected. This is because DOS is only a real-mode operating system. The result is a real performance penalty, in some cases dramatically less.

The kernel is supported by the file KRNL286.EXE. This file handles the file management and DOS inter-face. USER.EXE is the user interface routine, and GDI.EXE is the graphic primitives for the screen interface. HIMEM.SYS is the driver for extended memory, and DOSX.EXE component is the Windows interface for this driver.

386 Enhanced Mode

When you run Windows in the 386 enhanced mode, you can take full advantage of the power of Windows.

- You can use the Clipboard to copy graphics or a selected part of the screen, even between DOS programs.

- You can run multiple DOS programs at the same time, each in its own virtual machine.

- The computer runs in a true virtual memory mode, even using the disk as an extension of memory. You have better protection between programs.

- File management is no longer dependent on DOS. A 32-bit virtual device driver is built in (FastDisk) that supports many disk controllers.

- You have more control over how DOS applications use memory and the processor.

- You can use shortcut keys to switch between DOS applications.

- DOS applications can run full-screen or windowed.

- All Windows applications run in a single *virtual machine*—a system that does not interface directly to any physical input or output. Memory, disks, the video, printer, and keyboard are all addressed logically instead of physically. The 386 processor can support multiple virtual machines, all running at the same time without interfering with each other. All Windows applications run in a single virtual machine. Each DOS application runs in a separate virtual machine.

For the 386 enhanced mode, you will need a 386 or 486 processor with 2 megabytes of extended memory or more. This mode supports multiple DOS sessions at the same time and virtual machine processing, but it can be slower than standard mode. Virtual machine processing means that the processor is managing several programs at once in memory, each application using the processor on a shared basis and its own section of memory. Here are the important characteristics of Windows in 386 enhanced mode:

- Some of the Windows kernel runs in 32-bit protected mode.

- Windows programs run in a 16-bit protected mode but can have 32-bit protected-mode components.

- Windows supports virtual memory. The disk is used as a memory extension.

- Windows multitasks DOS and Windows applications.

- The Windows DOS extender (DPMI) is available to Windows programs and DOS programs.

- DOS applications can run in real, 16-bit protected, 32-bit protected, or virtual 86 modes.

Managing Memory for Speed and Performance

- DOS applications can run in the background.

- DOS applications run as preemptive multitasking. Windows programs run nonpreemptive (see "Multitasking with Windows" later in this chapter).

- DOS applications can run in a window. Each DOS application runs in its own virtual machine.

- DOS applications can use expanded memory.

- DOS applications can use extended memory if using DPMI.

- All Windows applications run in a single virtual machine.

> **Tip:** Use the 386 enhanced mode with 386 or 486 machines to permit breaking the 640K barrier for both Windows and DOS applications. (DOS applications can do it only by using the DPMI). You also have the advantage of virtual memory and preemptive DOS multitasking (see "Multitasking with Windows").

In the 386 enhanced mode, Windows runs in protected mode. Windows switches to real mode only when accessing DOS, such as for file I/O. With Windows 3.1, this switching is no longer necessary if you are using the FastDisk option (see Appendix B). Up to 4 gigabytes of memory can be addressed in theory; however, practical reality limits this. The current version of Windows was developed to run on a 286 and therefore uses a 16-bit addressing mode. This means you are limited to 16 megabytes of physical memory. Applications can be developed for 32-bit addressing for Windows, but such applications will not run on a 286 processor.

Memory in this mode is *virtual,* which means if you don't have enough physical memory for what you need to do, Windows uses the disk as an extension of physical memory for up to 64 megabytes. The swap file in this mode can be permanently installed to a specific location on the disk, and Windows can access it without using DOS (which means faster swap operations). Memory is paged to the file in 4K memory blocks, using an LRU (least-recently-used) algorithm. If you haven't used an application for a while and memory is tight, that's the one Windows is most likely to page to disk. The paging management is completely hidden from the user and, indeed, even the application programmer. The maximum size of the virtual memory depends on the size of the swap file, but it defaults to four times the size of the physical memory. If you have a 4-megabyte system, Windows can use a maximum swap file size of 16 megabytes.

The Windows 3.X 386 enhanced mode is really a combination of two distinct technologies. The first is the 8086 virtual emulation support, which was the same technique used with earlier Windows/386 and DESQview. The second (and new to Windows) is the DOS extender technology (DPMI), which is also used in the standard mode.

Figure A.4 shows the memory map for the 386 enhanced mode. To the left is the memory map for Windows applications. To the right is the memory map for each DOS virtual machine. Every DOS application has its own DOS machine.

Memory management in the 386 enhanced mode is much like that in standard mode. That is, discardable memory is moved to the disk instead of being thrown away, which enables it to be reloaded if needed again. Windows uses some translation buffers in reserved memory (UMBs) to communicate data between its own protected mode and that of the real-mode DOS.

Managing Memory for Speed and Performance

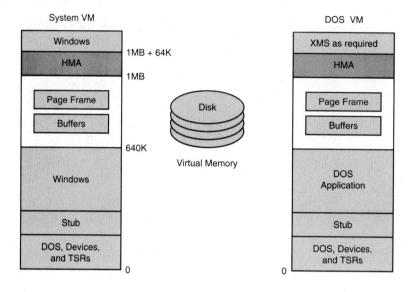

Figure A.4
Memory map for the 386 enhanced mode.

DOS applications can run concurrently in the 386 enhanced mode, each in its own window. Each application thinks it has its own 8086 processor and 8086 address space, that is, 640K. To use extended memory, the DOS program must use DPMI. Even if the DOS program was "ill-behaved" in earlier versions, it will still run. Even graphic programs or programs that write video directly to memory can run. You can use the Clipboard to transfer data between DOS applications, including graphic images in a DOS program. Unlike real or standard mode, 386 enhanced mode does not require DOS applications to be swapped to disk. Instead, they are *preempted;* the processor is switched between them in memory. This is automatic. A real-time process can't hog the processor. You can define the percentage of time each process gets. This enables you to tune each application for its processor needs. Peripherals (printers, communication ports, etc.) are viewed as virtual devices and output to each is managed by Windows.

Each DOS virtual machine inherits the DOS environment that started Windows. A TSR loaded before Windows is started is available for all DOS programs started under Windows.

Tip: You can save memory by maximizing the memory available to Windows before starting it. Whatever conventional memory is lost on starting will be lost to each DOS process.

Windows can simulate expanded memory for a DOS application. The DOS application's call for expanded memory is intercepted by Windows, which then uses extended memory to simulate expanded memory.

Tip: When running Windows in this mode, install all memory as extended memory. The only exception is if you have DOS programs running outside of Windows that need expanded memory. Then use the EMM386.SYS driver for these programs. Whatever memory is allocated for this expanded memory will not be available for Windows, however.

In the 386 enhanced mode, Windows runs in protected mode and uses buffer areas in the reserved I/O memory area for communication with DOS, which always runs in the real mode. These buffer areas are called the *translation buffers*, and are the window through which DOS and Windows can communicate in their respective modes. I/O calls, file transfers, and network interfacing are all done through the translation buffers. Most of the time Windows can find enough room for these buffers, but in some systems there may not be sufficient space in the reserved memory I/O. If this happens, you have two alternatives: eliminate the page frame for simulating expanded memory for DOS or place the buffers in conventional memory.

To eliminate the expanded memory page frame, edit the `[386enh]` section of SYSTEM.INI to include the line **ReservePageFrame=false** (see Appendix G). This will allocate the translation buffers first. If you set this value as `true`, the expanded memory page frame will be allocated first, placing the translation buffers in conventional memory. It an all or nothing proposition. The buffers are either all in reserved I/O or in conventional memory. If in conventional memory, they will reduce available memory for each DOS application.

Note: If EMM386.SYS is used to support expanded memory, the translation buffers are always placed in conventional memory. All available UMB space is used for expanded memory management. Don't use this driver for 386 enhanced mode unless you have DOS 5. With DOS 5, EEM386.SYS can be used to install drivers and TSRs to UMBs above 640K.

APPENDIX

A

Performance Tip: Make sure that plenty of memory is available for the applications before starting Windows. If Windows is started in a low memory situation, it will run very slowly because it will use the disk swap file to extend the physical memory available and will spend a lot of its time swapping data to the disk.

Performance Tip: A big advantage of the 386 enhanced mode is that the 386 runs in a virtual mode, which offers some protection to the programs from each other. If a DOS application hangs in this mode, use Alt+Esc, Alt+Tab, or Ctrl+Esc to return to Windows. Save all documents that are open. Then return to the DOS application and use Terminate from the Settings option of the Control menu to kill the DOS application. If using Windows 3.0, exit Windows and reboot.

The core layer now is a virtual layer, and each virtual machine has access to the device-independent driver. Windows and all Windows applications are in a single virtual machine. Each DOS application is in another virtual machine. The kernel is KRNL386.EXE. It performs the memory management, file I/O, and program loading. USER.EXE handles the user input and output. GDI.EXE contains the graphic primitives, and HIMEM.SYS is the extended memory manager. WIN386.EXE is the interface to the extended memory manager. It is also the scheduler, managing the processor between the

Managing Memory for Speed and Performance

various virtual machines. A variety of virtual device drivers are installed also, one for each device (printer, mouse, keyboard, etc.).

Windows 3.1 is still limited to a segmented architecture, with segments being a maximum of 64K in size. In a true 386 protected mode, you can have a 32-bit flat memory model and run everything in one large (gigabytes) segment. Windows does have a DLL library with it for supporting true 32-bit applications, but it is not well supported yet. If a developer develops a program for this library, it won't run on a 286 processor.

The Intel Processors and Windows

The three modes of Windows correspond to specific processor modes supported by the Intel processors used in DOS-based machines. The Intel 386 processor can really run in any of four modes. Here is a brief review of those modes and the corresponding Windows mode: 8088 (real), 80286 (16 bit-protected, standard), 80386 (32-bit protected—not yet implemented in Windows), and 8086-virtual (386 enhanced).

8088 (Real Mode)

The 8088 processor mode is supported by all Intel processors from the early 8088 of the IBM XT to the 80486-based processors being marketed today. A 16-bit address bus is used to address a maximum of 1 megabyte of memory. DOS applications support this mode exclusively except for some newer applications that use a DOS extender. Early versions of Windows supported this mode as a real mode.

80286 (16-Bit Protected Mode)

This 80286 processor introduced this mode, which is supported by the later 80386 and 80486-based processors. Up to 16 megabytes can be addressed. This, like the 8088 mode, is a segmented architecture, with the segments limited to 64K each. *Protected* implies that memory assigned to one program cannot be altered or used by another program; that is, one program cannot crash another. Windows runs as 16-bit protected when installed for standard mode.

80386 (32-Bit Protected Mode)

This mode was introduced with the 80386 processor, and is also available with the 80486. Up to 4 gigabytes can be addressed in this mode. It is still a segmented architecture, but the segments can be up to 4 gigabytes in size. This mode is also called the flat model because everything can be run in one big segment. In the 386 enhanced mode, some portions of Windows run as 32-bit protected. Windows applications can be written for this mode, but if so will not run on an 80286. Support is also minimal. For this reason, most Windows applications are written for 16-bit protected.

Virtual 86 (V86)

Virtual 86 is another mode introduced with the 80386 processor. In reality, it is a 1MB protected mode. A program running in V86 mode thinks it is running in real mode, when (in reality) it is under a V86 control program with the processor as a virtual machine supporting multiple real-mode machines. DOS applications in Windows' 386 enhanced mode are running in Virtual 86 mode. In the 386 enhanced mode, DOS programs can use the DPMI to switch to 16-bit or 32-bit protected mode, giving them access to megabytes of memory.

Multitasking with Windows

Now let's look at how Windows handles multiple applications. *Multitasking* is the process of having more than one program executing at a time. Windows supports two types of multi-tasking. Recognizing when each type is used and its limitations are important.

Windows supports *nonpreemptive multitasking* for Windows applications. When running multiple Windows applications, each application is periodically given control of the processor. It is the responsibility of each application not to hog the resources of the machine. Files should be opened only as they are needed, and I/O ports must be released for other applications. Developers must take these requirements into consideration when writing their programs. Windows can give control to an application, but the application must return control promptly. This is an inherent weakness of Windows, and won't be solved until there is a Windows NT, OS/2, or other operating system that supports preemptive multitasking in which Windows always remains in control.

With DOS applications running under Windows, it is a different story. In the standard mode, there is no DOS multi-tasking, since only one DOS application is running at a time. When switching between a DOS program and Windows, the DOS program is swapped out to the disk and suspended.

In the 386 enhanced mode, however, Windows supports true DOS preemptive multitasking. Each DOS application is running in its own 1-megabyte virtual machine, and the processor can manage each and protect each application from the others. If the program needs more than a normal 640K of memory, it must access extended memory using the DPMI standard. Windows provides each DOS application with a defined time slot in turn. True preemptive multitasking is done for the DOS applications. Windows is viewed as another task, and all Windows applications are switched in or out as a single virtual machine in a single time slice. You can also tune each DOS application and Windows, editing the PIF files for the amount of processor time each should have when active. When the time slice is up, Windows switches to another task. The 386 Enhanced option in Control Panel provides other options also. You can have a single foreground program that owns the display and keyboard, with others running as background programs—printing, calculating, transferring a file to or from a system, or compiling.

Now for specific examples. When you start an application (DOS or Windows), it is launched with its window open and active. In computer talk, that application has the *focus;* that is, it accepts keyboard input. Other windows may be open, but they do not have the focus or keyboard. If an application window is open but does not have the focus, it is said to be a *background application*. What happens here depends on whether it is a DOS or a Windows application. If it is a Windows application, Windows will continue to give it as much processing time as possible. When idle time is detected, Windows will work on the background application. That's fine for printing and spreadsheet calculation in the background, but if the Windows application in the background is a communications program transferring a file, it may or may not work. It all depends on if the foreground application is releasing enough time for the file transfer to take place properly. This problem won't be solved until Windows has true preemptive multi-tasking.

If you switch away from a DOS application (putting it in the background with the window still open), the story is different. In the standard mode, the background DOS application is suspended. There is no background processing until you return to the DOS application. In the 386 enhanced mode, you can run DOS applications in the background by using either of two ways. The first is to install the DOS application so that the PIF file controls the amount of processing time the application will get. Another way is to activate the Control menu from the DOS application and then use the Settings command to select Background from the Tasking Options. Then choose OK.

When you are running an application in the background, you may occasionally get messages from it. When you get a message, what happens next depends on the type of message. Let's say that you get a message from Print Manager about a printing problem while you are working in Word for Windows or PageMaker. Most of the time you can just acknowledge the message by a click and continue with whatever you were doing. The background process is still held, however, and if you switch to it the message is still there. For a printing problem, you would switch to the Print Manager as soon as possible and try to resolve the problem. The icon displayed with the message box generally gives you a clue as to the severity of the problem: a red stop sign indicates a critical message, a yellow circle with an exclamation point indicates a warning, a green circle with a question mark is a request for verification, and a purple circle with an "i" is for your information only.

If you find an icon flashing, it indicates the program represented by the icon has a message. Restore the program from the icon and respond to the message.

Multitasking also means you can run multiple copies of the same program. For example, you could open two copies of Notepad, each with different data files. The second copy of the application will always use less memory than the first because certain parts of the program code are shared in memory. You can run additional copies of DOS applications, as well, and the icon name identification when minimized for each icon will be followed by one or more dots. Some programs, such as Control Panel, won't permit a second copy to be started. Most applications in the Main group window won't open a second copy, nor will Recorder (in the Accessories window).

Monitoring Memory Use

What if you get an out-of-memory message for Windows? This means Windows does not have enough memory to complete the designated operation. You can use the **A**bout option of the **H**elp menu of File Manager or Program Manager to monitor how effectively memory is being used. The dialog box shows the current mode and some memory statistics. If you are using expanded memory, you may see additional lines with information related to the expanded memory. Here is an explanation of two of the terms used in out-of-memory messages:

> **Memory**—the amount of memory left for use in kilobytes. This value will also include any available extended memory. In the 386 enhanced mode, the figure will include available virtual memory (disk-based), and this figure may be larger than the physical memory in the

system. If this value is less than 30K, you should start closing applications.

System Resources—the percentage of system resources that are free. The system resources are stored in two special buffers. Windows actually has three components: USER.EXE, GDL.EXE, and KERNEL.EXE. The first, USER.EXE, controls the keyboard, mouse, sound, COM port, timer, and related functions. GDL.EXE controls the graphics and printing. KERNEL.EXE is the manager and controls memory management and program launching. Each of these has a local heap, or its own data segment. Each is 64K. Each program launched uses a part of the USER.EXE heap, and icons, brushes, and pen use the GDL.EXE heap. It's quite possible in Windows to run out of local heap space even though there is plenty of memory left. The only alternative at this point is to shut down a Windows application or two. In fact, it is best to start shutting down things if the Free Memory Resources drops below 15 percent. The basic rule is simple: close applications you are no longer using. Windows 3.1 has improved the memory problem through better resource management, but the problem is still there and will be until we have Windows NT.

Memory Managers and Windows

Note: When installing a third-party memory manager, always back up the complete system first.

You can use any of several memory manager products to improve the memory management under both DOS and Windows. DOS 5 (see the next section) also includes a memory manager. Two of the leading products, Quarterdeck's QEMM-386 and Quailitas' 386MAX, both work with Windows. Both permit you to place drivers and TSRs in reserved I/O memory, thus releasing more conventional memory. QEMM-386 supports standard and 386 enhanced modes, 386MAX supports standard only. If you are running large DOS programs, you may find one of these useful. The QEMM-386 product also automates the fine-tuning of the memory manager and includes a utility called Manifest that gives a very detailed picture of your memory configuration, even offering hints for improving the current system configuration. The trade-off is that these programs steal upper memory blocks that Windows uses for buffering when switching to the real mode for disk operations. The result can be slower disk operations.

Note: Be sure, when using QEMM-386, that you have a version supported by the version of Windows you are using. Windows 3.0 requires version 5.11 of QEMM-386 or later. Windows 3.1 requires version 6 of QEMM-386. When running in the 386 enhanced mode, Windows requires a WINHIRAM.VXD virtual device driver that is normally supplied with QEMM-386 as well as with later versions of Windows. Microsoft's goal is that eventually you won't have to update QEMM-386 each time you update Windows. However, you will have to update WINHIRAM.VXD, which would be supplied with the new version of Windows.

QEMM-386 is really an expanded memory manager (EMS 4.0), but what is unique is that it is also an extended memory manager (XMS). You install Quarterdeck's QEMM-386.SYS instead of Windows' HIMEM.SYS and EMM386.SYS, and you have a compatible system that supports the upper memory blocks, high memory area, expanded memory, and extended memory. As with DOS 5, you can put DOS device drivers in reserved memory (above 640K). QEMM-386 launches Windows in protected mode (as DOS 5), maps extended memory into pages in the reserved I/O memory, and then maps TSRs, device drivers, and DOS system resources into reserved I/O memory. Although this is a very powerful program, installation is virtually automatic, even to the rebooting after everything is done. The result is that if you run CHKDSK after installing QEMM-386, you will be pleasantly surprised at the amount of conventional memory you now have. You can then run Manifest (included with QEMM-386) to get hints for managing your memory even better!

Although DOS 5 also contains a memory manager (see the next section), QEMM-386 offers several advantages over DOS 5:

- The availability of more conventional memory for DOS applications.

- Automatic configuration of device drivers and TSRs for the UMBs.

- Extensive memory management reporting facilities through Manifest. DOS 5 offers a MEM program, but it offers only limited reporting and is not as easy to use.

- A Stealth utility for converting ROM addresses to high RAM.

- Sharing of RAM for expanded and extended memory.

■ Better expanded memory support.

■ Improved management of the loading of TSRs and device drivers for best fit. DOS 5 loads them only in the order listed in AUTOEXEC.BAT and CONFIG.SYS.

■ A squeeze feature that temporarily increases the high RAM region during a program's loading and initialization.

Once the QEMM-386 driver is installed, you can use QEMM.COM to view your upper memory mapping for changes.

Here are a few tips for using QEMM-386:

■ Be sure you are using the latest version of QEMM-386.

■ If QEMM-386 fills the reserved I/O memory for expanded memory paging, there isn't room for the translation buffers in the 386 enhanced mode. The buffers are then placed in conventional memory, using space (about 30K) in every DOS virtual machine created.

■ Programs that use VCPI (such as Lotus 1-2-3 release 3.0) require you to use an EMBMEM parameter with QEMM-386 to set aside memory for their extended memory.

■ On some machines, QEMM-386 will place its 64K EMS page frame above E000. This will freeze the system in the 386 enhanced mode. In this case, use the QEMM-386 FRAME parameter to move the page frame lower.

■ The RAM parameter should be installed with the driver. If you fail to do this, Windows may not start in the 386 enhanced mode. The RAM parameter permits QEMM-386 to use the area between 640K and 1 megabyte. Use the EXCLUDE parameter to exclude areas that you do not wish QEMM-386 to use.

■ Use the NOSORT parameter. QEMM-386 normally sorts applications when memory of mixed speeds is used, permitting the first applications loaded to use the faster memory. This won't work in the 386 enhanced mode, so the safest alternative is to always turn NOSORT off.

■ Be sure HIMEM.SYS is disabled. If you try to install it with QEMM-386, it will take 3K of memory that QEMM-386 can't reclaim.

■ If QEMM-386 installs to a page frame of 9000, try to move it between C000 and F000.

■ In the CONFIG.SYS file, specify **DOS=HIGH**, but don't use UMB (`DOS=HIGH,UMB`). Use QEMM's **LOADHIGH**—not the DOS `LOADHI` and `DEVICEHIGH`.

■ In SYSTEM.INI, use **DualDisplay=true**, and add **EMMExclude=E000-FFFF** (see Appendix G).

■ Always use these parameters with the driver: RAM, NOSORT, NOFILL, and NOSHADOW.

■ QEMM-386 can create page frames outside of upper memory, but Windows cannot work in the 386 enhanced mode with page frames outside of upper memory if they are assigned. Use QEMM.COM to view the memory allocation, and then use the FRAME parameter to move the page frame if necessary.

Memory management products all work in a similar manner. The memory manager communicates the status of the memory under its control to the Windows memory manager in a low mode by using a virtual device. This virtual device has a filename with the extension VXD. When Windows is started, VXD communicates the status of *all* memory to Windows in the low mode. After this is done, the SYS driver file becomes dormant. Windows can then enter the 386 enhanced mode,

where it takes responsibility for managing memory as long as Windows is loaded. All EMS and XMS calls (that would have been handled by the SYS driver) are now handled by Windows. Both the VXD and SYS files must be in the same directory.

> **Tip:** Because installing memory managers can cause lockups or system destruction, take two precautions before installation. First, back up the entire system. Second, create a boot diskette for quick recoveries.

DOS 5 and Windows

DOS 5 is an updated version of MS-DOS that is designed for better memory management and support of Windows. Although you can run Windows with earlier versions of DOS, you will probably find it worth the cost to upgrade. DOS 5 includes many features that you once had to obtain by buying the commercial memory manager products. With DOS 5's improved memory management, you can put your TSR and device drivers above 640K as well as put some parts of DOS in the HMA, releasing even more conventional memory.

> **Tip:** Always load DOS high when using Windows (`DOS=HIGH`). DOS uses the HMA area very efficiently and leaves more conventional memory available. Load DOS high even when using another memory management product. Don't use the HMA for application programs.

Managing Memory for Speed and Performance

DOS 5 uses two modules for managing memory. They are HIMEM.SYS and EMM386.SYS. (Both are also included with Windows.). HIMEM.SYS is the extended memory manager (VCPI, since DPMI is not supported). DOS 5 will run on a 286 or 386 processor. EEM386.SYS is used in addition if you have a 386 system. It permits you to load TSRs and drivers in the UMBs from 640K to 1MB, and also supports expanded memory management. Even if you don't need the expanded memory, load this driver if you have a 386 or later. It permits you to put your drivers and TSRs high.

DOS 5 doesn't manage the upper memory blocks quite as well as some of the commercial products. You will have more conventional memory left if you use many of the commercial products. DOS 5 also requires that the UMBs be contiguous, whereas QEMM-386 can manage scattered blocks. DOS 5 uses more conventional memory overhead for managing memory—8K versus the 2K for most of the others. QEMM-386 is about 5K. DOS 5 also has limited tuning for memory management in comparison with other products. Finally, DOS 5 loads the device drivers and TSRs in the order they appear in CONFIG.SYS or AUTOEXEC.BAT. Other products generally load the drivers and TSRs to get the best fit.

Always use the latest version of HIMEM.SYS with DOS 5 and Windows. Use the DIR command to examine the dates of these drivers on your system. If Windows is already installed when you install DOS 5, install the HIMEM.SYS with DOS 5.

The basic device driver area of CONFIG.SYS in DOS 5 may look like something for a 386/486 machine:

```
DEVICE=HIMEM.SYS
DEVICE=EMM386.EXE. NOEMS
DOS=HIGH,UMB
DEVICEHIGH=ANSI.SYS
```

This loads DOS to the HMA, which is the segment immediately above 1MB of memory. The expanded memory driver (EEM386.SYS) is used to reserve some UMBs in the memory between 640K and 1MB, and uses the UMBs for the device driver ANSI.SYS. If you need some expanded memory for DOS applications (an EMS page frame), use RAM instead of NOEMS. If not, use the EEM386 driver only for supporting the use of the drivers in the UMB area. (See Appendix G for information on editing CONFIG.SYS.)

In the same way, you can load TSRs to the UMBs by using the LOADHIGH command in AUTOEXEC.BAT:

```
LOADHIGH MIRROR /tc-100
LOADHIGH DOSKEY
```

First load as resident any programs that take more memory to initialize than to run. (See Appendix G for information on editing AUTOEXEC.BAT.) MIRROR is an example of such a shrinking TSR. Not all device drivers and TSRs can be loaded high. If you experience problems with a driver or TSR on loading high or if the system locks up, switch back to low. Also, DOS 5 is not as clean on managing this loading as most commercial memory management utilities. TSRs and drivers are loaded in the order you list them, and you may not get an error message if a driver or TSR doesn't load high. You can also experience lockup if there isn't enough UMB room for the drivers. Check the loading with the command MEM /c. Then reorganize to put the larger programs first. DOS 5 won't tell you on booting if it can't load some drivers or TSRs high that you specified for loading high. Use MEM /c at the DOS prompt to check what is really loaded high.

If you use the MEM /c command within a Windows virtual machine (from a prompt created by Windows in 386 enhanced mode), you will see only the memory of the virtual machine.

With DOS 5, you cannot use EEM386.SYS when running Windows 3.0 in the standard mode with an 80286 processor.

You can use it only with 386/486 machines in the 386 enhanced mode. If you try to start Windows in the standard mode, you will get a message telling you that Windows won't run in standard mode and the loading will terminate. With Windows 3.1, the EEM386.SYS driver supports standard mode.

Since DOS 5 can load high and can load drivers to UMBs as QEMM-386, many users question if QEMM-386 or another memory manager is needed. QEMM-386 will free up more conventional memory than DOS 5. If you have DOS applications that are memory hungry, use QEMM-386 (however, there will be less memory for the Windows applications). You also have more tuning flexibility. Finally, with QEMM-386, TSRs and drivers automatically load for a best fit.

Tips for Memory Management

Here are a few tips for general memory management:

■ Add as much physical memory as you can afford. Standard mode supports up to 16 megabytes. The 386 enhanced mode supports up to 64 megabytes, with 16 of it in physical memory and 48 additional megabytes of disk memory.

■ Invest in DOS 5. Load DOS high, and load drivers and TSRs high if using an 80386 or later.

■ If not using expanded memory, add **NoEMMDriver=yes** to the [386enh] section of SYSTEM.INI (see Appendix G).

Managing Memory for Speed and Performance

- [ ] Use a permanent swap file with an 80386 or later system if you are using 512-byte sectors (no third-party disk drivers).

- [ ] Use FastDisk if the controller supports it.

- [ ] Use only the TSRs and drivers that are necessary.

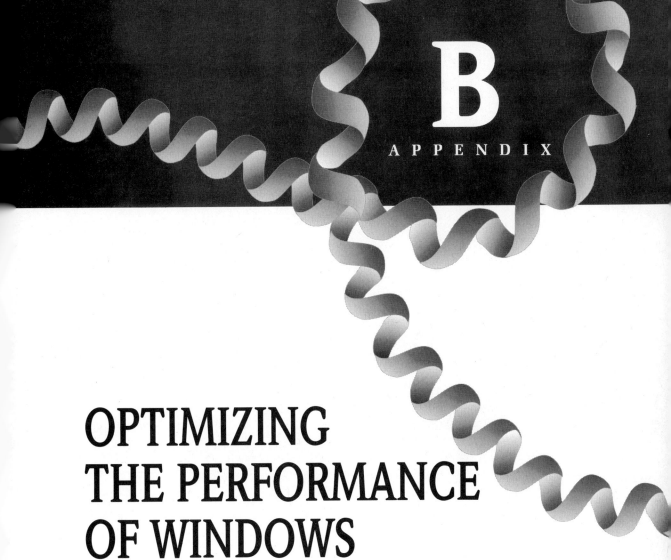

B

OPTIMIZING
THE PERFORMANCE
OF WINDOWS

This appendix will give you some tips on how to optimize
Windows on your system for maximum speed and performance. This includes swap file management, memory
management, disk management, and the role of disk
caches and RAMDrives in Windows.

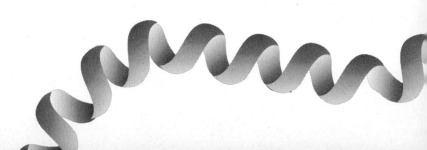

Which Mode?

If you have a 286-based computer, you are limited to running Windows in the standard mode only. If you have a 386/486 processor with enough memory, however, you can use standard or 386 enhanced. Which mode is better?

If using Windows 3.0, you will find that Windows runs somewhat faster in the standard mode on a 386. If you are running only Windows applications with this version, you will gain more stability and some speed by staying in the standard mode. If you are running DOS applications under Windows, you will want the 386 enhanced mode. This gives you the virtual memory support for DOS applications that enables them to run in the background, and it provides clipboard support.

If you are running Windows 3.1 on a 386 or 486 machine and you have the physical memory, use the 386 enhanced mode and forget the standard mode. With the 386 enhanced mode, you might have the advantage of Windows internal 32-bit file management system (if using FastDisk) as well as improved DOS support. If you have a 386 or 486 processor but lack the physical memory, purchase the memory and use the 386 enhanced mode.

Using the TEMP Directory

The AUTOEXEC.BAT file should include a SET command (see Appendix G for more on editing AUTOEXEC.BAT) that sets the TEMP directory for Windows, such as:

```
SET TEMP=C:\TEMP
```

Optimizing the Performance of Windows

Many application programs (both DOS and Windows-based) use this directory for temporary files. Programs should normally delete their temporary files on exit, so any files here can usually be deleted. Over time, this directory has a tendency to get trashed from abnormal program terminations. For this reason, you may wish to clear it as part of the normal bootup procedure. Under some conditions, however, its contents should not be cleared. For example, if your word processor keeps working files here and someone trips on the power cord, you may need that temporary file to recover. Some programs permit you to do this. The solution is simple. Let AUTOEXEC.BAT clear the directory on booting. If you wish to keep a file saved in the TEMP directory and to recover from a crash, boot from a diskette that does not clear the TEMP directory.

Tip: One of the major causes of hanging programs and computer lockup is inadequate space in this TEMP directory. Most application programs (including PageMaker) simply aren't smart enough to detect when this directory is full.

It may seem advantageous (in terms of speed) to put the TEMP directory on a RAMDisk. You can try it, but remember a few things. First, in some cases a temporary file can be very large. For example, it you print with PageMaker to a Hewlett-Packard PaintJet XL (in color), expect to need several megabytes in the temporary file. Most RAMDisks aren't large enough.

If you have at least 4 megabytes of RAM, consider using the extra as a RAMDisk. It can dramatically speed up some

applications that use temporary files. Be sure, however, that you do have enough RAMDisk for the temporary files.

Using Swap Files

Windows uses the disk as an extension of memory, swapping applications and even parts of executing programs to disk as necessary. This swapping is done through the use of *swap files*. Swapping in the 386 enhanced mode is managed differently than swapping in the standard mode.

Note: Never install a swap file to removable media.

Swapping in 386 Enhanced Mode

In the 386 enhanced mode, swapping is done by using either a permanent or a temporary swap file. A *permanent swap file* is a hidden file created on the disk as an extension of memory. It is a permanent file that is never deleted, and can use a large amount of space. Using a permanent swap file is the fastest and most efficient way to install Windows.

If disk space is at a premium, turn off the permanent swap file and use a *temporary swap file*. If no permanent swap file has been created, Windows automatically creates a temporary swap file on starting. When you exit Windows, the temporary swap file is deleted.

Note: Using a permanent swap file does not speed file input and output during normal execution. The permanent swap file helps speed performance only when you are swapping between applications. To speed up the file I/O, you should consider using FastDisk.

Tip: If possible, install Windows for the 386 enhanced mode with a permanent swap file. This ensures maximum speed, secure swapping, and better control. Windows can access this file without using DOS. You cannot create a permanent swap file on a network drive or on a RAMDisk. You can use either, however, for a temporary swap file. With Windows 3.1, you can find out which type of swap file is currently in use by starting Control Panel and choosing 386 Enhanced and then **V**irtual Memory. With Windows 3.0, you can find out by choosing Setup from the Main group and reading the last line of the dialog box displayed.

With Windows 3.1, you can use Control Panel on the Main program group to install or change the swap file by using this procedure:

1. Compress the disk you plan to use for the file by using a compression or defragmentation utility. The permanent swap file can be installed only to *contiguous disk clusters* (clusters that are sequential). Compressing will maximize the contiguous disk clusters on the disk. Exit Windows and do this from DOS by using a compression utility.

2. Comment out the `load=` line of WIN.INI by preceding it with a semicolon (see Appendix G).

3. Remove all TSRs from the system and start Windows in the 386 enhanced mode.

4. Close all applications except Program Manager.

5. Start Control Panel and choose the 386 Enhanced icon.

6. In the 386 Enhanced dialog box, choose **V**irtual Memory. The Virtual Memory dialog box will appear (see Figure B.1).

7. Click **C**hange>> to edit the current setting (see Figure B.2) and enter the new values. Select None if you do not wish to use a permanent swap file.

8. Exit and close the dialog boxes.

Figure B.1

The Virtual Memory dialog box.

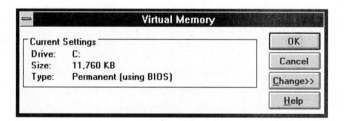

Note: You can create permanent swap files only on disks that are partitioned with the DOS FDISK utility and are using 512-byte sectors. Permanent swap files can't be created when a third-party partitioning program has been used, such as Disk Manager or SpeedStor. The only exception is the COMPAQ ENHDISK.SYS utility. You can check your system by using a utility that provides this disk information, such as the Disk Info option of PC Tools.

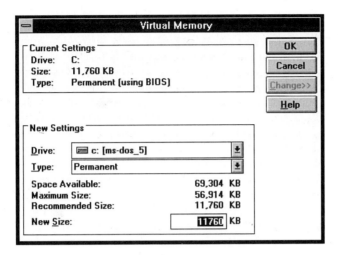

Figure B.2

Entering new values for the swap file.

The permanent swap file will be created as a hidden system file called 386SPART.PAR. An additional SPART.PAR file is also created as a hidden file. Keeping these files hidden protects them from inadvertent deletions. To see them, you can turn off the hidden attributes by using the **F**ile Properties command of File Manager.

Performance Tip: Place the permanent swap file in the root directory on your fastest drive or on the one with the most space, depending on your needs. Do not put it on a RAMDisk. That would be self-defeating since you are sacrificing real memory to get the same amount of virtual memory.

You don't have to use the recommended swap file size. This space extends your physical memory. Use a lower value than recommended and increase it only if you get a message about being out of memory and if the system resources percentage (using **H**elp **A**bout) is sufficient.

With Windows 3.0, use the following steps to create or edit a permanent swap file:

1. Compress the disk you plan to use for the file by using a compression or defragmentation utility. The permanent swap file can be installed only to *contiguous disk clusters* (clusters that are sequential). Compressing will maximize the contiguous disk clusters on the disk.

2. Comment out the `load=` line of WIN.INI by preceding it with a semicolon (see Appendix G). No other programs should load with Windows.

3. Remove all TSRs from the system, reboot, and start Windows in the real mode by using the command **WIN /r**.

4. Close all applications except Program Manager.

5. Choose **R**un from the **F**ile menu.

6. Enter **C:\WIN\SYSTEM\SWAPFILE.EXE** in the dialog box and choose OK (or use the drive and directory containing the Windows system files).

7. If a permanent swap file already exists, you will see a message. Choose to delete the current file and create a new one.

8. Choose the disk drive from the dialog box, using the **N**ext Drive command as necessary. You will see a dialog box showing the largest possible permanent swap file size that you can build, as well as a recommended file size. For the initial installation, it is generally best to use half the free space available.

9. Select **C**reate. The permanent swap file will be created or changed.

10. Exit Windows and restart it in the 386 enhanced mode.

To delete a permanent swap file with Windows 3.0, follow the previous procedure until the first dialog box is displayed. On this box, choose to delete the current file and choose OK. To change the size of the swap file or the disk drive on which it resides, compress the disk and recreate the file.

If you choose not to use a permanent swap file, Windows will create a temporary swap file on starting. By default, this file will be in the Windows directory. The name will be WIN386.SWP. You can define the drive for the temporary file by editing the `PagingDrive` parameter of the SYSTEM.INI file (see Appendix G for information on editing SYSTEM.INI). Set this parameter to your fastest disk. It is always placed in the root directory if the \WINDOWS directory is not used, and the directory can't be changed. Do not set the drive to a RAMDisk. The size of this file defaults to 1024K on starting. You must restart Windows after editing the SYSTEM.INI file because SYSTEM.INI is read only on starting.

You can turn off disk swapping completely (if disk space is at a premium) by adding the line **Paging=no** in the `[386enh]` section. You can limit the file size by editing the parameters `MinUserDiskSpace` (defines the space that must be kept free on the drive in kilobytes) and `MaxPagingFileSize` (defines maximum size of a temporary file in kilobytes). The `swapfile=` parameter in WIN.INI doesn't do anything. It's a holdover from an older Windows version.

B
APPENDIX

Note: You can use a temporary file on a network drive if you have a fast server and a root directory that is not read-only access, if you are not using Novell Netware, and if there is enough free space. This practice is not recommended, however. To set the temporary files to the server, edit the `PagingDrive` parameter of the SYSTEM.INI file to the network drive.

When doing backups, delete the swap file first to save time and tape (or diskettes). For Windows 3.1, to delete the swap file use 386 Enhanced from Control Panel. Choose **V**irtual Memory, select **C**hange>>, and then set the **T**ype to None. Then choose OK.

For Windows 3.0, use these steps to delete the file:

1. Comment out the `load=` line of WIN.INI (see Appendix G) by preceding it with a semicolon. No other programs should load with Windows.

2. Start Windows in the real mode using `WIN /r`.

3. Use **F**ile **R**un and enter `C:\WIN\SYSTEM\SWAPFILE.EXE` to start Swapfile (or use the appropriate directory) and choose to delete the swap file.

4. Boot from a boot diskette (without any TSRs) and do the backup.

5. Compress the hard disk drive with Windows from DOS.

6. Start Windows in the real mode again and rebuild the swap file.

Optimizing the Performance of Windows

If you can't create a permanent swap file in the 386 enhanced mode...

Be sure that you first have defragmented the disk drive you plan to use with a compression utility such as Central Point's Compress. Be sure you are using a drive partitioned with the DOS FDISK utility. Permanent swap files can't be created when a third-party partitioning program has been used, such as Disk Manager or SpeedStor. You must have at least 1.5 megabytes of free contiguous space on the disk to install a permanent swap file. You can't create a swap file on a network drive.

Swapping in Standard Mode

When Windows is running in real mode (Windows 3.0) or standard mode (Windows 3.0 or 3.1), swapping still occurs, but *application swap files* are used instead. There is no permanent or temporary swap file. When you switch away from a particular application, a portion or all of the application is put in an application swap file. Multiple application swap files can be created for different applications. When you exit Windows, all application swap files are deleted. The files are normally kept in the directory named by the TEMP environment variable. To change the location of the swap files, edit the Swapdisk parameter of SYSTEM.INI [NonWindowsApp] section (see Appendix G).

Note: Place the swap files on a hard disk with at least 512K of free space. If possible, use your fastest drive. If no location is specified in SYSTEM.INI, Windows will place

continues

continued

the swap files in the \TEMP directory. Avoid using a RAM disk for the swap files. If you use a RAM disk for swap files, Windows will simply be moving applications in memory and you will gain no advantage.

Making SCSI Drives Work

Windows can do very low-level interfacing with the disk, particularly with (1) Windows 3.1 for general file management and with the permanent swap file in 386 enhanced mode or (2) Windows 3.0 in the 386 enhanced mode when using a permanent swap file. In some cases, you can choose between hard disk drivers provided with Windows or drivers provided with the disk controller. In addition, the rules can change when you are using DOS 5. For the Adaptec AHA 154x series adapters, your best alternative is usually to use the ASPI drivers (ASW 1410, version 2.0 or later) shipped with the host adapter. Remember that you can't use a permanent swap file with third-party partitioning programs, like Disk Manager or SpeedStor.

If you have been using Windows and have upgraded to a new disk controller using the SCSI interface, you should install Windows again. This will modify the configuration automatically for the new disk controller. (Be sure to save WIN.INI first!)

Making Third-Party Disk Drivers Work

If you have a line in CONFIG.SYS that installs a special disk driver for your disk, it should work with Windows. The only precaution is that you should not install a permanent swap file or FastDisk.

Using a Disk Cache

Windows is highly disk-intensive. Unless it is running in 386 enhanced mode with megabytes of extended memory, you will see that the hard disk is doing a lot of work as you use Windows.

You will find that a disk cache will almost always improve the system's speed and your productivity. A *disk cache* acts as a memory buffer for disk reading and writing. Several sectors of the disk can be read to the cache at a time. If Windows needs more data from the same sectors, it can get the data faster by accessing the cache than by reading the disk again. Instead of writing to the disk, the program has to write only to the cache. The cache software can then write to the disk in the background. Windows includes its own disk-caching utility, SMARTDrive.

Unlike earlier Windows versions, Windows 3.1 has an excellent SMARTDrive 4.0, and can cache both reading and writing (Windows 3.0 uses an older version 3.x). Also, SMARTDrive 4.0 now supports Bernoulli, some hardcards, and some SCSI and WORM drives. In addition, SMARTDrive 4.0 can work with some third-party disk managers. SMARTDrive will also work with Stacker, but read the notes about Stacker in SETUP.TXT.

SMARTDrive is generally installed automatically with Windows. To install SMARTDrive manually, add the SMARTDRV.EXE driver to the Windows directory. Enter the corresponding installation line into the CONFIG.SYS file (see Appendix G) anywhere after the line defining the extended memory driver (HIMEM.SYS):

```
DEVICE=C:\WINDOWS\SMARTDRV.EXE
```

After installation you may wish to customize your use of SMARTDrive. The general form is

```
DEVICE=drive:pathSMARTDRV.EXE drive+|- /E:ElementSize
InitCacheSize WinCacheSize /B:BufferSize /C /R /L /Q /S /?
```

where the parameters and switches are those that are valid with Windows 3.1. Table B.1 gives the valid parameters and switches.

Table B.1

Valid Parameters and Switches for Windows 3.1

Parameter/Switch	Description
drive	Drive for caching. If *drive* is not specified, floppy drivers are read-cached, hard drives are read- and write-cached, and CD-ROM and network drives are not cached at all.
path	Path for SMARTDRIVE.EXE.
+|-	Enable (+) or disable (-) caching.
/E:ElementSize	The number of bytes moved at a time. Default is 8K.
InitCacheSize	Initial cache size (see text).
WinCacheSize	Minimum cache size in Windows (see text).

Optimizing the Performance of Windows

Parameter/Switch	Description
/B:*BufferSize*	Size of read-ahead buffer.
/C	Flush cache to hard disk.
/R	Clear cache and restart SMARTDrive.
/L	Prevent using SMARTDrive with UMBs. Use this option with DOS 5 with UMBs enabled.
/Q	Prevent display of SMARTDrive information on-screen.
/S	Display additional status information.
/?	Display on-line help.

Here is an example:

```
DEVICE=C:\WIN\SMARTDRV.EXE 2048 1024
```

The first number (2048) is the *InitCacheSize*, representing the normal memory size (in kilobytes) allocated to the disk cache. The second number (1024) is the *WinCacheSize*, defining the minimum size (in kilobytes) to which Windows can reduce the cache. Here's another way to look at it:

```
DEVICE=C:\WIN\SMARTDRV.EXE dos win
```

where *dos* is the DOS cache size and *win* is the Windows cache size.

When you are not running Windows and have extended memory, the cache is always running at the normal size (2048K here). If you start Windows in the 386 enhanced mode with the cache in extended memory, the cache is immediately reduced to the minimum size (1024K in this example) to provide as much room as possible for Windows. If the parameter is omitted, the cache is reduced to 0K (no cache).

Windows 3.1 defaults to a cache size of zero if total system RAM is less than 1MB. If total RAM is 2MB or more, it defaults to 256K. The table of default values is on page 540 of the *Windows 3.1 User's Guide*.

The starting cache size should be between 256K and 1024K. If memory space is available, the larger size is better. Increasing the cache size beyond 1024K generally does not improve performance by much.

Performance Tip: If your system has at least 512K of extended memory or 256K of expanded memory, you generally should install a disk cache.

Tip: You can tune SMARTDrive by printing the full status and examining the *hit rate*, or how often the computer gets the information from the cache instead of from the disk. To see the current status, enter: **SMARTDRV /S**.

Under certain conditions, Windows may install SMARTDrive with the following line in CONFIG.SYS:

```
DEVICE=SMARTDRV.EXE /double_buffer
```

This line is in addition to the normal AUTOEXEC.BAT SMARTDrive load line. SMARTDrive is actually two programs: a disk cache and a buffering program for certain disk controllers that need it. Some SCSI controllers use bus mastering. If the installation perceives buffering as a possible

Optimizing the Performance of Windows

problem, the double-buffering driver is added automatically on Windows installation in CONFIG.SYS.

To see if you can turn double buffering off, enter **SMARTDRV** at the DOS prompt. Look at the column labeled `Buffering`. You will see a `No`, `Yes`, or – for each driver. The – means that SMARTDrive can't determine if double-buffering is needed. If all lines read `No`, you can delete the parameter that specifies double-buffering in CONFIG.SYS.

If you are using Windows 3.0, the Windows 3.0 SMARTDrive included with it is not the best disk-caching program on the market. It caches disk reading, but not writing. Windows does a lot of disk reading, discarding code that is no longer used. For this reason, the Windows 3.0 SMARTDrive helps program management in Windows. Nevertheless, it is not the best product for general caching where both writing and reading are involved, such as with a database management product. Upgrade to SMARTDrive 4.0 or purchase a third-party disk cache. Several other disk-cache programs exist on the market, many of which will work with Windows 3.0 or later. These are faster and manage the disk transfers better.

If you have expanded memory, you can force the SMARTDrive to expanded memory by using the /a parameter. Otherwise, SMARTDrive uses extended memory by default. When you exit Windows, the cache always returns to the normal (DOS) size.

Performance Tip: The cache size is always displayed on booting. SMARTDrive will also display on booting the number of tracks and sectors that can be saved to the cache.

With the cache installed, reduce the number of buffers defined in CONFIG.SYS to 10 (see Appendix G). You don't need more than this with a cache. Here are some tips for setting the memory and size for SMARTDrive:

- If running 386 enhanced mode, keep the cache in extended memory.

- Install the cache as large as possible, particularly for database applications. However, you shouldn't need to use more than 2048K. Table B.2 shows some good starting values for normal operations.

- Try to keep the minimum cache size to 1024K. At lower values, caching is too small to be efficient.

- Increasing the minimum size above 1024K and the normal size above 2048K won't give you much improvement.

- Larger cache sizes will also tie up more conventional memory for managing the cache. SMARTDrive uses about 500 bytes of conventional memory per megabyte of cache for management.

- If using EMM386.SYS to emulate expanded memory, don't put the cache there. Don't cache to an emulator or you will lose speed.

- Be sure you are not using other cache programs with SMARTDrive, such as the internal cache of Quattro Pro or dBASE IV.

- Keep your disk compacted to improve the performance of the cache.

Optimizing the Performance of Windows

■ SMARTDrive is automatically disabled if a third-party partitioning software is installed (SpeedStor, Disk Manager, etc.).

■ For SCSI hardware, you may need to use the /b parameter with SMARTDrive or the SCSIHI.SYS driver instead.

System Memory	Normal Cache Size	Minimum Cache Size
1024K	320K	0
2048K	800K	0
4096K	2048K	1024K
6144K	2048K	1024K
8192K	2048K	1024K

Table B.2

Appropriate Starting Values for Normal Disk Caching

When you are using a cache, remember that rebooting or turning off the computer can cause a loss of data. Any data sitting in the cache that has not been written to the disk at the time is lost. This was not a problem with Windows 3.0 because the cache was read only. With Windows 3.1, however, this danger is real. As a precaution, SMARTDrive does try to protect the cache. SMARTDrive automatically writes the cache to the disk every 5 seconds. If you enter Ctrl+Alt+Del to reboot, SMARTDrive will flush its cache before the reboot. You can, however, force SMARTDrive to flush itself to the disk by entering the following command line at the prompt:

```
SMARTDRIVE /C
```

It is then safe to boot or turn off the computer.

B

APPENDIX

> **Performance Tip:** When you are using a disk cache with Windows, use extended memory instead of expanded. This is the default mode for SMARTDrive. Windows is more stable if there are no expanded memory programs running on startup.

Using RAMDrive

RAMDrive is a memory-resident utility that manages a specified memory area as if it were a drive. The RAMDrive has a drive letter, and it acts to the system like a disk drive, with two exceptions: it is much faster than a disk and it is *volatile*. If you turn off the power to the computer, the contents of the RAMDrive are lost.

Since Windows uses all of memory (including extended memory) anyway, allocating some to a RAMDrive generally doesn't make much sense, since it takes memory from what Windows would use. Using extra memory for a disk cache is a much better idea. There are a few situations, however, when you might wish to use a RAMDrive:

- You are using a diskless workstation where you have plenty of memory but no disk.

- You are running DOS applications in real or standard mode and wish to use the RAMDrive as a storage location for swap files.

- You are running an application that uses many small temporary files.

Optimizing the Performance of Windows

- You use several applications frequently. You could load these applications much faster from a RAMDrive than from a hard disk. Load them to the RAMDrive on booting; then start them from it.

- You have more than 4 megabytes of memory. You could use the extra as a RAMDrive, placing the temporary files there (**SET TEMP=***xxx*). This gives a speed improvement in some cases.

If you do need a RAMDrive, use the RAMDrive memory resident software to manage the memory. Avoid using other RAMDrive software because the software may conflict with Windows. Copy the RAMDRIVE.SYS driver to the Windows directory and add a line to the CONFIG.SYS file (see Appendix G) to install it:

```
DEVICE=C:\WINDOWS\RAMDRIVE.SYS 256 /E
```

where the number (256, here) specifies the amount of memory in kilobytes to allocate to the RAMDrive. Use the /e parameter to place the RAMDisk in extended memory. RAMDisk is automatically assigned as the next available drive in the system. Use /a to put the RAMDrive in expanded memory. If neither is used, the RAMDrive is placed in conventional memory. If using EMM386 to emulate expanded memory, don't place the RAMDrive there; it isn't efficient.

Note: Avoid the temptation to use RAMDrive as a fast disk for general installation. In the 386 enhanced mode, remember that Windows uses all available memory and then uses the disk to extend memory, swapping code out as necessary. When using a RAMDrive, you have less

continues

Using RAMDrive

continued

available memory, and swapping occurs sooner. Even though you are swapping to a memory-based disk, the net result is a slower system than if Windows had owned that memory in the first place.

The last reason mentioned for using a RAMDrive is very important for many users. In some cases, you can dramatically improve the performance of Windows by allocating the TEMP files to a RAMDrive. It depends on the memory you have, but keep at least 3 megabytes before trying a RAMDrive with what is left. Remember that using some scanners and printers may require megabytes of TEMP file space. For example, when you are printing with Hewlett-Packard's PaintJet XL, the entire color page is built as a file before it is sent to the printer.

If you are in standard mode and you wish to speed up DOS swapping without changing the printer's use of the TEMP file, try changing the swap file location to a RAMDrive instead. You can do this by editing the SYSTEM.INI [nonwindowsapps] section (see Appendix G) so that the swap file parameter points to the RAMDrive. Leave the TEMP directory on the hard disk (see the second point in the preceding list).

Don't try to use any other RAMDrives with Windows. In fact, if any other RAMDrive is installed, it will be removed when you install Windows. SETUP.INF defines the RAMDrive products that will be removed.

The general form of the RAMDrive load line is:

```
DEVICE=drive:pathRAMDRIVE.SYS DiskSize SectorSize
NumEntries /e /a
```

where:

    drive is the drive for RAMDRIVE.SYS.

    path is the path for RAMDRIVE.SYS.

    DiskSize specifies kilobytes for RAM disk.

    SectorSize specifies the sector size in bytes. Values can be 128, 256, or 512.

    NumEntries limits the number of entries in the root directory. The default is 64. The value can be 2–1024.

    /e places the RAM disk in extended memory.

    /a places the RAM disk in expanded memory.

Performance Tip: It is highly recommended that you specify /e or /a. If no switch is specified, the RAM disk is placed in conventional memory, which severely affects Windows performance.

Using Expanded Memory

You need expanded memory only if you wish to run a DOS application that uses expanded memory. Windows applications do not use expanded memory. (You may, however, wish to use the expanded memory driver with DOS 5 to load drivers and TSRs to upper memory.)

To support expanded memory with an 80286 processor, you must add expanded memory and a driver for this. Memory allocated for expanded memory will not be available to Windows. Do not use the EMM386.SYS driver for an 80286 processor.

The best alternative if you need expanded memory in 386 enhanced mode is to use the QEMM-386 product, which runs as expanded memory and simulates extended memory as Windows needs it.

If not using QEMM-386, you can use the EMM386 driver for expanded memory on a 386/486 machine. To install the EMM386 Expanded Memory Emulator, add the EMM386.SYS driver to the Windows directory and enter the following line to the CONFIG.SYS file (see Appendix G) anywhere after the command that installs the HIMEM.SYS device:

```
DEVICE=C:\WINDOWS\EMM386.SYS 640
```

where the path for the driver is specified and the number represents the amount of memory to allocate for expanded memory in kilobytes. Assign the minimum amount of expanded memory needed to support your programs. Reboot the computer to use the emulator. For more information on the options available, see your DOS manual.

Note: Most users will not be using expanded memory. If you use DOS 5, however, you may still wish to use this driver to allocate space in the UMB area for loading drivers high. See Chapter 2 for more details.

If you have an 80286 computer and need expanded memory for a DOS application, use an expanded memory board and the driver that came with the board.

Using FastDisk

Windows 3.1 supports a FastDisk feature that enables improved 386 enhanced support with certain hardware configurations. FastDisk offers the following advantages:

- Speeds up disk access in the 386 enhanced mode.
- Enables you to run more DOS applications at a time.

In short, FastDisk enables Windows to bypass DOS for disk I/O by using a 32-bit protected mode driver if your system meets certain conditions. The current conditions to use FastDisk are:

- The system can support the 386 enhanced mode.
- The disk controller supports the controller standard.

If the installation believes that the system is compatible for FastDisk access, you will see the option as a check box when you choose the 386 Enhanced option for Control Panel and choose **Virtual Memory**. You can then turn it on. You can also turn it on by adding **32BitDiskAccess=on** in the [386enh] section of SYSTEM.INI (see Appendix G).

Use great caution here. Just because the Windows installation believes FastDisk will work doesn't mean it will. Even though the check box may be there, it is turned off by default;

that is, the user makes the final choice. Back up the system before trying it. FastDisk will *not* work with SCSI or ESDI controllers. If you have an SCSI drive, try to find a controller that makes the controller look like a standard interface. Then you can use FastDisk.

Microsoft makes this FastDisk feature available, but it is up to the original equipment manufacturer (OEM) to decide to use it. Microsoft supplies only the single driver that supports this one controller. The OEM can write its own, if the manufacturer wishes, for its own machine. Microsoft is very supportive of this, and will supply the source code if the OEM wishes to try the challenge.

If you turn on FastDisk and it won't work with your system, the system may hang but you should not lose any data.

Loading TSRs

For more information on loading TSRs, see Chapter 10. You can create a batch file, WINSTART.BAT, and it will automatically execute when starting Windows in the 386 enhanced mode. Use this batch file to load TSRs that are needed only with Windows. They will not be available in the DOS virtual machines (see Appendix A), leaving more conventional memory free.

Optimizing Tips

■ If you are not using expanded memory, disable it completely by adding this line in the [386enh] section of SYSTEM.INI (see Appendix G):

`NoEMMIDriver=yes`

■ In the same section, set **ReservePageFrame=false** if no expanded memory is used. This will force Windows to allocate UMBs for the translation buffers before any page frame, keeping them in upper memory if the upper memory space is tight. This defaults to true, since Windows assumes you will need expanded memory.

■ SMARTDrive 4.0 can be loaded high, freeing up conventional memory.

■ Do not place a swap file on a networked drive.

■ Use a utility, such as Steve Gibson's SpinRite, to find and set the optimal interleave for the disk.

■ If you are using a memory expansion board that can be set as expanded or extended memory, configure it all as extended memory. Then use EMM386.EXE to emulate expanded memory (on a 386/486 system) for DOS applications as needed. Place the expanded memory driver first in CONFIG.SYS (see Appendix G) and then follow it by the HIMEM and EMM386 driver lines.

■ Use the RAMDrive only for the \TEMP directory, and only if you have more than 4MB of memory and enough extra to support the TEMP directory requirements (which can be large for graphic printing).

■ Load EMM386.EXE only if you wish to load drivers high with DOS 5 or to use expanded memory for DOS applications on a 386/486 machine.

B
APPENDIX

Help! I need to troubleshoot configuration problems.

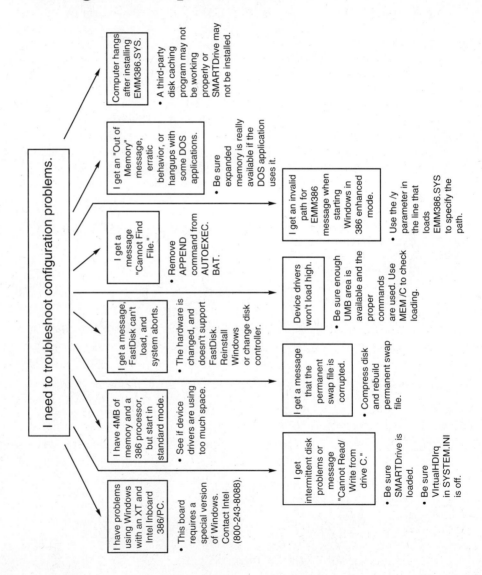

I need to troubleshoot configuration problems.

Computer hangs after installing EMM386.SYS.
- A third-party disk caching program may not be working properly or SMARTDrive may not be installed.

I get an "Out of Memory" message, erratic behavior, or hangups with some DOS applications.
- Be sure expanded memory is really available if the DOS application uses it.

I get a message "Cannot Find File."
- Remove APPEND command from AUTOEXEC.BAT.

I get a message, FastDisk can't load, and system aborts.
- The hardware is changed, and doesn't support FastDisk. Reinstall Windows or change disk controller.

I have 4MB of memory and a 386 processor, but start in standard mode.
- See if device drivers are using too much space.

I have problems using Windows with an XT and Intel Inboard 386/PC.
- This board requires a special version of Windows. Contact Intel (800-243-8088).

I get an invalid path for EMM386 message when starting Windows in 386 enhanced mode.
- Use the /y parameter in the line that loads EMM386.SYS to specify the path.

Device drivers won't load high.
- Be sure enough UMB area is available and the proper commands are used. Use MEM /C to check loading.

I get a message that the permanent swap file is corrupted.
- Compress disk and rebuild permanent swap file.

I get intermittent disk problems or message "Cannot Read/Write from drive C."
- Be sure SMARTDrive is loaded.
- Be sure VirtualHDIrq in SYSTEM.INI is off.

Optimizing the Performance of Windows

If you have a configuration problem, check for any recent hardware changes or edits of AUTOEXEC.BAT or CONFIG.SYS. Such changes should give you a clue to the source of the problem.

I have problems using Windows with an XT and the Intel Inboard 386/PC.

■ When using this board, you must have a special version of Windows. Contact Intel for more information (800 243-8088). If you already have Windows, the upgrade is free.

I get intermittent disk problems or the message "Cannot Read/Write from drive C."

■ If you are using an SCSI drive, be sure SMARTDrive is loaded. If using an Adaptec disk controller with an SCSI drive, you may need to use the `double_buffer` or /b parameter with SMARTDRV.SYS.

■ If you are not using SCSI but are using third-party disk managers (Disk Manager, SpeedStor, Innerspace, or *Vfeatures*), be sure `VirtualHDIrq` in SYSTEM.INI is off (see Appendix G). If you are using Windows 3.00a or later, Windows can detect when one of these products is in use and can turn SMARTDrive off. Avoid using a permanent swap file if `VirtualHDIrq` is off (see the `[386enh]` section of SYSTEM.INI).

I have 4MB of memory and a 386 processor, but Windows starts in standard mode.

Check the space allocated to device drivers and see if enough memory is really available. If RAMDrive or SMARTDrive is installed too large, there won't be enough left for the memory manager to start the 386 enhanced mode.

I get a message that my permanent swap file is corrupted.

Compress the disk drive containing the swap file. For Windows 3.0, restart Windows in the real mode and then create the swap file again by using **F**ile **R**un and executing SWAPFILE.EXE. For Windows 3.1, use Windows Control Panel, select 386 Enhanced, and rebuild the permanent swap file (virtual memory).

I get a message about interrupt conflicts, FastDisk can't load, and Windows aborts.

You probably modified your hardware from a standard controller and disk that support FastDisk to an SCSI controller and disk that don't. The best alternative is to reinstall Windows. The installation will recognize the new controller and set up everything properly.

The device drivers won't load to high memory on booting.

- Be sure that you are using a 80386 or 80486, that 350K of extended memory is available, and that CONFIG.SYS has the following (see Appendix G):

```
DEVICE=HIMEM.SYS              ; this must be before other commands here
DOS=HIGH,UMB
DEVICE=EMM386.EXE ram|noems   ; one of these switches must be included
DEVICEHIGH=xxxx               ; one of these must exist for each driver.
```

  In addition, AUTOEXEC.BAT must have a LOADHIGH command for each TSR to load high.

  Reboot, then type MEM /c at the DOS prompt, and press Enter to see if the drivers and TSRs are loaded high. If the drivers and TSRs still fail to load high, be sure there is enough space in the UMB area to load them. Some drivers and TSRs should not be loaded high and will cause the boot to hang. Make sure you have a boot diskette to recover before starting.

I get the error message "Cannot Find File."

- Remove the APPEND command from AUTOEXEC.BAT (see Appendix G).

On starting Windows in 386 enhanced mode, I get a message about an invalid path for EMM386.

- Add the parameter /y=path to the CONFIG.SYS command line that loads EMM386 (see Appendix G), where path specifies the path for EMM386.

Help! I need to troubleshoot configuration problems.

I get an "Out of Memory" message, erratic behavior, or hangups on some DOS applications.

Expanded memory support may not be available, even though you think it is installed. Be sure the DEVICE line for the EMM386.SYS driver in CONFIG.SYS contains the RAM parameter (see Appendix G).

The computer hangs after installing EMM386.

If a third-party disk-caching program is installed, it may not be working properly with EMM386.SYS. Load SMARTDrive instead. You may have a memory conflict problem with a network adapter, video adapter, or other card. A particular driver or TSR may not load high. Try switching each to conventional memory by removing the LOADHIGH (AUTOEXEC.BAT) or DEVICEHIGH (CONFIG.SYS) command.

HARDWARE INTERRUPT MAP FOR PC-AT AND 80386/ 486 COMPUTERS

Many of the adapter cards in the computer are assigned a specific hardware interrupt, or IRQ. This interrupt is set with a switch on the adapter card. No two adapter cards should share the same interrupt. Table C.1 lists the interrupt numbers.

Table C.1

Hardware Interrupts for PC-AT and 80386/486 Computers

IRQ	Description
0	Timer
1	Keyboard
2	Cascade to interrupt 9
3	COM2 and COM4
4	COM1 and COM3
5	LPT2 (parallel printer port)
6	Floppy disk controller
7	LPT1 (parallel printer port)
8	Real-time clock
9	Cascade to interrupt 2
10	Reserved
11	Reserved
12	Reserved, mouse port on PS/2
13	80x87 math coprocessor
14	Hard disk
15	Reserved

In addition, many cards may have a DMA number assigned or an address assignment. Cards should not share duplicate DMA or address assignments.

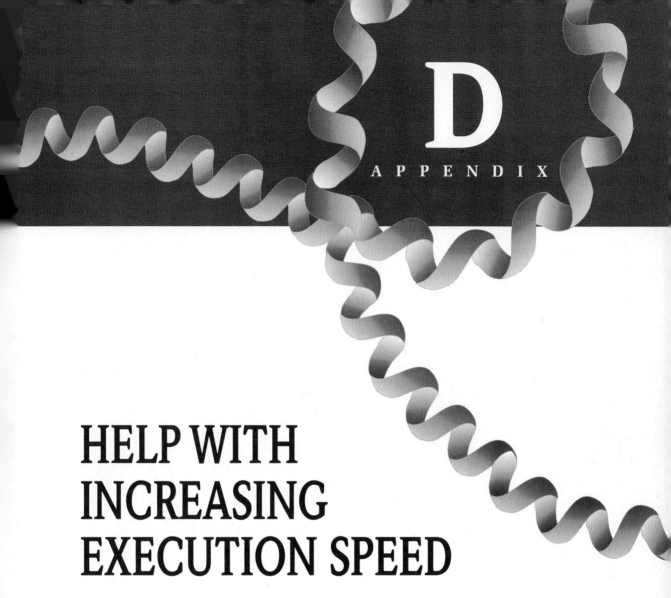

D

APPENDIX

HELP WITH INCREASING EXECUTION SPEED

This appendix offers suggestions for increasing the speed of Windows' execution. The suggestions are grouped into two categories: hardware and software.

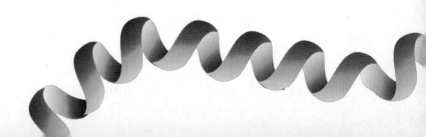

D
APPENDIX

Using Hardware to Increase Windows' Execution Speed

To increase Windows' execution speed, follow these guidelines for hardware:

- When purchasing hard disks, look for disk access times of 30 milliseconds or less and disk interleaves of 2:1 or 1:1.

- Use a system with a 386 or 486 processor. A 386SX processor is better than a 286, and the cost difference is small. DX machines are faster than SX machines, and faster clocks (33 MHz versus 25 MHz) mean more speed. A good standard office machine now is a 386DX running at 25 MHz.

- When using a 286 processor, use lots of memory. Five megabytes of memory with a 286 is faster than a 386SX with 1 megabyte.

- Use plenty of extended memory with 286/386/486 systems. Use a 386 machine and plan for at least 4 megabytes of total memory for good productivity. *For most systems, adding more extended memory is the single most important upgrade for increasing speed.*

- Use a 16-bit video adapter, and (if possible) purchase a VGA adapter with a coprocessor or accelerator.

- VGA is faster than EGA. Windows is more efficient with VGA than EGA.

Using Software to Increase Windows' Execution Speed

To increase Windows' execution speed, follow these guidelines for software:

- Windows is very disk intensive; that is, it does a lot of disk reading and writing. Use a disk-organizer software utility frequently (such as PC Tools' Compress) to reduce disk fragmentation. Periodically run the utility outside of Windows.

- Use a disk cache. Windows includes a SMARTDrive to use for caching if you have extended or expanded memory. Use SMARTDrive with Windows 3.1. With Windows 3.0, better commercial versions are available that are faster and work with Windows.

- If running in 386 enhanced mode, use a permanent swap file instead of a temporary one. Be sure to compress (defragment) the drive first and install from the real mode (Windows 3.0) or standard mode (Windows 3.1). When backing up, delete the swap file from the hard disk first (to save space on the backup tape or diskettes). Rebuild the swap file after backing up.

- Fine-tune the use of memory when using standard applications with the PIF Editor.

- Use FastDisk if your system will support it.

- For DOS applications in 386 enhanced mode, turn off the High Graphics option of the Monitor Ports section under Display Options when you are using text applications.

D

APPENDIX

- For the 386 enhanced mode, set `ReservePageFrame=false` in the SYSTEM.INI file under `[386enh]` (see Appendix G) if you are not using expanded memory with any applications.

- Check the video driver and be sure it is the latest one for your adapter. Sometimes, updating a driver can improve speed by a factor of up to 25. New drivers are often enhanced for Windows. Running 16 colors instead of 256 will increase speed by a factor of 3 to 10.

- Use a lower-resolution video driver.

- Maximize your windows. When several window frames are visible, some processor work is involved in tracking the various windows and keeping track of which one the cursor is over. (You won't gain much speed with this, however.)

- Use fewer windows. All Windows applications share a single virtual machine. You can't control the processor time that each application uses. Using fewer windows and applications ensures that fewer processor cycles are stolen from the foreground application.

- When using a disk cache, set `BUFFERS` to 10 in CONFIG.SYS (see Appendix G).

- Optimize the settings for SMARTDrive.

- If you have more than 4 megabytes of memory, you may wish to use the extra as a RAMDrive and place the temporary files there (`SET TEMP=xxx` in AUTOEXEC.BAT). This will give a speed improvement in some cases.

- Keep WIN.INI small. Remove applications and fonts that you no longer use (see Appendix G). Windows keeps WIN.INI in memory, and large WIN.INI files mean more disk swapping. Also, this file is written to the disk each time it is updated from Control Panel or another program—with the Colors option of Control Panel this means each time an OK button is pressed.

- If a foreground DOS application is running slowly, a background process (including the Print Manager) may be eating up the processor time. Setting the application's PIF to **E**xclusive may speed things up, suspending the background process. If you are running a background process, give the DOS application more time. Set priority to at least 400. Run full-screen. If the DOS application is text-based, be sure the Monitor Ports box of the PIF is unchecked. If running text and graphic programs together (such as Lotus 1-2-3 and Allways), run full-screen with **V**ideo Memory set to High Graphics and Retain Video **M**emory on.

- Font scalers slow down the display and printing. Some are better than others, however.

Applications

Many applications have tricks that you can use to dramatically improve speed. Here are two examples:

Microsoft Excel

- Use a macro to prompt for the file to open on starting, using Esc to abort to a new worksheet.

- In the INI file options, set `Maximized=1` to open Excel with a maximized window (see Appendix G).

■ Organize the worksheet, keeping assumptions in a separate area for easy updating. By taking the time to organize, you will increase your overall productivity because you reduce your errors.

■ When creating a worksheet, enter the data first. Then enter formulas and, finally, do the formatting.

Word for Windows

■ Learn to use style sheets. This simplifies formatting, improves productivity, and forces standardization.

■ Set **T**ools **O**ptions for maximum performance: turn off the display of pictures, turn off Table **G**ridlines, and turn off **T**ext Boundaries.

■ When changing printers, select **F**ile **P**rinter Setup and then click OK to rebuild the WIN.INI file. This will speed up the display.

E

THE ANSI CHARACTER SET USED BY WINDOWS 3.1 TRUETYPE FONTS

The following chart shows the ANSI character set used by Windows 3.1 TrueType fonts. To enter any of these characters, hold down the Alt key and press 0 plus the ANSI code on the numeric keypad. Characters that are new to Windows 3.1 are

printed in bold text. These characters are not supported by the Wingdings or Symbol TrueType fonts. If these characters don't appear when you type the ANSI code, check to be sure that you're using a TrueType font.

Character	ANSI Code
Backspace	8
Tab	9
Linefeed	10
Carriage return	13
Space	32
!	33
"	34
#	35
$	36
%	37
&	38
'	39
(	40
)	41
*	42
+	43
´	44
-	45
.	46

Character	ANSI Code
/	47
0	48
1	49
2	50
3	51
4	52
5	53
6	54
7	55
8	56
9	57
:	58
;	59
<	60
=	61
>	62
?	63
@	64
A	65
B	66
C	67

continues

Character	ANSI Code
D	68
E	69
F	70
G	71
H	72
I	73
J	74
K	75
L	76
M	77
N	78
O	79
P	80
Q	81
R	82
S	83
T	84
U	85
V	86
W	87
X	88
Y	89

The ANSI Character Set Used by Windows 3.1 TrueType Fonts

Character	ANSI Code
Z	90
[	91
\	92
]	93
^	94
_	95
`	96
a	97
b	98
c	99
d	100
e	101
f	102
g	103
h	104
i	105
j	106
k	107
l	108
m	109
n	110
o	111

continues

APPENDIX E

Character	ANSI Code
p	112
q	113
r	114
s	115
t	116
u	117
v	118
w	119
x	120
y	121
z	122
{	123
|	124
}	125
~	126
'	130
ƒ	131
"	132
…	133
†	134
‡	135
‰	137

The ANSI Character Set Used by Windows 3.1 TrueType Fonts

Character	ANSI Code
S	138
‹	139
Œ	140
'	145
'	146
"	147
"	148
•	149
–	150
—	151
™	153
s	154
›	155
œ	156
Ÿ	159
Space	160
¡	161
¢	162
£	163
⊗	164
¥	165
¦	166

continues

Character	ANSI Code
§	167
¨	168
©	169
ª	170
«	171
¬	172
-	173
®	174
¯	175
°	176
±	177
²	178
³	179
´	180
µ	181
¶	182
•	183
¸	184
	185
º	186
»	187
¼	188

Character	ANSI Code
½	189
¾	190
¿	191
À	192
Á	193
Â	194
Ã	195
Ä	196
Å	197
Æ	198
Ç	199
È	200
É	201
Ê	202
Ë	203
Ì	204
Í	205
Î	206
Ï	207
Ð	208
Ñ	209
Ò	210

continues

Character	ANSI Code
Ó	211
Ô	212
Õ	213
Ö	214
×	215
Ø	216
Ù	217
Ú	218
Û	219
Ü	220
Y	221
Ð	222
ß	223
à	224
á	225
â	226
ã	227
ä	228
å	229
æ	230
ç	231

The ANSI Character Set Used by Windows 3.1 TrueType Fonts

Character	ANSI Code
è	232
é	233
ê	234
ë	235
ì	236
í	237
î	238
ï	239
ð	240
ñ	241
ò	242
ó	243
ô	244
õ	245
ö	246
÷	247
ø	248
ù	249
ú	250
û	251
ü	252

continues

Character	ANSI Code
y	253
ṕ	254
ÿ	255

The ANSI Character Set Used by Windows 3.1 TrueType Fonts

F
APPENDIX

GLOSSARY

Active application. The application that appears in the window and that has the current focus for any keyboard input. The active window's title bar will be a different color or pattern from that of an inactive application.

Active printer. The printer to which a port is assigned.

ANSI character set. A numeric coding standard for characters and other symbols defined by the American National Standards Institute (see Appendix E).

Applet. Any one of the small application programs included with Windows, such as Microsoft Paintbrush.

Application. A program that supports a functional role for the user. Spreadsheet programs, word processors, and desktop publishing software are all examples of application programs. Application programs that require Windows are called *Windows Application Programs,* or *Winapps.* In Windows, application programs are often called *tools. See also* **Tool** and **Winapp**.

Application icon. An icon used to represent an application when no windows of the application are open.

Application Program Interface (API). A set of defined interfaces used by an environment or operating system for communicating with an application program. A defined standard or language for writing a program with functions and procedures. Windows has an API that is defined by the Windows SDK. The SDK is used by programmers to write Windows applications. The Windows API can be extended with DDLs. *See also* **DDL**.

Application swap files. Files used in real or standard mode for swapping applications to disk.

Attribute. A characteristic of an object, such as its color. Object attributes can be changed with tools in application programs. Files can also have attribute bits stored with the file in the directory to indicate whether the file is read-only, is hidden, has been backed up, etc. You can change the attribute bits of a file by using File Manager.

Authoring system. A system for creating—or authoring—a multimedia product.

AUTOEXEC.BAT. A file of DOS commands that is automatically read and executed on booting. You can modify this file to customize your system.

Backfilling. Defining the memory of an expanded memory card, making it available for use as conventional memory (see Appendix A).

Background application. An application that is running under Windows but does not have the focus of the keyboard or an active window. Printing, spreadsheet calculations, communication file transfers, and compiling are applications that typically can be run as background applications.

Batch file. A file containing a sequence of DOS commands. Batch files have a BAT extension.

BIOS (Basic Input/Output System). The basic part of the operating system (often in ROM) that does the initial power-on testing, loads the rest of DOS from disk, and supports some of the input and output operations for applications.

Bit map. An image stored as a bit array.

Boot. A small program in ROM that can be used to start the computer. Also, the process of reading this small program and starting the computer. A *cold boot* tests the computer and then starts it. A *warm boot* only restarts the computer.

Buffer. A storage area that holds data to be printed or transferred to or from the disk.

Byte. The smallest addressable unit of a computer's memory.

Cascading menu. A submenu that can be dropped down when the user initiates a command from the menu bar. The display of both the menu bar and the dropdown menus is handled by Windows.

Cascading windows. A method of arranging the windows on the desktop so that they overlap, with the title bar of each visible.

Check box. In dialog boxes, a type of control that acts as a toggle, either on or off.

Click. To press and release the mouse button quickly. For a right-handed person, the left mouse button is normally the one that is clicked.

Client. An application that receives an object from the server application that produced it. *See also* **Server**.

Client area. The portion of a window available to the application program. The title bar, menu bar, and scroll bars are all outside of the client area. Also called the *work area*.

Clipboard. A temporary storage area used by Windows to transfer data between programs or documents. The Clipboard can also be used for moving or copying data within an application.

Close. To remove an application or document from the desktop.

Cluster. The smallest addressable unit of storage in the directory of a disk. Clusters are normally about 2 to 4K.

Command button. A type of dialog box control used to initiate action.

Compound document. A document with many types of objects created by a variety of tools (applications).

Computer. A system that is capable of acting on instructions (programs) to accomplish a desired task.

CONFIG.SYS. A special file that is read on booting and that is used in configuring the system and loading special drivers.

Controls. In dialog boxes, objects having predefined behaviors that are consistent for all Windows applications. The five basic control types for input are command buttons, option buttons, check boxes, list boxes, and text boxes.

Control menu. A menu activated by clicking the Control-menu box. It is common to all application windows and provides options to minimize, maximize, move, and size the window. It can be altered by the application program.

Control-menu box. A box located at the upper left of the window and identified by a horizontal bar. Clicking the Control-menu box causes the Control menu to be displayed.

Conventional memory. The first 640K of memory used by MS-DOS for applications.

Cursor. An indicator on the screen. A *mouse cursor* shows where the mouse action (click, drag, etc.) will be initiated. An *insertion point* is a cursor used in some programs (such as word processors) to show where characters typed from the keyboard will be inserted.

Data files. Files used by a program to store information.

DDL (Dynamic Data Libraries). A method of extending the Windows API for custom applications.

Default printer. The active printer when Windows is started.

Delivery system. A system for playing a multimedia product.

Desktop. The screen background on which the various windows are displayed.

Dialog box. A type of predefined window that contains controls. Dialog boxes are one of the primary methods of receiving user input in a Windows application program.

Directory. A catalog or index of the files stored on a disk. The topmost directory is called the root directory. All others are subdirectories. *See also* **Subdirectory.**

Disks. A magnetic storage media for data.

Disk cache. An area of memory used to manage and improve disk access.

Display. *See* **Monitor**.

Document window. A window used within an application for documents. In Word for Windows, the working document is displayed in a document window. In Excel, a document window is used for the spreadsheet.

Downloadable fonts. Fonts that are stored on the computer's hard disk and sent to the printer as they are needed.

DPMI (DOS Protected Mode Interface). An extended memory DOS extender that works with Windows, permitting DOS applications to address extended memory.

Drag. To move a screen object by placing the mouse cursor on an object, pressing a mouse button, and moving the mouse. For example, you can move a window by dragging the title bar.

Driver. A special software routine for interfacing with printers, the mouse, or the keyboard. Drivers permit you to customize your system for your specific needs.

Dynamic Data Exchange (DDE). A name used by Microsoft to signify the process of passing data between Windows applications. When a DDE hot-link is created between applications, the data in one is updated automatically when the data in the other changes.

Dynamic-Link Library (DLL). A Windows feature that permits executable code modules to be loaded and linked on demand. The library code is stored as DLL modules. This is in contrast to DOS programs, which are compiled and linked to a single executable file in which the code is bound to specific memory addresses after linking. With DLL, the linking (and consequent binding to memory locations) is not done until execution, and then on demand. This method conserves memory, permitting unused code to be released. It also permits code to be shared by several programs in memory. The disadvantage is a loss of speed, since the linking must be done as the program executes. The DLL feature means that Windows is *extensionable;* that is, a programmer can expand the API to meet specific needs.

Expanded memory. A type of memory supported by all Intel processors (XT- and AT-compatible machines) in which pages of memory above 1 megabyte are temporarily placed in the 1-megabyte address space (see Appendix A).

Extended memory. The physical memory beyond the 1-megabyte limitation of conventional memory. Only the 80286 and 80386 processors or later can use extended memory, and then only when running in protected mode. Windows supports extended memory in standard and enhanced modes.

Extension name. A suffix used with the filename to indicate the type of file. For example, the BAT extension indicates a batch file, such as WP.BAT.

File. A group of related data stored as a single unit.

Floppy disk. A round, flat piece of Mylar or other material coated with a magnetic surface for the storage of data.

Focus. The area on the window where keyboard input will be received. Which window has the focus is normally determined by the mouse, but the location of the focus can also be controlled by the user within the program. For example, an application program can set the focus to any control in a dialog window.

Font. A typeface (font family) in a particular style, such as Times Roman Bold.

Foreground application. An application that has the active window and keyboard focus.

Full-screen application. A DOS application that occupies the entire screen when it is executing rather than using a window.

Group. A collection of programs treated as a unit by the Program Manager.

Group icon. An icon that represents a group.

Group window. A window used by the Program Manager to display the items in a group.

Grouped controls. Controls in a dialog box that are grouped to act as a unit, such as command buttons and check box controls.

Hard disks. One or more magnetic platters in a sealed enclosure that are used for the storage of computer data.

Hardware. The mechanical and electronic portion of the computer; the part of the system you can put your hands on.

High memory area (HMA). The first 64K of extended memory. It can be addressed as conventional memory with a little software trickery. DOS 5 can be stored in the HMA area.

Hinting. The ability to change the font's appearance with size.

Icon. A small pictorial representation of an object, application, or process. *See also* **Program-item icon**.

Iconic. A program state in which no window of the application program is visible, although the application is still in memory. Iconic programs are represented by a small icon at the bottom of the screen.

Inactive window. An open window that is not currently in use. Only one window can be active at a time.

Insertion point. The place where text will be inserted when the user begins typing.

Instance. A currently active copy of the application. Windows can have several copies of the same program in memory at one time, with each copy an *instance* of the program. Windows can share program code and data between instances.

Kernel. The part of the operating system that provides basic services.

Keyboard. The primary input component of the computer. Keyboards vary in design and key placement.

Link. To establish a dynamic relationship between the data in a source document and a destination document. Links are created in Windows by using DDE. *See also* **Dynamic Data Exchange.**

List box. A type of dialog box control permitting selection from a list, such as a list of filenames.

Macro. A series of actions stored as a unit that can be activated from a single action. In effect, a macro is a type of program.

Maximize box. A box located at the upper right of a window and identified by an up arrow that permits a user to zoom the window to maximum size.

Memory. An area in the computer that stores data. In the computer architectures of today, memory can be used to store programs or data. This permits a program to operate on another program as data. (This is how a BASIC interpreter works.)

Menu. Command options that are displayed to the user. Windows supports a first-level menu selection in a menu bar, and each item in the menu bar can support a pulldown menu as a second-level menu selection. As a third level, cascading menus

can be supported from the pulldown menu items. Menus can be dynamically created or altered by a program. In addition, programs can dynamically alter menu items.

Menu bar. A first-level menu displayed as a horizontal bar. It is displayed above the client area and below the title bar.

Messages. The primary method used within Windows applications for communicating with another program and the system.

Message box. In a program, a pop-up window that contains a brief message, with an optional icon, variable display, title bar, buttons, and response options.

Minimize box. A box located at the upper right of a window and identified by a down arrow that permits a user to reduce the window to an icon appearing at the bottom of the screen.

Modal dialog box. A dialog box that is activated by the system (system modal) or application (application modal) and that must be responded to before execution can continue. Modal dialog boxes are used for input.

Modeless dialog box. A dialog box that permits the user to continue to use other windows while the box is being displayed. Modeless dialog boxes are normally used for output only.

Modem. A device that converts computer data into a form that can be sent over a telephone line or radio link and, conversely, converts computer data from a telephone line or radio link to a form that can be processed by a computer.

Monitor. The video display used to view the computer output. The monitor is designed to support one or more graphic modes (*see* **Video adapter**). Multiscan monitors can adapt automatically to a wide variety of video adapters.

Mouse. A computer peripheral device that permits working with objects on the screen in a more natural way, such as by pointing or dragging.

Multimedia. A general term that encompasses full-motion video, hypermedia, interactive video, and other concepts.

Multimedia Extensions (MME). A software product for extending Windows to include the multimedia API.

Multitasking. An environment in which several applications execute simultaneously and share a single processor and other resources.

Network. An interconnected system of computers and other resources for sharing information.

Nonclient area. The area of a window that contains the menu bar, title bar, size box, minimize box, maximize box, and scroll bars. The artwork for the nonclient area is controlled by Windows, not the application program. However, the application can define some aspects of the nonclient area, such as the options of the menu bar.

Nonpreemptive multitasking. The application has exclusive control of the processor and determines when it releases the processor. There is no limit to the amount of time the application can hold the processor. The Windows system runs in a nonpreemptive mode, managing the requests of the various applications for the processor. *See* **Preemptive multitasking**.

Object. A related group of items. A piece of data created and edited in a Windows application. Examples of objects in a word processing program would include documents, paragraphs, sentences, words, and characters. In a spreadsheet program, the objects would be the spreadsheet, rows (or columns), or cells.

Object Linking and Embedding (OLE). A method of embedding an object in a document while maintaining with it information about its source. Double-clicking on the object loads the document object to the source program.

OOP (Object-Oriented Programming). A programming method in which various objects are created (windows, dialog boxes, icons, cursors, etc.) and pieces of code are attached to them.

Operating system. Software that manages and supervises the resources of the computer. OS/2, Windows NT, and UNIX are examples of operating systems. DOS is called an operating system, but it is really more of a control program.

Option button. A type of dialog box control used to select one item from a group, such as the modem speed or serial port in a communications program.

Page frame. An area within the upper memory block (640K to 1MB) that is the designated expanded memory page. The page frame itself can be a maximum of four 16K pages.

Parameter. A qualifier included with a command to more specifically define what the command is to do. For example, you can include a data filename as a parameter with a word processing file to start the program with that file. You can use /l as a parameter with Microsoft Word to start it with the last file for editing.

Path. A sequence of directory names that defines the location of a file.

Peripherals. External computer system components such as the printer, modem, and mouse.

Permanent swap file. A file used in the 386 enhanced mode of Windows 3 for swapping applications if memory becomes full. Access is directly from Windows, bypassing DOS. *See* **Temporary swap file**.

Pitch. A unit of measurement for fixed-spaced (monospaced) fonts such as Courier or Prestige. The pitch is measured in characters per inch.

PIF file. A file that is used when you are executing standard applications from Windows and that defines how the program should be managed.

Point. A unit of measurement of a font's height. A point is $1/72$ of an inch.

Port. A channel for sending data to or from the computer. DOS computers support up to four serial and three parallel ports.

Preemptive multitasking. The process of giving a specific application a specific amount of time (slice) on the processor. The application must relinquish control of the processor at that time, whether the task is finished or not. The application is suspended until the next available time slice. DOS applications run as preemptive applications under Windows using the time-slice settings determined by their PIF files. *See* **Nonpreemptive multitasking**.

Print Manager. An application included with Windows that permits the printing of files while continuing to work with an application.

Printer. A computer peripheral for producing a hard copy of the computer's output.

Processor (also called the CPU). The part of the computer system that reads, interprets, and acts on the program instructions.

Program. A set of instructions that can be executed by a computer to achieve a useful objective.

Program files. A file that contains instructions for the computer to execute.

Program Group. A set of programs treated as a logical unit by Program Manager.

Program-item icon. An icon in Program Manager that represents an action that can be initiated by selecting the icon. The icon can start a program, start a batch file, start a program with a data file, or start a Recorder macro.

Prompt. Text or other indicator displayed by the computer to indicate that the computer is waiting for input from the user.

Protected mode. A mode supported by 80286 processors, or later, that can address extended memory.

Random-Access Memory (RAM). The volatile memory of the computer. Memory that loses its information when the computer is turned off.

Raster fonts. Fonts provided as bit maps in a specific size and style.

Read-Only Memory (ROM). Memory that cannot be erased or rewritten by the user. A small ROM memory chip in the computer is used to test and start the computer when the computer is turned on.

Real mode. A processor mode that is supported by all Intel processors and is used by Windows and MS-DOS.

Rendering. A font creation process of scaling, applying hints, and rasterizing.

Reserved I/O memory. The memory space between the 640K limit of conventional memory and 1MB.

Resident fonts. Fonts internal to the printer. This excludes cartridge fonts.

Restore box. A box that appears at the top right of a window when the window is maximized and that permits the user to restore the window to its previous size. It can be identified by a double arrow.

Root directory. The primary, or main, directory on a disk. It is stored in a fixed physical space at the beginning of the disk.

Scalable fonts. Fonts provided as outlines for creating on the fly as bit maps or for creating permanent raster-font images of a specific size and style.

Scroll bars. An optional horizontal or vertical bar that is displayed in a window (at the right or bottom) and that permits the user to control the view of the logical window.

Scroll box. A small movable box within the scroll bar that can be clicked and moved by the mouse to affect the window display. Also called an *elevator* or *thumb box. See also* **Thumb box**.

Server. An application that donates the object used by the client application. *See also* **Client**.

Shortcut key. Predefined keystrokes that can be used as an alternative for menu commands.

Shrink. To iconize (minimize) an application.

Soft fonts. Fonts provided in raster images and stored as files on the computer. They are automatically downloaded as needed.

Spooling. A technique in a multitasking system that permits more than one task to use the printer. Print output is queued to a disk file, from which a spooler utility program prints the tasks in a FIFO (first-in, first-out) manner.

Subdirectory. A directory within another directory. *See also* **Directory**.

Surge suppressor. A device for protecting the computer from variations, spikes, and noises on the power line.

System unit. The computer box that contains the processor, memory, power supply, and disk drives.

Tape drive. A type of storage unit for storing data sequentially on a magnetic tape. It is useful for backing up large amounts of data.

Task. An open application.

Temporary swap file. A default file created in the 386 enhanced mode for swapping applications to disk if the memory becomes full. *See also* **Permanent swap file**.

Text box. A type of dialog box control permitting text entry and editing.

Thumb box. A small box within the scroll bar that can be clicked and moved by the mouse to affect the window display. Also called an *elevator. See also* **Elevator**.

Tiled window. A window that is placed on the screen adjacent to, but not overlapping, other windows.

Title bar. An optional bar at the top of a window that contains the program's title.

Tool. Anything for working with an object. In Windows, the application programs are tools. You can also have tools within a program, such as a brush or pen in a paint program.

TrueType. A font scaling technology used in Windows 3.1.

TSR (terminate-and-stay-resident) software. Memory-resident software. TSR software is a program that can remain in memory while another program is executing. Normally, a TSR program is activated with a special, or *hot key*, sequence.

Typeface. A graphic design common to all symbols of a set (characters, numbers, punctuation, etc.). A single font is supported in multiple sizes and styles (bold, italic, etc.). An example would be *Tms Rmn* (Times Roman).

Upper memory blocks (UMB). The partitions of the reserved I/O memory between 640K and 1MB.

VCPI (Virtual Control Program Interface). A DOS extender technology for enabling DOS programs to use extended memory. DOS programs using this technology are not supported by Windows in the 386 enhanced mode.

Vector fonts. Fonts provided as mathematical descriptions. Vector fonts can easily be resized.

Video adapter. The card or interface used to connect the monitor or display to the computer. Adapters are designed for different graphic modes such as VGA, Super VGA, EGA, and others.

Virtual machine. An engine that does not interface directly to any physical input or output. The Windows 386 enhanced mode is a virtual machine. Memory, disks, keyboard, and display are addressed logically instead of physically.

Volume. A single logical disk unit. Each disk has a volume name.

Wildcard character. A character used to represent another character or a group of characters. In DOS and Windows, an asterisk (*) is a wildcard character for matching a group of characters, and a question mark (?) is a wildcard character for matching any single character.

WinApp. A Windows application program, or a program that runs under, and is dependent on, the Windows environment.

Window. A rectangular area of the screen that is under the control of the user's application program.

Work area. *See* **Client area.**

G

APPENDIX

VIEWING AND EDITING AUTOEXEC.BAT, CONFIG.SYS, AND .INI FILES

If you have been a DOS user and are now migrating to Windows, you are aware of two DOS files on the C directory that are very important: AUTOEXEC.BAT and CONFIG.SYS. Both of these files are automatically read by the computer on booting and they define the system configuration. Both files are

modified when you install Windows. You can edit them, as necessary, using Windows Notepad to support your hardware and system configuration. For the edits to become effective, you must always reboot after saving these files. Before editing these files, make sure that you create a boot diskette.

When you configure Windows or use Control Panel, the configuration information is saved in a series of INI files. Before Windows 3, a single WIN.INI file was used for the configuration information. Windows 3.0 and later versions provide a series of INI files:

WIN.INI modifies the startup parameters for Windows and contains general configuration information for Windows and any installed application programs.

SYSTEM.INI defines hardware-specific parameters for Windows.

PROGMAN.INI is the configuration file for the Program Manager.

WINFILE.INI is the configuration file for the File Manager.

CONTROL.INI is the configuration file for the Control Panel.

In addition, various applications have their own INI file that defines configuration specifics. For example, if Excel version 4.0 is installed, you will find that the file EXCEL4.INI is in the Windows directory and that it defines the current Excel configuration. All of the INI files are dynamic in the sense that they are constantly updated as you use Windows.

Viewing and Editing AUTOEXEC.BAT, CONFIG.SYS, and .INI Files

Tip: You can place comments in INI files by starting the line with a semicolon. Comment on the changes you make and why you make them.

Thus, AUTOEXEC.BAT, CONFIG.SYS, and the .INI files control how your system works. From time to time, you may need to edit these files manually to optimize your system's performance and eliminate problems. The following sections explain how.

Viewing and Editing AUTOEXEC.BAT, CONFIG.SYS, and .INI Files

Each of these files is a simple ASCII file and can be edited with any text editor, such as Windows Notepad. WIN.INI is often updated from within Windows automatically, such as when using Control Panel. The only files you should edit with an editor, however, are generally AUTOEXEC.BAT, CONFIG.SYS, WIN.INI, and SYSTEM.INI. It's useful to learn how to edit these files, for in so doing you can introduce a wide range of customization into your system and Windows. This appendix will show you how to do this.

Note: AUTOEXEC.BAT and CONFIG.SYS are read only when your system is started. WIN.INI and SYSTEM.INI are read only when Windows is initially started. If you use an editor from within Windows (such as Notepad or Sysedit) to edit a file, the edits will not take effect until your system (and Windows, if necessary) is restarted. If you made changes to WIN.INI and they don't take effect, reboot and restart Windows. If changes still fail to take, look for duplicate lines in the files (setting the parameter to two different values).

Caution: Never use Control Panel and an editor at the same time to update WIN.INI. An editor will make changes to a copy of the WIN.INI file and then save it to memory. If you try to make changes with Control Panel at the same time, writing the edited file to memory will overwrite the Control Panel changes.

Performance Tip: For maximum speed and productivity, keep WIN.INI small. Windows keeps the entire WIN.INI file in memory as it works, which means a larger file leaves less memory for other programs. Microsoft encourages those who develop Windows applications to keep program-specific parameters in a separate INI file, such as the EXCEL.INI file that is used for Excel. Remove applications from this file that you no longer use with a utility such as PROGSET (from *PC Magazine*).

Windows provides a special editor for editing your configurations: *Sysedit*. You will find this little jewel in the SYSTEM subdirectory of Windows. This editor automatically saves backup copies with an SYD extension. If you use it to modify files, you will always have a backup.

Performance Tip: Install Sysedit as a program by locating it with the File Manager and dragging the file icon to a Program Manager group. You can use **F**ile **P**roperties to assign either of two icons to it. Sysedit is then always available.

Sysedit works much like Notepad, but it opens WIN.INI, SYSTEM.INI, CONFIG.SYS, and AUTOEXEC.BAT on starting. Then all four windows are available for editing. One caution in using it, however: Sysedit is limited to files of 35K or smaller.

Following are instructions for using Sysedit to edit a system file. Keep in mind that no matter which text editor you use, you should always save a backup copy of the file you're editing, save the newly edited file, restart your system (if necessary), and restart Windows.

1. From the Windows 3.1 Program Manager, choose the **F**ile menu and then choose the **R**un command.

2. Type `C:\WINDOWS\SYSTEM\SYSEDIT.EXE` in the Command Line text box of the Run dialog box; then click OK. Alternatively, use the **B**rowse command button to find the SYSEDIT.EXE command.

3. Windows displays the System Configuration Editor, with CONFIG.SYS, AUTOEXEC.BAT, WIN.INI, and SYSTEM.INI files each in a document window.

4. Change to the document window for the file you want to edit by using the **W**indow menu.

5. Edit the file as needed.

6. Select the **F**ile menu and then choose **S**ave to save the file.

7. Choose E**x**it from the **F**ile menu to leave Sysedit.

8. If you've edited AUTOEXEC.BAT or CONFIG.SYS, exit Windows and reboot your system for your changes to take place. If you've edited WIN.INI or SYSTEM.INI, exit and then restart Windows.

Viewing and Editing AUTOEXEC.BAT, CONFIG.SYS, and .INI Files

I

INDEX

INDEX

1-800-HELP! with Windows 3.1

1-800-HELP! with Windows 3.1

1-800-HELP! with Windows 3.1

1-800-HELP! with Windows 3.1

1-800-HELP! with Windows 3.1

H

1-800-HELP! with Windows 3.1

I

I N D E X

1-800-HELP! with Windows 3.1

1-800-HELP! with Windows 3.1

1-800-HELP! with Windows 3.1

starting programs
  as icons without running,
    125
  DOS icon in Main group,
    125
  double-clicking program
    item icons, 124
  from associated data files,
    126
system status, 115-116
programs, 609
  active after termination,
    111-112
  DOS
    CHKDSK, 12-13
    EXPAND, 33
    MEM, 116
    MEN, 27
    SETUP, 16-17, 21-23, 83
    SHARE.EXE , 15
  FREEMEM shareware, 116
  groups, 604, 610
    scrambled or missing,
      82-83
  icons reverting to defaults
    when minimized, 128-129
  pop-up, 355-357
  starting
    in Program Manager,
      124-126
    Windows with, 129
    with Windows, 130
  Startup
    running/minimizing at
      opposite times, 131
    starting Windows
      without, 131

TSR (terminate-and-stay-
  resident), *see* TSRs
see also applications, software, utilities
prompts, DOS
  changing in DOS applica-
    tions under Windows, 383
  instead of Windows starting,
    72
Properties (Program Manager
  File menu) command,
  117-118, 122-124
proportional fonts, 240
protected mode, 507, 528-529,
  610
  running applications in
    Windows, 357-358
protected-mode software,
  running under Windows, xlv
PrtScrn key, 301, 389-393, 398
Publisher's PowerPak (Atech
  Software), 250-251

Q

QEMM-386 memory manager,
  534-537
question mark (?) wild card
  character, 613
queues, 319-320
  active after termination, 112
  changing printing priorities,
    321
  controlling error-message
    display, 322
  network, 488-491
  print jobs, 320-321
quitting Windows, 109-112

1-800-HELP! with Windows 3.1

I N D E X

1-800-HELP! with Windows 3.1

1-800-HELP! with Windows 3.1